Property Investment

2nd Edition

David Isaac

Professor of Real Estate Management, School of Architecture and Construction, University of Greenwich

John O'Leary

Senior Lecturer, School of Architecture and Construction, University of Greenwich

palgrave
macmillan

This edition first published 2011 by
PALGRAVE MACMILLAN

Palgrave Macmillan in the UK is an imprint of Macmillan Publishers Limited,
registered in England, company number 785998, of Houndmills, Basingstoke,
Hampshire RG21 6XS.

Palgrave Macmillan in the US is a division of St Martin's Press LLC,
175 Fifth Avenue, New York, NY 10010.

Palgrave Macmillan is the global academic imprint of the above companies
and has companies and representatives throughout the world.

Palgrave® and Macmillan® are registered trademarks in the United States,
the United Kingdom, Europe and other countries

ISBN-13: 978–0–230–29024–2 paperback

This book is printed on paper suitable for recycling and made from fully
managed and sustained forest sources. Logging, pulping and manufacturing
processes are expected to conform to the environmental regulations of the
country of origin.

A catalogue record for this book is available from the British Library.

A catalog record for this book is available from the Library of Congress.

10   9   8   7   6   5   4   3   2   1
20   19   18   17   16   15   14   13   12   11

Printed and bound in Great Britain by the
MPG Books Group, Bodmin and King's Lynn

To Ruth and Pat, thanks for everything.

By the same authors

Property Development: Appraisal and Finance (D. Isaac, J. O'Leary and M. Daley)
Property Finance (D. Isaac)
Property Valuation Principles (D. Isaac)
Property Valuation Techniques (D. Isaac)

Contents

Preface to the Second Edition

In this second edition, John O'Leary has joined David Isaac to revise and update a work which was originally published in 1998. Since that time a number of new agendas have emerged which are of importance to the topic of property investment and the authors have tried to reflect these changes in this new edition. Four key areas in particular have come to prominence and which have influenced the updating as follows:

1 Sustainability has become a fast moving and significant topic for all of those who work in or derive an income from property investment in its various guises. This edition of the book has therefore tried to assess the implications of sustainability for both residential and commercial property investment.
2 The credit crunch which took place broadly between 2007 and 2009 but whose reverberations linger on, raised significant challenges for residential and commercial property investors. This edition of the book has tried to reflect upon those experiences and to consider the extent to which risk reduction techniques can mitigate against these globally induced and volatile market swings.
3 The private rented sector has witnessed a revival under its new marketing brand of buy-to-let and thus greater prominence has been given in this edition to residential property investment.
4 Since 2007 major property companies whose business is to trade in and manage portfolios of commercial property have had the opportunity to benefit from a more favourable tax regime by converting to Real Estate Investment Trusts (REITs). This edition of the book has therefore looked at some of the key investment performance issues which have arisen from the introduction of UK REITs.

As in the first edition, opportunities have been taken to illustrate principles wherever possible by including worked examples. This has particularly been the case in those chapters which explore the property appraisal techniques which are often used to assess viability or inform decision-making in residential and commercial property investment.

Finally, we would like to thank Helen Bugler and Neha Sharma at Palgrave for their patience and support in helping us to complete this edition of the book. Thanks also to Martin Barr for his initiative and value adding suggestions which helped get the draft of this edition of the book into production.

Caveats

This book should not be relied upon as a basis for entering into transactions without seeking specific, qualified, professional advice. The authors can take no responsibility for any damage or loss suffered as a result of any inadvertent inaccuracy within this text.

David Isaac and John O'Leary
School of Architecture and Construction
University of Greenwich
2011

Acknowledgements

The authors and publishers wish to thank the following for the use of copyright material in this second edition: the RICS for permission to reproduce the chart showing the proportion of transactions between 10, 15 and 20 per cent bands in Chapter 7; and to Cengage Learning for permission to reproduce the utility functions diagram in Chapter 9 which originally appeared in Lumby and Jones (2006).

Every effort has been made to trace all the copyright holders, but if any have been inadvertently overlooked, the publishers will be pleased to make the necessary arrangements at the first opportunity.

Abbreviations

ARLA	Association of Residential Letting Agents
ARY	all risks yield
ASF	annual sinking fund
BREEAM	Building Research Establishment Environmental Assessment Method
CAPM	Capital Asset Pricing Model
CGT	capital gains tax
CML	capital market line
CoML	Council of Mortgage Lenders
CPI	Consumer Price Index
CSH	Code for Sustainable Homes
CSR	corporate social responsibility
DCF	discounted cash flow
DRC	depreciated replacement cost
ERV	estimated rental value
FRI	full repairing and insuring [lease]
FTSE	Financial Times Stock Exchange [100 companies]
GDP	gross domestic product
GDV	gross development value
IPD	Investment Property Databank
IPF	Investment Property Forum
IRFY	inflation risk-free yield
IRR	internal rate of return
JV	joint venture
LEED	leadership in energy and environmental design
LTV	loan-to-value ratio
NPV	net present value
NTV	net terminal value
pa	per annum
PBIT	profit before interest and tax
PEST	political, economic, social and technical [change analysis]
PFI	private finance initiative
PPP	public–private partnerships
PTAL	public transport accessibility level
PUT	property unit trusts
PV	present value
RADR	risk-adjusted discount rate
REIT	Real Estate Investment Trust
RFR	risk-free rate
RICS	Royal Institution of Chartered Surveyors
RLA	Residential Landlords Association
RPI	retail price index

SWOT	strengths, weaknesses opportunities and threats [analysis]
UCO	Use Classes Order
USS	Universities Superannuation Scheme
VOA	Valuation Office Agency
YP	years' purchase

1

Introducing property investment

Aims

This chapter aims to introduce some key property investment concepts in order to provide a foundation and a vocabulary for what follows in the book. The chapter also seeks to reveal some of the dilemmas and challenges which are faced by both the novice and experienced property investor. The chapter rounds up by considering how heightened concerns with sustainability are beginning to influence property investment decision-making.

Key terms

>> **Yield** – an annual rate of return expressed as a percentage of the capital value of an investment such as a tenanted commercial property which is producing a rental income stream. The yield will vary over the life cycle of an investment property because rental income will change and there will be periodic revaluations of the capital value, such as when the building is sold.

>> **All risks yield** – the expression 'all risks' implies that the investor has considered all the risks and potential rewards in arriving at a purchase price which is then reflected in the yield.

>> **Capitalization** – the process of converting an income stream from an investment into a capital value. For investment properties this would normally involve the conversion of the annual rental income into a capital

value by using a multiplier called the Years' Purchase in perpetuity abbreviated to *YP in perp*. The YP in perp. is the reciprocal of the yield.

>> **Reverse yield gap** – the difference which sometimes manifests itself between the prevailing rate of annual interest on what is considered to be a risk free investment such as government gilt-edged stock and a lower all risks yield which may have arisen from the purchase of an investment property. By accepting a lower initial rate of interest on the property investment relative to what is available on gilts (the reverse yield gap) the property investor is signifying an expectation that both the capital and rental value of the property will grow in future to ultimately outperform the risk-free interest rate obtainable on gilts.

>> **Corporate social responsibility** (**CSR**) – the degree to which an organization recognizes that it should consider the impacts of its activities on the environment and a wider group of stakeholders than just its shareholders or immediate clients. CSR, which is sometimes articulated in an organization's mission statement, is strongly linked to whether an organization recognizes and acts in a sustainable way, such as in the types of buildings it develops or chooses to lease.

>> **Sustainability** – there are numerous overlapping definitions of sustainability, however it is widely acknowledged that sustainability has *environmental, economic* and *social* dimensions and that sustainable decisions in these three fields will be those which do not compromise the ability for future generations to make their own sustainable decisions.

>> **Triple bottom line** – recognition that decisions should be evaluated on more than just financial performance, as environmental and social gains or losses should also be considered.

1.1 Introduction

This chapter plays an introductory role in the book by beginning to explore some of the key property investment terms and concepts. For example a discussion is begun on why property investors need to factor in risk, inflation and an opportunity cost when expressing their investment expectations in the interest rate which is commonly referred to as a yield. The focus in the chapter and indeed throughout the book is mainly on commercial property sector. However where it is felt appropriate, there is reference to residential property investment which in recent years has taken off in the form of buy-to-let. The chapter considers the unique characteristics of property investment in comparison with other investment media such as gilts and equities which, from an investor's perspective, are easier to get into and out of. The chapter rounds up by considering how growing concerns with sustainability are beginning to influence the thinking if not the practices of those involved in the property industry.

1.2 The rationale for property investment

A building can be owner-occupied or rented and the latter is an investment property. Investment properties come in all shapes and sizes and for example include high street shops, offices on business parks, industrial and warehouse

Figure 1.1 Riverbridge House, Anchor Boulevard, Crossways Business Park, Dartford

units, pubs and leisure premises, buy-to-let residential property and even whole farms. Investment properties therefore feature in all sectors of the property market. In some property sectors such as residential, most of the housing stock is owner-occupied or managed by social landlords with a relatively small proportion of private rented properties. However it is estimated that around 43 per cent of the commercial property market is made up of tenanted investment properties with the remainder being owner-occupied.

Riverbridge House (see Figure 1.1) is a 5,148 m² B1 building at Crossways Business Park, Dartford in North Kent. The building was developed on a speculative basis so that when it is fully tenanted it becomes a rent-producing investment property.

What distinguishes property investments like the above building is that there is a non-occupying owner who is primarily interested in receiving the income in the form or rent and in monitoring the capital value. The owner is therefore mainly interested in the *investment value* of the property while the occupier who may be a business or a household, will be primarily interested in the *use value* of the property. Of course the two types of value are intimately linked because a property which is highly useful for an occupying business or household will tend to be sought after in the market place and this will normally sustain the underlying investment value.

When there are periodic downturns in property markets, some investment properties may become vacant and it may be difficult to find tenants for new investment properties being brought to the market for the first time. Lengthy voids, which are a characteristic of a recession, might suggest that a property has been a poor investment for its owner. However investors in property need to take a longer-term view when compared with investors in more liquid investment opportunities. Thus the real picture on whether a property has performed well as an investment might only emerge by examining its performance over a number of years rather than considering a relatively short time horizon during which the economy might not have been functioning particularly well.

The investment market for property cannot be seen in isolation from other investment markets. The application of funds to property reflects competition from other forms of investment. The decision to invest in a particular type of investment will be the outcome of a comparison between the returns and security offered by different types of investment media. Thus the investor's knowledge and analysis of alternative investment opportunities is important. The application of financial appraisal techniques to property investment is a key factor in identifying investment performance and thus signifying its attractiveness relative to other forms of investment.

Oprea (2010) agrees that feasibility analysis does have a legitimate role to play in rational property investment, as the purchase of an investment property essentially places considerable sums of money at risk in anticipation of receiving future cash receipts. As Oprea explains regarding property investors:

> They are in effect buying a set of assumptions about the project's ability to generate the anticipated revenue. (2010: 59)

Setting aside the potential for indirect investment in property by purchasing shares in property companies or investing in Real Estate Investment Trusts (discussed later), direct investment in property will usually require a loan. This simply reflects the scale of investment required. For example, even for the most modest buy-to-let residential investment, the property investor will probably still need a mortgage which will amount to perhaps 65 per cent of the value of a property. The ability of the borrower to meet mortgage repayments will be assessed by the lender against the expected rental income stream from the property.

The buy-to-let scenario above represents perhaps the simplest arrangement, but for higher value commercial properties the situation is more complex. For commercial properties such as office blocks or shops, finance is generally raised by corporate entities, such as property companies, using existing property and other assets as collateral. Large corporate investors will also tend to purchase a portfolio of assets which may include individual properties which have high unit value. However by comparison those properties may only represent a minor percentage of the overall value held in a portfolio, given multimillion pound investments in other assets such as shares and bonds which typically make up the bulk of value held in institutional investment portfolios.

Property and property investment plays a significant role in the wider economy. Property is a factor of production, it is also a corporate asset and it is also an investment medium. As a factor of production, property provides the space in which economic activity and production takes place. The efficiency and costs of such space will affect the cost of goods and services produced. As a corporate asset, property forms the major part of asset values in companies' balance sheets and the majority of corporate debt is secured against it. As Sayce *et al.* (2006: 190–3) confirm, despite fluctuations in the attractiveness of property as an investment asset, it remains a modest but important type of investment held by individual investors and the financial institutions.

Qualities of an investment

An investment essentially involves an initial outlay of money in order to recoup a future income stream and/or a future capital repayment. One way of analysing what is required of an investment is to use a check list of questions and answers. The key question is what an investor expects from an investment, to which the answers might be:

- security of capital;
- security of income from the capital invested;
- regularity of income;
- ease of purchase and sale of the investment;
- low cost of purchase and sale of the investment;
- divisibility which enables parts of the investment to be sold off if necessary; and
- security in real terms, wherein the value increases at least in line with inflation.

Table 1.1 on page 6 compares these desirable characteristics to a number of possible investment opportunities and finds that some investments inevitably outperform others, particularly regarding start-up costs and the security of the investment. The additional key variable is whether the return outstrips inflation and this is considered in the final row of the table.

Real security

The last characteristic in Table 1.1 considers the real security of the investment, which is whether it will hold its value over time by matching or outperforming the rate of inflation. If there is decline in capital value or income in real terms, then the investment is inflation prone.

However, deciding on which measure of inflation to use as a benchmark is not as straightforward as it once was, as the long standing measure of inflation: the Retail Price Index (RPI) has a competitor in the form of the Consumer Price Index (CPI). The essential difference in the two measures is that the CPI does not include residential mortgage repayments and therefore tends to generate a lower annual inflation rate than is recorded by RPI. On that basis it is perhaps not surprising that the use of CPI has its supporters in government and officialdom. However it is still common practice in the UK to use RPI as the measure of inflation where there are clauses in contracts concerning payments which are to be 'index linked'. Perhaps the underlying loyalty in the use of RPI in contracts is partly inertia and partly that there may be an underlying sentiment that the more broadly based RPI is a more 'honest' reflection of the inflation rate.

In reality each individual and each company has a different inflation rate depending on specific consumption patterns. Thus if individuals are renting property in the public or private sectors they will experience different inflation rates to those who are outright home owners or those who are still paying off

Table 1.1 The characteristics of different investment assets compared

Characteristic	Type of investment					
	Tenanted house	Tenanted prime high street shop	Shares	Gilts	Building society accounts	Premium bonds
Security of capital	Probably, but depends on market conditions, quality and location	Yes, unless an out of town retail centre is opened nearby	No, companies and their share prices can collapse completely	Yes, although some erosion is possible when traded	Yes	Yes
Security of income	No	Probably, although some retailers fail in recessions	Depends on company performance	Yes	Yes, although interest rates may vary	No, but windfall gains are possible
Regularity of income	Yes when tenanted	Yes when tenanted	Yes, although dividends may sometimes be withheld	Yes	Yes	No
Ease of purchase and sale	No	No	Yes	Yes	Yes	Yes
Low cost of purchase and sale	No	No	Yes	Yes	Yes	Yes
Divisibility	No	No	Yes	Yes	Yes	Yes
Real security/growth (hedge against inflation)	Yes over the long term	Possibly depending on location	Depends on company performance	Normally	No	No

a mortgage. An individual's inflation rate is also influenced by age, income, marital status and lifestyle as these factors largely determine specific consumption patterns. However, from the property investor's perspective, while there is some choice on which inflation benchmark to use, it would be reasonable to look at annual inflation as measured by the broadly based RPI to see if the growth of rental and capital values has kept up with that measure of inflation.

To provide a simple example, the comparative chart below uses data compiled by the Department for Communities and Local Government in England on average house prices and the Central Statistical Office's RPI record of annual inflation. An arbitrary start date of 1987 provides a sufficient time-series to establish whether the average price of an average London terraced house has kept pace with inflation over that time span. By comparing the bottom line index figures, the cliché that bricks and mortar provide a hedge against inflation is borne out in the long term. This is one of the reasons why investors have been attracted to the buy-to-let market.

The above comments presuppose that the buy-to-let investor has retained their investment for the longer term, which is probably not the case for many investors in this market. While inflation has increased annually at modest rates with only one very marginal negative value in 2009 the annual changes in housing values are far more volatile with significant growth in some years contrasted with falls in four of the 23 years being examined. Thus timing is an issue for the investor if they are only planning to stay in this market for the short term. This market does seem to reward the investor who is able to stay in the market for the longer term in order to ride out the few years when capital values fall. For example to have purchased a property at the end of 1991 and then to have sold the property two years later would have seen a property investor facing a considerable loss.

Time-series data like those shown below always have to be treated with some caution, as averages hide a multitude of individual variations, especially in a broad category such as terraced houses across a city such as London. Some properties will no doubt have performed way above average because they are close to amenities, good schools, transport connections and are in fashionable parts of London. Other properties will have performed below average because of numerous factors including poor housing condition, remoteness from social infrastructure or the presence of negative externalities in the particular area.

The figures in Table 1.2 on page 8 are also silent about the income generation of the properties which is important for buy-to-let investors and also whether the rate of capital value increase above inflation provides a significant enough return relative to the interest rate available on other investments.

The quality of an investment from an economic point of view must be a comparison of the return against the risk. The return is not just the cash flow arising but also the relationship between the original outlay and the return when the asset is sold. The cash flow needs to be considered relative to the original outlay, ongoing costs, future income and capital revenues. Thus investors are not only looking for a hedge against inflation but a margin above that to compensate for the risks involved and this matter is returned to later in this chapter.

The type of investment chosen is related to a number of factors which will differ according to the investor. An investor may for example have a particular tax status or ethical considerations may affect investment choices.

Table 1.2 Time-series data on house price changes

Year	Annual RPI %	RPI index	Average London terraced house price £	Annual % change	Terraced house price index
1987	4.2	100	65,187	25.3	100
1988	4.9	104.2	81,660	10.9	125.3
1989	7.8	109.3	90,588	−1.7	139
1990	9.5	117.8	89,037	5.6	136.6
1991	5.9	129	93,990	−16.9	144.2
1992	3.7	136.6	78,120	2.2	119.9
1993	1.6	141.7	79,851	5.6	122.6
1994	2.4	144	84,310	4.3	129.4
1995	3.5	147.5	87,957	4.1	135
1996	2.4	152.7	91,584	16.1	140.6
1997	3.1	156.4	106,292	7.9	163.2
1998	3.4	161.2	114,720	27.2	176.1
1999	1.5	166.7	145,925	18.0	224
2000	3	169.2	172,223	8.9	264.4
2001	1.8	174.3	187,493	15.9	287.8
2002	1.7	177.4	217,327	20.2	333.6
2003	2.9	180.4	261,284	14.6	401.1
2004	3	185.6	299,399	2.4	459.6
2005	2.8	191.2	306,591	5.5	470.6
2006	3.2	196.6	323,344	12.2	496.3
2007	4.3	202.9	362,650	−0.3	556.6
2008	4	211.6	361,563	−5.2	554.9
2009	−0.5	220.1	342,676		525.9

Capital risk and growth

Capital security is obviously important to a prudent investor. Until the credit squeeze which began in 2007 it was unheard of for a bank in the UK to get into difficulty and thus bank accounts were not thought to be at risk. However with the failure of Northern Rock and the need for the UK government to take size-able stakes in a number of other high street banks, even this hitherto safe haven is now less secure than it once was. In general terms however, money deposited in banks and building society accounts is unlikely to be at significant risk, whereas alternative investment opportunities such as shares or works of art may lead to a partial or complete loss.

When the concept of security is considered, the relationship between security in real terms and in money terms need to be examined. Security in money terms ignores inflation whereas security in real terms considers the potential erosion of the purchasing power of money which inflation can bring. To identify its true purchasing power, income needs to be discounted by the rate of inflation to find the security in real terms. This discount may be compensated to some extent by any interest received on deposits. Real capital growth in property would require the growth in the capital to outstrip the rate of inflation. However such an analysis, while concentrating on inflation, ignores other elements which make up interest rates. Besides allowing for inflation, an interest rate will also need to compensate for delayed consumption and risk, so that there are three components reflected in the rate of return or yield on an investment:

- an element which provides compensation for the time preference of money;
- an element related to inflation which exists to maintain the real value of the return; and
- an element for a risk premium.

These three elements can be considered in a little more depth in the following paragraphs.

The time preference element

This element exists as compensation to the investor who cannot spend money which has been invested and will have to wait until the investment is sold. The compensation principle stems from the view that individuals prefer to have money available now rather than later, so that it is readily available to spend on consumables of one kind or another. The interest rate offered therefore needs to be sufficient to entice individuals to invest their money and thereby delay consumption.

The inflation allowance

The inflation allowance which forms a component of an interest rate should reflect the investor's anticipation of inflation and this may differ depending on the economic assumptions held by the government and other investors. At this point the analysis can show the relationship between market rates of interest which are inclusive of inflation and real rates of interest. This is given by the equation:

$$(1 + \text{real rate of interest}) \times (1 + \text{rate of general inflation})$$
$$= (1 + \text{market rate of interest})$$

or $(1 + i) \times (1 + g) = (1 + e)$

so $i = ((1 + e)/(1+g)) - 1$

Where i is the real rate of interest, g is the rate of general inflation and e is the market rate of interest, all as decimals. As an example, if the rental growth (at market rate = e) is 6% and the rate of inflation (g) is 7% the real rate of growth can be seen to be negative, around −1% or more precisely:

$$i = (1.06/1.07) - 1 = -0.0093$$

The risk premium

This is the addition to the risk-free interest rate to take into account the risk of the investment. There is a trade-off between risk and reward, for additional risk a greater reward is expected by the investor and vice versa. By dividing the real rate of interest into its elements of time preference and the risk premium, the element of the risk premium can be exposed. Thus:

$$(1 + i) = (1 + d) \times (1 + r)$$

Inserting into equation above: $(1 + d) \times (1 + r) \times (1 + g) = (1 + e)$

Here d and r are the time preference and risk elements respectively, rearranging:

$$e = ((1 + g) \times (1 + d) \times (1 + r)) - 1$$

If the risk element was taken out of the above equation, a risk-free return (RFR) would be:

$$RFR = ((1 + i) \times (1 + d)) - 1$$
$$\text{and } e = ((1 + RFR) \times (1 + r)) - 1$$

Multiplying out:

$$e = (1 + r + RFR + rRFR) - 1$$

But rRFR will be small and an approximation is e = RFR + r, thus the market rate of interest is equal to the risk-free rate plus the risk premium attached by the market.

Income risk and growth

Most investments involve an initial capital outlay followed by a stream of income which provides a return, perhaps culminating in a capital receipt on resale of the asset. This is a simplification, as while investments should generate a return some may only do so at the end of the holding period. For example, a vintage car is likely to generate a loss of income up until the time when the asset is sold. At that point the car may realize a higher price than was initially paid because it is valued by a select group of collectors of such cars. In the property world, investment property companies will receive income periodically from rents and they would also seek capital appreciation but a property trading company is likely to rely on the sale of completed project alone.

If an investment is generating an income, that income is never entirely immune from risk. For example the income or dividend payable from investing in ordinary shares bears some risk. This is not just because of absolute changes of income declared by the directors of the company in which shares are held, but also because the rate of return for the individual is related to the price paid for the shares. Thus if an individual purchases £1,000 worth of shares at the beginning of the year in order to obtain an annual dividend of 5 per cent and the income of £50 is duly paid, the investor is 5 per cent better off so long as the share price remains constant. However if the shares are sold at the end of the year when the prevailing market price has fallen to £950 there has obviously been no overall gain for the investor. Of course if the share price had strengthened by the time the shares were sold at the end of the year, the investor would have seen a greater than 5 per cent annual return.

A similar principle applies to government gilt-edged stock whose official market trading title is either Treasury or Exchequer Stock but which are more commonly referred to as gilts. For example, assuming that the issue price of long dated gilts is £100 and the declared nominal rate is 8 per cent then £8 per annum will be paid to the investor by the government. This return is called a *coupon* and it is usually paid in two equal instalments, which in this simple example would be two payments of £4 six months apart. If the stock is purchased at a price higher than the issue price which is referred to as the face value, then, as the £8 income is still paid, the yield is lower for the purchaser. Conversely if the gilts subsequently change hands for less that £100 then the yield becomes higher.

Consider the following example of 30-year 6 per cent Treasury Stock which will be redeemed in 2028. At the time of writing this gilt-edged stock had 18 years until redemption and thus would be considered 'long dated' by the market. At the time when this stock was issued in 1998 the rate of 6 per cent was deemed by the government to be sufficiently attractive to tempt investors to buy the stock and thereby invest in government debt. The government has not so far defaulted on its obligation to pay the rate of interest on any gilts it has issued and nor has it failed to repay the original sum on the redemption date. In that sense, investment in gilts is risk free, but as will be discussed this does not mean that there are no risks at all.

To reflect the relative security provided by the government, the rate of return on gilts will not be as high as might be achievable on riskier investments such as shares or property.

6% Treasury Stock issued in 1998, redeemable in 2028.
In June 2010 this stock was quoted as:

Purchase price	£123.73
Interest only yield	4.85%
Gross redemption yield	4.24%

The interest only yield is simply the relationship between the current quoted purchase price of the gilts and the annual income. In the above case there would be £6 per annum income, so the calculation to determine the interest only yield would simply be: $6/123.73 = 0.04849$ which rounded up is 4.85 per cent.

The gross redemption yield includes the receipt of a capital sum at the end of the life of the investment which reflects the original face value of the gilts i.e. £100 or multiples thereof to reflect the quantity held. This gross redemption yield also reflects the timing and value of all remaining coupons on the assumption that an investor who has paid £123.73 for every £100 lot will hold the gilts until redemption. This is a little unlikely as the gilts are more likely to be traded many times before redemption.

The calculation of the redemption yield is an internal rate of return appraisal taking account of the timing of coupons over the whole period until redemption. It is not necessary to delve into this particular aspect too deeply in this book; however those who are particularly interested in this specialized subject can

Table 1.3 Return on gilts over a three-year holding period

Scenario A in which base rates do not change over the three-year holding period

Year	Expenditure	Income	Net cash flow	Event
0	1,237.30	0	−1,237.30	Purchase gilts
0.5		30	30.00	First half of the annual income of 6%
1		30	30.00	Second half of the annual income of 6%
1.5		30	30.00	First half of the annual income of 6%
2		30	30.00	Second half of the annual income of 6%
2.5		30	30.00	First half of the annual income of 6%
3		1,267.30	1,267.30	Second half of the annual income of 6% plus sale of the gilts
Internal Rate of Return =			4.85%	

consult the UK Government's Debt Management Office (www.dmo.gov.uk) or the Bank of England (www.bankofengland.co.uk) where the formula for calculating the gross redemption yield can be obtained.

To illustrate the general principles at work, *Scenario A* in Table 1.3 above assumes that an investor decided to purchase £1,000 face value of the above gilts in June 2010 at the then market price of £1,237.30 and held these gilts for three years before selling them on. The investor would therefore be entitled to three years of annual income of £60 plus whatever the market was paying for the gilts when they were sold. The price achieved on sale three years later will be affected by changes in the base rate. However if the base rate remained unchanged then it could be expected that these long dated gilts would achieve a similar value on resale.

It would be unusual for base rates to remain unchanged over a three-year period and if base rates were to rise or fall then gilt traders would expect the income return on gilts relative to the trading price to rise or fall by a similar margin. *Scenario B* on page 13 (Table 1.4) therefore explores an example where base rates have risen by 1.5 per cent over the three-year holding period to illustrate the implications for the trading price of the gilts in that event.

In scenario B therefore it is assumed that in the interests of the wider economy, the Bank of England Monetary Policy Committee decided to gradually raise interest rates from what was a historically unprecedented low rate of 0.5 per cent at the beginning of the three-year period to 2 per cent by the end of it. Investors in long dated gilts could be expected to respond to this 1.5 per cent

Table 1.4 Return on gilts when the base rate rises

Scenario B in which base rates have risen 1.5% over the three-year holding period

Year	Expenditure	Income	Net cash flow	Event
0	1,237.30	0	–1,237.30	Purchase gilts
0.5		30	30.00	First half of the annual income of 6%
1		30	30.00	Second half of the annual income of 6%
1.5		30	30.00	First half of the annual income of 6%
2		30	30.00	Second half of the annual income of 6%
2.5		30	30.00	First half of the annual income of 6%
3		974.88	974.88	Second half of the annual income of 6% plus sale of the gilts
Internal Rate of Return =			–3.37%	

increase in base rates by expecting around a 1.5 per cent increase in the income returns on gilts. Thus a 4.85 per cent return may have been acceptable when base rates were 0.5 per cent but investors could be expected to require a 6.35 per cent return from gilts when base rates were 2 per cent three years later. Thus for the £1,000 face value of 6 per cent long dated Treasury stock in the example above, investors in the market would then expect to pay closer to 60/6.35% = £944.88 which when added to the final coupon of £30 in year 3 below generates the figure £974.88.

In the unlikely event that the original purchaser had not monitored the market and offloaded the gilts before the interest rate rises, then the internal rate of return (IRR) for holding the stock for three years in scenario B would have been a small loss signified by the –3.37 per cent return. The mathematics and significance of the IRR as an evaluative tool is explored fully in Chapter 5 where there are worked examples. However at this stage it might best be thought of as a convenient way for an investor to make comparisons between investments based upon what is paid out to acquire the investment and what is returned over the holding period.

Thus it is not entirely true to say that investing in gilts is risk free, although the current rate of return on gilts is often used as a proxy for the 'risk-free rate' against which to compare returns on other perhaps riskier investments. When purchasing gilts when base rates are particularly low, the value paid in the market will be tempered by the risk that in the near future base rates might rise, causing a loss of exchange value to gilts. Conversely when interest rates are historically high, investors might purchase gilts in the expectation that base rates cannot remain high indefinitely and as the base rate falls, the market exchange value of gilts is likely to rise commensurately. Market sentiment on where base rates are likely to go in future will therefore play a role in determining the trading value of gilts.

1.3 Characteristics of property investment

Durability, uniqueness and cost

Land is both more durable and often more expensive than other commodities and those who purchase it for future income or use must forgo present consumption to do this. If purchasers buy properties for personal use then they are in the position of receiving an income equivalent to a rent which they would otherwise have to pay if they did not own the property. Property is thus purchased for investment as well as consumption purposes. Land is heterogeneous in that each piece is different and each property is unique by location. However despite the differences there are some common characteristics enabling a degree of substitution between one property and another.

In the residential market the price of property is high relative to individual earnings and in most regions in the UK the average house price represents up to eight times the regional average annual income. Thus people have to borrow to buy property and the availability and price of credit has an important bearing on demand. During the height of the credit squeeze in 2009 the inability of particularly first time buyers to access mortgage loans saw average house prices fall between 10 and 15 per cent depending on the region. Legal factors have a significant effect on the supply and demand for property. For example there have been periods in the UK when rent acts sought to control rental levels in the private rented sector and this led to a dramatic decline in private investment in that sector.

Psychic characteristics

The psychic effect relates to the feel-good factor associated with owning land and property and the ability to see 'something concrete' in one's investment. The ownership of something tangible such as land or bricks and mortar will bring kudos to the owner. The ownership of a period house set in its own grounds or a penthouse flat in a fashionable area will inevitably bestow upon the owner a sense of security and achievement. There is an undeniable status and prestige associated with the ownership of buildings such as these and this can transfer to the corporate sector where landmark buildings with sustainability credentials may be sought by large companies for public relations and corporate image reasons.

Social characteristics

The ownership of land and buildings has historically been linked to social responsibility and the French expression: *noblesse oblige* implies that with wealth, title and landownership comes social responsibility. In the modern context there are ethical considerations related to property investment which will be considered further towards the end of this chapter when the concept of CSR is explored.

At a subliminal level there is an expectation that the owners of properties will take responsibility for their upkeep as not to do so (particularly in a residential context) would be seen as not keeping up with implied but unwritten social obligations. The public realm has entered the popular vocabulary and it is clear that where buildings and spaces are maintained properly there is less chance of those areas attracting vandalism and graffiti which might lead to further deterioration. Development proposals can affect amenity and those proposals which are not 'in keeping' with the character of an area will tend to attract objections from third parties.

There may be a responsibility in ownership related to the local community and its activities and it is often the case that where residential owner-occupation levels are high there tends also to be signifiers that the residents are active at least in terms of the ubiquitous neighbourhood watch committees. Similarly retailers who feel that they have a stake in their town centre will tend to become active in the town centre management group. This is not to say of course that those individuals or companies in rented property cannot or do not play a stakeholder role in their communities, but that ownership strengthens the likelihood that individuals or firms will become active defenders of 'their patch' as they have an added financial incentive to do so.

Economic characteristics

The rational investor will always be concerned with the economic characteristics of property investment, and this relates to the risk and return profile of an investment. There are a number of aspects to this relating to risk and return of capital and income, the costs of managing the asset and the taxation of income and capital. Other aspects which affect the risk and return are the timing of in- and out-flows of income and capital. The life of the asset is associated with this, as is the concept of depreciation in value over time. Risk and return is also related to the liquidity of the asset and the extent of ongoing management obligations. These economic considerations can now be considered in a little more detail, and there are two elements to consider: *capital* risk and growth and *income* risk and growth.

Inflation hedging characteristics

The example earlier which looked at the increase in average terraced house prices across London relative to inflation over the same period suggested that that particular type of housing in that particular location did outperform inflation. In crude terms therefore the housing could be seen as a hedge against inflation. However the growth in housing values particularly in cities like London has been fuelled by particular set of circumstances which includes low housebuilding rates relative to the growth in demand. It would be unwise to assume that this inflation beating performance is true of all residential property types in all areas and nor should it automatically be assumed that all commercial property sectors in all locations outperform inflation.

However discussion around interest rates inevitable raises the question of whether in general terms, investing in commercial property can be a hedge against inflation. As far back as 1995 Matysiak *et al.* used a multivariate analysis of long-term total returns from commercial property relative to inflation over the period 1963–93. They found no evidence that property returns provide a hedge on an annual basis against inflation. More recently Baum revisited the issue:

> Data suggests a strong correlation between rents and inflation in the long run, and the cash flow might (although subject to deterioration and obsolescence) be expected to increase in line with inflation over a long period. (2009: 28)

However Baum adds the caveat that because the income stream on commercial property is usually stepped to reflect five-year rent reviews, during the interim periods the income is fixed and therefore prone to inflation. Thus there are some similarities with the housing example previously discussed in that the inflation hedging principle could apply on condition that the investor takes a longer-term view and is sensible about the specific properties to invest in.

Legal characteristics

The two principal estates in land are freehold and leasehold. Other legal interests also exist such as easements, restrictive covenants and licences. Freehold properties are those which the owners hold absolutely and in perpetuity. The owner may be in possession as an owner-occupier or they may be absent but receiving rents arising from leases or tenancies. In that case they will have become property investors. Leasehold properties are subject to legal agreements allowing the lessees rights over the property for a term of years. Freehold and leasehold interests are defined as 'legal estates' by the Law of Property Act 1925 and these are enforceable against anyone. Other interests are termed equitable interests and can be enforced against some people only. Leasehold and equitable interests are carved out of the freehold interest. At the end of a lease there is a reversion to the landlord, however, this has been restricted by government legislation. For instance, the Rents Acts affect short leases and the Leasehold Reform Act affects long leases, the Agricultural Holdings Act affects agricultural land and the Landlord and Tenant Acts affect commercial property.

There are two principal types of lease, the first of which is a *building* or *ground lease* which enables the lessee (the party taking the lease) to erect buildings on a site. These leases tend to be long leases because of the commitment to build and are therefore usually 99 or 125 years in duration but could be as much as 999 years.

The second type of lease is an *occupational lease* which enables occupation of both land and buildings. A conventional lease pattern here might be for 20 or 25 years with the rent being reviewed every five years and possibly a break clause at the half way stage. However in recent years shorter occupational leases of between five and 10 years have been agreed in response to the economic climate and the desire from businesses to achieve a more flexible relationship with their leased premises.

Sub-leases are granted by lessees and carved from their leasehold interest,

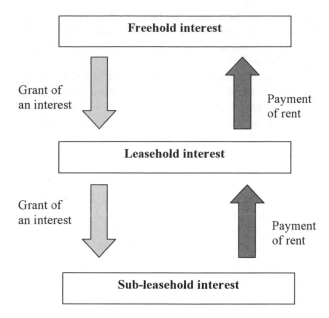

Figure 1.2 The relationship between freehold and leasehold interests in commercial property

although there will normally be legal conditions which will have to be met before sub-letting can take place or indeed assignment of a lease to a third party. However in general terms there is a hierarchy of leases and subleases as shown in Figure 1.2 above.

Other interests include restrictive covenants and easements which are restrictions on the use of land created by a freeholder or leaseholder. A restrictive covenant is a contractual obligation in a deed. An easement is a right under common law which burdens one piece of land for the benefit of another. Easements include rights of way, rights of support and rights of light and ventilation. Interests in land have to be distinguished from permissions to enter upon land such as licences, and this distinction is summarized in Table 1.5 as follows.

Table 1.5 Legal and equitable interests in property

Legal interests	Equitable interests

Legal estates such as:
     freeholds
     leaseholds
 Legal rights over land:
     easements
     covenants
	Grants under wills or settlements such as:
	     permissions to enter land
	     licences

It is neither possible nor necessary in this book to unravel all of the legal complexity raised by leases, sub leases and other estates in land; however those who wish to explore this topic in more depth could examine a specialist legal text such as Smith (2008).

As well as legal interests, land is also constrained by government statutes. For example, the government can intervene in the landlord and tenant relationship with legislation which provides security of tenure or to enable tenants to extend their leases in certain circumstances. Local authorities also have statutory control over the development and use of land through the Town and Country Planning Acts and over the construction of buildings through the Building Regulations. There is a myriad of legislation relating to the use and condition of premises including the Offices, Shops and Railway Premises Act, the Factories Act, the Fire Precautions Act, the Housing Acts and Health and Safety legislation. From time to time property investors will therefore require specialist legal and accounting advice and this is yet another distinguishing feature which sets property investment apart from investment in other media such as gilts and equities.

Basic tax characteristics

Net of tax or after tax returns are those which are of interest to investors. Gross funds (pension funds and other investment funds which do not pay tax) would not want to take on income taxed at source as this reduces their return. Where a differential exists between the treatment of capital and income taxes, investors who pay high income tax may opt for a low income return but a large capital growth. Tax rate differentials between income and capital gains have been largely brought into line but tax allowances may moderate an individual's tax burden. Tax shelters such as capital allowances in construction are important as is the tax treatment of losses in offsetting profit elsewhere, as these may improve returns to a portfolio of investments.

Because of the leverage exerted by the large corporate property investors over the commercial property sector, funds are usually able to acquire new tenanted property investments from developers net of acquisition and stamp duty costs which are in effect absorbed by the developer. One of the key tax advantages for large property companies in converting to Real Estate Investment Trusts (REITs) was that they would become exempt from tax on their property trading activities. This enables a larger tax exempt surplus to be passed on to REIT investors who would then individually be liable for tax on income. Effectively a REIT avoids double taxation on its property investment activities.

For small investors capital gains tax (CGT) is also a significant issue for what might be relatively modest gains from investments. For example if an individual had purchased a £150,000 portfolio of shares and had held the investment for several years before selling the portfolio for £200,000 to make a capital gain of £50,000 that gain would be subject to CGT. In August 2010 the rate of CGT for a standard tax payer in the UK was 18 per cent (28 per cent for higher rate tax payers) on gains over £10,100. Thus the small investor would normally pay an 18 per cent tax on a gain of £39,900 (£50,000 –10,100) which would be £7,182 leaving the investor with a net capital gain of £42,818.

For the buy-to-let investor the CGT liability could be reduced as there are tax allowances which include legitimate expenditure on acquiring the property in the first instance (stamp duty, survey and solicitors' fees for example) and any costs of improvement and costs of disposal (agents' fees). For the buy-to-let investor the taxable element might then look as follows:

Purchase modest property for buy-to-let purposes:	£150,000
Cost of acquisition (stamp duty, survey and legal fees):	£3,500
Costs of improvement:	£10,000
Costs of disposal:	£2,500
Value on disposal:	£200,000

Basic CGT calculation:

Difference between purchase and sale value:	£50,000
Deduct allowances (total costs of acquisition, improvement and disposal):	£16,000
Net gain therefore: £50,000 − £16,000 =	£34,000
Taxable element: £34,000 − allowance of £10,100 =	£23,900
Tax payable: £23,900 × 18% =	£4,302

However the UK government has spent considerable sums of money propping up an ailing banking sector between 2008 and 2009 and in a raft of measures termed *quantitative easing* designed to prevent the economic situation worsening. The result has been that in one way or another, there has been a reduction of tax returns to the Exchequer and increased public expenditure. While the policies and the spending may have been necessary, most analysts expect taxes to rise across the board going forward from 2010 in order to relieve the massive public debt which has accumulated. One of the taxes which will inevitably be reviewed at each budget by the Chancellor of the Exchequer is CGT and some observers expect this tax to rise and/or thresholds and allowances to change so that the tax revenue to the Exchequer is increased. It is difficult to predict with certainty how any Chancellor of the Exchequer will adjust taxes like CGT, as such proposals and their release at budgets is shrouded in secrecy up until they are made public (usually in the Chancellor's budget speeches). However it is perhaps obvious that the incidence and timing of tax and indeed awareness that taxes are likely to change are of obvious importance to investors large and small.

Time issues

The timing of receipts is important, especially if an investor is dependent on one or two investments. For a larger investor, a portfolio of investments may balance out the timing of cash flows. Rent on commercial property is usually paid quarterly in advance and monthly for residential buy-to-let properties. Thus even for commercial property, rent is receivable more regularly than share dividends or gilt coupons which are paid half yearly. The importance of timing in investment is often to match income with liabilities.

Life cycle characteristics

The life cycle of an investment is important. Gilts will have a market exchange value which gradually converges on its face value as the redemption date approaches. However there is a difference between gilts with a term and those without (such as undated Consols), in the same way as leasehold and freehold property. A lease will incur costs at review of the rent or when a lease comes to an end and reinstatement works may have to be carried out under the lease. Freeholders with leases which are not prime property will, in particular, encounter disruption to their income flows as tenancies end and when voids may occur while marketing and negotiation takes place in order to relet a building.

Depreciation and obsolescence

Depreciation is the wearing out of an asset over time and this may lead to a loss of income as an asset becomes less attractive and there will also be a loss of capital value as the asset becomes less saleable. Depreciation in property may require refurbishment or complete redevelopment. Either solution will require capital outlay and loss of income during the reconstruction process. For example, the Savoy Hotel in London's Strand was closed in 2009 for a three-year refurbishment programme during which time there is obviously no income from paying guests.

Depreciation can be caused be economic factors (such as a fall off in demand for the asset) or physical factors (such as a deterioration of the fabric of the building or a loss of aesthetic attractiveness as the building ages) or functional (relating to the design and use of the building) or a combination of all three. Land should be distinguished from buildings in this analysis, as land will tend not to depreciate unless it becomes contaminated or is affected by misuse or bad neighbour development. Buildings will depreciate although this may be curable by timely maintenance or it may be incurable in which case the term obsolescence is used. Depreciation is a specialized topic which is discussed more fully in Chapter 7.

Obsolescence can be further divided into factors which are integral to the building or which are extrinsic and driven by wider factors in the external environment. For example obsolescence which is caused by factors which are integral to the building manifest themselves in outdated facilities, décor or design by which a building has been left behind by changes in taste, expectation and technology. These factors are sometimes mirrored in a deterioration of the aesthetic qualities of a building as it ages, particularly where external facades weather poorly and the building begins to look like a dated concrete edifice. In that situation it will become increasingly difficult to let the building and it will probably have become obsolete. Extrinsic obsolescence relates to changes in external markets such as a global shift in the location of production. For example a whole car plant can be rendered obsolete because a multinational car manufacturer makes a strategic decision to shift production activity to a country where labour rates are cheaper. Redevelopment for another use is often the only solution when this happens, as there may be no other users interested in the car plant or those that are have made the same decision to off-shore their production activity in order to remain competitive alongside their business rivals.

In the age of satellite technology there is a degree of functional obsolescence attached to the BT Tower in central London, pictured above (left). However the option to redevelop what the owners probably feel is an obsolete telecommunications tower on a valuable site is not available, as this is a listed building. This dilemma is often faced by owners of commercial buildings which have been listed but whose original function has moved on requiring that a new use be found.

The Bristol Shot Tower pictured above (right) has been listed as an example of a twentieth-century industrial building where innovative construction technology was employed. The industrial use has now ceased and this presents a challenge for the owners to find a new use for this listed building. Sometimes there is considerable delay before a viable alternative use can be found. Even when an alternative has been identified the plans for internal and external alterations have to be approved by the local authority in consultation with English Heritage.

The *Well Hall Coronet* below was designed by Andrew Mather and opened in 1936. The building was listed grade II in 1989. However the cinema closed

in 1999 when multiplex cinemas in more accessible locations captured the cinema going market. There ensued a 10-year search for an acceptable alternative use, during which time the building deteriorated to the point where it featured in English Heritage's Buildings at Risk Register.

For the Well Hall cinema above Cathedral Properties obtained planning and listed building consent from the London Borough of Greenwich in late 2008. The consents enabled part redevelopment and part conversion of the cinema for a mixed use scheme containing retail, residential, offices and leisure uses. The plan retained the distinctive façade of the building and part of the auditorium, which was to be made available as a resource for student film-makers. From a heritage perspective there will always be a debate about the granting of such consents as some would view this as a successful outcome while others would say that it was a pragmatic compromise.

As well as becoming obsolete because the original use of the building is no longer viable, buildings can also become obsolete due to the decay of the environment and changes in the location of industry. For example the movement towards larger ships and containerization in the late twentieth-century saw most of the major European ports relocate to deeper water estuary locations leaving behind swathes of redundant warehouses around old dockland centres. This kind of locational obsolescence presents a significant challenge in terms of regenerating older dockland areas. A further analysis of depreciation related to the valuation of property and buildings is undertaken in Chapter 7.

Transferability and divisibility

There are higher transfer charges related to the sale and purchase of real property than for other competing asset classes. There is also a time element involved in property transactions which can be costly in terms of accrued interest charged during the period of the transaction and there can also be adverse effects in situations requiring a forced sale. If the property market enters a downward phase in a particular sector or location, it may be difficult to dispose of a property and the investor may well be left holding an undesirable asset. In that scenario the owner may have to seek professional advice on alternatives such as a change of use on a temporary or permanent basis or complete redevelopment of a site.

The complexity of property transactions also carries some risk and the process of due diligence which involves the verification of title and land searches will add time and cost to the transaction to prevent fraud and mistakes from happening. The flow chart below in Figure 1.3 which was inspired by Darlow (1983) depicts some of the key stages which will typically be undergone during what can be a lengthy acquisition process for a substantial investment property. Even some of the apparently straightforward headings in the chart can disguise a layer of complexity. For example, climate change has meant that a greater proportion of commercial and residential properties are now prone to flooding and some of those properties are virtually uninsurable. Thus part of the search process will now commonly involve the inspection of Environment Agency flood risk maps.

There has also been increased reuse of brownfield sites for housing and commercial developments and a proportion of these sites will at one time have

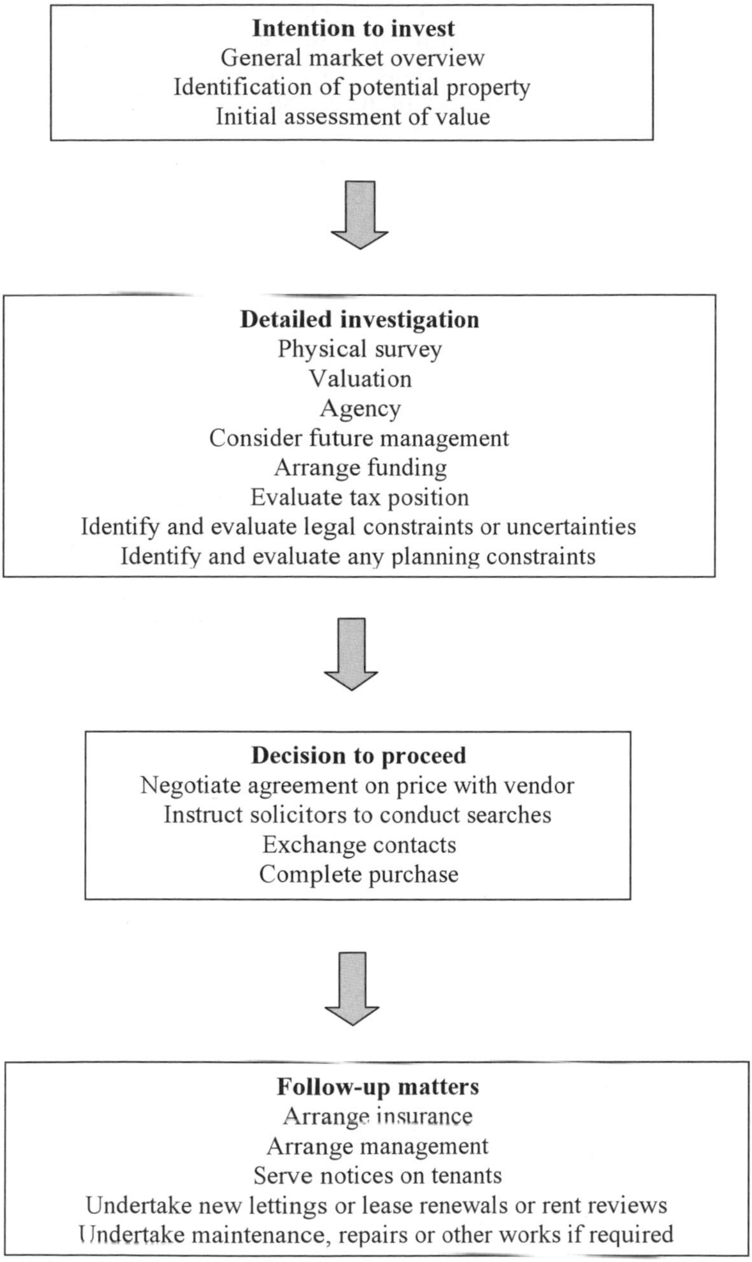

Intention to invest
General market overview
Identification of potential property
Initial assessment of value

Detailed investigation
Physical survey
Valuation
Agency
Consider future management
Arrange funding
Evaluate tax position
Identify and evaluate legal constraints or uncertainties
Identify and evaluate any planning constraints

Decision to proceed
Negotiate agreement on price with vendor
Instruct solicitors to conduct searches
Exchange contacts
Complete purchase

Follow-up matters
Arrange insurance
Arrange management
Serve notices on tenants
Undertake new lettings or lease renewals or rent reviews
Undertake maintenance, repairs or other works if required

Figure 1.3 Stages in property acquisition

been contaminated and then remediated. Purchasers will need to see guarantees that the remediation work was conducted properly and that there are no latent liabilities which could cause problems for the new owner at a later stage.

Newer commercial properties may also be encumbered by claw-back clauses enabling the original landowner to share in future property value uplifts which are sometimes referred to as overage. There may also be complicated section 106 agreements which can create ongoing obligations on the new owners of a building. This is not to say that these constraints automatically become 'deal breakers' but that their presence needs to be detected through diligent research by the purchaser's professional team and then interpreted, as these factors will almost certainly have an effect on the value of an investment property.

In contrast to the complexity set out above, competing investments like gilts and equities can be bought and sold with relative ease within a day and if the market value of a particular share or gilt falls to a predetermined point a computer programme can trigger a sale before the price falls too far. There is a central market in these share assets with publicized prices, so there is knowledge of the net income that will be received. The delay in property transactions and the nature of offers made in property contracts can lead to terms being renegotiated up to exchange of contracts. These situations create additional risk and uncertainty which can lead to abortive costs. Transfer costs on competing investments can amount to less than 1 per cent of the price being paid for the asset, whereas with a major property transaction costs are likely to be over 5 per cent when stamp duty, professional and legal fees are accounted for.

In comparison to stocks and shares which can be purchased in small lot sizes, the indivisibility of property presents difficulties. This has led to experimentation in property unitization in order to break down the equity invested into smaller parts which are more feasible when compared with the purchasing power and risk profiles of a wider range of investors. Similarly investment in property company shares provides some indirect exposure to the property assets held by the major property companies and this matter is discussed further towards the end of this chapter.

Management obligations

Compared with traditional investment opportunities, one of the distinguishing features of real property investments are the ongoing management obligations. The challenges of managing property assets include collecting rents, dealing with repairs and refurbishments, marketing when there are voids and negotiation of lease terms and rent reviews. Armatys et al. (2009: 94) point out that these challenges and ongoing obligations can mean that management costs will be somewhere between 0.5 and 15 per cent of the rental income. A figure at the lower end of that spectrum will arise for buildings which are let to a single tenant on a full repairing and insuring (FRI) lease, while a higher cost will attach to a multi-let building whose tenants are occupying on internal repairing only leases. The management of property therefore involves ongoing costs and it requires informed judgements about what to do and when.

Even with an FRI lease, the purchase and ownership of property requires informed management to deal with the technical and legal issues which can arise. This is particularly true of large multi-let commercial properties such as shopping malls and office blocks whose leases are of different durations and where rent review patterns are varied. There are numerous pieces of legislation to be considered, requiring professional advice and maintenance and management problems will be more involved when there is not an FRI lease. The risks include potential tenant default leading to voids, accidents and liabilities, deleterious substances (like asbestos which may have been used in the construction of the buildings), dangerous structures, nuisance generated by the building and so on. For these reasons direct commercial property investment is unlikely to be an attractive proposition for the small investor, although there are obviously direct investment opportunities in the residential buy-to-let sector (as discussed in Chapters 3 and 8).

1.4 Economics, valuation principles and property investment

Economic principles

Land is a scarce resource and its supply is limited. The use to which land is put can obviously be changed as can the intensity to which land is developed, however in the long term the supply of land could be said to be fixed. Expensive projects such as land reclamation may be feasible in the long term but the affect on the overall supply of land would be marginal. Value, when related to land, was of great interest to the classical economists who used the concept of economic rent to describe payments to land because it is a factor of production which is unable to adjust its supply readily to changes in the level of demand. Land therefore has a degree of monopoly and economic rent was thus earned in the form of higher prices for land because of its scarcity.

As well as limitations on the supply of land for any type of development, in the short run the supply of new property entering a market is inelastic. This is because of the time required to identify and purchase suitable sites, obtain planning consent and to assemble sufficient finance and construction capacity to carry out what might be a lengthy construction process.

An economic representation of these constraints is set out in Figure 1.4 on page 26 where the steeply sloping supply schedule: S–S is contrasted by a flatter and therefore more elastic demand schedule: D–D. This could for example, represent the quantity of commercial floorspace or housing stock in a town or city. For the purposes of this discussion the supply-and-demand relationship represents office floorspace in a city. The change in demand represented by the shift from D–D to D^1–D^1 represents a growth in demand from incoming firms and existing firms expanding and looking for additional office space.

However it takes a number of years for developers to respond to these demand signals by constructing new buildings, marketing and finally letting them. Thus the supply of new office floorspace lags behind demand by several years. However there will always be at least a small volume of supply coming forward in the office development pipeline, representing schemes which were conceived several years earlier. In the short term however the supply response is inelastic relative to demand from office tenants and the consequences will be

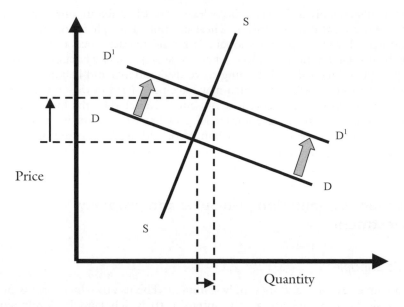

Figure 1.4 Supply and demand for office floorspace

significantly higher rates of growth in price (office rents in this case) relative to the quantity of supply coming on to the market.

However markets are dynamic concepts in which the equilibrium point seldom rests in one place for very long. Figure 1.5 below represents the situation several years later when the supply schedule has begun to respond to demand as signified by its flatter gradient. Developers have now brought new

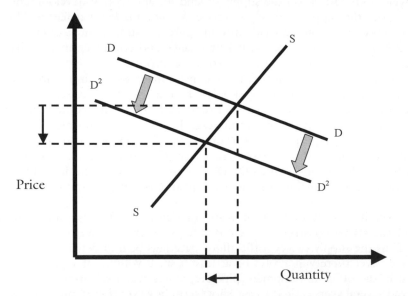

Figure 1.5 A new equilibrium in the supply-and-demand relationship for offices

office blocks onto the market given the prospect of being able to let the offices for higher rents. However by the time the additional supply begins to flow, businesses have begun to downsize as a response to declining economic conditions and thus demand drops from D–D to D^2–D^2. The results are a sharp drop in rental values just at a time when more office stock is arriving on the market. Developers of these schemes will probably be facing lengthy void periods or the need to offer tenants inducements such as rent-free periods. In some localities a proportion of the vacant second hand stock could well be converted to a more profitable use and this will typically see office blocks converted into apartment blocks.

Some property valuation principles

Valuation is a matter of opinion arising from an individual's assessment of all the relevant factors. Different weights and adjustments are made to the various factors under consideration when a valuer is using one of the methods of valuation. With experience and knowledge of the particular property market, a valuer should be able to generate valuations which are credible and robust and which should assist clients in this decision-making processes. Computer software can assist with assembling and analysing market data and it can reduce the time spent in constructing mathematical formulas required to carry out the calculations. However, in the end there is no substitute for sound judgement in the framing and adjustment of key variables which are the ingredients in the valuation process.

Fundamentally a valuer's role is to identify the market value for a property prior to a market transaction. This is a responsible role, as to put a property up for sale at too low a valuation will probably see the vendor lose money, while a valuation which is too high will raise unreasonable expectations and will see a property remain unsold or un-let on the market for perhaps lengthy periods of time. Property valuation therefore aims to assess the *market value* of a property, an internationally agreed definition of which is contained in the *RICS Valuation Standards* and which states:

> The estimated amount for which a property should exchange on the date of valuation between a willing buyer and a willing seller in an arm's-length transaction after proper marketing wherein the parties had each acted knowledgeably, prudently and without compulsion. (2010a: 46)

Despite this clear definition, the concept of market value is not as straightforward as it might at first appear. Economists discuss value in terms of utility, but this is of no practical use when trying to determine the specific value of a property in the market. A price may be achieved through a market transaction but the figure may not always equate with the value placed on the asset prior to the transaction by a valuer. Similarly general market sentiment may place a value of £X on an asset however when it is actually sold it achieves £Y to the surprise of most players in the market.

The difference between the price achieved on the sale of a property and the value placed on the property before the sale arises for a number of reasons. For instance the quoted market value of gilts or shares can quickly be obtained from the internet or the daily newspapers and investors active in those markets will expect to pay the quoted market price. In contrast, the price of an office building might be more difficult to obtain. It may be that an identical office block has just been sold and this potentially provides a useful indicator for the price of the block being valued.

The sale of the office block being used for comparison could however reflect a number of anomalies from what might be expected in a perfect market situation. For example it might be discovered that the deal reflected the need for the vendor to achieve a quick sale for corporate cash flow reasons. Alternatively the purchaser may have paid above what might have been expected, as the site formed part of a larger site which a developer was assembling for redevelopment. The comparison property might have been affected by legal constraints of one kind or another which affected its value but which were not obvious to any third party not immediately involved in the deal. There is a whole host of reasons why real property is bought and sold and the economic environment in which transactions are taking place is constantly changing, making the process of valuation more an art than a science.

Besides the problem of assessing the value of a property in advance of a transaction there is also a problem of assessing asset value or worth when a property is retained by an individual or corporation. Property could therefore be valued for a number of reasons, for a mortgage, compulsory purchase, insurance reinstatement or tax reasons. These valuations do not necessarily lead to a transaction which can support or contradict the valuation, thus the valuation of a property is adjusted according to the purpose for which it is required. Determining the circumstances and purpose for a valuation is therefore crucial to a valuer's work, as summed up by the anecdote attributed to an anonymous estate agent, who when asked to add 2 plus 2 by a particularity innumerate client, replied:

'Are you buying or selling?'

The following hypothetical example illustrates some of the challenges faced by property valuers. A recently developed and fully let office building of good specification in a town centre has become available for sale on the investment market and bids are invited from institutional investors. The building is generating an annual net rent of £250,000 and although there is scant evidence it seems that similar properties in the locality have changed hands recently to reflect an all risks yield of 7 per cent. The comparable evidence therefore suggests that the building might have a value in the region of:

(1/0.07) × £250,000
YP 14.29 × £250,000 = £3,572,500

The valuer acting for the vendor has analysed the comparable market evidence and has considered all relevant information including the condition and quality of the building, the terms and duration of the lease, the timing of rent reviews, the reliability of the tenant, the location, floorspace availability on the market and its take up rate. A valuation of £3,700,000 is put on the property generating an expectation that after a period of marketing, a property investor who may

Table 1.6 Bid pattern to acquire an office building

Number of bids by value (£)

2,750,000 to 3,000,000	3,010,000 to 3,250,000	3,260,000 to 3,500,000	3,510,000 to 3,750,000	3,760,000 to 4,000,000	4,010,000 to 4,250,000	4,260,000 to 4,500,000	4,510,000 to 4,750,000
X		X	X	X	X	X	
		X	X	X	X		
		X	X		X		
			X				
			X				
			X				

well be a financial institution, will pay around this figure to acquire the investment. Subsequently a number of offers are made by property investors to create the pattern shown in Table 1.6 above.

Clearly the majority of bidders placed a subjective worth on the property similar to the value arrived at by the vendor's valuer. This is perhaps not surprising, as valuers acting for prospective purchasers will have followed a similar process to determine the value. Indeed if those individuals were chartered valuation surveyors they would almost certainly be working to the guidelines set out in the *RICS Valuation Standards* (2010a) also known informally as the *Red Book* which at the time of writing is in its 6th edition. While the Red Book allows a degree of professional judgement and the selection of an appropriate valuation method by the valuer, it would be expected that practitioners conforming to these standards should arrive at similar valuations.

However, as the chart above suggests, the successful purchaser was willing to pay a price which does not appear to be prudent but which does outbid the competition to secure the asset. That purchaser might also have been taking a much more optimistic view about the data than were other prospective purchasers and in doing so is taking on more risk than other bidders were willing to tolerate. That judgement might have been driven by the investor's desire to obtain some exposure to the market in this particular location and property sector. Other bidders might already enjoy that exposure through investments already held and thus were less motivated to increase their offers.

Assuming the price paid was then £4,300,000 a new comparable statistic becomes available which suggests that the all risks yield for this type of asset in this particular location is: 250,000/4,300,000 = 5.8 per cent. The sale price achieved also reflects an uplift of more than 10 per cent on the original valuation of £3,700,000. While the vendor would probably be quite happy with this outcome, there arises a question of whether the valuer was negligent in failing to get closer to the sale price achieved. Where sales values have fallen well below a valuation it is not unknown for vendors to seek a remedy in the courts by suing the valuer for professional negligence. Litigation over property valuations has been a feature of the credit crunch and ensuing recession because some large property investors have experienced significant capital mark downs on commercial property assets. The important topic of valuation accuracy is discussed further in Chapter 7 of the book.

The simple example above illustrates that markets tend to be shaped not by the middle ground or what some might refer to as prudent market sentiment, but by purchasers who are knowingly or naively outbidding the competition to secure the asset. This stretching principle can only be sustained so far until a market correction process asserts itself, as capital values cannot continue to outstrip rental performance indefinitely.

Rental growth must also sustain some relationship with the growth rates achieved by the companies and firms who pay those rents. In aggregate the performance of those firms is measured by national gross domestic product (GDP). If growth in GDP was, for the sake of argument, consistently 3 per cent per annum, there is no reason why rental growth on commercial properties could be sustained in the longer term at say 5 per cent per annum. If that were the case, the rental cost of floorspace would ultimately become too expensive and the companies occupying the space would either collapse financially or downsize their space requirements or exercise break clauses and relocate to where premises were more affordable. One of the reasons why a number of large UK companies have 'off-shored' some or all of their back office and call centre functions to emerging countries is that the occupation of office space in the UK is amongst the most expensive in the world.

A similar market correction process operates periodically in the residential property market where increases in sales values can only continue for so long before first-time buyers are priced out of the market because the lending multiples against income have been stretched beyond safe limits. Ultimately the market has to fall back to price individuals back into the market so that sales chains can establish themselves.

Rates of interest and yields

A yield is important to an investor, as it indicates an annual level of earnings from an investment. For example it is perhaps obvious that if 15 per cent is the yield on an investment then it is a fair expectation that £15 per annum will be earned for every £100 invested. If the yield is 5 per cent then £5 is earned. Thus 15 per cent as a yield is obviously more attractive than 5 per cent but the concept is more complicated because the yield also indicates the risk associated with the investment.

Investments vary considerably in their risk characteristics but a general principle is that those investments which have higher risk will need to offer a higher return in order to tempt investors away from safer investments. For example drilling to find new gas or oil deposits off shore in deep water locations carries a tremendous risk that (a) this expensive process might not detect any commercially exploitable fields and (b) that something could go wrong necessitating lost production, a huge environmental clean-up bill and probably expensive litigation. The potential rewards for investors considering investing in a venture like this must therefore be significant, as investors could face a 100 per cent loss in the worst-case scenario.

The payback period is also a critical element in investment analysis and yields can be compared simply by establishing how long they will take to pay back the original capital invested. A 20 per cent yield on £100 generates an annual income of £20 which over five years will nominally have matched the initial £100 invested. An investment with a 5 per cent yield will have a nominal payback period of 20 years. Risky investments tend to have earlier payback periods so that after the nominal payback milestone has been reached any additional earnings could be seen as profit. However this rule-of-thumb approach is a little crude, as it ignores the time preference value of money which is based upon the principle that £1 available now is worth more than £1 in one year's time.

The yield that an investor expects from a property investment is determined by the interplay of a number of countervailing forces. At a strategic level the investor will want the highest yield that can be obtained from any particular type of investment and there is therefore a need to compare yields from different asset classes. Risk then comes into the picture as the greater the perception of risk the higher will be the yield expected. However acting in the opposite direction is the weight of investment interest in the particular asset. For example in the hypothetical example the majority market sentiment placed a value of around £3,700,000 on an asset which was generating an annual income of £250,000. Thus those investors would have been happy with an initial yield of £250,000/£3,700,000 = 6.8%. However the successful purchaser was willing to pay more to outbid the competition for the investment and thus was willing to accept a lower initial yield of £250,000/£4,300,000 = 5.8%.

The above is an example of yield compression, which is caused by the weight of money in a market competing for investments which appear to have future growth potential. This can occasionally drive initial yields down on the most desired investments, so that the initial yield is lower than can be achieved on so called risk-free investments such as gilts. In the property market this 'reverse yield gap' occasionally happens when prime shops in prosperous high street locations are targeted by a number of funds competing to secure the property because they feel that this type of asset has considerable rental and capital growth potential. Cautious market analysts would also see the occurrence of a reverse yield gap in property as a sign that investor expectations had risen too high and that the market was overheating.

Rates of interest are considered here in the context of nominal rates of interest, a concept introduced earlier in the chapter when gilts were being discussed. If a company sells stock to investors, it needs to offer an interest rate to tempt investors away from less risky investments such as gilts. So if the gilt rate in the market was say 6 per cent a company shares issue would have to match or improve upon that rate to tempt investors away from investing in gilts. A number of factors will shape the rate at which the shares are first offered but in this simple example the company directors decide that 10 per cent is the appropriate yield. So at the time the stock is issued the picture is as follows:

Nominal rate of interest:	10%
Nominal price of stock:	£100
Annual income therefore:	£10

The price of the stock may start at this level but the price will inevitably change over time but the £10 annual return will still be offered on the original £100 nominal value of the stock. However the rate of interest will change if the trading price of the stock falls as follows:

£100 nominal stock now valued in the market at:	£80
Annual return still offered:	£10
Rate of interest (yield) therefore = £10/£80 =	12.5%

A £10 annual return is still being offered because it is based on the par value of the stock, par value being the original offer price. So the only time when the nominal rate of interest is a true reflection of the relationship between the nominal annual interest and nominal face value is at the date of issue. There is at that point in time a clear relationship between income, yield and capital value. If the rate of interest or yield is 10 per cent and the capital value of the investment is £100, then the expected annual income is £10. By working back from this calculation, if an investment produces an annual income of £10 and the investor requires a yield of 10 per cent, the price paid by the investor is £100 and this is the basis of the investment method of valuation.

The investment method of property valuation

Most investors seek to obtain a return on their investments either as an annual income or a capital gain, the investment method of valuation is traditionally concerned with the former. Where the investor has a known sum of money to invest on which a particular return is required the income can be readily calculated from:

$$\text{Income} = \text{Capital} \times \frac{i}{100} \text{ where } i = \text{rate of return required}$$

For example if £10,000 is to be invested with a required rate of return of 8 per cent the income will be:

$$\text{Income} = £10,000 \times \frac{8}{100} = £800 \text{ per annum}$$

In this type of problem the capital is known and the income is to be calculated. In the case of real property the rental income is known, either from the actual rent passing under the lease or estimated from the letting of similar properties and the capital value is usually calculated. The formula above has to be changed so that the capital becomes the subject:

$$\text{Capital} = \text{Income} \times \frac{100}{i}$$

What capital sum should be paid for an investment producing £800 per annum and a return of 8 per cent is required?

$$\text{Capital} = £800 \times \frac{100}{8} = £10,000$$

This process is known as 'capitalizing' the income, in other words converting an annual income into a capital sum. It is essential that the income capitalized is 'net' that is clear of any expenses incurred by the investor under the lease so that the formula becomes:

$$C = NI \times \frac{100}{i} \text{ where } C = \text{Capital}$$
$$NI = \text{Net Income}$$
$$i = \text{Rate of Return}$$

For given rates of return $100/i$ will be constant, for example:

Rate of Return 100/i
8% 12.5
10% 10
12% 8.33

This constant is known as the Present Value of £1 per annum, or more commonly in real property valuation, Years' Purchase in perpetuity (abbreviated to YP in perp.). The formula can thus be finally modified to:

$$C = NI \times YP$$

Where C is the capital value, NI is net income and YP is the years' purchase. The YP in perp., calculated by using $100/i$ will only apply to incomes received in perpetuity from freehold interests let at a full market rent or rack rent. Incomes to be received for shorter periods use a YP calculated using a more complex formula (shown in section 5.4 of Chapter 5) or as identified from tables of constants in Parry's Valuation and Investment Tables.

The traditional approach of Parry's Tables was to assume that the rental income was received annually in arrears whereas in practice it is received quarterly in advance. Although the tables now include both options, much traditional valuation uses the assumption of annually in arrears income for simplicity, although later in the book there will be examples of quarterly in advance valuations. At this stage of the discussion it should be noted that whatever income basis is used to estimate the capital value of an interest in real property, three elements are required:

1 The net income to be received.
2 The period for which the net income will be received.
3 The required yield.

Elements (1) and (2) above will be obtained from the lease of the subject property or if the property is un-let, an estimate of the rental value will be obtained from lettings of comparable properties. Item (3) will be obtained from analysis of sales of comparable investments. A valuer must therefore have knowledge of both the letting and investment markets in order to bring together credible variables to carry out a basic investment method calculation. For example, assume that prime shops in a prosperous city centre have an initial yield of 5 per cent and that the annual net rack rental income of one such shop is £250,000. The valuer's calculation to determine the capital value of the freehold interest of the shop might look as follows:

Net annual rental income: £250,000
Years' Purchase @ 5% in perpetuity 20 YP*
Capital Value £5,000,000

$$*YP = \frac{100}{Yield} = \frac{100\%}{5\%} = 20$$

1.5 The property investment market

A historical perspective

Property investments can be created in the first instance by developers who find and acquire sites, erect buildings and then let them to tenants and this creates the property investment market in the UK. This arrangement is thought to have evolved out of the development of the landed estates where historically the landed gentry were divorced from those engaged in manufacturing and commerce. However at some subliminal level in the British psyche there is suspicion regarding the rent-collecting landlord who is often bracketed with the land speculator; both of whom have been demonized in works of fiction from the Victorian era until the present day. This is in marked contrast to the positive portrayal of risk taking entrepreneurs who because they make or invent things for a market are deemed to be honest, hard-working and value adding. There are also theoretical traditions dating back to Adam Smith and Henry George which explore the monopoly value of land and which imply that the ability to collect rent from land or buildings is undeserved. From that perspective rental income and indeed capital gains from property are seen as an 'unearned increment' and therefore a legitimate target for taxation in various forms. Perhaps ironically by the twenty-first century many employees in the public and private sectors have pension policies whose performance relies, at least in part, upon the unearned increment.

A full debate on the historical origins and continuing legitimacy or otherwise of the landlord and tenant relationship in the residential or commercial property sectors in the UK is beyond the scope of this book. However in practice the landlord and tenant model has remained durable in the UK particularly in the commercial property sector where REITA (2010) estimate that around 50 per cent of properties are rented by business tenants although other estimates put it at around 43 per cent. Because of the statistical difficulties in the face of such a large stock of properties what could safely be said is that there is between 50 and 60 per cent owner-occupation of commercial real property by firms and companies in the UK. However even for the owner-occupying businesses the focus is more upon company performance, labour productivity and profit generation from the production of goods and services rather than the investment returns arising from property ownership. Indeed it is not unusual for companies to sell the freeholds of the properties they occupy on a sale-and-leaseback basis, so that the sale receipts can be used as working capital to support the development of the business.

The nature of the property market

The market is made up of a number of types of investment which produce different types of income. For instance: rack rented freeholds, reversionary investments, secure ground rents, short term leasehold profit rents, turnover rents and so on. The type of investment will determine the amount and timing of the income stream.

The property market is fragmented geographically and by sector and despite the best efforts of companies such as Estates Gazette through EGi and CoStar the transactions in the market are not systematically recorded on a frequent or regular basis. It is true that transactions are ultimately recorded by Land Registry and that public access to this data has helped transparency. However the recording of transactions with Land Registry takes place sometime after a sale has been achieved and thus the data is not as instantly available as it might be in a share dealing situation. In some locations and property sectors there may be lengthy periods during which there are no transactions. Overall it could therefore be said that there is imperfect knowledge in the property market. Property is diverse and each property has unique characteristics so the market is unstructured. There is restriction of movement into and out of the property market because of time constraints and legal and financial considerations.

The nature of investment markets generally

There are three major areas of traditional investment opportunity (ignoring gold, commodities and works of art) which are fixed interest securities (a collective name for bonds and government gilt-edged stock), company stocks and shares (sometimes referred to as equities) and real property. The world's major stock exchanges provide a market for listed shares and fixed interest securities such as those issued by governments, local authorities and public bodies. However, by contrast, the market in real property is fragmented with no central market place.

Centralized markets assist the transferability of investments on a national and global basis, as does the fact that stocks and shares can be traded in small lots thereby providing divisibility and liquidity. In contrast, a decentralized market, such as exists for property, will tend to have high costs of transfer of investments and there will be an imperfect knowledge of transactions in the market. Regarding imperfect information, companies such as CoStar have improved the situation in recent years with a regularly updated commercial property data base which is available on a subscription basis. However as Srivatsa et al. point out:

> One of the long-standing issues with the property investment market has been the lack of data due to infrequent property valuations and transparency concerns surrounding the direct property market. (2009: 24)

Srivatsa et al. (2009) note that at best, commercial property portfolios in the UK are likely to be revalued on a monthly basis and this does not therefore compare well with the transparent and instantaneous updating of gilt and share prices in central stock exchanges.

The factors discussed above make property difficult to value and there may also be an absence of any recent comparable market transactions for the valuer to analyse. The problems of valuation relate to difficulties of trying to relate comparable transactions to properties being valued or even trying to assess what transactions could be considered comparable. Because of the nature of the real property market and its barriers to entry, individual investors have tended to stay out of particularly the commercial property investment market and this has been reinforced by the channelling of savings into more accessible and mainstream financial products such as ISAs (Individual Savings Account), premium bonds, pensions of various forms and insurance products.

Markets are risky places

Different types of property such as retail, industrial and offices have different risk and return profiles and so they may be more or less attractive to different types of investor. The risk profile for an investment property will also vary depending on location and whether the market perceives the property to be prime (best quality) or secondary or tertiary. Property investors will also look at the covenant of the business tenant(s) the duration, terms and conditions of the lease and whether it contains any break clauses.

In the UK the codes of practice governing advertising standards require that where financial products which have some risk attached are being promoted there needs to be an explicit warning (usually provided in the small print) that there are risks as well as potential returns which potential investors need to consider. The wording used by REITA is typical of the risk reminders that are used:

> The value of investments and any income from them, can go down as well as up as a result of market and exchange rate movements and you may not get back the amount you originally invested. Past performance is not necessarily a guide to future performance. (2010)

History shows that the same is true of property investments as they are subject to market dynamics which may at any time be conducive to capital and income growth while at other times can result in the value of property falling.

Economists have debated the direction of cause and effect between conditions in the wider economy and the performance of the property market. One possible answer is that a 'clumsy' over-supply of property leads to its devaluation and this in turn triggers a depressive multiplier effect on the rest of the economy. An alternative explanation is that recessionary conditions in the wider economy cause the devaluation of property. A property crash seems to occur when both of these conditions prevail simultaneously.

Given that the demand for property is essentially derived from individuals and companies and that when they are financially secure they may demand more property (or bid up the price of the existing stock of property) most would agree that the causal relationship is that the performance of the wider economy will in the end determine the financial performance of property. For example if the financial services sector decides to downsize and reduce staff numbers this will ultimately be felt in a reduced requirement for office space and this will lead to a fall in office rents. Similarly in the residential sector a sustained and significant growth in unemployment will usually have the knock on effect of reducing house prices and private rental levels.

The next question which arises is whether property cycles are regular and therefore predictable. However, even the expression 'property cycle' can be misleading as it implies regular and smooth oscillations in a helical shape around an axis. Research in the 1990s by the Investment Property Databank and the University of Aberdeen (1994) found that over a 30-year period the depth and duration of these fluctuations was not regular, predictable nor subject to any formula. Rather than a smooth cycle the property market seems to experience periods of around 15 years during which there is irregular annual growth before shorter periods of two or three years which see market correction during which values fall back.

There will always be volatile periods in the wider economy and sometimes sustained periods of recession are experienced despite the best efforts of governments to create economic stability through monetary and fiscal policy. Those recessionary periods will inevitably depress property values such as 1973 to 1974 and 1989 to 1991 and more recently in the credit crunch which began to take effect towards the end of 2007 and extended into 2010.

During periods of market turbulence it is sometimes difficult to determine whether the economy will go further into recession, or bottom out or begin to recover. There are helpful quarterly commercial market surveys provided by RICS which chart movements over time on topics such as 'new occupier enquiries', 'floorspace availability' and 'lease lengths and inducements'. The RICS surveys also capture the opinions of surveyors working in different regions throughout the UK in terms of whether they feel the market is strengthening, weakening or remaining unchanged. For example the RICS (2010b) market survey for the first quarter of 2010 provided a mixed picture in which there was still a considerable overhang of unoccupied space on the market but that the extent of inducements (such as rent-free periods) needed to attract office tenants was gradually reducing. Surveyors in different regions were reporting that rents particularly in the office sector were beginning to harden after two years of falls.

It is however only with the benefit of hindsight that the picture becomes clear. This is not helped by differences of opinion from analysts some of whom take a pessimistic view of the future while others interpreting the same market data, will take an optimistic view of the future. The uncertainty also triggers a search for 'recession proof' investments so that money will switch in and out of investment media such as shares, gilts, cash deposits, commodities and different types of investment property in a search for the best returns.

Institutional investors in the property market

Property is only one of a number of competing investment media and major investors will assemble a portfolio of different investments to reflect their attitudes to risk and return. Portfolio composition should also be diversified in order to reduce risk, so that the under-performance of one type of asset could be counterbalanced by the stronger performance of other asset classes. At a sophisticated level fund managers also look for negative correlations between assets, so that when the value of asset X falls it is likely that the value of asset Y will rise creating an in-built insurance policy. Fund managers will also look at subdivisions of asset classes, so that within the property element of a portfolio there will be a spread of different property types such as retail, offices, leisure industrial and warehousing. Similarly within the equities element of a portfolio fund managers might decide to spread share ownership to reflect exposure to different industrial sectors. It is for this reason that major institutional portfolios will tend to contain a mix of equities (shares) purchased from domestic and overseas markets, gilts, different types of property and other assets such as cash deposits and commodities.

Dubben and Sayce (1991) reported that back in 1989, 77 per cent of the value of a typical UK institutional portfolio (such as that held by a pension fund) would be held in equities, 12 per cent of the portfolio value would be held in gilts, 8 per cent would be held in property and 3 per cent would be held in cash and other investments. Of course the asset proportions within investment portfolios do not remain static for very long, as fund managers are constantly reviewing their acquisitions so that poorer performing elements can be replaced by better performing assets. By 2010 Mercer reported that for a typical UK pension fund portfolio, 50 per cent of the value was held as equities, 41 per cent in gilts, 2 per cent in property and 7 per cent in other assets such as cash deposits. To illustrate that average figures such as these can disguise some variation the composition by value of the Universities Superannuation Scheme Limited (2010) was:

Equities: 68%
Fixed interest securities: 12.5%
Property: 10%
Alternatives, including commodities and cash deposits: 9.5%

The relatively modest proportion for property in portfolios probably reflects the fact that by 2010 property had experienced two years of devaluation which had been triggered by the credit squeeze. The general downturn in economic activity had also made it difficult to let some commercial properties at competitive rents without offering tenants incentives such as lengthy rent-free periods. In those circumstances fund managers had not surprisingly looked to transfer funds to other asset classes such as gilts, equities and commodities such as gold, which in combination might perform better than property in fragile market conditions.

The generally modest proportion of property assets held by financial institutions is sometimes at odds with academic opinion which suggests that funds should increase their exposure to property given its potential for portfolio diversification and income and capital growth in the long term. However perhaps Baum best sums up the situation by stating that:

Property is usually described as a medium-risk asset. Its returns should therefore be expected to lie between those produced by equities and those produced by bonds, and its risk profile should be similarly middling. (2009: 26)

While the proportion of property held by financial institutions seldom gets into double figures in percentage terms, this does not mean that the funds are not major players in the commercial property sector given the sheer size of these funds. Property is also the prime investment held by the top 24 UK quoted property companies whose combined capitalization is reported by REITA in 2010 to be £3.7 billion, while the 22 UK REITS have a combined capitalization of £21.3 billion.

What affects values in the property market?

The international situation can affect levels of confidence in the property market but probably not as dramatically as in the stock market. Interest rates will affect borrowing and therefore activity in the new and second-hand markets for property. The state of the national economy affects the confidence of investors and land prices and rents will tend to be higher in areas where the local economy is thriving. The levels of disposable income available affects house prices and the amount available for investment.

Government policy and legislation affect property values. For example, changes to tax rates on income and capital gains from property will affect the investor's return. Government can encourage or discourage investment through monetary policy or by applying more stringent environmental standards on buildings through changing the building regulations.

In recent years the government has stopped short of legislating to outlaw upward only rent reviews in return for an undertaking from the property industry to attempt to achieve the same objective through a voluntary code of practice. It is correct in principle for government to challenge this historically derived practice which is unjustified and anti competitive. If the upwards only principle were applied to other commodities or markets, consumers would quite rightly complain if there were (for example) upward only price changes on goods in supermarkets or on the price of airline tickets or mortgage interest rates or upward only petrol prices. However government interventions whether indirect or direct and however well justified, increase the degree of regulatory risk from the investor's perspective and this has knock on effects on property values.

Location is obviously important, so for example the demand for space in an office block may be contingent on its position within a central business district which benefits from diverse transport infrastructure and attractive surroundings. Fashion and the presence of recreational and leisure facilities can stimulate demand which affects property prices. Regeneration and gentrification of formerly 'average areas' can see property prices rise significantly and residential estate agents will confirm the uplift in housing values generated by the presence of a good school in a district. The promise of and realization of infrastructure improvements such as extensions to the Docklands Light Railway, underground systems or Crossrail or even the reduction of rail journey times through improved signalling and the introduction of new fast trains will also have positive effects on property values.

The design features of properties can affect value and these may include the presence or absence of onsite parking spaces, the efficiency and versatility of the internal layout and whether there are any sustainability features which will make the building cheaper to operate in the long term. Tenure may affect the property price as a property may be freehold or leasehold and this is an important area of valuation analysis which is discussed later in the book. The condition, state of repair and appearance of a building will also affect value as will the quality and capacity of building services. The latter includes heating, air conditioning, lifts and trunking which will enable buildings to stay abreast of changes in information and communications technology.

The potential for extension, renovation, change of use and/or redevelopment will affect a property's value. The ease of purchase and sale which in other words is its transferability, will affect the property price. Prices will be depressed if a transaction takes a long time to complete, as property investors are often paying interest on monies used for purchase. A lack of information can affect property price, because of the nature of the investment, people will not generally buy a property investment unless they have full details of the investment.

Decision-making in the property market

Given the interplay of variables such as those described above and their potential effect on property values, analysts involved in large value transactions might model combinations of positive or negative factors in order to strengthen the objectivity of their decision-making. There are well known business decision-making tools which include the SWOT analysis (strengths weaknesses, opportunities and strengths) as described by Cole (2004) or the PEST analysis described by Mullins (2007) which looks at political, economic, social and technological change which may take place. These types of exercises can be adapted to consider the investment prospects of property acquisitions.

For example consider a recently developed and fully let B1 unit (which can be lawfully used for offices, light industry or research and development activity) on a business park which is gradually being developed in a prosperous area. The business park has good motorway connections and is a little unusual in that it also benefits from a good commuter rail service. The B1 unit does not have a green label such as a BREEAM accreditation although in other respects it has a full complement of modern services, is visually attractive and achieves an 85 per cent gross to net floorspace relationship. There is a single business tenant who is three years into a 20-year FRI lease which has five-year rent reviews with a break clause at year 10. A SWOT analysis could be carried out for this property investment prospect which might look as shown in Table 1.7 opposite.

Decision-making aids like the SWOT analysis do not make the investment decision, but they do help the decision-maker identify those factors which are most likely to materialize and affect value going forward.

Rates of return in the property market

The annual rates of return from a wide sample of commercial and residential property investments have been tracked over the long term by Investment Property Databank (IPD) whose periodically updated indexes provide investors with a picture of the rental and capital performance of property. For example IPD's Residential Investment Index recorded total returns of 11 per cent for 2009 marking a turnaround from the previous two years when total returns for this sector fell. The total return recorded by IPD for 2009 comprised a 2.9 per cent rental income return and an 8.1 per cent return for capital growth. For

Table 1.7 Example of a SWOT analysis in a property investment context

Internal factors

Strengths	*Weaknesses*
At only 3 years old the building is relatively new and aesthetically appealing. The gross to net floorspace relationship is efficient and there is plenty of parking on site.	The building does not have a green label such as a BREEAM rating and thus is not a sustainability leader.
The building is let to a single tenant on a long lease making management easier. A rent is passing and thus there are no voids or rent-free periods to consider.	The rental income is dependent on a single tenant who if defaulted would leave no other income stream. It might be difficult to find a new tenant to occupy the whole building.
There is a rent review in two years' time, when the income could increase.	
The lease is FRI so there will be no significant outgoings for the investor/purchaser.	
The site is accessible to public transport and there is good highways access.	
The building has an unrestricted B1 use and thus is versatile and could be used by a wide range of businesses.	

External factors

Opportunities	*Threats*
It is likely that there will be a trend away from car commuting and the adoption of green travel plans. This would free up some of the parking space on the site which subject to planning consent could provide an opportunity to extend the building.	Future legislation could require expensive upgrades and retro-fitting, perhaps to comply with reducing carbon footprints.
The building has been designed on a modular basis and similar buildings have had upper floors added. There is thus an opportunity to extend the building by adding upper floors if necessary.	There might be changes to the tax regime which threaten income and/or capital value.
	Newer buildings will appear on the business park and these will probably be 'greener' with technological advantages making them more efficient to operate. Such buildings will probably be easier to let and will probably command a rental premium.
	There could be changes in working cultures which see more employees working remotely or from home. There could be an economic downturn. In either case, the occupier could decide to downsize its office space requirements and exercise the break clause at year 10 of the lease.

residential property therefore, the IPD index was signifying a recovery during 2009 for a hitherto beleaguered investment sector.

IPD also produce an index for 'all property' which represents the commercial property sector comprising retail, offices and industrial. For 2009 total annual returns to this sector were put at 3.5 per cent by IPD based upon a rental income return of 7.4 per cent set off against negative capital growth at −3.6 per cent.

The snapshot view of just one year can be misleading particularly in this case which reflects a year during which there has been a gradual recovery from a property recession. Because of the lack of liquidity associated with property investment and the costs involved in property transactions, property investors are unlikely to buy in and buy out of direct property investment within one year. Exposure to property would need to be longer in order for capital growth and income to compensate for the transaction costs involved. REITA (2010) for example suggest that the exposure to direct property investment would need to be for a minimum of five years to justify the costs of investing and then divesting of a property asset.

Investors such as the pension funds and insurance companies have perhaps a clearer view on what might reasonably be expected in terms of rates of return from different asset classes. These funds have long experience and data regarding the actual performance of the assets which they have bought and sold. One such occupational pension fund in the UK is the Universities Superannuation Scheme (USS) Limited (2010) which as the name suggests pools contributions from employers and employees in the higher education sector in order to reinvest those funds in a portfolio of assets. Those investments are then expected to perform in a manner which will match the call on pensions from those retiring from the university sector. The USS suggests that because property is medium risk, it therefore warrants a medium return relative to gilts and equities and when an allowance is made for inflation the real annual rates of return which are expected are:

Equities (shares): 5%
Property: 3.75%
Fixed interest products (bonds and gilts): 2%

1.6 Direct and indirect investment in property

Background

In the 1950s and 1960s, the modern corporate property investor and property developer began to emerge as a response to the shortage of commercial property following the destruction of buildings in the Second World War. There had also been shortages of resources which curtailed all but essential construction projects, but as the economy began to recover the pent up demand for commercial property revealed itself. This resulted in rental levels of property developments increasing while generally low inflation saw fairly static building costs. The other major stimulants to property development and investment were fixed interest rates and the ability to finance deals with 100 per cent debt finance without any equity input.

The growth of property companies during the 1960s relied on a strategy of refinancing a development on completion with a fixed interest mortgage for 20 to 30 years. Financial institutions also provided finance for the developments during this period and there was a link-up between developers and institutions. Over this period, financial institutions such as insurance companies, started to secure a greater share in the equity returns available from property by purchasing shares in the property companies. Another tactic used by the financial institutions to increase their equity exposure to property developments was to make their mortgage debenture loans convertible to shares in the event that a development was successful.

In the late 1960s and early 1970s developers began using sale and leaseback arrangements to enable developments to be financed in the construction phase using short-term bank finance, following which the completed schemes were sold. Because of the close working arrangements which evolved between developers and their institutional funders it was perhaps not surprising that the institutions (pension funds and insurance companies) began to take on some of the more proactive roles which were previously seen as the sole province of the developer. For example, institutions began purchasing developable sites and then secured a property development partner who in exchange for cheap building finance would carry out the scheme and then sell or lease it back to the fund.

The 1960s was then a period which saw experimentation, creativity and risk taking in how to fund and develop large commercial schemes. Unfortunately this also gave rise to an impression that property development was a means to 'get rich quick' and too many speculative copy-cat ventures were brought forward in the late 1960s and early 1970s on ever flimsier financial and marketing grounds. This over-speculation came at a time when interest rates and building costs began to rise. There was also reduced commercial tenant demand for space which led to income voids. Circumstances had become much more challenging for the property developer and some found that it was difficult to meet profit expectations while others got into difficulties by accumulating interest charges on costs which could not be paid off. In the end there was a calamitous property crash in 1974 necessitating the Bank of England to launch a financial rescue package called the 'Lifeboat' in order to prop up the secondary banking sector. The latter had become over-exposed to what had become the very risky commercial property sector.

There are perhaps some similarities between the property crisis described above and the more recent one in 2008 and 2009 which was triggered by excessively risky mortgage lending in the USA and the UK. In the UK the Bank of England had to step in with a government backed (and tax payer funded) rescue package.

In the 1980s and 1990s the revised approach to funding was that the funder was invited to purchase the site and provide funds for the building contract. Interest would be rolled up during the development period and added to the development costs. On completion and letting of the building, the profit on development was paid over to the developer. This method of project funding enabled developers to build up a turnover by basically matching their site finding and project management skills with the institutional investors' funding. Such approaches greatly reduced the risk exposure of the developer to the project, as forward funding meant that the project was financed for the development period at a lower interest rate than market levels. However the trade off for reduced risk was that the capital sum received by the developer at the end of the project was reduced, as the funding institution would value at a higher yield (to generate a lower capital value) in order to recoup the interest lost during construction.

Many of the models of property development funding described above such as sale and lease back were further refined during the 2000s. There were also innovations around partnerships and joint ventures which saw greater risk sharing in developments between different stakeholders such as the developer, funder, landowner and local authority. Government agencies and regeneration vehicles also became more involved in development particularly in regeneration areas where the property market has historically been fragile. The expression 'slicing' became increasingly used to denote equity sharing arrangements in developments of various types. The government also promoted the Private Finance Initiative (PFI) and Public Private Partnerships (PPP) as ways of channelling private capital and development expertise into the provision of public capital projects. It is beyond the scope of this book to explore in any depth the diverse ways which now exist to structure property development, but those who are particularly interested in this topic could examine Dubben and Williams (2009) or Isaac *et al.* (2010).

Indirect property investment

The discussion above charts a gradual evolution of the equity involvement of financial institutions in particularly commercial property development and investment. However in the end these funds represent the pooled savings and investments of millions of people who are therefore indirectly (and probably unknowingly) investing at least some of their deposits in property. Of course this is not the only way that the small investor could obtain some investment exposure to property and as far back as 1965 property bonds were made available to the general public. These insurance linked bonds were similar to investments in property unit trusts.

Indirect investment methods have evolved since the 1960s and there is now a more diverse market of property investment media. Smaller institutions wanting to take a stake in commercial property but lacking the size of resources to invest directly can use indirect routes into property in common with other small investors. The main indirect property investment routes are described by REITA (2010) and these include property company shares (which include shares in those companies which have REIT status) self-invested personal pensions, property syndicates, property unit trusts (authorized and unauthorized) property bonds usually tied to unit linked life assurance schemes and property derivatives. Some of these vehicles are highly specialized and investors would need to seek advice from an independent financial advisor were they contemplating investment in some of these vehicles. However, perhaps the most obvious indirect route to property investment is to purchase some property company shares.

Purchasing property company shares including those in REITs, overcomes some of the disadvantages of direct investment discussed earlier in this chapter.

Shares are available in smaller units and can be easily traded and it is thought that property shares offer some protection against inflation because of the durability of assets held by a property company. The shares of a property investment company where most of the revenue is derived from rental income also provide the investor with a high degree of income security. Thus property company shares have traditionally been seen to provide both an element of protection against the effects of inflation and greater security to the investor.

There are two types of publicly quoted property company in which shares may be purchased. The first type of property company normally holds property for long periods and takes the majority of its revenue from rental income. These companies include the largest property companies in the UK such as Derwent London, SEGRO (Slough Estates Group) British Land, Hammerson and Land Securities. Since 2007 these companies have converted to REIT status to benefit from the internal tax advantages. A REIT does not have to pay corporation tax or capital gains tax on its property trading activities and should therefore be able to retain a larger proportion of it profits for distribution in dividends to shareholders. Development is more risky and the rules on REIT status in the UK prevent the more risk bearing property companies from becoming REITs. However REIT property companies are not entirely prevented from undertaking some development, so long as it remains a minority part of the company's business activity.

The second type of property company is sometimes referred to as a trading property company, because it specializes in developing and then selling completed developments. Thus the majority of the earnings for this type of property company come from disposals of completed properties rather than from rental income. Because of their higher risk profile these companies are debarred from becoming REITs. Indirect investors in commercial property therefore have a choice between the modest returns likely to arise from investing in the less risky REITs or perhaps the possibility of better returns but higher risk from investing in non-REIT property companies.

1.7 Housing and the property investor

Background

The discussion above has focused upon the evolution of property development companies and their changing relationship with funding institutions in the context of the development of commercial property. Included in this broad category are office blocks, shopping centres, retail warehouse parks, business parks, industrial and warehouse estates, marinas, leisure developments and mixed use developments of various kinds. The majority of text books which deal with property development and investment tend to focus on the commercial property sector, as housing development and investment raises a different set of issues which are quite reasonably treated as a specialized field. However, one of the key changes that have taken place since the first edition of this book was published in 1998 is the growth in residential buy-to-let property investment. A whole new range of mortgage products has developed in response to this market and there is some speculation that Real Estate Investment Trusts (REITs) could be configured to contribute to the supply of rented housing in the UK, given that REITs are already used for this purpose in the USA. Thus while the central focus of this book does largely conform to the genre by focusing on commercial property, it is not felt appropriate to ignore the residential investment sector entirely. The introductory discussion here on buy-to-let residential investment is therefore supplemented by further discussion and examples in Chapters 3 and 8 of the book.

The development and funding of housing has been heavily influenced by successive government policy, which in recent decades has either implicitly or explicitly endorsed the principle that home ownership is the 'natural' tenure. This policy assumes that as a household's income rises, the 'natural' desire line is from rented property into intermediate tenures (such as shared ownership or shared equity) and then on to outright ownership. Of course not all households are in a position or want to make that journey while others have the income or wealth to skip over the earlier stages and straight into home ownership. There are also academic debates which challenge the legitimacy of this orthodoxy. However it is hard to challenge the underlying set of values held by most individuals who express a desire to get a foot on the housing ladder. While it might not be expressed as such by individuals, the concept of 'housing wealth' is widely understood and valued.

Given that home ownership aspirations are embedded in government housing policy, private sector volume housebuilders have come to dominate housing production and their principle product is not surprisingly housing for open market sales to owner-occupiers (although in fact most owner-occupiers will be supported by a mortgage). The smaller affordable housing sector has different historical origins based upon meeting housing needs rather than market demands. That sector has developed its own unique and quite complicated funding protocols which are coordinated and codified by the government's affordable housing champion: the Homes and Communities Agency.

Affordable housing was until the early 1980s mainly the concern of local authorities. However since then, there have been changes in thinking on how affordable housing should be procured and then managed. In recent years this has seen a strengthening of the housing association sector and a growth in the provision of shared ownership properties alongside social rented property. Some volume housebuilders such as Bellway Homes have also set up specialized not-for-profit divisions in order to qualify as affordable housing providers with the government's Homes and Communities Agency. Although the output of affordable homes from that particular route is miniscule when viewed from a national perspective, it does signify the transition from state provided affordable housing to a mixed economy of provision. This policy change has enabled some valid experimentation with different delivery models, so that there is now more diversity in procurement methods, management of stock and tenure.

In theory the innovations described above should have resulted in a decent home to meet the needs of all income groups. However in reality there has been consistent under-building of housing over several decades and as the Barker Review (2004) revealed the under-supply of housing has fuelled house price inflation over the long term. The result has been that ever increasing income multiples are needed by borrowers to achieve their first foot on the housing ladder. That particular elastic band can only be stretched so far and the unfortunate consequence of some of the over-stretch that has taken place (as reported by the Council of Mortgage Lenders, 2010) has been a rise in 2009 and 2010 of both borrowers falling behind with their mortgage repayments and in home repossessions. In simple terms the growth in house prices over many years has simply outstripped the growth in incomes and this has priced out of the market an increasing proportion of aspirant first-time buyers.

In any market where there is under-supply and prices rise, it is not long before these signals stimulate investment interest. Ordinarily new supply would be switched on in a market to meet demand and prices would gradually come down to a new equilibrium level. However as discussed earlier in this chapter, the supply of real property (including housing) has an inelastic response to demand. Indeed there are those who harbour conspiracy theories in which housebuilders act as a cartel which deliberately restrains the rate of production to keep prices high, although it is not possible to prove or disprove these theories here.

Buy-to-let residential investment

The impact of buy-to-let investors has had a mixed impact on the housing market depending on the perspective taken. On the one had the presence of buy-to-let investors could be said to be a good thing in that housebuilders now have more demand for their output as they now have both customers who wish to purchase for occupation and those who wish to purchase for investment. All things being equal this should have stimulated a higher volume of housing development. However this has not been the case in the UK housing market, in which output during the credit squeeze years of 2008 and 2009 fell dramatically because of reduced credit availability and uncertainty in the general state of the economy. The presence of buy-to-let investors in the housing market has not therefore been significant enough to have raised the output of housebuilders.

From a social policy perspective some would argue that the presence of residential buy-to-let investors has exacerbated problems of housing affordability because investors can typically outbid a proportion of first-time buyers and those on low incomes. This, some suggest, has artificially sustained house prices which needed to fall further in order to price those households into the market. The intermediary role played by the buy-to-let investor from this perspective is parasitical in that (a) it has not brought forward a genuine new supply of properties and (b) it has seen investors acquire properties that might otherwise have been purchased by first-time buyers. Discussions around the topic of buy-to-let investment can therefore be value laden and perhaps the landlord and tenant relationship is less straightforward than might appear to be the case for commercial property. The topic has here been introduced and will be taken up again in Chapters 3 and 8 where there is a fuller discussion on residential buy-to-let investment.

1.8 Sustainability and property investment

Sustainability and the triple bottom line

One of the most significant changes which have taken place since the publication of the first edition of this book in 1998 is the concern over climate change and the ensuing commitments by governments around the world to try to reduce carbon emissions. These commitments, whether in formal protocols or arising from a shift in consciousness, require that individuals and organizations find more sustainable ways of going about their business. Most readers will be familiar with at least one definition of sustainable development and those that are familiar with the concept would probably improvise an interpretation of the widely cited definition from the 1987 Brundtland Report:

> Development that meets the needs of the present without compromising the ability of future generations to meet their own needs. (World Commission on Environment and Development (Brundtland Report) 1987)

Authors such as Pivo (2005) have suggested that when applied to property investment decisions, the concept of sustainability should be understood and accounted for across three dimensions:

- rigorous economic analysis;
- assessment of the environmental consequences; and
- assessment of the social consequences.

These three dimensions of sustainability have become known as the triple bottom line. In a perhaps idealistic scenario governments and businesses would only embark upon projects or investments that showed a gain across all three of these bottom lines. However in some circumstances that ideal might appear a little utopian and not practically achievable or even measurable. Perhaps the next best alternative might be to say that projects or investments should only be embarked upon where there might be a gain against one or two of the budget headings while there was a neutral effect on the other budget heading(s). The fall back position might then be that (a) at least the negative consequences on one or two of the bottom lines was acknowledged and accounted for and that (b) the identified negative consequences could be offset against the gains made on the other fronts. Although now of questionable environmental integrity, the concept of carbon offsetting is an example of this third approach.

As pointed out by the RICS (2009a) accounting across a triple bottom line is a concept now widely understood by business, government and the property industry. Conscious of international obligations to reduce carbon emissions and national policies aimed at fostering more sustainable development, professional bodies have recognized that they have a role to play in encouraging their members to think, act and provide advice to clients which is consistent with these 'public interest' concerns.

The preeminent property profession in the UK is the RICS and it provides advice to its members (who are chartered surveyors) on how they may make constructive 'interventions' at different points in the property life cycle in order to support the principles of sustainability. The RICS (2009b) describe the stages in the property life cycle as:

Stage 1: Greenfield/estate management.
Stage 2: Planning and procurement.

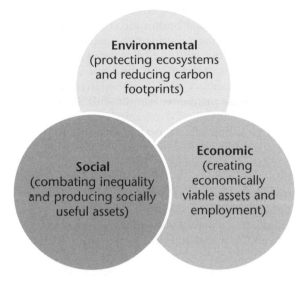

Figure 1.6 The three dimensions of sustainability

Stage 3: New construction.
Stage 4: Occupation and use.
Stage 5: Demolition and remediation.

The RICS advice to the different types of chartered surveyors active at each of the five stages is quite detailed and it is beyond the scope of this book to explore all of the permutations. However, by way of example, the RICS (2009b: 60) advise those surveyors who are involved in commercial property practice during stage 1 of the property cycle that:

> During the purchase, sale and leasing of real estate, where the surveyor is acting as an agent, broker or auctioneer in the purchase, sale and leasing of commercial real estate, consideration can be given to researching and iden-tifying those key sustainability aspects of the real estate which could be considered by the purchaser. These include:

> • the energy use and carbon emissions of the building (important for those organizations participating in Emissions Trading Schemes);
> • the Energy Performance Certificate;
> • water consumption (and any technologies introduced to reduce this);
> • pollution and nuisance, light, dust, etc;
> • potential traffic disruption from operations, etc.; and
> • the provision of alternative public transport (not just car parking spaces).

Further advice is given to these surveyors by the RICS (2009b: 61) during stage 1 of the property cycle when they become involved in the interface between landlord and tenant. At that point there is potential to explore the use of green leases which incentivize both parties to improve the performance of the building so that carbon emissions, water use and waste can be reduced. It is clear therefore that professional bodies are contributing to promoting practices by their members which are conducive to achieving sustainable outcomes in the development, acquisition and use of property.

While the concept of sustainability and the triple bottom line may be widely understood, the ability to measure positive or negative impacts against the three bottom lines in a systematic manner is fraught with difficulty. These difficulties reduce the ability of individuals and companies who are concerned about triple bottom line effects to compare competing investment opportunities. While there is a search for reliable metrics (or ways of measuring and reporting) the debate and research on this issue is still in its infancy. As Lorenz and Lutzkendorf (2008) point out, even evaluating the value difference that the sustainability features of a building may have on just one of the bottom lines i.e. the financial dimension is still beyond the abilities of the valuation profession. While acknowledging the practical difficulties Lorenz and Lutzkendorf urge that an appropriate and usable methodology be found as they feel that:

> a huge untapped market potential exists for sustainable property investment products and consulting services [and that] sustainable buildings clearly outperform their conventional competitors in all relevant areas (i.e. environmentally, socially, and financially). (2008)

In common with writers such as Lorenz and Lutzkendorf the RICS has issued guidance for its chartered surveying valuers which if it were paraphrased might quite reasonably suggest that 'yes sustainability is out there, but it's too difficult to put a precise value on it just yet':

> Although sustainable principles may be embedded in the policies of property owners and occupiers, translating them to their property decisions has been difficult. An important contributory reason for this is that not all aspects of sustainability translate easily or demonstrably into market value, yet they nevertheless exist. However, currently little is known about their impacts on value and it is important, therefore, that claims of relationships that cannot be evidenced are considered cautiously. (RICS 2009a: 5)

Regarding the difficulties with accounting across the triple bottom line when evaluating investment properties, Kimmet (2009) confirms that not only are the economic aspects difficult to pin down but that the social aspects of sustainability are also hard to measure. For some at least, the social dimension of sustainability, which concerns increased productivity and social well-being, are less visible and therefore will be continued to be viewed as the 'softer and politically correct' part of sustainability rather than a core aspiration. As Kimmet states:

> The benefits of sustainable commercial property investment (SCPI) in both existing and new products, get measured in micro (energy efficiency, recycling etc) and macro terms (greenhouse gas reducing, carbon footprinting, less resource depleting, etc) but are nearly always environmentally based. (2009: 471)

Thus a sustainable property asset is often considered, not unreasonably, to be one which produces less waste and is more energy efficient and therefore must be more environmentally benign. The 'green accreditation' bestowed on buildings through the use of BREEAM (Building Research Establishment Environmental Assessment Method) in the UK and LEED (Leadership in Energy and Environmental Design) in the USA tend, not unreasonably, to focus upon measures which reduce carbon footprints. Less is said explicitly about the social usefulness of property, which is ironically where the economic bottom line can best be sustained. There lies ahead therefore the challenge for property investment practitioners and theorists to demonstrate how socially responsible investment decisions can underpin economic viability.

The role of corporate social responsibility (CSR)

There perhaps remains in the sustainable development and investment debate a latent suspicion that addressing environmental and social concerns will in some way impact negatively on the economic bottom line. This is despite authoritative reports such as the Stern Review (2006) which set out convincing evidence that not to take action on at least environmental issues will ultimately impact negatively upon the financial bottom line.

As Jones *et al.* (2009) note a helpful development over the last decade is the growing corporate awareness and adoption of policies on CSR. Those authors note that there is some historical antecedence to CSR in that some companies, charities and branches of government have long recognized that there are wider than economic obligations when operating within communities. The early green movement championed the concept of responsible 'stewardship' of the earth's resources and this today would translate into the adoption of carbon reduction targets and wider sustainability practices by government and companies which sets the modern context for CSR policies. Jones *et al.* (2009) pull together a number of academic views on why companies adopt CSR policies and a synthesis of those contributions appears to centre on the following corporate motivations:

- A sense that organizations have a moral obligation to act as good citizens by setting good examples through actions and decisions.
- That companies accept that they need to obtain license or legitimacy from other stakeholders in order to operate.
- That companies feel a need to keep up with their peer group by conforming to society's norms and expectations on what companies should be achieving.
- That companies, like individuals, care and want to develop positive reputations amongst peers, clients and stakeholders. This may have a positive spin-off in strengthening the corporate brand.
- That companies pragmatically respond to pressures from shareholders and other stakeholders to raise their aims and ambitions above just making profits.

These motivations have led various organizations to articulate their CSR policies in a public way. It is also not surprising that there is a strong link between the adoption of CSR policies and a commitment to act in a sustainable way. However the adoption of CSR policies amongst organizations is mixed and even where CSR policies have been adopted there are differing degrees of commitment to taking action in line with these policies. The property sector is no different to any other sector in this respect as the RICS confirm:

> Whilst some participants in the market have advanced knowledge of sustainability matters and have adopted stringent corporate social responsibility (CSR) policies that include property investment and occupation matters, others have not. Hence in forming a judgment as to the extent to which sustainability factors will impact on valuation, the attitudes of those likely to be in the market for the subject property, both as occupier and owner, are relevant. Often it may be difficult for such factors to be quantified; nevertheless it may fall within the remit of the valuer to provide some qualitative comments. (2009a)

The market for sustainable buildings

Research by Eichholtz *et al.* (2009) on the financial performance of green office buildings in the USA found a marginal uplift in rental and capital values for buildings which had a green accreditation of one kind or another. In the USA that accreditation is usually represented by either a Green Star label or a LEED accreditation.

In the UK the picture is not quite as clear cut and as RICS confirm (2009a) this is partly because valuers currently lack the appropriate methodology to place a monetary value on any sustainability uplift attributable to the green credentials of a building. However as the earlier quote from the RICS confirms valuers are encouraged to make qualitative notes on the extent that market sentiment has been influenced by sustainability issues.

Valuers of commercial properties in a UK context are also faced with a vast stock of 'non-green' buildings in contrast to a minority of new buildings coming forward, only a minority of which exceed the minimum requirements in the building regulations sufficient to attract a green accreditation. In the UK most readers will be aware that the green benchmarking of commercial properties is normally reflected in a BREEAM rating which is measured independently against eight categories which include energy use, water consumption and transport. A weighted scoring system then determines which of the following standards can be awarded to reflect the building's sustainability: 'Pass', 'Good', 'Very Good', 'Excellent' or 'Outstanding'. Dixon *et al.* (2009) reported that only about 7 per cent of new office developments attract a BREEAM rating of 'Good' or above each year.

From the occupiers' perspective, the British Council for Offices (2009: 25) suggests that:

> Fundamentally, occupiers need their offices to deliver three things:
>
> Productivity
> Good value for money
> Prospect of best place to work

> But for an increasing number of occupiers, there is a fourth factor to be addressed – they wish their offices to convey a message, subliminal or

blatant, about the underlying ethos of their organisation, typically in terms of their 'corporate social responsibility' (CSR) and in order to assist recruitment and retention of the best staff.

Dixon *et al.* (2009: 61–85) looked at this issue in a little more depth in their research on the search criteria used by companies when seeking new office space. That research suggested that despite growing awareness of the importance and applicability of sustainability by those who produce and use commercial investment properties, progress towards delivering genuinely sustainable commercial buildings has been slow. This was thought to be because of a 'circle of blame' in which occupiers report that they are not offered sustainable buildings and so they remove this ambition from their search criteria. Developers then claim that there is no real market demand for sustainable buildings from either occupiers or investors, while property investors claim that developers do not bring forward sustainable properties and so these do not feature prominently on their acquisitions list.

The British Council for Offices who are strong advocates of the business case for building more sustainable buildings have reached similar conclusions in that change needs to be demand driven:

> Occupiers and buyers have to keep demanding high-performance buildings in order for developers to build them. Only when the demand side of the commercial office world embraces the cost savings from productivity gains and reduced absenteeism in addition to operational savings, will there be a true business case for green buildings. (2009: 35)

In their research Dixon *et al.* (2009) looked at the connection between the aspirations of companies seeking new office space and their policies on CSR. There was some correlation between companies which had explicit policies on CSR and their ultimate choice of offices, which tended to be BREEAM rated. These companies, which were in the minority in the sample, were able to identify the benefits of occupying sustainable buildings which went beyond energy reduction and reduced bills to increased employee productivity, flexibility of space and adaptability. However the research found that it is still the case that the search criteria for companies seeking new office space was in the following order of priority:

- location;
- availability;
- building quality;
- running costs;
- design; and
- sustainability features.

While sustainability features are ranked in last place by companies, the research team suggested that there remained an implied sustainability weighting in location and running costs, even though for most office occupiers the prime concern under 'running costs' was the rent. The overall conclusions reached by the research team were that sustainability issues were likely to creep up the agenda of companies seeking new premises but that the development of a market distinction for sustainable buildings in the UK was still very much in its infancy. This conclusion was largely confirmed by GVA Grimley and the CBI whose corporate real estate survey at the end of 2009 followed two difficult years for businesses and the property market. It seemed that difficult economic conditions may have been an additional reason why firms were cautious about paying a rental premium in order to occupy a sustainable building, as GVA Grimley and the CBI stated:

> As the survey has shown, keeping costs down is one of the main priorities for business at the moment. So it is no surprise that property costs and rent are two of the highest concerns when buying or leasing new space and that one of the main reasons for choosing a sustainable building is the reduced costs of operating in it. However, firms are unwilling to pay anything other than marginally more for a sustainable building. This may be because of a perceived lack of belief that the additional rent will see additional costs recouped, or it may be that non-financial benefits are not as valued at the current time as the financial ones. (2009: 7)

1.9 Summary

The ambition of this chapter was to introduce some preliminary property investment terms and to place both residential and commercial property investment in a wider context in which investors are faced with different investment opportunities. It was suggested that even so called 'risk-free' investments such as government gilts, still attract some risks depending on when the investor buys and sells. Risk in this sense is the chance that the investment will not earn the anticipated rate of return, rather than a risk that all of the money tied up in the investment will be lost. That can happen with shares if a company fails, so investors would expect a higher rate of return on their share dealings given the higher risks involved. Property comes some way between both of these investment media, as there will always be a tangible asset which can be sold or redeveloped even if the financial performance of the property may sometimes disappoint. Thus property investments should be seen as reflecting a modest rate of return relative to the modest risks involved.

Because of the professional advice, fees, management responsibilities and taxes involved in investing and divesting of property, this type of investment is more likely to suit the medium to long-term investor seeking to diversity a portfolio of investments. It is for that reason that some of the largest investors, particularly in commercial property, are the insurance companies and pension funds. There are however ways for smaller investors to obtain indirect exposure to the performance of property and one such vehicle is the tax efficient REIT which perhaps has yet to realize its full potential in the UK given that the concept was unfortunately launched at the onset of the credit squeeze.

The chapter rounded up by looking at sustainability and how this concept will gradually come to influence property markets, as occupiers will gradually become more discerning about the sustainability credentials of the buildings they purchase or lease. However at present the picture is mixed, partly because not all organizations have adopted coherent CSR policies and partly because property valuers do not yet have an adequate toolkit in order to clearly identify a sustainability uplift in a property's rental or capital value. However it is likely that the ground swell of enthusiasm behind this project will see progress being made quite rapidly in the near future. A number of the key themes and concepts introduced in this chapter will be explored in more depth in the chapters which follow.

References

Armatys, J. Askham, P. and Green, M. (2009) *Principles of Valuation* (London: EG Books).

Barker, K. (2004) *Review of Housing Supply – Delivering Stability: Securing our Future Housing Needs* (London: HM Treasury). Available in e-format at: www.barkerreview.org.uk

Baum, A. (2009) *Commercial Real Estate Investment – A Strategic Approach*, 2nd edn (London: EG Books).

British Council for Offices (2009) *2009 Guide to Specification* (London: British Council for Offices).

Cole, G. A. (2004) *Management Theory and Practice*, 6th edn (London: Thomson Publishing).

Council of Mortgage Lenders (2010) *Market Commentary, May 2010*, available only in e-format at: www.cml.org.uk/cml/publications/marketcommentary

Darlow, C. (ed) (1983) *Valuation and Investment Appraisal* (London: Estates Gazette).

Dixon, T., Ennis-Reynolds, G., Roberts, C. and Sims, S. (2009) 'Is there demand for sustainable offices? An analysis of UK business occupier moves (2006–2008)', *Journal of Property Research*, 26(1).

Dubben, N. and Sayce, S. (1991) *Property Portfolio Management: An Introduction* (London: Routledge).

Dubben, N. and Williams, B. (2009) *Partnerships in Urban Property Development* (Chichester: Wiley-Blackwell).

Eichholtz, P., Kok, N. and Quigley, J. (2009) *Doing Well by Doing Good? An Analysis of the Financial Performance of Green Buildings in the USA*. RICS Research Report (London: RICS).

GVA Grimley (2009) *CBI/GVA Grimley Corporate Real Estate Survey* (London: GVA Grimley). Available in e-format at: www.gvagrimley.co.uk

Investment Property Databank and the University of Aberdeen (1994) *Understanding the Property Cycle* (London: RICS).

Investment Property Databank (2009) *IPD UK Annual Property Index* (London: Investment Property Databank). Available in e-format at: www.ipd.com

Isaac, D., O'Leary, J. and Daley, M. (2010) *Property Development, Appraisal and Finance*, 2nd edn (Basingstoke: Palgrave).

Jones, P., Hillier, D., Comfort, D. and Clarke-Hill, C. (2009) 'Commercial property investment companies and corporate social responsibility', *Journal of Property Investment and Finance*, 27(5).

Kimmet, P. (2009) 'Comparing "socially responsible" and "sustainable" commercial property investment', *Journal of Property Investment and Finance*, 27(5).

Lorenz, D. and Lutzkendorf, T. (2008) 'Sustainability in property valuation: theory and practice', *Journal of Property Investment and Finance*, 26(6).

Matysiak, G, Hoesli, M., MacGregor, B. and Nanathakumaran, N. (1995) 'Long-term inflation-hedging characteristics of UK Commercial Property', *Journal of Property Finance*, 7 (1).

Mercer (2010) *Asset allocation survey and market profiles* (London: Mercer). Available in e-format at: www.mercer.com/assetallocation

Mullins, L. J. (2007) *Management and Organisational Behaviour*, 8th edn (Harlow: Financial Times, Prentice Hall).

Oprea, A. (2010) 'The importance of investment feasibility analysis', *Journal of Property Investment and Finance*, 28(1).

Pivo, G. (2005) 'Is there a future for socially responsible property investment?', *Real Estate Issues*, 30(1).

REITA (2010) *The Personal Investor's Guide to Property*. Available in e-format at: www.reita.org

RICS (2009a) *Sustainability and Commercial Property Valuation, Valuation Information Paper 13* (London: RICS).

RICS (2009b) *Sustainability and the RICS Property Lifecycle* (London: RICS). Available in e-format at: www.rics.org

RICS (2010a) *RICS Valuation Standards*, 6th Edition (London: RICS).

RICS Economics (2010b) *RICS Commercial Market Survey, First Quarter 2010* (London: RICS). Available in e-format at: www.rics.org

Sayce, S., Smith, J., Cooper, R. and Venmore-Rowland, P. (2006) *Real Estate Appraisal: from Value to Worth* (Oxford: Blackwell).

Smith, R. J. (2008) *Property Law*, 6th edn (Harlow: Longman).

Stern, N. (2006) *Stern Review of the Economics of Climate Change* (London: HM Treasury and Cabinet Office).

Srivatsa, R., Smith, A. and Lekander, J. (2009) 'Portfolio optimisation and bootstrapping', *Journal of Property Investment and Finance*, 28(1).

United Kingdom Debt Management Office (2005) *Formulae for Calculating Gilt Prices from Yields*, 3rd edn (London: United Kingdom Debt Management Office). Available in e-format at: www.dmo.gov.uk

Universities Superannuation Scheme Limited (2010) *Statement of Investment Principles*. Available in e-format at: www.uss.co.uk

World Commission on Environment and Development (Brundtland Report) (1987) *Our Common Future* (Oxford: Oxford University Press).

2

Property investment markets

Aims

This chapter explores some of the peculiarities of the property investment market which distinguish it from more conventional investment markets which trade in stocks and shares. The chapter explains why the property market is a risky domain for both corporate investors who tend to target commercial property assets and smaller investors who tend to target residential buy-to-let properties. Both residential and commercial property markets experience periods of volatility and even when prudent research is undertaken and professional advice sought, the risks will never be entirely dissipated.

    The chapter seeks to provide some indication of the overall scale of the property investment market and why large corporate investors have focused upon commercial property but have largely ignored residential property. There is discussion on key issues such as trends in lease terms which have a bearing upon investor risk and asset values.

Key terms

>> **Arbitrage** – the process by which participants in a market will seek to buy low and sell high by judging when an asset is undervalued relative to its returns. Arbitrageurs, or market traders in common parlance, will then sell the asset on when they sense that its value has peaked. The combined action of market traders acting on this principle will bring assets to their true market value and will tend to equalize the returns from groups of similar assets which have similar risk profiles.

>> **Globalization** – the process by which national economies, cultures and technologies become interconnected in a global network facilitated by communication and trade. Although the economic dimension of globalization is most

often discussed, the cultural and technological dimensions should not be underestimated. There are critical perspectives which can be taken on globalization. It can be seen as signifying human progress by widening trading opportunities, expanding markets and enabling the dissemination of ideas and technologies. It has also been criticized for reducing everything to a lowest common denominator and price and that it erodes cultures and is exploitative, widening inequality between rich and poor nations.

>> **Property cycle** – not as the name suggests a regular or predictable cycle governed by any known formula, but the name given to the peaks and troughs in property values which seem to occur every 10 to 12 years. The term describes the process of market adjustment which takes place when too much property is produced relative to the demand for it. The trough part of the cycle usually follows a long period of sustained economic growth at the end of which the banks have often become overexposed to toxic property loans.

2.1 Introduction

The market for investment property is well established in the UK. However, because there is no central exchange or dealing floor, some effort is required on the part of investors to interpret and participate in the market. This is not helped by the fact that there is imperfect information in the property market despite the best efforts of companies such as CoStar to bring transparency with their Focus database which records commercial property market transactions. To some extent the Rightmove website provides a similar facility for the residential property market although it is fundamentally a marketing service for properties which are available for sale or rent rather than a systematically researched database on transactions.

Commercial or residential property investments will each have their own particular characteristics and thus professional advice will almost always be required when an investor is considering whether to acquire a property asset. The property market is thus a hazardous place for the layperson to invest in.

This chapter will consider the size of the property investment market and some of its peculiarities such as the periodic cycles which see values rise and fall over relatively short periods. The chapter will also look at the nature of leases which structure the relationship between tenants and property investors in both the commercial and residential property sectors.

2.2 An overview of property investment markets in the UK

From an investor's perspective there is not one homogenous property market but several specialized sub-markets in which there are also regional differences. However, the first and perhaps obvious distinction is between residential and commercial property investment.

The commercial property investment market

Investors in the commercial property market tend to be large companies and finance houses which purchase commercial properties such as shops, offices and industrial units in order to lease them out to business tenants (the characteristics of investors are explored in Chapter 3). Thus commercial property is a large category of building types and can be anything which is not housing or agricultural land.

In 2005 the Investment Property Forum (IPF) tried to estimate the size of the UK commercial property market and the proportion of the market which is invested rather than owner-occupied. Although this sounds like a relatively straightforward statistical exercise, the IPF research team had to make a number of assumptions and construct a bespoke methodology in order to bring together and make sense of different datasets. IPF acknowledged (2005: 6) that there was a range of uncertainty attached to the out-turn figures which were at best indicators of the size and patterns within the property market rather than representing a definitive picture.

Despite some uncertainty over the precision of the IPF figures, the work sheds some light on the broad patterns of commercial property investment. For example IPF estimated that in 2003 the overall stock of commercial property in the UK had a capital value of £611 billion of which 33 per cent was retail property, 26 per cent offices and 21 per cent industrial. Thus 80 per cent of the total stock by value was made up from these three core commercial property types. The remaining 20 per cent comprised hotels, pubs, leisure outlets and public service buildings. The IPF reported (2007: 3) that these figures were subsequently updated to the end of 2005 at which point the total value of the commercial property stock was thought to have been £762 billion but that the percentage distribution between property sectors within that stock remained unchanged.

Of the total stock of commercial buildings IPF estimated that 43 per cent by value was owned by investors, which when applied to the 2005 updated figures equates to something like £328 billion. The balance of 57 per cent was estimated to represent £434 billion of owner-occupied commercial property. However, property investors had targeted the high value end of the market and by default owner-occupying businesses tended to own lower value properties on a metre squared comparison. Thus while investors might own 43 per cent of the commercial stock by value, when measured by floorspace the invested proportion of the stock was around 20 per cent of total commercial floorspace. The 43 per cent value headline figure also concealed marked differences between different property sub-sectors. Thus 61 per cent of retail property by value is owned by investors, with corresponding figures of 63 per cent for offices but only 23 per cent for industrial.

The IPF research also looked at geographical spread of investment property and found that there was an even spread across the country of retail investment property. Thus the large corporate investors had shown enthusiasm for acquiring prime shops and well located retail warehouses which were trading well in all parts of the UK. However investment patterns for offices and industrial property were much more focused upon London and the South-East of England, as investor sentiment clearly expected stronger rental and capital growth to take place in these localities for these types of property.

The residential property investment market

In contrast to the commercial property market discussed above, the residential property investment market is dominated by smaller investors with very few

Table 2.1 A summary of UK housing tenure

Estimated total UK housing stock in 2007	Owner-occupied	Privately rented	Rented from a housing association (registered social landlord)	Rented from a local authority
26.6 million	69.5%	12.4%	8.4%	9.7%

large corporate investors. Residential property investors purchase houses and flats in order to become residential landlords by letting property to tenants in the private rented sector.

Historically in the UK the private rented sector was much larger than it is today. In the 1950s around 50 per cent of all households rented from a private landlord, 30 per cent were owner-occupiers and the balance of 20 per cent rented mainly from local authorities with a small proportion renting from charitable trusts and housing associations. By the 1980s the private rented sector had shrunk to below 10 per cent of all households but has since grown gradually to reach the level shown above in Table 2.1 which is based upon a summary of UK housing tenure statistics produced by the Department for Communities (2010a).

The shrinkage of the private rented sector has been discussed in detail in housing texts such as Kemp (2010: 122–39) and is partly to do with government-imposed rent controls in the 1950s and 1960s which had the effect of reducing profitability for investors in the sector. The exodus of investors from housing coincided with a mass council house building programme and the development of the new towns which widened housing choice for many households. From the 1980s onwards housing associations were encouraged to build up their stocks so that by 2007 as Table 2.1 shows, they were almost as large a landlord as local authorities.

The proportion of the housing stock held by local authorities declined significantly due to central government policy which curtailed local authorities' capital-building programmes and encouraged stock transfers to housing associations. Many council tenants also took up their new right to buy their properties. Increasing affluence enabled more households to take on a mortgage and to become owner-occupiers. Of equal importance was a change in social attitudes by which individuals and families began to have realistic aspirations to become home owners.

The outcome of these changes is revealed in Table 2.1 which shows that just under 70 per cent of the homes in the UK are now owner-occupied. Within the home ownership category the Office of National Statistics (2009) estimates that 44 per cent of homes are owned outright with the balance of 56 per cent being purchased with a mortgage. Those readers who are particularly interested in the extent of outstanding mortgage debt could look at Wilcox (2008) or statistics collated by the Council of Mortgage Lenders at www.cml.org.uk.

On the basis of the above summary therefore the UK's private rented sector contains around 3.3 million dwellings. The sector has experienced a minor revival from 1991 when there were just over 2 million properties in the sector.

Research by Ball (2007) for the Investment Property Forum drew upon Office for National Statistics data which suggested that the overall asset value of housing in the UK in 2006 was £3,915 billion. Given that the proportion of that stock held by private landlords is around 12 per cent then the total value of private rented stock is in the order of £470 billion. As noted above this compares with a 2005 estimate that the total value of the invested commercial stock was around £328 billion.

Given the different statistical base dates, the very large figures involved and the necessity in statistical exercises like this for adjustments and assumptions to be made, there is little value in prying too deeply into the figures. The key point however is that the total estimated value of the private rented sector at around £470 billion appears to be easily larger than the total value of the commercial property investment sector at £328 billion. Thus either considered as 3.3 million homes or as a sector whose total asset value is greater than that of the commercial property investment sector, the private rented sector should not be seen as a minor branch of the property investment market. It is in fact the largest single element in the property investment market.

Despite the scale of the residential property investment market Ball (2007) notes the relative lack of enthusiasm on the part of financial institutions for investing in the sector. Thus what Ball refers to as the 'weight of wealth' argument has not persuaded large corporate property investors to become heavily involved in the private rented residential market. There are of course some notable exceptions such as the UNITE group plc which specializes in student housing, but the general position is that the private rented sector is dominated by smaller non corporate investors. This surprised Ball (2007: 21) who having reviewed data produced by Investment Property Databank (IPD) and Paragon Mortgages also noted that the real returns over a 25-year-period from residential property investment were superior to the returns on commercial property investment. Even over shorter timeframes and in the context of specific portfolios of properties monitored by IPD the superior asset performance of residential over commercial is clear from IPD's headline figures in Table 2.2 below.

Ball (2007) also noted that there was an imperfect correlation between the booms and slumps in the commercial property market and the residential market and that by avoiding residential investment investors may have been missing an opportunity to reduce risk through portfolio diversification. Ball also noted that the booms in prices in the residential market were stronger and the slumps shallower than for commercial property.

Even the summary figures from IPD above seem to support Ball's observation in that the three years leading up to 2009 encompassed the core credit crunch year of 2008 which saw dramatic write-downs in the value of commercial property

Table 2.2 Headline figures from IPD's Residential Investment Index for 2009

	Annualized total return %		
Time-frame	Over 3 years	Over 5 years	Over 9 years
Residential property	3.1	6.8	10.0
Commercial property	−8.0	1.8	5.9

portfolios reflected in the −8 per cent annualized returns in the IPD index for the three-year period. Over the same period the performance for residential property was still positive at 3.1 per cent despite the effects of the credit crunch, although down on the longer-term average of 10 per cent.

Given the available data, it seems illogical that institutional property investors have been systematically favouring commercial property over residential property. Ball notes that this pattern is not specific to the UK as elsewhere in the world large institutional investors have preferred to focus their investment attentions on commercial rather than residential property. The reasons for this pattern may lie in the need for additional management expertise because managing housing is far more resource intensive than managing the average business park office unit let on full repairing and insuring terms. Ball also notes the churn factor that characterizes the private rented sector where households tend to move on in quick succession. This is mainly because rented accommodation is seen as a temporary arrangement for many households rather than an end destination. In the commercial property sector where leases are longer, there is less need for repetitive marketing and reletting.

There are also economies of scale that can be achieved by corporate investors when buying large commercial properties which cannot be achieved when appraising and purchasing single residential properties. Thus the fine-grain nature of the residential market and the variability within it simply lends itself more to smaller investors who may be able to devote the time and attention needed for the detailed and more complex challenges of residential property management.

Finally there is perhaps the underestimated and implicit factor which might best be thought of as the transactional interface between landlord and tenant. In the commercial property sector the relationship is normally between corporate landlord and business tenant both of whom will tend to use professional intermediaries when engaging with one another. The additional customer focus, cultural adjustment and ability to micro-manage situations when a corporate landlord engages with a household is not a challenge that many large corporate organizations have an appetite for, nor the staff skills base to deal with. There may therefore be a cultural reluctance on the part of decision-makers in large investment organizations to becoming residential landlords. In combination, these factors perhaps go some way towards explaining why large corporate investors continue to prefer commercial rather than residential property investment, despite the better financial returns from the residential sector.

2.3 Volatility and cycles in property markets

There is a history of cycles in the property sector which have connection with the wider business cycle. Cyclical movements in the property market are most evident in the office development and investment markets although buy-to-let investors will also testify to quite dramatic rises and falls in residential property values in recent years. It is not necessary to review the whole history of these peaks and troughs which began to occur from as far back as the Second World War; however a summary of some of the more notorious episodes will serve to illustrate how complex the circumstances can be surrounding the rise, fall and then recovery of property markets.

Even a brief review of these cycles would seem to suggest that there is a lack of collective memory and an inability of participants in the property market to learn from past mistakes. It appears almost as if the lessons have to be relearned each time. However that is something of an overgeneralization as very few experts in any field were able to predict the unprecedented credit crunch which emerged due to global factors in 2007 and which saw the first run on a UK bank for over 100 years. In the event the government stepped in and took the bank: Northern Rock into public ownership in order to try to stabilize the situation.

A history of peaks and troughs

The selected examples of peaks and troughs in the world of property which follow illustrate the complex interplay of variables which play out over time and which give rise to the boom-and-bust phenomenon. One such episode began in the late 1960s when developers began experimenting with sale and leaseback, by which a property development was financed during the construction stage using bank finance and then sold on completion. A shortage of commercial floorspace had became apparent at the time and the institutions (the insurance companies and pension funds) saw an opportunity to purchase development sites and then use building agreements and agreements for lease with developers.

At the time, developers borrowed short term against their developments because they believed that rising asset values would counterbalance the deficit finance. Some developers ignored cash flow and borrowed against the antici-pated increase in the capital value of their properties to meet the income short-fall between rental and interest payments. Essentially elements of the development industry and the funding institutions had become too confident and ceased to appreciate the real risks that the bubble could burst. The bubble did burst and there ensued a serious property crash in 1974/75 which brought to a grinding halt the growth that had been experienced during the 1950s and 1960s.

At the time of the property crash there were high interest rates in the after-math of the oil crisis of 1973 and this coincided with reduced tenant demand and inflation of building costs. In combination these factors meant that profit levels on speculative property developments were not achieved because of income voids during which interest charges on outstanding debt accumulated. Highly geared property companies had been fuelled by debt finance provided under fairly lax lending criteria. Accounting conventions at the time had disguised the sharply negative cash flows of a number of property companies which had embarked upon major development schemes. Secondary banks which had become heavily committed to property began to collapse. It became impossible to sell a property and it was not possible to borrow on it. Brett (1990) records that property shares at the time collapsed as did the direct market in property.

Another volatile episode in property markets began in the early 1980s when a recession and rising unemployment had affected the demand for property and commercial rents fell along with capital values. Property lagged behind the rest of the economy in its recovery and there was not another property boom until 1986–7. The institutions were now less important as providers of funds for property and their net purchases dropped as they re-weighted their portfolios towards equities and gilts, disappointed with the performance of their property assets.

A development boom, funded by the banks, then began as they were prepared to lend on individual developments and roll up the interest until the property was disposed of. Thus some developers became traders rather than investment companies. By the beginning of the 1990s the rental growth had tailed off and the market was collapsing because there were no buyers for the glut of completed developments which had reached the market at the same time. The banks had to extend their development loans beyond the development period because there were no institutional funders in the market. Development loans were thus converted to investment loans, committing banks to reluctantly remain in the market.

The most recent roller coaster in property markets is linked to the credit crunch which manifested itself most severely in the UK during 2008 and 2009. The credit crunch had its origins in the sub-prime mortgage market in the USA where a significant number of loans were made to borrowers who had no reasonable prospect of being able to meet repayments. The ensuing wave of repossessions by lenders had a catastrophic effect on the housing market in parts of the USA.

Because these loans were refinanced using mortgaged-backed derivatives and collateralized debt obligations in the global financial markets, the uncertainty created by the volume of loan defaults was sufficient to destabilize financial markets which had previously experienced 10 years of growth. The expression 'toxic loan' began to be used to reflect the fact that too many institutions had indulged in high-risk lending against overvalued property assets and as a consequence they were unlikely to see their money again. Some financial institutions had simply become overexposed to toxic loans and financial stakeholders in those institutions also began to suffer losses which prevented them from doing business. A negative chain reaction had been triggered in the world's financial markets.

In the UK there had also been some imprudent lending by banks in both the residential and commercial property markets. Credit had become too easily available to just about anyone who wanted to borrow and the effect was to stoke up property values well beyond what could reasonably be supported by incomes. Borrowers in both the residential and commercial property markets had overstretched themselves and loans could not be repaid and thus the toxic loan phenomenon took hold on this side of the Atlantic as well.

In September 2008 Lehman Brothers Bank collapsed and around that time the situation had become so precarious that over one weekend the government was monitoring the possibility that the high street banks' ATMs would cease to provide cash and that salaries would not be paid. The fear was that the whole credit system would grind to a halt. In the event, the crisis passed but it was probably a very near miss.

In the housing market values had simply become unaffordable and a process of market correction had to set in to bring prices down to sensible ratios against the income of borrowers. In some regions in the UK the average house price to annual income ratio had risen to an unsustainable 12:1 when historically the safe building society lending ratio had been 3:1.

Housebuilders who had purchased sites against expectations that housing

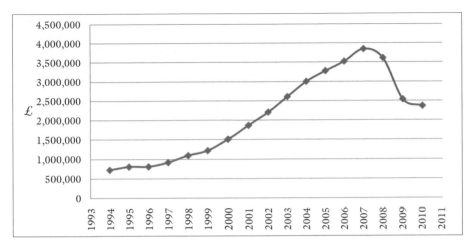

Figure 2.1 Average value per hectare of residential building land with planning consent in England

Data based on: Department for Communities and Local Government (2010b)

values would rise or at least remain at prevailing rates by the time the developments were completed were now facing falls of 20 to 30 per cent in the value of completed projects. Figure 2.1 produced from data collected by the Department for Communities provides an indication of the movements in the average value per hectare for residential building land with planning consent in England, excluding London.

Some half-completed housing schemes were taken into receivership and others were disposed of cheaply at auctions. Large developers simply mothballed sites, effectively sitting on their land to ride out the recession and wait for housing values to rise again. With the fall in housing values, the spectre of negative equality and repossessions by lenders began to stalk the housing market in a manner not seen since the early 1980s.

The commercial property sector was not immune, as depressed consumer spending saw companies downsize and suspend expansion plans or exercise break clauses in leases. The fragile financial services sector also saw cost cutting and redundancies to underline the general contraction of business activity which was taking place. Commercial developments which had begun on-site several years earlier had now arrived in a market where there was little if any tenant demand. In order to secure business lettings, developers had to offer significant inducements, including lengthy rent-free periods. For 2009 the Valuation Office Agency (2010) reported a fall of 15 per cent in headline rents in the central London office market and that was on the back of a similar fall during 2008.

By 2010 a degree of stability had become apparent and this was partly due to the effects of the government injecting billions of pounds into the economy during 2008 and 2009 under the principle of quantitative easing. The Bank of England Monetary Policy Committee had also played its part by bringing down and sustaining the base rate at an unprecedented low level of 0.5 per cent in order to help companies nursing loans and to enable some borrowing to take place where business expansion was possible.

The rate of recovery from this particular recession is predicted to be slower than following previous cycles. This is because the coalition government elected in 2010 embarked upon a round of deep public spending cuts to try to recover some of the public sector debt which had accumulated during the previous two years when the government purchased large equity stakes in banks to keep the financial system functioning. Those cuts will see redundancies in the public sector and in agencies which derive most of their income from the government. The campaign to reduce the size of the public sector will inevitably reduce the amount of money circulating in the economy and in such a situation it is unlikely that, particularly for commercial property, there will be any significant growth in property values over the short term.

However, property markets, in the same manner as the wider economy, tend to recover after about two years of recession and in 2010 some very ambitious development projects such as the Shard of Glass at London Bridge were begun on-site. The expectation was that this type of scheme would emerge two years later onto a rising property market. More pessimistic market pundits were predicting a double-dip recession on the basis that the cuts in public spending would have a negative multiplier effect throughout the economy. Thus in the middle of property and development cycles, the complex interaction of government policy, global economic shocks, domestic banking practice and consumer behaviour make it very difficult to determine whether a cycle has further to fall or whether the storm has run its course and the recovery has begun.

2.4 Theory and property cycles

The above discussion on recent boom-and-bust periods in the property market reveals that the volatility is caused by external factors in the wider economy in combination with factors integral to the property industry. Regarding external influences, the commercial property investor is essentially providing a facility (floorspace) which is a factor of production required by other businesses. Thus the expression 'derived demand' is often used to describe the occupier market for investment properties. The strength of that demand for space will depend on how successful companies are in their business endeavours and this in turn will be affected by the interplay of a number of macroeconomic factors. These include the volume of consumer spending, financial and business confidence in the economy, the price and availability of credit, government fiscal policy and movements in interest rates.

Levels of personal debt are also a factor, as during periods when consumers are carrying high personal debt consumer spending on goods and services will be depressed, reducing retail turnover which ultimately has negative consequences for retail rents and capital values. The credit crunch and the ensuing credit squeeze by banks essentially made it harder for households to take out new mortgages and the knock-on effect was a dampening of residential property values.

There are also factors which are internal to the property industry which affect property cycles and these include the development lag which is essentially the inflexibility by which the overall stock of buildings can be increased. This lag is also experienced when there is a glut of one type of property such as offices for which there is insufficient demand, but there is pressing demand for another type of property such as housing. While market signals may suggest conversion of one type of property into another or redevelopment of sites, time is inevitably required to obtain the necessary consents, raise finance, tender contracts and then carry out the conversion or redevelopment work. Thus the supply response in property is said to be inelastic relative to demand.

While it is obvious that there are recurrent and quite dramatic fluctuations in property markets the word 'cycle' which is often used implies that these fluctuations are regular and governed by a law or formula which makes them predictable events. Unfortunately for the property investor and those funding property transactions this is not the case, although this has not stopped some very worthy efforts at mapping the linkages between property cycles and wider economic cycles.

The Barras (1994) model, for example, suggests that when there is an economic boom there is usually credit availability and business confidence is high. Property developers then tend to embark upon ambitious speculative schemes but by the time these developments become available several years later, the economy may have moved into a recessionary stage and this depresses the achievable property rents below what would have been needed for developments to be viable and for bank loans to be repaid. This scenario manifested itself in 2010 in Dubai where a generation of ambitious speculative office, retail, housing and leisure developments reached completion and became available on the market just at a time when that locality began to experience the effects of a global recession. A number of hitherto successful property developers were reported to have defaulted on significant property loans.

The property slump described by Barras may last through the next business cycle, but because of the surplus of property there will be no shortage in the next upturn. When the next long cycle of development picks up it will tend to be demand driven with minimal speculative development because the banking system still has debts outstanding from the last boom. Thus another long cycle will need to proceed before the necessary preconditions will be in place for another speculative boom. Barras suggests that this is why property booms occur in every second long cycle of development and in every fourth short cycle of business activity.

Another model of the property cycle emerged from RICS-sponsored research in 1994 which described three phases:

1 In the early stages of an economic upturn, rental growth is likely to be dampened by the surplus of space from the previous recession and development boom.
2 In the second phase, continued economic expansion faces a shortage of space; commercial rents begin to rise rapidly and this triggers a spate of development starts. Since these developments will not reach the market for a year or more, the second phase of rapid rental growth is likely to be as long as a typical economic upswing. In the interim period the shortage of space will often worsen, and rental growth will accelerate to reach a peak. Developers reacting purely to current market conditions will be encouraged to start more development.
3 The third phase is likely to begin with weakening or falling tenant demand for space. As recessionary conditions begin to manifest themselves, buildings

triggered in the early part of phase two will be completed. The consequent fall in rental values puts a sharp stop to development schemes in the pipeline, although the surplus of newly completed space continues to rise, as the schemes started at the peak of the boom fall into recession.

The research concluded that if the property industry has lacked foresight, it is because property cycles are built into the workings of the economy and property directly. These cycles can never be smoothed out, but with better understanding there is a chance that appropriate responses can be made which might to some extent mitigate the impacts (McGregor *et al.* 1994).

2.5 Globalization and property investment

The UK once had an empire which covered half of the globe and formed the basis for the exchange of goods, services, ideas and to some extent culture within and outwith the boundaries of that empire. Of course in recent times empires have given way to powerful trading blocs such as the European Union within which trading barriers are at least theoretically removed to provide a semblance of a free market. Thus the basis for international trade and economic activity which forms the bedrock of globalization is nothing new to countries such as the UK which historically have had to develop their ability to trade beyond national boundaries.

The globalization of the investment markets for a whole variety of asset classes was stimulated by the abolition of exchange controls for investment funds in the late 1980s in the UK. At about the same time the banks became interested in globalization as a way of expanding their lending activities by servicing the needs of their corporate clients who were increasingly operating on a global basis.

Given rapid advances in information technology it was inevitable that these transnational trading relationships would be strengthened and that national financial markets would gradually become part of a global network of trading opportunities. Financial markets are now for the most part globalized, deregulated and relatively free for investors to trade in. Thus stateless finance, outside the jurisdiction of any one country and its regulatory institutions can have a significant effect on markets anywhere in the world.

With advances in the ability to access different global financial markets there has also been a behavioural shift on the part of investors in that they no longer see significant geographical barriers to their investment portfolio building ambitions. Thus it is not now seen as unusual for a Korean pension fund to purchase a multimillion pound office tower in London Docklands as part of its investment portfolio, as was the case in 2009. Indeed it makes perfect sense for large funds such as these to operate on a global basis in order to diversify their investment portfolios and spread risk, so that asset values are not overexposed to the economic performance of one particular nation.

The globalization of property investment is not a new phenomenon: Scandinavian, Japanese, Arabian, American and German investors have been active in the London property market since the 1980s and continue to have significant holdings there. Indeed one of the early development catalysts in London Docklands in the 1980s came from the development of the first office tower at Canary Wharf by a North American property development and investment company Olympia & York. As well as direct investment, Maxted and Porter (2007) also record the significant role played by international banks, particularly those from Germany, in terms of funding commercial property development and investment purchases in the UK. Of course globalization is not unidirectional and UK banks and property investors are also holding and investing in some of the most valuable real estate in most of the major cities in the world.

Innovations in funding property investment have run in parallel to the globalization of financial and property markets. In particular the introduction of Real Estate Investment Trusts (REITs) in countries such as the USA, Australia, Spain and the UK has gone a long way towards providing a tax-efficient solution to the inherent illiquidity of property as an investment. There also remains the opportunity for global investors to buy shares in UK commercial property companies which have not converted to REIT status because they are more focused upon development than property management, although in that case the same tax benefits do not arise for the investor.

The REIT model still has some way to go in the UK as at present it is solely focused upon commercial property and has yet to be rolled out for residential property investment. Thus if a UK investor wishes to gain some exposure to a residential REIT they will have to look at for example the American markets. In some senses therefore the UK residential property investment market remains (to coin a pun) rather domestic if not parochial and is largely untouched by the effects of globalization. This is partly because it is so atomized relative to the large concentrations of commercial real estate found in the major UK cities and which are identifiable and attractive investment opportunities for major global investors.

2.6 Market efficiency

The concept of market efficiency rests upon the idea that the prices of assets being traded will adjust instantaneously to reflect all the available information about market conditions and the anticipated returns relative to the risks involved. The degree of market efficiency therefore relies on the ability of arbitrageurs (dealers or market players) to recognize when prices are out of line and to make a profit by driving them back to an equilibrium value through collective buying and selling activity. Thus arbitrage is based upon the principle that dealers are able to spot opportunities to buy low and sell high or at least sell higher, so that ultimately assets will be traded at their correct price. The principle of arbitrage is central to market efficiency and is supposed to result in the optimum allocation of resources. However, for this principle to function, the market must approximate a perfect market which has the following characteristics:

- The market needs to be frictionless without transaction costs and taxes.
- There should be no constraining regulations limiting freedom of entry and exit for investors.
- All traded assets should be perfectly marketable.
- All services in the market should be provided at the average minimum cost, with all participants price takers.

- All buyers and sellers should be rational in that they seek to maximize their utility.
- There should be many buyers and sellers so that it is not possible for monopolies or cartels to fix prices.
- Market informational should be costless and received simultaneously by all active participants in the market.

In reality no market could ever satisfy all of these conditions in their entirety, although it is possible to relax some of the assumptions so that while they are not met in totality there might still be a 'fairly efficient market'. With regards to investments in property a distinction would need to be drawn between direct investment through buying commercial or residential properties and indirect investment such as buying shares in a property company or REIT. It is evident that indirect investment in REITs and property company shares more closely approximates the principles of a perfect market and where the concept of arbitrage is likely to take effect. Specialist investment traders would in this context build up knowledge surrounding the performance and upcoming programme of property companies by assessing annual company reports, announcements from the board and half yearly results. The whole monitoring and research process by traders helps to build a picture of whether the shares of any particular company in the sector represented a true reflection of the underlying value of the company.

Regarding direct investment in specific properties, the perfect market assumptions of costless information, a frictionless marketplace and many buyers and sellers are not met absolutely in every subsector of the property market. Nor are all property assets perfectly marketable as some properties will have legal or physical encumbrances. There will also be a difference in price between leasehold and freehold property and in the former case whether a property is tenanted or not.

Perhaps what might be said is that with direct property investment the twin concepts of arbitrage and the perfect market make a little more sense when a particular property subsector or group of properties is under consideration. Thus in a city centre where the rental yield on buy-to-let two-bedroom apartments is known to be 7 per cent and that monthly rents for these properties are £1,000 it is likely that buy-to-let investors will value this kind of asset at around £170,000 as at that price the annual return of £12,000 would represent a return of 7 per cent (a fuller analysis of buy-to-let appraisal is tackled in Chapter 8). However, given that home owners currently represent around 70 per cent of all households, investors will only represent a small fraction of the bidders in any housing market. Thus in the example above, if there was a context of a shortage of housing, available mortgage credit and pressure to get on the housing ladder, those seeking to purchase properties as a home rather than an investment might bid up the price of the available two-bedroom apartments to well over £170,000. In that scenario buy-to-let investors would have far less influence on the market price of these assets.

For commercial property, an example might be a particular type of retail unit which normally commands an initial yield of 6 per cent. The collective action of the investors who buy and sell this type of property will have far more influence in bringing the purchase price of this type of asset into line relative to the rental income stream. Through the process of arbitrage therefore, the market price of a property asset becomes the present value of future returns expected by the participants in the market, discounted at a rate which reflects the risk-free rate plus an appropriate risk premium. A fuller discussion on how investors might determine the risk rate is provided in Chapter 9.

2.7 Lease structures

There are some obvious and basic differences between commercial and residential leases and which structure landlord and tenant relationships in the two property markets. To begin with it is quite possible in the commercial sector for a landlord to pass onto a business tenant the full repairing and insuring obligations under covenants in a lease. However, that is seldom, if ever, possible in a residential landlord–tenant relationship, where far more of the ongoing management obligations remain with a landlord than is normally the case in the commercial property sector. In the commercial sector it is also possible within the terms of a lease for a tenant to assign their leases to another business which then takes up the rent paying and other obligations set out in the lease for the remainder of the term. This is seldom if ever legally possible in a residential context.

In terms of lease length, in the residential sector the assured short-hold tenancy effectively enables a flexible relationship which does not commit either party to longer than a six-month term. This provides flexibility for both parties and for example enables the landlord to review the rent when one short-hold tenancy ends and a new tenancy begins. Lease lengths in the commercial sector will typically be much longer than six months (see Table 2.3 which summarizes commercial lease lengths) although will increasingly include break clauses which potentially shorten the length of leases in practical terms. The payment of rent will normally be quarterly in advance in the commercial sector and monthly in advance in the residential sector.

Commercial leases

In the years leading up to the publication of the first edition of this book in 1998 the institutional lease had become a central feature of the commercial property investment market in the UK. The dominance of this type of lease reflected the influence of the financial institutions in the property market as it structured the power relationship firmly in favour of commercial landlords and against business tenants. Thus at that time, most major commercial property investments owned by financial institutions were let on 25-year leases containing five-year upward-only rent reviews and on fully insuring and repairing terms. Since then the length of the average commercial lease has shortened dramatically. Edwards and Krendel (2007: 9) explain that it does not make sense for business tenants to commit themselves to buildings for 25 year terms when in all probability the pace of technological change could render a building obsolete after 15 years.

Also in the years leading up to the first edition of this book, privity of contract had enabled landlords to pursue the tenant who had originally signed the lease in the event that an assignee had defaulted on the rent. Legislation has subsequently outlawed privity of contract and there are other important changes to

Table 2.3 Key features of commercial leases

Change to key features of commercial property leases

Year	Average lease length in years	Average lease length in years taking break clauses into account	Proportion of leases with break clauses	Average rent-free periods in months
1999	9.6	8.7	No data	No data
2000	8.9	8.2	No data	3.6
2001	9.1	8.4	No data	4.0
2002	8.8	7.8	16%	5.8
2003	7.8	6.8	21%	5.6
2004	7.3	6.4	20%	5.8
2005	7.1	6.2	21%	6.2
2006	6.6	5.7	23%	5.8
2007	7.2	6.2	23%	5.7
2008	7.0	5.9	28%	6.2

commercial leases which have effectively taken the institutional investor out of the comfort zone and into a situation where there are more risks.

Table 2.3 has been compiled using data from the British Property Federation and Investment Property Databank *Annual Lease Review for 2009* and it shows that dynamism in the business world has generated more flexibility for business tenants and thus a rebalancing of the power relationship between landlord and tenant. Not only have leases become shorter but they are increasingly containing break clauses and rent-free periods. A code of practice has also been in place for several years, which seeks to end upward-only rent reviews which are quite rightly seen by the government as a restrictive practice.

The figures in Table 2.3 are averages for all commercial property sectors based upon a broad survey of over 75,000 tenancies over the time-series. Thus the data are representative of the trends in the wider commercial property market. However, as with all averaging exercises there are embedded trends which are not apparent, such as a propensity for lease lengths to increase with the size of property and for there to be longer leases in the retail sector than for the office sector. Similarly shorter rent-free periods have been granted by landlords in the industrial and retail sectors than for the office sector.

Whichever way the data are interpreted, there is an undisputed trend towards more flexible lease terms for business tenants. There are a number of drivers behind this trend, one of which is that property managers acting for corporate tenants are more aware of their property options. Thus when faced with the offer of a long lease with rent reviews, facilities managers will compare the alternative of a commercial fixed-rate mortgage which will enable a company to purchase a property outright. Depending on the rent sought and terms offered by a commercial landlord, purchasing a property might be a better financial arrangement for an established company.

Business tenants are also now more likely to use professional advisers who have the capability to negotiate much harder regarding lease terms, particularly in the context of fragile property markets. Tenants who represent a strong covenant will also be seen as desirable longer-term tenants and so landlords have been more flexible when negotiating with these tenants. There has also been an influx of foreign businesses into the UK who with their professional advisers and financial backers are less prepared to tolerate rigid lease terms. Thus in order to stay abreast of global trends and to remain a place where companies can do business competitively, the UK commercial property lease has had to evolve to become more business tenant friendly.

2.8 Property market research

The scale of investment required particularly for direct investment in large commercial properties which have yet to be let will necessitate some market research to ascertain a realistic estimated market rent. An overview of the supply and demand position for the particular type of property in the locality is therefore a helpful first step.

On the demand side of the equation it would be prudent to identify the type of tenant who might be in the market for the particular property in the particular locality and what their property expectations might be. The RICS (2008: 6) has summarized the influences on occupier demand as:

- the location of the property;
- access and the availability of transport routes;
- car parking facilities;
- amenities attractive to tenant and/or purchasers;
- the scale of the development in terms of sale or lettable packages;
- the form of the development; and
- market supply, including actual or proposed competing developments.

If the investment were offices, then Barkham (2002: 57) suggests that at a strategic level a view needs to be taken on whether a locality is traditionally a destination for large international or national companies and government departments or whether the locality fulfils more of a regional or local function whose business community is really based upon smaller companies local authority offices with some indigenous company expansion.

On the supply side, rises in property rents will generally indicate a shortage of supply of that type of space, but this conclusion requires further analysis. The supply of space is essentially a sum which combines that proportion of the existing stock which is available for letting plus new speculative development arriving on the market which remains to be let. The demand side of the equation is represented by the take up rate represented by the historical pattern of lettings in a locality. The calculation is:

$$\frac{ND_t + (ES \times NV_t)}{TU_t}$$

where: ND_t is new development expected to arrive on the market over time period $_t$

ES is existing stock

NV_t is the percentage of existing stock expected to become available over time period $_t$

TU_t is the average take up rate on an historic basis for time period $_t$

For example let it be assumed that time period $_t$ is one year and that the formula is applied to a city where the total stock of office floorspace: ES is 500,000 m^2. Historic data suggest that the total lettings of office space: TU in the city averages 50,000 m^2 each year. A survey of the projects already embarked upon on site suggests that a number of new office developments will emerge onto the market over the coming year to add 30,000 m^2 of floorspace. Historic data also suggest that on average each year 4 per cent of the existing stock becomes vacant as leases expire or break clauses are exercised. Thus from the existing stock of offices 20,000 m^2 of floorspace is expected to became vacant and available for reletting. Inserting the variables into the formula gives the following outcome:

$$\frac{30,000 + (4\% \times 500,000)}{50,000} = 1$$

In this deliberately simplified example the equation balances and suggests that on a strictly quantitative basis the market is in equilibrium. This is because the take-up rate of office floorspace each year balances the supply provided by a proportion of the existing stock becoming vacant plus new developments arriving from the development pipeline. Of course in reality in most towns and cities there will seldom be a perfect balance between the supply and demand for floorspace over any time period and the picture is usually one of disequilibrium.

What is perhaps of most interest to an investor are wide discrepancies between supply and demand. Thus where there is a dearth of supply relative to the historic take-up rate this might suggest development or investment opportunities. Conversely where the rate of vacancies in the existing stock is high and there is a high volume of new development coming onto the market, the combination may grossly exceed realistic demand. In that scenario rents and capital values will tend to fall and long rent-free periods might have to be offered to attract the few businesses looking for premises. Property investors would need a special reason for becoming exposed to such a market.

A broad quantitative analysis is useful for providing an overview of the supply-and-demand relationship which exists in a locality and is one reason why the property journals *Estates Gazette* and *Property Week* provide regular commercial property market data and commentaries on different regions and cities within the UK.

The quantitative overview is helpful for a developer who may be planning a large speculative scheme which would distort the floorspace equilibrium in a town or city. In that case the developer and the financial backers would need to be confident that there was some special justification for the dramatic increase in supply planned relative to the usual rate of take-up. Market research might in that context be able to ascertain whether the developer was about to flood the market with unwanted space. For example the justification might be provided by knowledge of planned infrastructure improvements, or that the government had earmarked the locality as a strategic growth point, or that the local authority had secured funding for regeneration and environmental improvements. Knowledge about the timing of infrastructure improvements might help a developer devise a phasing programme over a number of years so that new floorspace could gradually be absorbed by the market.

Market research should also be able to identify qualitative issues. For example research might reveal that the real demand in a locality was from footloose media and IT businesses who were seeking new and environmentally sustainable office space and that the vacant proportion of the existing stock was now so dated that it was unlettable. Thus a purely quantitative picture of supply might not pick up the fact that empty second-hand office blocks in the locality were never again likely to be let but which were in reality future redevelopment sites.

Changes in technology and working cultures may lead to changes in the demand for space. For example the British Council for Offices (2009) reports that in recent years companies have been using their premises more intensively so that the average space per employee has been reducing. There has also been a trend towards more flexible work patterns with homeworking or teleworking for part of the working week combined with hot-desking. However this trend has not gone as far as some were predicting and the workplace model has proved to be far more durable than might have been supposed; the office-based working week is far from a redundant concept.

The commissioning of market research to provide an arm's-length perspective on these issues is thus money well spent when a multimillion pound investment is being contemplated. At the other end of the scale where individual residential buy-to-let properties are being considered for purchase it is obviously not necessary to embark upon corporate-style market research. However a prudent buy-to-let investor would make some common-sense deductions and enquiries with local agents to ascertain who the likely tenant populations were and what types of property were they looking for, how difficult or easy it might be to let properties in the locality and what rents could reasonably be expected. Buy-to-let investors should also be looking at how accessible the location was and how diverse was the employment market in that area given that a high proportion of private rented tenants are younger, upwardly mobile junior professionals who will ultimately move onto home ownership.

2.9 Summary

There are fundamentally two property investment markets, one in residential property and one in commercial property and there is very little overlap between the two types of investor which inhabit these markets. The commercial property investment market is dominated by large corporate investors some of whom operate on a global basis, while the residential property investment market is dominated by more numerous smaller investors based mainly in the UK. Judging by the volume of academic books written on the topic of commercial property investment and the fact that there are some very high-value individual commercial properties, it might be supposed that this sector had the highest aggregate value. However this is not the case and while the private rented sector in the UK may only represents 12.4 per cent of the total housing stock, the combined capital value of these 3.3 million homes easily exceeds the combined capital value of all commercial property investments.

It is however one dimensional just to focus upon the store of value held in a particular property sector, when an investor is principally interested in the returns achievable from a particular sector. Here again there are surprises in that the better returns in recent years have consistently been achieved from residential rather than commercial property investment. Curiously the lure of superior financial performance has been insufficient to tempt all but a few specialized corporate investors into the private rented sector. The reasons may be a combination of inertia, a lack of appetite for the management challenges which present themselves to residential landlords and perhaps a subliminal degree of cultural resistance to the concept of residential landlordism. This also explains why the UK REIT only exists in the commercial property form and not in a residential form.

There are also some limitations around the private rented sector which make it rather a specialized investment sector. One of the obvious factors is that home ownership in the UK has already reached nearly 70 per cent of tenure and government policy continues to champion home ownership as the 'natural' tenure. The core business of building societies has after all evolved almost entirely on this direction of travel and which coincides with as a legitimate popular aspiration for home ownership. In parallel there is in the UK a strong welfare theme underpinning the provision of affordable housing where there is a strong tradition of not-for-profit provision by housing associations and local authorities. Thus in this scenario the buy-to-let investor is providing for a minority niche market of tenants who by default do not currently fit within either of the tenure categories discussed above.

In contrast the commercial property sector is inhabited by businesses which are not necessarily aspiring to become owner-occupiers of their premises, but are operating to make profits to satisfy (in many cases) shareholders. Businesses are more pragmatic about who owns the means of production and if this involves leasing rather than owning property, then that is a matter to be determined by a financial appraisal which identifies which option is most cost-effective for the business.

Thus the residential buy-to-let investor is participating in a market against the grain of popular home ownership aspiration while the commercial property investor is engaging in a market driven by cost and value objectives rather than owner-occupation ambitions. A company looking for premises will simply look at commercial mortgage repayments and weigh them against rental payments.

The chapter also confirmed that property markets are volatile places for investors and that the periodic booms and slumps are felt most severely in the offices market and less severely in the residential market. The latter appears to experience shallower troughs but stronger peaks in value over time. Despite some useful theorizing around why property cycles occur, there is as yet no definite formula which can be used to predict when the next property peak or trough will occur.

References

Ball, M. (2007) *Large-scale Investor Opportunities in Residential Property: An Overview* (London: Investment Property Forum).

Barkham, R. (2002) 'Market research for office real estate', in S. Guy and J. Henneberry (eds), *Development and Developers: Perspectives on Property* (Oxford: Blackwell).

Barras, R. (1994) 'Property and the economic cycle: building cycles revisited', *Journal of Property Research*, 11(3), winter: 183–97.

Brett, M. (1990) *Property and Money* (London: Estates Gazette).

British Council for Offices (2009) *Guide to Specification* (London: British Council for Offices).

British Property Federation and IPD Ltd (2009) *BPF IPD Annual Lease Review 2009* (London: British Property Federation and IPD Ltd).

Department for Communities and Local Government (2010a) *Statistical Table 101: Dwelling stock: by tenure, United Kingdom (historical series)*. Available at: www.communities.gov.uk

Department for Communities and Local Government (2010b) *Statistical Table 563: Housing market: Average valuations of residential building land with outline planning permission*. Available at: www.communities.gov.uk

Edwards, C. and Krendel, P. (2007) *Institutional Leases in the 21st Century* (London: EG Books).

Investment Property Databank (2010) *IPD UK Residential Investment Index* (for 2009). Available in e-format at: www.ipd.com

Investment Property Forum (2005) *The Size and Structure of the UK Property Market* (London: Investment Property Forum).

Investment Property Forum (2007) *Understanding Commercial Property Investment: A Guide for Financial Advisers* (London: Investment Property Forum).

Kemp, P. (2010) 'The transformation of private renting', in P. Malpass and R. Rowlands (eds), *Housing, Markets and Policy* (Abingdon: Routledge).

McGregor, B., Nanthakumuran, N., Key, T. and Zarkesh, F. (1994) 'Investigating property cycles', *Chartered Surveyor Monthly*, July/August: 38–9.

Maxted, B. and Porter, T. (2007) *The UK Commercial Property Lending Market: Year End 2006 Research Findings* (Leicester: De Montfort University).

Office for National Statistics (2009) *Wealth in Great Britain – Executive Summary of the Main Points from the Wealth and Assets Survey 2006/2008* (ed. C. Daffin). Available in e-format at: www.statistics.gov.uk

Royal Institution of Chartered Surveyors (1994) *Understanding the Property Cycle: Economic Cycles and Property Cycles* (London: RICS).

Royal Institution of Chartered Surveyors (2008) *Valuation Information Paper 12: Valuation of Development Land* (London: RICS).

Valuation Office Agency (2010) *Property Market Report 2010*. Available in e-format at: www.voa.gov.uk

Wilcox, S. (2008) *UK Housing Review 2008/2009* (Coventry: Chartered Institute of Housing; London: Building Societies Association).

3

Property investors

Aims

This chapter acknowledges that it is futile to try to categorize and discuss all of the many organizations and individuals who now invest in either residential or commercial property. Thus the chapter does not attempt to comprehensively capture all categories of investor, but it does try to identify some of the principle organizations and individuals who invest in property. The chapter explores the motivations of these key investor types which drive them to commit often considerable sums of money over lengthy periods of time in property assets.

Key terms

>> **Real Estate Investment Trusts – REITs** are commercial property companies which benefit from tax exemption on their property trading and letting activities. REITs must restrict development to a minor part of their business in return for preferential tax status, and they must distribute 90 per cent of their profits to shareholders.

>> **Property Unit Trusts – PUTs** enable investors to purchase units which reflect the value of a portfolio of commercial properties. A PUT is unlikely to hold all of its assets in property, as some liquidity is needed to match any short-term deficit arising from an imbalance between investment and redemption of units. PUTs are open ended in that additional assets will be purchased if investor funds exceed redemptions. PUTs benefit from some tax efficiencies which can be attractive for small corporate and individual investors looking to gain some indirect exposure to property investment.

>> **Investment trust company** – a company exempt from capital gains tax which manages a portfolio of property company shares. By investing in a trust, investors can benefit indirectly from exposure to a diverse portfolio of shares in property.

>> **Liquidity** – the ease or difficulty of converting an investment into its cash equivalent. Investments such as shares are highly liquid because they can quickly be converted into a cash sum representing the prevailing market value. Property investments are far less liquid, as while they may have an up-to-date valuation, the realization of an equivalent cash sum through a sale will normally require a period of marketing followed by a detailed process of exchange which will typically involve negotiation, legal searches and due diligence. There might also be a third-party funder involved and satisfying their requirements will add time to the process of exchanging a property title for its cash equivalent.

3.1 Introduction

There is perhaps no such thing as the typical property investor, which is perhaps a contradictory statement at the start of a chapter which attempts to put property investors into categories. Property investors differ both in the scale of funds that they have available to invest in property and whether they invest *directly* by purchasing or part-purchasing a property or whether they invest *indirectly* by purchasing shares in larger organizations which own investment properties. Thus a property investor may be somebody who has purchased one buy-to-let residential property or an individual who has some shares in a property company. At the other end of the scale, a property investor can also be a pension fund which owns several shopping centres and office blocks, the combined value of which might represent a small percentage of the overall investment portfolio held by the fund.

Property investors are therefore a diverse group and this diversity has increased over the last 20 years as the opportunities to invest directly and indirectly in commercial and residential property have expanded. The media through which investors may gain some exposure to property is likely to continue to develop and thus it is likely that the investment community will also continue to widen and diversify.

This chapter therefore acknowledges that there is an ever expanding universe of property investors and that the investment media those investors use will continue to evolve. The ambition of the chapter is however to try to provide some broad definitions and shape to the discussion by trying to frame some broad categorizations of investor types and motivations. Similar categories have been identified by authors such as Havard (2008: 58–63) although greater emphasis will be given here to the residential buy-to-let investors who take their place alongside larger corporate property investors such as the financial institutions, property companies and foreign banks.

3.2 The scale of property investment in the UK

Before looking at broad categories of property investors and their investment ambitions, it is worth providing a reminder on the scale of investment made in property in the UK, data about which was discussed in Chapter 2. However because of the sheer size of the stock of commercial and residential buildings in the UK and the fact that property values are constantly moving, there are practical difficulties in identifying reliable financial totals at any point in time. Helpfully some estimates have been produced which at least provide an indication of the value held in the stock of buildings and how that is distributed between owner-occupied property and invested stock. For example the Investment Property Forum (2007: 3) reported that in 2005 the UK stock of commercial buildings was notionally worth £762 billion and that approximately half of that stock was owned by property investors, thus around £381 billion by value. This estimate of the invested part of the commercial property stock is of a similar order of magnitude as totals discussed in Chapter 2.

Most observers expect the proportion of the invested stock of commercial property to grow marginally given a recent trend in sale and leaseback transactions where owner-occupying companies have decided to sell either the freehold or a long lease on their properties. These deals have enabled companies, such as supermarket chains, to sell and then lease back the premises for operational purposes. This process releases capital tied up in properties to be redeployed in other corporate activities such as implementing development or expansion plans.

With regards residential property the size and total value of the stock in the UK is much larger than for commercial property. However the proportion of the residential stock owned by property investors is much smaller than for the commercial sector and was put at 12.4 per cent in 2007 (Communities and Local Government 2010). Given the volatility in house prices, it will always be an imprecise exercise to try to place an accurate value on the total residential stock and to disaggregate this into different sectors such as owner-occupied and private rented. However a guide has been provided by Ball (2007: 15) who suggested that in 2006 the asset value of all dwellings in the UK was £3,915 billion, so that if approximately 12 per cent is invested stock, then that sector of the market was worth approximately £470 billion at that time. The key point is that the total value of residential investment stock is considerably larger than the invested proportion of the commercial property sector. Ball predicted that the private rented sector would grow annually by 3 per cent. However there is a strong countervailing force which will limit the expansion of the private rented sector and that is simply the prevalent social ambition to become a home owner.

3.3 Investors in private rented residential property

Given that the residential private rented sector is larger in value terms than the stock of invested commercial property it seems logical to begin a discussion on investor types and motivations by looking at the residential sector. To some extent this approach runs counter to more conventional discussions on property investment where the commercial sector tends to dominate. This is because there is a degree of glamour attached to the commercial property sector where large lot sizes customarily change hands for headline-grabbing figures, while transactions in the more diffused residential market attract far less attention. There is also perhaps a stereotypical degree of mystique and sophistication associated with large-scale, high-risk investment in commercial property which perhaps does not feature to the same degree for residential property investment.

Traditionally therefore the centre of interest in academic and professional journals has tended to be commercial rather than residential property investment. However, in recent years, the rather dowdy and some would say exploitative reputation of residential landlordism has gone though something of a born-again transition, emerging under its new marketing badge as buy-to-let. The latter is now seen as a perfectly modern and acceptable investment activity for typically the comfortable middle classes to indulge in; subject of course to acceptable returns.

Kemp (2010: 128) explains that the newfound respectability for investing in the private rented sector has a number of drivers including the deregulation of rent controls in the wake of the Housing Act 1988. Since then, assured short-hold tenancies have effectively allowed private landlords to levy market rents while tenants have no right of extension to their tenancies beyond the term of the short-hold agreement (usually six months or one year). Thus if a buy-to-let investor wants to exit from private rented market, he or she only has to wait for the expiration of the current tenancy to sell the property. Alternatively the property can be marketed and sold while still tenanted as the purchaser will be fully aware that there is no obligation to extend the letting beyond the expiration of the current tenancy. Thus there is now an easy-in and easy-out dimension for the private landlord plus the ability to achieve open market rents applicable to the locality plus the potential for capital growth on the final sale.

Another obvious factor behind the revival of the private rented sector was, as Kemp (2010: 132) explains, the introduction from 1996 of more competitive buy-to-let mortgages following an initiative by the Association of Residential Letting Agents (ARLA). Statistics produced by the Council of Mortgage Lenders (2010) show that in 1998 only two years after the ARLA initiative, there were already 28,700 buy-to-let mortgages in the UK. The market for this type of product quickly developed so that by the end of 2010 there were 1,290,000 buy-to-let mortgages and although the housing market had been through several years of decline, the number of buy-to-let mortgages was still showing year-on-year growth.

The enthusiasm shown, particularly by novice landlords to enter the buy-to-let market, is also linked to historically low interest rates which reduce risks considerably. There has also been a well-publicized decline in the performance of many private pension schemes and so many of those who are in a position to supplement what will be underperforming pensions, will have at least thought about becoming a buy-to-let landlord. In this context independent financial advisers have been able to identify the capital growth potential of buy-to-let investment. Financial advisers have also been able to advise their clients on the flexible mortgage products which mortgage providers have marketed in recent years, revealing a far more entrepreneurial engagement with this market than hitherto. Some would say that the middle classes have found their new pension plan and its name is buy-to-let.

Historically, Wilcox (2008: 23–4) confirms that the private rented sector was dominated by small risk-averse investors and in that respect little has changed. Recent data reviewed by Wilcox suggest that almost 40 per cent of all residential investors own only one investment property. At the other end of the scale, large corporate residential landlords who own 100 or more properties only represent around 5 per cent of all investors in the sector. Another indicator of the dominance of the small investor in the sector is that approximately 75 per cent of all residential property investors own nine or fewer properties.

Ball (2007: 26) who has reviewed similar data confirms the dominance of individual small investors in the buy-to-let market, although also reports upon the growth of corporate investment in the specialized student accommodation market. In that residential sub-market the UNITE group plc (2009) has been assembling a portfolio of purpose-built student properties in London and other cities which have large student populations. UNITE has evolved a flexible model which can involve development of new purpose-built blocks or the acquisition and conversion of existing property or by forming joint ventures with university partners. Despite the best endeavours of UNITE, only 9 per cent of student housing is purpose built and managed on a commercial basis. The student accommodation market remains dominated by privately owned housing let in multiple occupation (so-called HMOs) which accounts for 51 per cent of all student accommodation. University halls of residence provide 22 per cent of student housing. The balance is made up by students living in parental homes.

Despite the threat of higher university tuition fees and developments in distance and blended learning programmes, there has been sustained growth in the number of students enrolling on conventional attendance mode university programmes in the UK over the last 10 years. This reflects a widely held expectation that 'going to university' signifies social progress and can lead to a well-paid professional career. The university experience is also now seen increasingly as the norm for many whose parents would not have contemplated attending a university. The demand stems from both home-based students and increasingly from overseas students who are targeted by the universities' international marketing and recruitment teams. Professionally accredited university programmes are also seen as an accepted route into a second career for older students under the banner of lifelong learning. The drivers behind the sustained growth in student numbers are therefore diverse and are unlikely to dramatically abate in the near future and thus companies such as UNITE are looking to broaden their market share through partnerships, direct development and property acquisitions.

The corporate progress and expansion plans of the UNITE group plc for the student accommodation market have not so far been mirrored in the wider residential rental market, where as was noted above, the market is atomized and dominated by small independent investors. The development of residentially focused Real Estate Investment Trusts (REITs) as seen in the United States has not so far been a feature of the UK market. One of the factors inhibiting the incursion of large corporate property investors into the residential market may be the requirement for more intense management and expertise around property selection, acquisition, management and disposal. The REIT model could also crystallize some uncomfortable and difficult-to-resolve conflicts of interest for a REIT board of directors. On the one hand they have an obligation to maximize investors' returns, but they would also have to respond to tenant requests for what might be costly responsive repairs, property maintenance and refurbishment.

In the social rented sector registered social landlords (housing associations) and local authorities are not burdened with the obligation to make profits for shareholders but face a myriad of other statutory duties to maintain decent housing standards. In the social sector there has therefore been an accumulation of property management experience and more of a culture and practical ability to respond systematically to tenants' needs. The tenant-centred housing management culture and capacity to deliver on an organizational scale has not developed to anything like the same degree in the private sector and this has left a void in the private rented sector which has been filled by small independent residential landlords. That model has evolved and could be thought of as fit for purpose for the local peculiarities and challenges found in the private rented sector. Apart from the specialized student market, there are no signs that this model is likely to be seriously challenged by an incursion of large corporate landlords into the private rented market in the UK.

3.4 Financial institutions

Private independent investors who have accumulated sufficient equity as leverage for a buy-to-let mortgage now have a relatively easy route to becoming a residential landlord and the mathematics involved is explored in Chapter 8 of this book. However because of the significantly larger average lot size in the commercial property sector, individuals are unlikely to become direct investors in, for example, an office block or an out of town shopping mall. Primarily for that reason research conducted for the Investment Property Forum in 2007 confirmed that only 3 per cent of the total value of the UK's commercial property invested stock was held by private investors. Another factor explaining this small proportion is probably that individuals of very high net wealth are unlikely to want all of their investable wealth exposed to the performance of an individual property. It is more likely that wealthy individuals will prefer to spread risk and seek tax efficiencies by investing indirectly in an intermediary organization which owns investment properties. The latter would typically own a diverse portfolio of investment properties, so that if one or two underperformed the overall performance of the portfolio would not be jeopardized.

The term 'financial institution' which frequently occurs in property related books like this one, principally refers to insurance companies and pension funds. These organizations effectively pool enormous annual pension contributions and insurance premiums and they then seek to invest those funds in relatively low-risk assets which have reliable long-term return profiles. Because the institutions are investing their own funds rather than borrowed money, the element of capital appreciation as opposed to income generation is important. There are seldom any problems of an income deficit, a concern which can beset property companies which may be highly geared, i.e. relying heavily on borrowed money. Property investment is a long-term commitment of funds with significant transfer costs and purchase time (up to six months) which restricts opportunities for short-term dealings. Thus the barriers and slower pace of investment and divestment in property and the longer-term horizons needed for this type of asset does not deter the financial institutions who have similar long-term perspectives.

The income and capital returns on what are often vast portfolios of assets is designed to at least match or ideally exceed predicted liabilities to pay pensions or to meet claims on insurance policies. The financial institutions long-term objectives and the vast sums at their disposal, make them ideal investors in the longer-term investment performance of prime commercial properties. Thus over many years the leading insurance companies such as Standard Life, Legal & General, the Prudential and Aviva (formerly the Norwich Union) and numerous occupational pension funds have built up significant property portfolios but which in turn represent only a small proportion of their overall investment portfolios.

The larger insurance companies and some of the very large pension funds have internal departments specializing in property. The professional staff in these departments has the expertise and resources at their disposal to initiate development, as well as advising on the purchase and management of existing investment properties. Some of the larger life insurance companies have a long history of investing in property and their enthusiasm for gaining exposure to property has tended to be greater than that demonstrated by pension funds. Dubben and Sayce (1991) have suggested that this is because insurance companies are more likely to possess in-house experts whose role it is to take responsibility for property investment decisions, whereas pension funds are thought to outsource some of these specialized functions. The relationship between longer term capital growth generated by property investment and the maturation of endowment policies is also thought to be a factor which has strengthened the commitment of the insurance companies to property.

Commercial property therefore holds attractions for the financial institutions in terms of its income generation and capital growth potential. With regards to capital growth, the Investment Property Databank (IPD) has compiled time-series data which demonstrate real capital growth from a representative portfolio of commercial properties. Thus there is some evidence that investing in commercial property provides at least a reliable hedge against inflation. Property is also thought to be a good diversifier in an investment portfolio because of low volatility of returns and low correlation with the performance of shares and gilts.

Financial institutions also need liquidity in order to meet that proportion of total liabilities which will arise in the short term. Procedures are therefore put in place to protect policy holders and one such test is that the cost of meeting all liabilities in the unlikely event that they all became redeemable in the short term should not exceed 90 per cent of the total value of all assets held. The need to demonstrate that these types of obligation can be met implies liquidity and thus it would be counterproductive for an institution to become overexposed to property. This is simply because shares and gilts are far more liquid assets, and it is no surprise therefore that these media form the bulk of most institutional investment portfolios. The outcome of the interplay between the need to retain liquidity set against the good 'slow-burning' performance of property as a portfolio diversifier, is that financial institutions customarily hold a relatively small but important part of their overall investment portfolios in commercial property.

Because the owners of large commercial properties are often financial institutions, individuals might not be conscious of the fact that the performance of their pensions or their endowment policies will in some small way be contingent on the long-term performance of commercial properties. As discussed above the institutions have considerable experience in managing portfolios of commercial property and research undertaken for the Investment Property Forum (2007: 3) confirms that the institutions constitute the largest single ownership category of invested commercial property in the UK, holding 28 per cent of the total value of the invested stock.

The history of the involvement of financial institutions in commercial property is lengthy and so for the purposes of this chapter will be summarized. Those readers who wish to learn more about the historical ebbs and flows in the commercial property investment market could examine Baum (2009: 64–91). However, the brief historical perspective here will begin in the 1950s when financial institutions were essentially passive lenders to property developers and purchasers of completed developments. Thus it then became established practice that as part of bearing the risks of development, property developers would take on short-term bank loans to finance a development. The expectation was that the completed development would be purchased by either an owner-occupier or a financial institution, enabling repayment of the short-term bank debt and the realization of a profit by the developer. Insurance companies at that time also played a role in refinancing developments by providing long-term fixed-interest loans; an approach which was tenable when inflation was negligible and did not erode the real value of returns.

Financial arrangements and cooperation between developers and financial institutions gained impetus at that time because of the short supply of commercial space in the face of significant demand which saw rental and capital growth. When inflation became more of an issue in the 1960s and 1970s the passive fixed-interest long-term loans which the institutions had previously provided to developers, became less feasible as a business model. Some of the leading financial institutions began to rethink their approach to property development and investment.

A more entrepreneurial approach to property emerged on the part of the institutions, as they began to use sale and leaseback agreements with developers. Under these agreements the freehold of a development property could be sold by a developer to an institution, which then leased the site back to the developer who then completed and let the scheme to business tenants. Early deals had no provision for rent reviews but by the late 1960s and early 1970s review periods became standard in the agreements. Rent reviews enabled the owners of these assets to benefit from periodic uplifts in rental income, effectively providing inflation-proof returns.

The sale and leaseback or lease and leaseback agreements could be tailored to suit the specifics of the development and the requirements of the parties involved, however a key theme reflected in the agreements related to risk transfer. Thus the obligation to market and let a scheme to occupational tenants and/or undertake the asset management obligations to secure rental income and conduct rent reviews could be negotiated between the parties. In these negotiations financial institutions invariably had most financial leverage, enabling them to secure discounts for themselves when agreeing to purchase a completed scheme. Alternatively, institutions were able to secure ongoing equity participation in the rental income and any growth in that income over the longer term.

Another manifestation of the institutions taking a more central role in developments was their ability to link the funding of a development with a pre-sale agreement, under which the developer received development finance at preferential rates. The pre-agreed sale to the institution was capitalized at a rate which reflected the reduced risk borne by the developer given a guaranteed end sale and preferential development finance. This enabled the institutions to acquire fully let property assets on more advantageous terms and with tighter control over the design and specification of the development. Eventually the institutions began to carry out their own developments using their own funds and contracting a developer who then received a project management fee with some additional incentives. Equity sharing, sale and leaseback and related funding and development partnerships have evolved considerably from that time and are now quite complex reflections of the balance of risk and return perceived by the parties involved in a development. It is not the purpose of this chapter or this book to delve into this specialized area of development; however those wishing to learn more about this topic could examine Dubben and Williams (2009).

Smaller financial institutions seeking some direct exposure to commercial property but lacking the size of resources to carry out development or to meet 100 per cent of the asking price for particular property assets, can enter into partnerships with larger funds or property companies. The partnering principle is not restricted to smaller funds and for very large, high-risk property developments even well resourced and established funds might choose to form partnerships so that they are not overexposed to the financial performance of one mega-property. Thus *Estates Gazette* (30 October 2010) reported the formation of partnerships in 2010 to fund very large office developments in the City of London. One of these schemes is the 47-storey office tower in London's Leadenhall Street dubbed the Cheesegrater and which is shared equally between British Land and Oxford Properties. Nearby the 37-storey office development dubbed the Walkie Talkie on Fenchurch Street saw a partnership form between Land Securities with 50 per cent ownership, Canary Wharf Holdings with 15 per cent ownership with the remaining 35 per cent owned in equal proportions by CIC, Qatar Holdings and Morgan Stanley.

3.5 Property companies and Real Estate Investment Trusts

Taking even a relatively small direct share of a large commercial property development could result in overexposure for a smaller investment fund or a wealthy individual investor. In those circumstances indirect investment in a vehicle which has exposure to commercial property investments is often a more sensible alternative. There are a number of indirect routes to commercial property investment for smaller investment funds and individuals and these include purchasing shares in a property company or a Real Estate Investment Trust (REIT). The two types of organization have similarities and a degree of overlap in their activities. However a key distinction is that the core business of a property company is development, while a REIT must show that at least 75 per cent of its business is the management of rental property. The balance of a REIT's business activity may however include property development and so long as such properties are held for a minimum of three years before disposal, the receipts arising will be tax exempt under the REIT rules.

A non-REIT property company will derive less than 75 per cent of its income from property rental and trading, simply because it has pursued a different strategy and one which exposes it to perhaps more risky but potentially higher rewarding property development activity. A REIT however has already been able to establish a property portfolio through acquisitions and/or development and has opted to focus upon asset management in order stay within the REIT rules and in so doing avoid corporation tax. The trade-off is that while a REIT's annual income will not be dominated by potentially high-earning but riskier development activity, there is likely to be moderate sustainable growth from property trading and management. Because the income arising from that latter activity is tax exempt, a larger fund remains for distribution to shareholders.

As the name implies, a property company holds all or most of its assets in property and thus ownership of shares in such a company is a surrogate for direct property investment. Shares are traditionally thought to possess some advantages over direct property investment in terms of the ability to liquidate share holdings rapidly in the event of rapidly rising or falling markets. Shares are also thought to benefit from gearing which can increase the returns to equity (shareholders) given that borrowing will tend to account for the major part of funding a property development. Shareholders are also thought to benefit from the entrepreneurial skill and wisdom of boards and expert staff who identify and realize development opportunities and who determine stock selection and property management strategy. The drawback of share ownership in a non-REIT property company compared with direct property investment is the double incidence of tax which is captured in corporation tax and again at the investor level so that a shareholder is in effect taxed twice.

The value of shares in a listed property company bears some relationship to the value of the property owned by the company and the income derived from property trading, but the link is not a direct one. Property company shares will fluctuate on the market depending on the reported value of property owned by the company but also depending on wider market sentiment. The latter is affected not just by changes in policy and legislation which affect the property sector, but also by a myriad of factors such as the overall state of the economy and the performance of other global markets, particularly those of the USA and Japan.

Although theoretically there should be a close correlation between a property company's share price and the value of properties held, the stock market has tended to take a very cautious view of property companies on the basis of the perceived risks which are specific to the property sector. Thus there is some awareness in the markets of a property cycle which seems to cause the value of assets to rise and fall over time and this gives rise to latent concerns that the book value of property assets might not always be realizable in reality. There are also investor concerns regarding liquidity in that some property assets are so large that there are too few potential purchasers in the market to create any buoyancy around price, should an asset need to be sold. Property is also a very tangible asset requiring ongoing management and it can be subject to depreciation. Shopping centres for example, will need periodic upgrading to maintain footfall and competitiveness with other nearby shopping centres. For all of these reasons and as confirmed by Sayce *et al.* (2006: 241) the stock market has traditionally discounted the value of property companies' shares against the net asset value reported in company accounts. Property company shares can therefore trade at a disadvantage against what the market perceives to be other more liquid and dynamic stock available on the market.

To try to overcome these disadvantages and to try to put property companies on more of a level playing field with other listed companies REITs were first experimented with in the USA in 1960. Legislative changes introduced then, enabled companies which owned property and mortgages to convert to REIT status and in that guise to pay dividends to shareholders arising from property investment and trading without prior deduction of corporate taxes.

REITs are 'closed ended' in that the market value of what is a fixed quantum of shares in these publicly quoted companies will fluctuate in response to market sentiment. Thus when the activities of a REIT excite investor interest, the share price will tend to rise and where annual reports suggest disappointing results then this will probably have an adverse effect on the share price. Occasionally the board may decide to issue more shares to raise additional equity, particularly when major acquisitions or developments are envisaged.

The tax efficiency of the REIT model was thought to work well in providing an additional conduit for a wider range of investors to gain exposure to property investment. REITs were therefore felt to have a beneficial effect on liquidity in property markets and the model was replicated in a number of countries beyond the USA with varying degrees of success. It was not until 2007 that publicly listed property companies in the UK first had the option to convert into a REIT and by doing so, would benefit from tax exemption on earnings from property investment and trading activity.

In return for the favoured tax status a UK REIT must meet certain operational requirements, which include distributing at least 90 per cent of profits arising from rental income to shareholders. This provision was supposed to go some way towards addressing the discount to net asset value disadvantage which confronts property companies in the market and which was discussed above. Of course the tax liabilities which individuals may have on their earnings arising from their REIT shares (as on any other income source) are not exempt from tax, but the REIT measure at least removed double taxation on profits.

When considering whether to invest in a property company or REIT a prudent investor will examine annual company reports to assess the quality of property assets held in the portfolio. Thus the age, location and tenure of individual properties will be important as well as the investment's relative importance in the portfolio. The different types of property and the proportion held overseas should also be considered. The markets and investors also place importance upon the perceived quality of management in the company, although this can be a little subjective as it is based upon the reputation of individuals rather than the actual difference that individuals make to a company's strategy and decision making. Investors will usually look at the sources of income to the company and this relates to the quality and reliability (sometimes referred to as the covenant) of the business tenants secured in high-income-bearing properties within the portfolio.

Investors will also be interested in the capital structure of the company and in particular whether there is high gearing which implies a degree of risk. The latter relates to the potential for interest rates to rise and which would require a higher proportion of income to be used to service interest charges on debt. REIT boards of directors keep property portfolios under review and will occasionally request that assets be disposed of when it is thought that the best rental or capital growth period may have passed for a property. Disposals or part disposals also allow the reduction of exposure to the performance of single very large properties. Asset disposals enable a property company or REIT to reduce debt, so that gearing remains within comfortable limits. The interest cover test under the REIT rules requires that the income stream from properties held by a REIT must equate to at least 125 per cent of interest repayments due.

The boards of property companies and REITs understand that the market is naturally interested in this type of information and they therefore try to reassure existing and potential investors by setting out their strategies and trading positions in annual and interim reports. For example, British Land is a leading UK REIT with an extensive commercial property portfolio which was valued at £8.5 billion in 2010. High-profile properties within this portfolio include the Broadgate office complex in the City of London (50 per cent ownership) the Meadowhall regional shopping centre on the outskirts of Sheffield (50 per cent ownership) and Regents Place and Ropemaker Place which are large office led developments in central London (both of which are 100 per cent owned).

British Land's annual report (2010) describes a strategy of acquiring well positioned shopping centres, superstores, department stores and out of town retail property. Retail property represents approximately two thirds of the British Land property portfolio by value with retail warehouses being the largest single property type representing 31 per cent of the total value of the portfolio. The balance of the portfolio is made up by prime central London offices. British Land's annual report explains that the capital value of the property portfolio grew by 13.5 per cent over the financial year 2009–10. However what might appear to be an impressive annual performance needs to be seen against the backdrop of several years when the valuations of properties held in REIT portfolios fell by similar margins due to credit crunch induced financial uncertainty.

Leading REITs such as British Land therefore have strategies which target the acquisition of prime properties which are usually tenanted. These properties are then entrusted to asset management teams. British Land was able to report that in the year leading up to 2010 it had been very successful in meeting this objective with an occupancy rate of 99 per cent for its retail property and 93 per cent for its offices. The overall occupancy rate for the combined portfolio was 97 per cent given the higher proportion of retail in the portfolio. This is a very impressive statistic during an economic downturn when commercial property owners will typically see some of their tenants go into receivership, leading to potentially lengthy void periods when a property is being marketed and relet. British Land was able to report that during 2009–10 only 0.6 per cent of its retail tenants had gone into administration while none of its office tenants had.

Potential investors in REITs such as British Land will also be interested in the average lease length of the tenancies in the portfolio and British Land were again able to report an impressive statistic for 2009–10 when the average lease length to first break option or expiry was 12.9 years across the whole portfolio. A related statistic is that only 6.8 per cent of the total rental income from British Land's portfolio was subject to expiry or a break clause option within three years. Thus in the short to medium term the bulk of this REITs income could be deemed to be secure. However when seen in isolation, statistics like this can be misleading and experienced investors would make comparisons with benchmark data provided by the IPD and by examining the performance of other leading REITs. The annual reports produced by REITs enable sensible comparisons to be made on strategic as well as detailed issues. Thus the reports will reveal information on major acquisitions and portfolio strategy, asset management performance as well as detail such as the degree of indebtedness, gearing ratios and earnings per share. Evaluative criteria which could be used to compare company performance, is discussed in Chapter 10 of this book where aspects of financial management and evaluation are explored.

3.6 Banks

During the credit crunch the spotlight fell heavily on the main clearing banks because of what was felt to be a cavalier culture which had developed around lending to individuals and organizations. The banking sector's reputation was not helped by the requirement for some very public government bailouts to keep the banking system functioning. Events in 2010 in Ireland exposed large and some would say foolhardy loans which banks there had made to property developers against speculative developments which remained unsold and unlet following completion. It is likely there that the banks will have to write off considerable loans made against residential and commercial property developments.

The banks therefore stand accused of casual and high-risk lending on property development which is thought to have fuelled the financial crises experienced in recent years in the USA, UK and Ireland. However putting to one side the popular tendency for 'bank-bashing' these institutions are still seen as a legitimate source of funds when a developer is considering a scheme. This is because even though the loan to value ratios offered by banks will reduce during difficult economic periods, developers will still need to use debt finance to part fund large schemes, simply because equity will seldom stretch far enough. Even when a developer does have sufficient equity it would seldom make commercial sense to use all of it to fund a development, because greater rewards can usually be earned by using equity selectively to gear several different projects.

Conventionally a bank's role is mainly to provide a developer with short-term lending to cover a large proportion of land acquisition and construction costs. As Maxted and Porter (2007) have shown, in aggregate the scale of bank lending against property development has tended to grow year on year despite periodic economic crises. The loan to value ratio offered by a bank to a developer will vary depending on the specific project risks, the state of the economy and a bank's existing exposure to property at any point in time. Assuming that a developer can contribute sufficient equity and can meet a bank's other terms and conditions, the developer will draw down the loan in instalments to match the rate of development progress. Interest charges will typically be rolled up over the development period. The developer will then normally seek to repay the capital and interest by either refinancing a development when it is completed or by repaying the debt from receipts arising from the sale of the development.

3.7 Property unit trusts and investment trust companies

Authorized property unit trusts (PUTs) invest directly in property allowing investors in a PUT to gain indirect exposure to commercial property in the same way that a unit trust offers investors exposure to a share portfolio. PUTs will tend to target smaller commercial properties than those acquired by financial institutions and REITs, so that the smaller scale of the PUT portfolios is not overexposed to the performance of any one property.

A unit holder has a legal claim to a fractional part of a PUTs portfolio. In contrast to company shares which are traded on the Stock Exchange, units in PUTs cannot be traded in a secondary market and need to be acquired or redeemed directly from the PUT. Investing in a PUT enables a small investor to benefit from portfolio diversification and specialist management without requiring the individual expertise and financial resources which would be needed if investing directly in the same investment portfolio.

The structure of a PUT is similar to unit trusts which invest in portfolios of company shares, in that there is a board of trustees advised by executive management. The management of the PUT takes care of the day to day running of the fund and reports to the board on strategic issues. The board of trustees in turn have a fiduciary duty to the unit holders to ensure that there is transparent reporting and that there are regular independent valuations of the portfolio. While property companies can sometimes be highly geared, the borrowing of PUTs is usually modest.

There are also unauthorized property unit trusts which are specialist vehicles only open to tax exempt funds such as pension funds and charities.

The value of units in property unit trusts (PUTs) are determined directly by the valuation of the property portfolio held by the PUT. Thus the value of the portfolio is divided by the number of units held in the fund and after allowance for the PUTs expenses this value becomes the unit price of the fund. The managers of the PUT then operate the market at this price by disposing of units whose owners wish to sell and by issuing units to new investors. There is a margin between offer and bid prices to cover costs of transfer of the units.

PUTs are 'open ended' in that there is some correlation between investment funds flowing into a PUT and the acquisition of new investments by fund managers. Conversely when investors move out of a PUT the liabilities arising must be met by the PUT. Given that investments will seldom equal redemptions in the short term, it is necessary for a PUT to hold a proportion of its investments in liquid assets such as cash, gilts and equities so that fluctuations in sales and investments can be managed. Should these operating buffers be exhausted due to a high volume of withdrawals, there are mechanisms which can be invoked by PUT managers which effectively set up temporary moratoriums on redemptions in order to prevent a run on a PUT.

PUTs benefit from some allowances against corporation tax but not to the same extent as a REIT. A distribution made by a PUT to its unit holders will be treated for tax purposes as dividends on company shares, although individual unit holders may qualify for tax credits on those distributions. Corporate investors who pay corporation tax at the small companies' rate will also have the whole of their tax liability arising from PUT earnings covered by a tax credit. PUTs are free from capital gains tax arising on the disposal of property although unit holders will be subject to any capital gains tax arising from the disposal of their units.

Investment trust companies purchase and hold shares in UK and overseas property companies. Because they are not investing directly in properties in the same way that a PUT or REIT does, an investment trust avoids the costs of acquisition and property management and can respond more flexibly to market movements given that shares are a very liquid asset in comparison to direct property investment. Investors in these companies benefit from indirect exposure to a diverse portfolio of property related shares held by the trust and so risk is diluted. However the trusts cannot escape the effects of the discount to net asset value described above in this chapter in relation to property companies. An investment trust is a quoted company and closed ended unlike a PUT.

In addition these specialized investment vehicles there are also the traditional institutions which hold property such as the church, the crown and local authorities who own a large portfolio of investment land from bequests, death intestate and government purchase. Although these properties are generally considered to be operational, they are now subject to normal investment performance criteria for accountancy purposes.

3.8 International investors

Large-scale commercial property investment has for many years been a global phenomenon, and research cited by the IPF (2007: 3) estimated that around 15 per cent of the total value of the invested stock in the UK is owned by overseas investors. UK property investors are similarly active in other countries' commercial property markets and for example Hammerson (2009) which is one of the largest REITs in the UK with a £5.1 billion property portfolio, holds 34 per cent of that portfolio in the form of French shopping centres.

There are varying degrees of permeability in terms of the ease of participation in some international property markets but the general international trend has been towards more openness and transparency. There is an incentive for different international property markets to gradually harmonize their valuation methods, reporting standards and tax regimes, as this will assist in the free flow of capital. The latter may be an important element in providing a diverse source of funds to underpin modernization, redevelopment and investment.

The UK is a relatively open property investment market and London is perceived by overseas investors to be an internationally important, stable and diverse business location. For these reasons a number of overseas property investors now hold considerable commercial property portfolios in London. It should be noted that because the residential property investment sector is more atomized compared to the commercial property sector, the focus of overseas property investors is almost entirely upon commercial rather than residential property. This applies equally to indirect property investment because the UK does not yet have any residential REITs but has since 2007 had a number of commercial property REITs.

Given that overseas property investors are more active in the prime 'large lot' commercial property sector then it is perhaps not surprising that overseas purchasers tend to be financial institutions, property companies or construction companies. Overseas investors come from an ever widening pool of countries led by institutional investors from Germany, Ireland, the USA, Scandinavian and Arabian countries. Among the reasons why these investors target prime commercial property particularly in London, is to diversify risk by gaining exposure to economic cycles and growth rates which differ from their own domestic markets. Although the ripple effects of the credit crunch saw a number of overseas investors divest of property assets in London it is unlikely that this represents the permanent withdrawal of overseas property investors, indeed there has been renewed interest on the part of investors from Japan and South-East Asian countries. Given the rapid economic progress being made in India and China, it is very likely that institutional investors from those countries will increasingly begin to make their presence felt in London's commercial property market.

3.9 Summary

There is an ever widening community of investors in the UK who have acquired some exposure either directly to residential or commercial property or indirectly via specialized investment vehicles such as Real Estate Investment Trusts (REITs) or property unit trusts (PUTs). It would probably require a whole book to systematically categories all of the different types of property investor and then to assess their motivations and investment strategies. This chapter has therefore been selective by trying to indentify some of the key market players and their investment aspirations.

Despite the higher profile given to commercial property, the total value of invested residential property in the UK is larger than the total value of the invested commercial property stock. The stock of private rented residential property has increased in recent years due mainly to the influx of buy-to-let investors to that market. Those investors account for almost 1.3 million buy-to-let mortgages which have enabled typically small investors to acquire one or a small number of properties. These investors will have accumulated sufficient equity to supplement loan to value ratios offered by buy-to-let mortgage providers. Large corporate investors have not shown the same enthusiasm for the private rented residential market, although there have been some successful corporate incursions into the specialized student accommodation market.

Financial institutions continue to show interest mainly in large prime commercial properties which then in turn represent a small percentage of a typical institutional investment portfolio. The latter are dominated by shares and gilts which have the advantage of greater liquidity over direct investment in property. The institutions have enormous pooled pension contributions and insurance premiums to invest and property represents a good portfolio diversifier which has shown modest but consistent long-term real growth in rental and capital value. Property investment therefore helps institutions meet their ongoing liabilities to pensioners and insurance policy holders.

REITs are publicly listed property companies which have accumulated significant commercial property portfolios through acquisitions and development. Borrowing continues to play and important part in maintaining those portfolios. Providing a REIT continues to base its core business on trading and managing properties and to distribute at least 90 per cent of its income to shareholders, then it will continue to benefit from tax exemption on that activity.

Small investors could decide to purchase shares in a REIT or they might prefer to invest in property units trusts (PUTs) which have accumulated portfolios of smaller properties supplemented by shares and gilts to provide some liquidity. PUTs also benefit from specific tax exemptions although PUTs are open ended, meaning that additional assets will need to be purchased when investments exceed redemptions. Conversely properties may ultimately need to be sold where there is a long-term trend of investors redeeming units rather than purchasing them.

Property investment has been a significant global investment activity for at least the last three decades and that trend is likely to continue in the near future as funds from around the world try to gain some exposure in overseas property markets in order to spread risk. Thus while a proportion of the invested commercial stock in the UK is owned by overseas corporate investors, UK property companies also own sizeable overseas property investments. The general trend for trade barriers to weaken and tax and accountancy standards to harmonize will probably stimulate a greater volume of international property trading in future.

References

Ball, M. (2007) *Large-scale Investor Opportunities in Residential Property: An Overview* (London: Investment Property Forum).

Baum, A. (2009) *Commercial Real Estate Investment: A Strategic Approach*, 2nd edn (London: EG Books).

British Land Company plc (2010) *Annual Report and Accounts 2010* (London: British Land Company plc).

Council of Mortgage Lenders (2010) 'Buy to let lending showing modest signs of recovery' (CoML press release,11/11/10; in e-format at: www.cml.org.uk).

Department for Communities (2010) *Table 101 Dwelling stock: by tenure, United Kingdom (historical series)* (London: Department for Communities and Local Government). Available in e-format at: www.communities.gov.uk

Dubben, N. and Sayce, S. (1991) *Property Portfolio Management: An Introduction* (London: Routledge).

Dubben, N. and Williams, B. (2009) *Partnerships in Urban Property Development* (Oxford: Wiley Blackwell).

Hammerson plc (2009) *Annual Report 2009* (London: Hammerson plc).

Havard, T. (2008) *Contemporary Property Development*, 2nd edition (London: RIBA Publishing).

Investment Property Forum (2007) *Understanding Commercial Property Investment: A Guide for Financial Advisers* (London: Investment Property Forum).

Kemp, P. A. (2010) 'The transformation of private renting', in P. Malpass and R. Rowlands (eds) *Housing Markets and Policy* (London: Routledge).

Maxted, B. and Porter, T. (2007) *The UK Commercial Property Lending Market: Year-End 2006 Research Findings* (Leicester: De Montfort University).

Sayce, S., Smith, J., Cooper, R. and Venmore-Rowland, P. (2006) *Real Estate Appraisal from Value to Worth* (Oxford: Blackwell).

UNITE Group plc (2009) *Annual Report and Accounts 2009* (Bristol: UNITE Group plc).

Wilcox, S. (2008) *UK Housing Review 2008/2009* (Coventry: Chartered Institute of Housing; London: Building Societies Association).

4

Types of investment

Aims

This chapter will look at the characteristics of properties which are most commonly acquired by investors including residential property and in the commercial sector shops, offices, industrial and warehouse units.

The chapter also explores some of the legal and physical constraints which can limit the range of uses to which a property may be put, thereby affecting investment value. There is also discussion which explores the extent to which investment buildings need to have a green certification such as BREEAM for non-domestic buildings and Code for Sustainable Homes for housing.

Key terms

>> **Use class** – in the UK the lawful use to which a building may be put is defined by 14 use classes in the Town and Country Planning Use Classes Order. Each class has its own alphanumeric code, for example A1 is shops, B1 is business and D2 are buildings which may be used for assembly and leisure. Properties such as launderettes, scrap-yards and car showrooms do not conform neatly with any of the 14 use classes, so by default they fall into a miscellaneous category called *sui generis*. Although it will usually be obvious, solicitors acting for a property investor will normally conduct inquiries to confirm the lawful use class for a property before it is acquired.

>> **BREEAM** – the Building Research Establishment Environmental Assessment Method contains ratings of pass, good, very good, excellent and outstanding which are awarded to non-domestic buildings to reflect their degree of sustainability. The ratings reflect the degree of improvement over the statutory minima required by the building regulations. The certification

is based upon a weighted scoring system which assesses a building against eight categories such as energy use, water consumption, land use and ecology. Certification is made by an independent assessor for either new or existing buildings, for example where a building is being refurbished. There is currently no legal obligation on building owners or occupiers to obtain a BREEAM rating. However an increasing number of organizations now have CSR policies which create a self-imposed obligation that the buildings they procure and use should have a benign effect on the environment. This will mean that buildings will have to have a 'green badge' which at present for commercial buildings in the UK is signified by a BREEAM rating.

>> **Code for Sustainable Homes** (**CSH**) – is the housing counterpart for BREEAM. The CSH also has a weighted scoring system which is used by independent assessors to measure the sustainability of housing against nine categories which include energy and CO_2 emissions, water consumption, materials, waste and health and well-being. A CSH assessor may award stars against a housing development to signify its overall sustainability. The award of one star ★ signifies entry level, which is a home that is 10 per cent more sustainable than the minimum required by the building regulations. The award of 6 stars ★★★★★★ is the highest award for what is a zero carbon home. New housing does not currently have to attract a specific CSH level and could post a zero return. However the Homes and Communities Agency in England will stipulate a specific CSH level when they are contributing public money to an affordable housing development.

4.1 Introduction

When adding properties to their investment portfolios, property investors in the residential or commercial sectors will assess the degree of versatility of property. While a property may currently be fully let and producing an income stream, the prudent investor will consider what might happen if the building were to become vacant. The investor will thus try to assess whether the building could be relet reasonably easily to the category of occupiers who would normally be interested in occupying such buildings. If that versatility exists then it is likely that the asset will be able to hold its value and could therefore be divested of if necessary to other property investors.

Large corporate property investors exert considerable influence over the design of a whole range of commercial buildings as a condition of either providing development finance and/or the agreement to purchase completed projects. Institutional investors thus have leverage over developers and their architects and they will impose minimum specifications for items such as floor load-bearing capacity, ceiling or eaves heights, planning grid, column spacing, lighting and ventilation.

By meeting the investor's specifications a building will have appeal to the widest possible group of potential occupiers and this reduces an investor's risk. Indeed it has almost become a pejorative term to refer to a development as an 'investor's building' because this implies that because it is meeting all sorts of minimum specifications, the building will have no distinctive or aesthetic qualities. This is a little unfair, as some of the most iconic commercial landmark buildings designed by leading architectural practices in recent years have been funded by pension funds and insurance companies.

This chapter looks at the characteristics and legal constraints for core types of investment property which as discussed in Chapter 2 comprise residential and in the commercial sector: retail, offices, industrial and warehousing. Other property types such as leisure development only represent a small fraction of the overall value of the invested property stock and are rather specialized and so will not be discussed at any length in this chapter.

The issue of sustainability cannot now be ignored when investment buildings are being discussed and so the chapter will look at the emerging evidence on whether it is necessary for a commercial investment building to have a BREEAM rating or a buy-to-let residential property a Code for Sustainable Homes rating.

4.2 Location, location and location

Before looking at the specific characteristics of different types of investment property, some overview points regarding location are relevant because ultimately property does not have a value which is entirely independent from the economic performance of the area in which it is located. Thus in areas where there is high unemployment and where there has been a spate of company closures it is likely that property values in all sectors will be deflated. It is also likely that without significant regeneration effort or new infrastructure provision or an arts based revival or similar catalyst, that property values will fall. This is not to say that areas which are currently depressed should instantly be removed from a property investor's search list, as the most spectacular growth over time can come from investing in regeneration areas, where there is some risk but where there is a real prospect that an area can be transformed.

There are numerous examples in the UK where areas have been transformed through the concerted effort by a developer working in partnership with the local authority, a regeneration agency, the community and landowners. The term urban renaissance is often used where a vision for regeneration is promoted alongside commitments for spending on infrastructure. Regeneration success stories include Brindley Place in central Birmingham, which has been transformed through a commitment to high-quality urban design and place marketing. Other perhaps obvious examples include the Lea Valley in East London which hitherto would not have featured as a destination for a property investor, but part of the legacy which follows the Olympic Games and associated infrastructure improvements will be a considerable range of property investment opportunities.

The King's Cross railway lands in central London (pictured on page 98) would also have been considered off the map for major commercial property investors. However the concerted effort by the lead developer Argent and other stakeholders will see the phased realization of a dramatic mixed use development containing over 486,000 m^2 of offices on this 26 hectare brownfield site.

Where regeneration is concerned good judgement and research will be necessary to evaluate whether the critical mass of development and investment have been mustered to create the synergies needed to transform a locality. For successful investment there is a symbiosis where those promoting regeneration

Figure 4.1 King's Cross railway lands, central London

require investors to take some risks, while investors have to believe that those producing the strategies have captured a vision that can be delivered. Thus both parties need to believe that an area can be transformed.

Property investors will normally seek to invest in properties which are located in areas which have a buoyant and diverse economy and where there are good schools, transport connections, an attractive environment and a normal range of social and physical infrastructure. These characteristics will tend to suggest a prosperous area and which will probably be reflected in higher than average property values. It is however unrealistic to expect every locality to exhibit these ideal characteristics. Perhaps what a property investor might practically look for are localities which have a balanced set of characteristics relative to the national average or which are areas where regeneration is taking place and there is future potential. That latter would include 'areas on the rise', perhaps because of recent or planned improvements to transport infrastructure. For example, in England the Department for Communities has identified growth points where additional public spending will be targeted to improve infrastructure capacity to support growth.

The likely effects of regeneration initiatives and infrastructure improvements on the property market are picked up by *Estates Gazette* and *Property Week* which review different localities in the UK each week. CoStar's Focus service can generate 'town reports' which provide an overview about a locality. These reports draw upon existing datasets such as the census reports, business information collected by Experian, property data compiled by firms of surveyors and the property press and local authority reports and strategies. These types of reports are helpful because they bring together and summarize key themes such as demographic data and time-series data on commercial rents. For example the latter would help a property investor to determine whether there were any unusual or worrying trends in comparison to what had been happening elsewhere or benchmarked against the national average. Thus if office rents had fallen 5 per cent in a locality over the previous year, then that might not be such a concern if the national average fall in office rents had been 10 per cent because of an economic down-turn.

Regarding demographic data, census information can provide a local picture of the age profile, occupational groupings and proxy measures which are often used to assess the relative affluence of a location such as the proportion of households who own their own home. The Focus Town Reports also go a little further by drawing upon the Mosaic Consumer Classification produced by Experian. Examples of four of the 12 Mosaic classifications are shown below in Table 4.1.

The above types of classification could be derided as pseudo-scientific and some of the descriptors suggest soap-opera characters or stereotyping and some not used here could be construed as sarcastic and or even borderline offensive. However the underlying data are derived from the census of population and thus something is being said about the age structure, relative affluence of an area and ultimately the spending power in the immediate catchment area.

Although this type of analysis is unlikely to be a deciding factor for a property investor poised to make a commitment on a purchase, it might well confirm other pieces of information being used to build up a sense of what might or might not be viable in a particular locality. Snippets of information about local spending power are particularly important for investors who are active in retail and leisure property.

There are also some basic physical attributes regarding location which reasonably competent property lawyers acting for property investors should be

Table 4.1 Examples of Mosaic Consumer Classification

Mosaic Consumer Classification	Characteristics	GB average %
Symbols of Success	People with rewarding careers who live in sought-after locations, affording luxuries and premium-quality products.	9.7
Happy Families	Families with a focus on careers and home, mostly younger age groups now raising children.	11.64
Urban Intelligence	Young, single and mostly well educated, these people are cosmopolitan in tastes and liberal in attitudes.	7.35
Grey Perspectives	Independent pensioners living in their own homes who are relatively active in their lifestyles.	7.36

able to identify. Given the degree of climate change which has taken place in recent years, it is now important that Environment Agency flood maps are examined to identify the extent of flood risk affecting a property. This has implications for both the insurability and resale value of both commercial and residential property.

Property investors will also need to look at the physical context for their planned investments and to make some broad categorization of the area. For example are they investing in very functional 'built to a cost' properties sometimes found on edge of town retail parks where free surface parking for customers is part of the expected package. Property agents sometimes refer to the DIY and flat-pack furniture warehouses as 'shed land'. Alternatively an investor might be targeting a more sophisticated product such as high specification office development in the central business district of a city where there is good public transport.

4.3 Car parking, sustainability and investment properties

When property investors are considering the purchase of a commercial property such as an industrial unit or a retail warehouse or a business park unit, what they are in fact often looking at is a plot of land which contains a building surrounded by surface parking (or sometimes under-croft parking). The number of spaces provided will bear some relationship to the gross floorspace of the building. Similarly residential investors may be purchasing houses with off street garages or flats where there is an allocated on-site parking space. The availability of a sufficient quantity of on-site parking relative to the particular use is reflected in the value of the property.

To a large extent the parking provided in the existing stock of property whether it be commercial or residential, is a product of the application of local authority parking standards over many years. Those standards sought to avoid on-street parking and the potential for clogging up highways by ensuring that each new development had sufficient on-site parking spaces. Thus for flatted developments in a suburban setting, planning consent would not be granted unless there was one off-street parking space per flat with a few additional visitor parking spaces. Similarly for commercial schemes in edge or out of town locations the parking standards were expressed as minima which would need to be met when the scheme was being designed. It was only in very busy town and city centres that local authorities applied restrictions to on-site parking, by expressing parking standards as maxima.

Given the threats posed by climate change and government policy commitments to reduce carbon emissions, the rationale for providing on-site parking spaces in new developments has come under greater scrutiny. In the residential sector it is now common to come across either car-capped schemes where there are only a few parking spaces provided and entirely car-free schemes, particularly in city centres which benefit from a range of public transport options.

For property investors the switch in attitudes around car parking provision gives rise to a dual market in which properties which might be 20 years old will probably come with what might be seen as a full complement of parking spaces. In contrast, very recent or planned developments will probably have a significantly reduced parking ratio. In the short term before the majority of the population learn to rely less on the car, there is likely to be a marginal value premium for developments which have what might be seen as 'normal' car parking provision. This is certainly true of apartments in urban areas which have an off street parking space in contrast to more recently built schemes. Large retail schemes such as Bluewater and the Metro Centre whose car parks are often oversubscribed in the peak trading weeks leading up to Christmas, illustrate that on-site parking provision is still seen as a draw for customers.

Given the priority to foster sustainable development local authorities will now normally require a green travel plan for a new development of any magnitude. Some companies, public sector and third-sector organizations are voluntarily implementing similar strategies retrospectively to reduce their carbon footprints in conformity with their corporate social responsibility policies. The emphasis in green travel plans and similar policies is to encourage employees to use public transport, walk or cycle to work. The very last resort is seen as providing car parking spaces on site as they encourage employees to drive to work. As mentioned above, in most city centres it has long been the practice to restrict on-site parking to no more than a handful of spaces in the basement of a major development which will normally include be some disabled parking bays, motorcycle parking spaces and secure cycle storage.

For developments on the periphery of towns and cities such as superstores, retail warehouse and business parks, there is seldom a developed public transport network and in some suburban and semi-rural settings there is only an infrequent bus service. It is accepted in these circumstances that there will be significant on-site parking but that the use of the car may be mitigated to some extent through employer promoted car sharing or cycling (with showers and lockers provided) where that is a practical option for some employees.

Where substantial development proposals are being evaluated by local authorities there will be a transport planning input and this will normally involve the compilation of a PTAL (Public Transport Accessibility Level) score. A PTAL effectively maps public transport provision to generate a score of between 1 and 6 which is used to govern the on-site car parking allowance for a particular development. Remote sites with poor public transport accessibility will typically attract a PTAL score of 1 and if that were a retail development then most customers would have little choice other than to use their cars to go shopping. At the other end of the continuum, city centre sites with good public transport accessibility will attract a PTAL score of 6 signifying that the site is well connected to public transport. In that setting customers or employees have a choice of accessible modes of transport to go shopping or commute to work.

The on-site parking allowances relative to the PTAL score will vary between local authorities who will make adjustments to reflect the remoteness or accessibility of the site under evaluation. For example, the parking standards in the London Plan (which applies to all London Boroughs) for a food superstore of over 4,000 m^2 which had a PTAL score of 1 and which therefore had poor accessibility, the standards allow a generous on-site parking standard of 1 space per 15 m^2 of gross floorspace in the development. Thus for a superstore which had a gross floorspace of 5,000 m^2 the on-site parking allowance in that context would be 5,000 ÷ 15 = 333 spaces. Conversely the standards are more restrictive for very accessible town centre sites which achieve a PTAL score of 6. In that context the parking standard for a superstore of 5,000 m^2 is 1 parking space per 25 to 38 m^2 of floorspace. Thus there is some choice in that a range is provided, so if a developer chose to adopt 1 space per 30 m^2 the calculation would be 5,000 ÷ 30 = 167 spaces. The latter would reflect a town centre site where other transport options were available. Ultimately with city centre metro style supermarkets there is no on-site parking provision.

Business parks and science parks which began to appear in the UK in the late 1980s were typically capitalizing on cheaper land on the edge of cities where there was good access to the motorway network and ideally a railway station and airport. These developments are low density with good landscaping and with a high ratio of car parking provision. Car parking standards for business and science parks are much higher than for traditional industrial estates and even now when there are attempts to restrict car commuting it is still possible to find recently completed business park units boasting a car parking provision of one space per 20 m^2 of lettable floorspace. However the norm might be a little higher with one parking space for between 25 and 30 m^2 of floorspace.

4.4 Use classes

The lawful use to which a building may be put is an issue that a property investor would check before acquiring a property. A check on the building's use class both confirms what a building can be marketed for and in terms of future flexibility should there need to change the use of the building to a different function. The issue is perhaps more salient to commercial property investors as residential investors will know that they are acquiring a house or a flat and will probably have no ambitions to change the use of the property from residential.

Ratcliffe *et al.* (2009: 82) explain that 'uses' are bundled together into legal categories in a statutory instrument called the Town and Country Planning Use Classes Order 1987 (as amended). The Use Classes Order (UCO) enables local planning authorities to grant or refuse planning consent for proposed changes of use although changes within a class do not require planning consent.

A summary of the current UCO is shown in Table 4.2. Those uses which do not conveniently fit into a class, such as car showrooms, scrapyards, launderettes, petrol stations, hostels and theatres, are deemed to be outside the UCO in a class of their own or '*sui generis*'. Changes to and from *sui generis* uses require planning consent.

The alphanumeric code in the left-hand column of Table 4.2 is often referred to in property marketing, conveyancing and legal agreements relating to property. For example it is quite common to see property agents' advertising boards above shops in any high street announcing that an A1 unit is available to let or is for sale. In legal terms this signifies that there is legal right to operate a retail business from the property as A1 is the 'Shops' class in the UCO and contains premises from which goods may be sold to the public and which also includes post offices, hairdressers, dry cleaners and sandwich shops. Thus, if an investor owned a vacant unit which had recently been tenanted by a hairdressers but was now attracting interest from a business which wanted to use the premises for a sandwich shop, planning consent for a change of use would not be required as the new use falls within the same class (A1) as the previous use.

However planning consent for a change of use would be required if a fast food operator wanted to use the premises as a restaurant, which is in Use Class

Table 4.2 A summary of the Use Classes Order

Use class	Title	Description
A1	Shops	Premises used for the retail sale of goods other than hot food. Includes post offices, travel agents, sandwich shops, hairdressers and internet cafes.
A2	Financial and professional services	Includes banks, building societies, betting offices and professional services which would normally attract visiting members of the public.
A3	Restaurants and cafes	Includes premises where food is sold and consumed on the premises.
A4	Drinking establishments	Public houses, wine bars and other drinking establishments.
A5	Hot food takeaway	Premises where hot food is sold for consumption off the premises.
B1	Business	Includes premises used as offices, research and development and light industry.
B2	General industrial	Includes factories normally found on industrial estates.
B8	Storage and distribution	Includes warehouses, but not retail warehouses which are contained in Class A1.
C1	Hotels	Includes guesthouses and boarding houses but not residential care homes where care is provided.
C2	Residential institutions	Premises where personal care or treatment is provided and to residential educational establishments.
C2A	Secure residential institutions	Prisons, secure hospitals, detention centres, military barracks.
C3	Dwelling houses	Residential use by single persons or a group of persons living together as a family. Can also include groups of up to 6 people living together as a household.
D1	Non-residential institutions	Non-residential buildings visited by members of the public, includes crèches, nurseries, museums, libraries and court houses.
D2	Assembly and leisure	Includes places of mass assembly such as cinemas, concert halls, indoor and outdoor sports arenas. Some debatable omissions from this class include theatres and motor sports which are *sui generis*.

A3. The local authority would in that scenario weigh up whether allowing such a change would result in an erosion of amenity or was contrary to policy. For example there might be a flat above the premises and the occupiers might well object to proposals to open a restaurant beneath them where before there had been a quieter, less aromatic use which operated during daytime business hours. The local authority is required to consider any third-party objections but is not bound by them. The authority will weigh objections in the balance as material considerations before reaching a decision on whether or not to allow a change of use. Where no objections arise it is likely that the local authority would permit a proposed change of use which did not compromise policy nor give rise to a detrimental effect on amenity.

Another use class which commercial property investors will be familiar with is Class B1 'Business' which includes buildings used as offices, or for research and development purposes or for light industry. In this context light industry and research and development activities might best be thought of as 'white coat' smokeless and noiseless activity which could pass a notional amenity test in that it could be carried out in a residential area without detriment to amenity. Thus if a property investor owned a building whose last tenant used it for research a development purposes but a prospective tenant wanted to us it for offices then planning consent would not be required as they are both contained within use class B1.

On first coming into contact with the UCO there is a natural response to see it as Orwellian bureaucracy gone mad. However experienced property investors will know that this type of control prevents the random erosion of property value from bad neighbour uses. In a residential setting where somebody had spent a considerable sum purchasing a home and a neighbour then decided to turn the large house next door into a car servicing and repair centre, this would have a serious detrimental affect both on the value of neighbouring houses and the amenity enjoyed by the residents. In these situations residents will soon be demanding that the local authority take action to return the car repair centre back to its lawful use as a house. It would be very likely that the local authority would take enforcement action in such a situation to restore the status quo.

In a commercial property context such as in a shopping centre or on a business park, the juxtaposition of different use classes can sometimes raise contentious issues. For example a property investor who had spent millions on a high specification B1 unit on a business park will want its neighbours to be high specification B1 business units and not (for example) retail warehouses, vehicle depots, recycling centres or scrap metal dealerships, which are perhaps better located on trade and industrial parks.

There will be occasions when a local authority is likely to resist a proposed change of use. For example a proposed change from a light industrial use (B1) in a residential area to general industry (B2) might well be refused on the grounds that it would create noise, vibration and HGV traffic generation.

Another sensitive change of use scenario arises out of concerns raised in recent years by the police and residents regarding the proliferation of bars, clubs and restaurants in town and city centres. These are A4 (drinking establishments) A5 (hot food takeaway) and D2 (assembly and leisure) uses. Many of those who live in or around town centres, feel that their amenity has been seriously eroded by an overconcentration of these 'night-time economy' uses.

Residents in these areas feel that saturation point has been reached and now want their local authorities to refuse planning applications which would give rise to more A4, A5 and D2 outlets.

Local authorities such as Westminster City Council are taking the issue seriously by carefully assessing the effect of each application for a new bar or club in streets which some feel are 'overheating'. Where consent is granted for further A4, A5 or D2 uses, the City Council may attach conditions which limit late night opening. Some authorities are considering whether to create permissive 'Entertainment Zones' where these uses are encouraged to locate, although outside of these zones there will be a presumption against new A4, A5 or D2 uses. Thus potential investors in leisure property will need to conduct some research if they are planning to acquire and turn a former retail unit into a night time use, to establish whether the tipping point has already been reached in the particular locality and where the local authority will probably refuse the proposal.

Gunne-Jones (2009: 28–30) sets out some of the permitted development rights provided in planning law which effectively grant exemptions from planning consent for selected changes across use classes. Examples of these exemptions include:

- From A3 (Restaurants) to A1 (shops) or A2 (financial and professional services).
- From A2 to A1.
- From B2 (industrial) to B1 (Business) or B8 (warehousing) within certain floorspace limits.
- From B8 to B1 within certain floorspace limits.

The rationale for allowing these exemptions is that there is likely to be an environmental improvement in these unidirectional changes, which property lawyers and planners refer to as the 'ratchet effect'. However consent would be required to go back the other way. From a property investor's perspective this has value implications because an A3 unit is more versatile as it can be marketed to all businesses which comply with the A1, A2 and A3 use classes. However an A1 unit is less versatile and could only be marketed (without a change of use) to businesses which would conform to the A1 shops class.

Another context where the commercial property investor may come into contact with the UCO relates to high street retail properties which in most localities will be subject to core retail frontage policies in local authorities' development plans. These policies attempt to prevent the erosion of prime retail frontages by restricting a change of use from A1 retail to other uses such as financial and professional services (A2) and restaurants and cafes (A3) pubs and bars (A4) and hot food takeaways (A5). The London Borough of Greenwich Unitary Development Plan contains policy TC17 which is a typical policy in this respect:

The Council will seek to protect the overall viability of town centres by designating Core (Primary) and Fringe (Secondary) Shopping Frontages in major and district centres, and by designating local centres in their entirety as Local Shopping Frontage. At ground floor level a minimum of 70% of

Core Frontage, and 50% of Fringe and Local Frontage, should be available for A1 retail use. (2006: 166)

In some town centres the A1 retail offer has already been seriously eroded because of the scale and quality of competition in the form of out of town regional shopping centres such as Bluewater, the Metro Centre, Meadowhall and Lakeside. These developments obviously capture trade from existing town centres where the footfall drops and where retailers begin to leave, vacating units which are then typically targeted by pub chains, fast food restaurant operators and slot machine arcade businesses. The latter is an example of a *sui generis* use. In these circumstances local authorities will try to resist a further loss of A1 units on policy grounds but this is sometimes a forlorn 'King Canute' exercise.

Where a local authority refuses a change of use from retail to another use there is often an appeal where the appellants, such as a fast food chain, argue that their proposed use is 'quasi-retail' and generates pedestrian flow like a shop. Planning inspectors who decide these appeals have to consider whether these arguments stand up to closer scrutiny as well as considering the government's overall policy framework for town centres. The latter is contained in the Department for Communities' (2009a) *Planning Policy Statement 4: Planning for Sustainable Economic Growth* which champions the vitality and viability of town centres.

The discussion on the UCO perhaps illustrates that particularly for the commercial property investor, there is no substitute for using experienced and specialist property solicitors to ascertain whether there are any legal restrictions which would impact upon the future use of a property and hence its investment value. For example, for more recently developed out of town retail warehouse units there is sometimes a section 106 agreement which places limitations on the type of retailing which can take place from the unit. This type of legal constraint is sometimes put in place by the local authority on policy grounds and may seek to limit retail activity on a particular site to bulky goods and flat-pack furniture but may prevent, for example, food retailing. These agreements run with the land and act as a form of restrictive covenant, overriding and narrowing what might have been possible under an un-fettered A1 use.

As well as the UCO another key area of legislation which the commercial property investor needs to be aware of and when necessary take specialist legal advice upon, is the Landlord and Tenant Act 1954 (part 2) and its associated secondary legislation. Retail, offices and industrial premises when let are collectively known as business premises and fall within the remit of the Act. Under the provisions of the Act, an occupying lessee has the right on the expiration of a lease to be granted a new lease at a market rent, unless the landlord can prove certain grounds for possession, such as redevelopment proposals or tenant/lessee breach of covenant. Landlord and tenant law has provided a stable framework over a long period of time in which the contractual arrangements between investor and occupier can operate.

4.5 Retail investments

Historically retail investments have been regarded as the best performing commercial property sector and this has been reflected in the yield that investors are willing to purchase at and which has tended to be lower than for most other forms of property investment. The reason for investors bidding down yields reflects the fact that the retail sector is based directly on consumer spending. Increases in consumption are quickly relayed to retailers who, during periods of economic stability, are able to pay competitive rents in order to lease shops in the best trading positions. Successful retailers are also more able to absorb rental increases at review, thus providing the investor with potential income growth. However these comments relate more to prime retail property which is well located in busy high streets or shopping malls or on successful retail parks. For secondary and tertiary retail units, it might be very difficult to achieve rental or capital growth and in some high streets and smaller town centre malls which have been affected by superior out of town retail competition, it will be difficult to find retail tenants at all.

Because there will always be some locational risk affecting retail property, experienced investors in this sector tend to look at the ranking of town centres produced by leading firms of surveyors. Investors will be particularly interested in whether particular town or city centres have been moving up or down the rankings and whether a centre is deemed to be a high risk because it has more than its fair share of retail firms which are themselves considered to be at high financial risk. The demise of Woolworths in 2008 is a case in point here.

Ignoring the non-prime areas of the retail market such as corner shops and units in suburban parades, the main areas of interest for retail property investors are prime high street shops and town centre shopping schemes (sometimes referred to as precincts or malls), retail warehouses and regional out of town centres. The discussion on retail property however begins by briefly explaining why food-based superstores do not feature at the top of the list of property investment assets.

Superstores

The majority of food-based superstores are owner-occupied by the large supermarket operators such as ASDA, Sainsbury's, Tesco, Safeway and Morrisons. However where a large supermarket is one of the large units on an edge of town retail park or where it forms an anchor unit in a medium sized shopping mall there may well be a joint venture arrangement where the developer is working closely with the supermarket from an early stage. The developer in that scenario may be a large property company which retains completed developments as investments and so there will be some long-term investment interest in the supermarket. The format is seldom developed on a speculative basis in order to be leased to a supermarket operator and then sold on into the investment market.

There has been some lease and leaseback activity in the supermarket sector by Sainsbury and Tesco where commercial mortgage-backed securities have been used as a way of raising capital against some stores. Using this model, the supermarket retains the freehold of the site but sells a lease which can be up to 99 years to a property company (normally a Real Estate Investment Trust) or investment fund which then agrees to lease back the building to the supermarket on a commercial occupancy lease which would normally contain a provision for index-linked rent reviews. Because the supermarket chain is already in occupation there is continuity of operation, but the lease and leaseback has released capital from the property which can be used to pursue an expansion programme by acquiring other sites where new stores can be built. The Real Estate Investment Trust or financial institution which has purchased the long lease receives a virtually risk-free rental income stream from the supermarket chain and which equates to a rate of return on whatever was paid to acquire the long lease. In this way British Land plc, which is one of the UK's largest REITs has built up the largest investment exposure to the supermarket sector with 102 stores.

Although the lease and lease back model does enable REITs like British Land to gain some exposure to the supermarket sector, that degree of exposure remains the exception rather than the rule. The leading supermarkets are locked in such fierce competition with one another that they independently target sites within particular residential catchment areas and then negotiate the planning system to ultimately develop a store that meets their trading requirements. In recent years this has seen the development of superstores with around 5,000 m^2 of trading space which fit in with supermarkets' strategic development programmes and supply chain logistics. The role of the property investor in the development and use of superstores is marginal to what has become a finely tuned corporate activity.

In recent years the leading supermarket chains have begun to look back within towns and cities in order to capture particularly the spending power of the working population. This has seen the introduction of *Express*, *Metro* and *Local* formats which are similar to large convenience stores but which do not offer the full range that is possible within a supermarket format. In that context the supermarket chains are more ambivalent about whether they own the freehold or leasehold of a property. These types of units might for example be around 450 m^2 on the ground floor of a large office building on a highly visual junction near a tube station in the central business district of a city. Here perhaps the property investor does have a role, and would probably be very happy to grant a long lease on such a property to one of the leading supermarket chains which represent very strong covenants.

The high street and town centre shopping malls

Town centre schemes incorporating shopping malls were a product of post-war developments, starting off in a basic open format precinct and gradually developing into the covered mall with high-quality finishes, facilities and climate control. In order for centres to meet modern expectations and to try to keep pace with the competition provided by regional out of town centres, town centre retail developments have needed regular refurbishment and in some cases complete redevelopment to make better use of a large prime central site. Many of these shopping centres are partnerships between local authorities and developers who share in the rental income arising from the development and Isaac *et al.* (2010: 85–100) explore some of the complicated income sharing arrangements which can arise in that context. Local authorities also have responsibilities for encouraging regeneration and ensuring that the retail offer in their town centres is as good as it can be. Local authorities are therefore stakeholders in a number of senses and they will often be enthusiastic partners with developers and investors when a town centre retail scheme needs to be rejuvenated. For example the partnership between Canterbury City Council and Land Securities recently saw the successful redevelopment of the Whitefriars shopping centre in Canterbury.

Town centre schemes present significant traffic and parking challenges, as on the one hand the success of a scheme might depend on the availability of a critical mass of parking yet on the other hand the town centre highway network may not have sufficient capacity to deal with the traffic generation at peak times. Thus traffic management is required and which has tended to use a combination of the price mechanism to regulate the turnover of parking spaces, distinguishing between short-term and long-term parking, the use of priority lanes and in some cases various forms of congestion charging at peak times to discourage car-borne shopping trips. Ultimately some compromises have to be brokered and a balance found between car accessibility and restriction.

However that balance can be struck as exemplified by centres such as the Glades shopping centre in Bromley, Kent where a high-quality shopping development has been skilfully inserted into a town centre around which there is an affluent middle-class catchment area which generates considerable spending power. The development is matched with extensive car parking, pedestrianization of the high street and good bus and train links to the high street.

Location is very important for high street shops whose income and thus rental levels are based on customer spending and thus a position which is convenient to shoppers and a layout which encourages sales is important. Property investors therefore tend to look closely at a shop's position within a high street or shopping centre relative to neighbouring lettings and pedestrian flows past or through the shop premises. The location is also important with respect to the town or city in which the shop is situated and a prudent investor will be considering whether there is potential for growth and whether the location is likely to be undermined by the development of competing shopping areas nearby.

Although 'town centre first' planning policies have been applied in the UK with varying degrees of commitment for over 40 years, the policy does not protect exiting town centres from retail competition absolutely. It is also recognized that for practical reasons some retail formats are better located in non-central or edge of town locations. Policy on this issue in England is contained in the Department for Communities' *Planning Policy Statement 4 (PPS4): Planning for Sustainable Economic Growth* (2009a) and similar policies have been adopted by the devolved administrations in Scotland and Wales. PPS4 contains the long established *sequential test* which is used to evaluate the most sustainable location for new retail development. The policy asks local authorities to consider whether the particular retail proposal could be accommodated satisfactorily in the town centre and if the conclusion is that it cannot, then other locations are considered in turn.

The decentralization of some retail formats reflects the interplay of increasing car ownership, the need for very large premises particularly for flat-pack furniture and carpet retail warehouses and because there is a degree of differentiation in the types of shopping trips that customers make. Thus for convenience or food shopping there is no pressing need to bring customers into what might already be congested town centres. Similarly a trip to a large flat-pack furniture retailer such as IKEA is not really a town centre experience. However high-value comparison shopping is something that is associated with town centre shopping and which is threatened when regional out of town shopping centres are developed.

The government's policy in PPS4 seeks to sustain the vitality and viability of existing town centres and hence the policy tries to channel retail property development which is focused on comparison shopping onto town centre sites wherever possible. The government is therefore trying to prevent the negative consequences of so called 'retail impact' on existing centres, a policy which is consistent with fostering sustainable development. Thus far in the UK consent has only been granted for the development of a handful of regional scale (over 50,000 m² of comparison shopping) out of town retail centres, the best known of which are Brent Cross, the Metro Centre, Meadowhall, Lakeside and Bluewater. In each case there was felt to be a combination of special circumstances which enabled the government (often following a public inquiry) to allow the development of these very large schemes. The developments were not unanimously welcomed and numerous third parties including neighbouring local authorities objected to these very large out of town centres.

Because of the gravitational pull that centres like the Metro Centre and Bluewater exert on their regional catchment areas (measured by drive time isochrones) the impact upon existing town centres is diffused across all of the shopping centres within the catchment area. However the centres which are closest to the regional out of town giant will experience the greatest retail impact, which can be measured either as a loss of trade, reduced rental value or reduced footfall. Some centres are able to withstand the competition better than others and typically it is the smaller and less diverse centres which are likely to suffer more than those which have critical mass and a diverse retail offer.

Retail impact can have consequences at a number of levels and from a property investor's perspective the concern will be the negative effect on retail rents and capital value. When a significant out of town centre is proposed in a locality some of the most prominent objectors will be institutional property investors who may have a significant financial stake in a town centre retail scheme. An example of retail impact upon property values is illustrated by the before and after effect of the opening of Bluewater in north Kent. The 150,000 m² development, which occupies a former Blue Circle chalk quarry, opened for trading in 1999. At that time Zone A retail rents in nearby Dartford were estimated to have fallen by 50 per cent and major retailers pulled out of that town centre. Some of the vacated retail units were taken by charity shops while others remained vacant for lengthy periods. Of course not all shopping centres suffered quite as dramatically as Dartford, and centres like Bromley which are on the outer reaches of Bluewater's 1-hour drive time catchment area were large and robust enough to withstand any significant retail impact.

To be able to fend off out of town retail competition, shopping centres must be accessible by different modes of transport and there has to be adequate car parking capacity. The design and tenant mix must support pedestrian flows and there should be a diversity of uses such as leisure, financial and restaurant facilities to encourage visitors. The catchment area should ideally reflect a diverse and buoyant local economy and be of an appropriate size relative to the development. A shopping centre must be managed effectively and an appropriately experienced town centre manager is often jointly appointed and funded by developers, investors and the local authority in order that an overview can be taken on, for example cleanliness, maintenance and policing. It is important that visitors to these centres leave with a favourable impression so that it is more likely that they will revisit the centre. From an investor's perspective effective property management will help to sustain rental value and provide good value for money for the tenants of the centre.

Regional out of town shopping centres

The design and management principles which were gradually learned over decades on town centre shopping schemes have been mapped onto the regional out of town centres with considerable success. In shopping malls the designer will have tried to achieve concentrated pedestrian flows in the malls and arcades and the selection of key tenants and the overall tenant mix are important factors in this respect.

To attract shoppers, the magnet or anchor stores will ideally be established department stores with an instantly recognizable brand name and these stores will normally be located where they will draw people along the malls past the smaller retail units. A successful model of this approach is provided by Bluewater in Kent, a regional out of town centre which relies mainly upon its M25 and M2 location to attract car borne shoppers from a very wide catchment area across the South-East of England. There is a railway station at Greenhithe from which there is a connecting bus service to Bluewater, however the majority of customers will arrive by car to occupy one of over 13,000 free parking spaces which are distributed around the mall to maximize customers' convenience.

Bluewater has three anchor units positioned at the corners of a broadly triangular twin level mall. The anchor units are occupied by Marks & Spencer (18,600 m²), House of Fraser (12,100 m²) and John Lewis (37,000 m²). Other major tenants include C & A, W H Smith and Boots. There are 10 flagship stores of between 465 m² and 13,000 m² and 260 smaller shop units. Planning the tenant mix, marketing and initial leasing took 15 months. The centre has traded well and in the weeks leading up to Christmas it is not unusual for the highways leading into the centre to be closed to further traffic as the centre is full to capacity. This is perhaps not surprising given that the centre is located in the relatively affluent South-East of England and that there is an estimated 9.6 million people living within the 1-hour drive time catchment area.

As well as a balanced mix of high street retail names to satisfy shoppers' expectations, modern malls like Bluewater will also provide a diverse range of restaurants in food courts, strategically placed coffee bars, a multiplex cinema, banks and building society branches and amenity space. Getting the balance right between these uses will help to underpin the attractiveness of the shopping centre and guarantee repeat customer visits.

Malls and arcades should be wide enough for pedestrian flows, but not too wide to lose the window shoppers' attention. While there is some variation between centres, a width of 15 metres for the mall narrowing to 6 metres for the arcades appears to work well. Modern centres will have atria which allow natural light to penetrate what is often a twin level galleried arrangement. Within a mall, the individual shop units will vary in size with anchor department stores ranging between 15,000 m² and 40,000 m². At the other end of the spectrum Lawson (2007: 13–11) points out that a small shop unit will have a frontage of 5.4 metres and depth of 13 metres and thus a gross internal floor area (measured between the internal surfaces of the external walls) of only 70.2 m². However a so-called standard retail unit could also have a frontage of up to 7.3 metres and a depth of 39 metres providing a gross internal area of 284.7 m².

From an investor's perspective very large high-quality regional shopping centres such as the Metro Centre, Brent Cross, Meadowhall, Lakeside and Bluewater represent an enormous capital investment which comes with considerable risk. The strong trading performance that these centres have makes them attractive investments, however even the largest property funds in the UK cannot easily accommodate these assets in their property portfolios. For example, the ownership of Bluewater is divided between four corporate property investors: the Prudential owns a 35 per cent stake, Lend Lease Europe Ltd owns 30 per cent, Lend Lease Retail Partnership owns 25 per cent and pension fund Hermes owns the remaining 10 per cent share.

Retail warehouses

In the UK retail warehousing first began to appear either individually or clustered on retail parks from the early 1980s when consumers began to show their enthusiasm for DIY and flat-pack furniture. Initially the locations were a little haphazard as retailers such as MFI, B&Q, Magnet, Halfords and electrical goods retailers took occupation in converted storage warehouses and industrial units on major roads. In these locations corporate retail brands could be advertised to passing motorists to maximum effect. Because some of the early retail warehouses were converted factories or warehouses the on-site car parking provision was often insufficient to cope with the considerable demand for customer parking. Gradually the format evolved and local authorities began to plan for this relatively new arrival on the retail scene by allocating land for retail warehouse parks adjacent to major junctions on orbital routes around towns and cities. Because of the land required to accommodate large plan buildings and considerable surface parking, it is not practical for retail warehouse parks to be accommodated in town or city centres. However the viability of this type of retailing depends upon it being proximate to centres of population and so it is seldom found entirely beyond the urban envelope.

In many cases, in order to provide economic buildings, the retailers deliberately avoid high specifications. A wide range of units within a park may be provided from 500 m² to 7,500 m². Surface parking is essential for these units, ideally at a ratio of one space to 20 m² of gross floor area.

Retail warehouses are much like superstores in that they depend on the car borne shopper and so again location is important with good road access, a prominent location to attract passing traffic and sufficient car parking. The developers are sometimes owner-occupiers but investors are very active in the sector. A retail warehouse will tend to have a more basic build standard and finishes than a superstore and many will be built using a steel portal frame with steel profile walls and roof and with partial brick or blockwork-built walls. Retail warehouses sell a wider range of goods than a superstore and the overall retail offer on a retail warehouse park will therefore tend to be quite diverse and will typically include electrical goods, DIY, motor accessories, home furnishing and carpets and sports goods.

One of the reasons investors have become more interested in retail warehouses is because the range of tenants on any particular development will be varied and this diversification reduces risk. Factory outlets are an extension of retail warehouse activities, an invention from the US, outlets provide the retail outlets from a particular manufacturer and carry stocks of overruns and perhaps discontinued lines. These outlets are especially popular for clothing and kitchenware and a number of these outlets have been established in the UK.

4.6 Offices

Over the last 50 years, the UK in common with other developed countries has gone through a process of deindustrialization which has seen a shift in employment away from engineering, scientific application and manufacturing towards the service sector and particularly the financial services sector. It is a moot point whether this equates to long-term progress for a nation, as there must ultimately come a point where there is overreliance on the service sector relative to design, manufacturing and other core industries which arguably are true value creators. There is in the UK a belated recognition that a diverse economic base is important and there is now action on the part of the government to try to promote engineering, science and manufacturing as careers for younger people in the hope that these sectors can be expanded. However in the short term at least, the office is where most people go to work as reflected in satirical TV series which portray life in and commuting to the office.

The shift of business activity into the service sector has seen considerable office development take place in all of the UK's major towns and cities and on edge of town business parks. In the 1980s there were predictions of a leisure society in which the working week would decline and where improvements in information technology would enable most to work from home. In fact what has happened is that the working week has if anything extended for most people and employees are now expected to have longer working lives in order to pay for retirement pensions. Forecasters also underestimated the sociological value of work and having a meaningful career and the importance of a psychological demarcation that most individuals need to make between home and work. While there are continuing debates about what might be a healthy work–life balance, for many the choices made around housing are still made on the basis of whether a location is within practical commuting distance of the office. Thus the signifiers suggest that 'going to work' and particularly going to work in an office is a durable model which is unlikely to alter dramatically in the near future, despite more flexible working patterns and the use of hot-desking by some companies.

What perhaps has changed in the last 20 years and which is of significance to the property investor, is a more pragmatic approach on the part of larger companies regarding the location of back office functions. Thus the prestigious headquarters office might be in the central business district of a principal city, although that office might in fact be quite small, reflecting the considerable costs of occupying space in such a location. The support functions and bulk of staff might then be located either on a peripheral business park or in a suburban centre where rental values could well be half of what it costs to occupy space in the central business district. When taken to its logical extent whole corporate functions have been out-sourced to countries such as India where wages and property overheads enable call centre functions (for example) to be delivered at a fraction of the cost that would be incurred if the same service remained in the UK.

There are however limitations on how far office functions can be outsourced offshore as there can be adverse customer reactions when the process is taken too far. For example high street banks have for many years been trying to entice their account holders to use online and call centre delivered services. However what might seem to be illogical from the prism of corporate decision-making, many customers still prefer to queue up in their local branch in order to talk face to face with somebody. Concerns about online security are also a factor reinforcing the habit of visiting the local branch of a bank for many customers.

For companies which need office space to operate but who are not owner-occupiers, the cost of occupying the space is the second largest expense after staff salaries and thus using office space efficiently will always be a corporate priority. As Baiche and Walliman (2000: 337) confirm, improvements in information technology have reduced the need for administrative and clerical support staff and companies now have flatter management structures. It is not now uncommon for middle managers and even senior managers to be expected do some if not all of their own word processing, data storage and spreadsheet work. While most offices are not entirely paperless, the e-storage of documents means that there is now less need for banks of filing cabinets in offices. Office equipment including personal computers, display screens and photocopiers have developed considerably and consume far less valuable office space than they once did.

Greater efficiency in the use of office space is therefore a factor of changes in a number of variables which include the decline in the number of office workers employed, a move to more open plan layouts in which there is a higher employee density, some flexibility in working patters such as hot-desking and reduced space demands for document storage and office equipment. Dixon *et al.* (2005) have produced some interesting conjectures on how the interplay of all of these variables might progress and impact upon the real estate investor. However at a more empirical level it is not surprising that the British Council for Offices (2009: 74) have identified a trend over time in which companies are using space far more intensively with the average occupational density now around 1 employee per 10 m² of net office floorspace.

At a strategic level research undertaken by the British Council for Offices (2009) identified a number of priorities which businesses expect their office space to deliver and which are:

- productivity;
- good value for money;
- prospect of best place to work; and
- conformity with corporate social responsibility policies.

To assist employee productivity, offices should provide a good basic working habitat in terms of thermal comfort, lighting and sound insulation. Essentially the working environment should be comfortable. In terms of value for money an office occupier is responsible for various outgoings and thus a building which does not raise significant repairs bills and is economical to run will obviously be a competitive product in the office occupier market. Display Energy Certificates which have become mandatory in the UK potentially go some way towards signifying a building's energy efficiency. However, the British Council for Offices points out there is as yet insufficient research to determine how this type of data actually influences the decision making processes of the average footloose office tenant.

Research in the USA by Eichholtz *et al.* (2009) suggests that there is a marginal capital and rental value premium for offices that have a sustainability accreditation under either the LEED or Energy Star labels, which are broadly equivalent to the BREEAM accreditation in the UK. It is too early to be definitive about the precise relationship between green building accreditation and value performance over time. However given the growing enthusiasm of companies in their adoption of corporate social responsibility policies, it is very likely that BREEAM rated office buildings will have an advantage in the office market as the British Council for Offices suggest:

> Sustainable offices, with their low carbon, energy-efficient and socially responsible approach to development, are more likely to comply with future legislation, thus decreasing the risk of premature obsolescence. Furthermore, occupiers keen to demonstrate their environmental commitment will increasingly seek out low carbon buildings, potentially leading to rental premiums. (2009: 38)

Office space needs to be flexible and offer the potential for sub division if multi-letting is required. In that respect an industry norm has evolved which is based upon a 1.5 metre planning grid. This modulus enables the arrangement of floorspace either on an open-plan basis or with part or full cellular division using partitions relative to structural columns spaced at 7.5 m, 9m or 12m. This type of floorplate enables an efficient net to gross relationship of around 85 per cent for buildings up to 10 storeys. For buildings over 10 storeys the increasing space which needs to be set aside to house lift cores and plant reduces the floorspace efficiency to significantly below 80 per cent.

Institutional investors expect their offices to have a minimum floor to ceiling height of 2.6 metres and floors should be able to take a load of 3 kN per m^2 with high load areas able to carry 7.5 kN per m^2. External cladding will also need to satisfy thermal and noise insulation requirements. In terms of internal finishes; suspended ceilings are now frequently used for concealing service runs and also suspended flooring. Commercial space may be let in a shell form in which the tenants fit out the space and finishes to their particular requirements.

The physical design parameters described above apply to office developments generally although there are concessions made where 'statement architecture' and landmark tower developments promoted at transport hubs in the central business districts of major cities. Thus buildings such as the Gherkin in the City of London and the Shard of Glass at London Bridge buck the trend towards standardization; however the overall package will remain very valuable because of the kudos associated with these developments.

The floorspace grid format described above will commonly be found on less prestigious city centre sites and will certainly be the norm for low rise business units on edge of city business parks. The latter format evolved from the 1980s science parks which were low density campus style developments in the USA. Those developments provided space for companies which sought to cluster around science and technology-based universities in order to exploit commercial spin-offs from 'blue skies' research. While location and quality of the environment are important in developments like this, a perhaps more important factor is the quality of the labour force in terms of its skills and entrepreneurial ability.

The success of science park development formats in the United States was thought to be because of the availability of highly capable individuals who could work on product design and development and who were the 'movers and shakers' providing the creativity and innovation behind new products. Areas such as Silicon Valley in California were based upon this concept, enabling different firms to utilize the skills of the local labour force and perhaps develop synergies in research and production which might not otherwise be attainable by a single company in isolated production.

In the UK an example of the genre is the Cambridge Science Park which began development in the 1980s and was thought at the time to provide a template for how this particular type of development could be rolled out throughout the UK. Despite the 'hi-tech' marketing hype, a lot of subsequent copy-cat developments failed to establish any meaningful synergies between university research and business activity. While there have been some successful collaborations in the fields of biotechnology and electronics there are sometimes practical difficulties in achieving a commercially viable technology transfer between companies and academic institutions. Gradually, in various locations, the claim to 'science' was quietly dropped and the term 'business park' became more prevalent. This also reflected the fact that a lot of the occupational demand was mainly from the financial and services sector rather than the technological or scientific sectors.

One of the pioneering and very successful business park developments in the UK is Stockley Park near Hillingdon in West London, which set the standard for low density business unit development in a high-quality landscaped environment. This development was begun in the mid 1980s and utilizes a large reclaimed brownfield site which has convenient links to the M4, M25 and Heathrow Airport.

Very large business parks such as Stockley Park tend to be developed on a phased basis. One of the consequences of this is that the new floorspace created gradually filters into the market over a lengthy period of time, so that supply does not swamp demand. In these situations the business park developer has the opportunity to market plots and notional buildings rather than actual ones. This enables companies who are potential occupiers of space to become involved in negotiations for pre-lets or in some cases they will seek to become owner-occupiers by purchasing the plot and the building outright. During these discussions companies can make known their precise building requirements so that a better match can be made between the size and specification of a business unit and an occupier's actual needs.

Using pre-lets or pre-sales as a trigger for plot development significantly reduces a developer's risk exposure. This is a particularly useful device during economic downturns when development loans are hard to obtain on competitive terms and when speculative development would be particularly unwise in any case. Phasing also helps a developer's cash flow, as once individual plots are developed and let, they can be sold as income producing packages to property investors. The capital receipts arising can then be used to develop the next plot and/or reduce bank debt whichever is the priority at the time.

Phasing enables a developer to gradually exploit all of the plots on a business park so that ultimately it will have been completed. For schemes as large as Stockley Park, the whole process might take between 15 and 25 years to accomplish. The rate of progress will depend on market buoyancy over the time frame and the capacity of infrastructure (in particular high capacity roads and their junctions) to keep pace with the incremental addition of new buildings on the business park. As each plot is exploited and a new building created, the increase in floorspace will increase the working population entering, using and leaving the site each day. Complicated legal agreements are brokered in these situations under which the developer is usually obliged to make staged payments to the local authority and/or the highways authority so that the cost of upgrading roads and services are not left to be met entirely by the tax payer. There are normally trigger mechanisms included in these agreements which, as a certain stage has been reached, prevent further exploitation of plots until a tranche of money has been paid to the relevant public body to progress infrastructure works.

The majority of units on developments like Stockley Park fall within the B1 use class, enabling them theoretically to be used for 'white coat' light industrial and R&D activity as well as offices. However the reality on business parks is that most B1 units will be occupied as perhaps the back offices for banks, the headquarters of retail firms, insurance company offices, professional consultancies, advertising agencies and other large employers within the service sector. Business parks also provide office space for government agencies, local government departments and even some third-sector organizations such as large housing associations and charities. While most of the units will be B1 units used as offices there will also be some B2 general industrial units and B8 storage and distribution units (discussed below).

Business parks are normally master-planned by a leading firm of architects so that districts within the business park are given particular identities underscored by careful management of details like signage and the implementation of a landscape strategy. Within the master-plan particular types of uses will be clustered and plots allocated for hotels, restaurants, a pub and a gym and there is even a golf course at Stockley Park. From an investment perspective, a master-plan creates certainty and ensures that the overall exploitation of the site optimizes value and attracts the best business tenants. The professional fees consumed in these exercises are, in the end, usually money well spent.

4.7 Industrial and warehouse units

Industrial and warehouse units are sometimes discussed interchangeably in the property press as if they were one homogenous group of properties. There is some validity in this approach as it does conveniently demarcate the big three commercial property investment markets as retail, offices and industrial. However industrial and warehouses are quite distinct in the way they are used, their design specification and in terms of the use class categorization which is B2 for 'general industry' and B8 for 'storage and distribution'. Thus the discussion which follows will draw distinctions between the two types of property under the respective subheadings.

Industrial

Investors in commercial property should ideally try to maintain a general sense of how the firms and businesses in the particular occupier market are performing, because in the end the financial performance of the property will have some bearing on how well the sector is performing. This is particularly true of the industrial sector which traditionally has been viewed by investors as risky, because it was felt that this sector was particularly vulnerable to economic downturns which would typically see company closures.

In the UK there has also been a trend over a number of decades which has seen the industrial sector contract while the service sector has expanded. For example, the UK was once a major car manufacturer but with the demise of Rover there is now very little in the way of this type of industrial activity. It is true that there remain some large plants, but even here the emphasis has switched from on-site manufacturing to assembly of imported components and completion of vehicle carcasses before they are delivered to car showrooms.

The general decline of large manufacturing plants has had the knock-on effect of reducing demand for smaller industrial units, the demand for which came from small tool-making and precision engineering companies. These firms customarily undertook specialized contract work for the larger engineering companies. Other sectors of heavy engineering such as shipbuilding and steel making have also declined significantly in the UK simply because of global price competition. Either the labour or raw material costs or both which feed in to the manufacturing process can often be found at lower prices in developing countries. The consequences of globalization in this sector of activity has therefore been that large former industrial areas in the UK have now been remediated and redeveloped to form large residential estates or retail parks and/or office parks.

Given the trend towards de-industrialization, the fully fledged industrial estate is most likely to be a legacy from the 1950s or earlier. Modern B2 industrial units are now less likely to be built as part of an integrated industrial estate but are more likely to be found as a minor component on a large business park where B1 units predominate. This is illustrated in Figure 4.2 where a relatively new B2 unit has been developed on one of the plots at Crossways Business Park in north Kent. Industrial units developed in such a context will benefit from an attractive environment, sufficient on-site parking for employees and visitors, adequate access for HGVs and access to the high capacity road network.

As well as the backdrop of gradual decline in industrial activity, one of the characteristics of industrial property is that it has often been 'built to a cost' to be very functional but seldom with the ambition to achieve a long life cycle. This type of property is therefore prone to depreciation and obsolescence, making reletting progressively more difficult as the building ages. Void risk is

Figure 4.2 Crossways Business Park, north Kent, showing a B2 unit 'to let'

therefore an issue particularly for the second-hand stock of industrial property. Industrial properties are also difficult to adapt to alternative uses when it is found that there is insufficient demand from industrial firms.

Even when redevelopment of an industrial site for a different use is contemplated it is not always in the best location for the envisaged new use and there might be problems with ground contamination, necessitating expensive remediation work. The response to these risks and uncertainties on the part of property developers and investors has often been to build industrial units to minimum standards and low life-cycle expectations, so that a site can be redeveloped within 20 years for something else. In those circumstances property investors tend to look for fast pay back rates and thus initial yields in the sector tend to be higher than for other property types.

Where industrial units are provided as part of a business park development, the developer will usually spread risks by providing a range of unit sizes to cater for different demands. Unit size may vary from small or nursery units at around 200 m^2 to conventional estate units of 500 m^2 up to 2,000 m^2. The smaller units can be terraced to achieve economies in cost and maintenance. A versatile industrial unit will normally have a clear internal height of 6.4 metres which will allow the full vertical extension of a fork lift truck as well as the installation of roof-mounted gantries. Clear internal space dimensions can be slightly lower than this and still be adequate for most industrial processes. Ancillary offices for industrial premises are generally provided at no more than 10 per cent of total space and sometimes this is provided as a part mezzanine floor. However the 10 per cent proportion may be varied where high-tech activity and a sales and delivery team need to be accommodated.

The design of most industrial units exploits the speed of construction, relatively light weight and high strength provided by a steel portal frame structure which also has the benefit of reducing the need for internal columns which could restrict movement of fork-lift trucks. The lower walls of these buildings up to 2 metres high will normally be brick and blockwork to increase strength and security. The roof and upper walls will often be steel profile sheeting combined with factory produced insulated panel systems supported by purlins. There should be heating, a sprinkler system and 3 phase power available. Most industrial units will be single storey and the floor slabs will need to be able to cope with loadings of 25 kN per m^2 with high strength areas which can deal with point loads of up to 36 kN per m^2.

Warehouse units

While the industrial property sector has experienced something of a decline in recent decades the same is not true for companies in the storage and distribution sector who have increasingly sought large warehouse units to support their business models. Even though there might be more reliance on imported goods, those commodities will still need to be stored, batched and then distributed efficiently to outlets and end users. Large companies particularly in the retail sector have evolved very sophisticated logistics models which use electronic rate of sales data from outlets to feed back up through the supply chain to stimulate deliveries from strategically located distribution warehouses.

The location of warehousing units and distribution parks is largely independent from the immediate local economy, as what is important is a strategic position on the motorway network which enables optimal use of delivery fleets on a regional, national and international basis. Thus for some businesses the drive time to the channel ports/Eurotunnel terminal will be at a premium while other businesses will need to be close to international airports or the main centres of population.

From a facilities management perspective, large warehousing units offer the potential to store production output and goods ready for distribution, offsetting the need for extensive storage space in relatively more expensive retail and manufacturing premises. Large warehouses provide flexibility in supply chain management and cost savings on property for large corporate enterprises.

In common with industrial units a steel portal frame construction is a sensible choice for warehouse construction as it is able to deliver the required clear internal space with minimum interference from vertical columns. Thus the business occupying the unit has a free hand on how to arrange the internal pallet and racking system and forklift truck circulation. This type of steel frame with cladding panels is also utilizing standard modular factory produced components. From a developer's perspective this provides considerable cost advantages, reliability and rapid build times. Thus the real challenge for developers in this sector is securing the large sites required in optimum locations and securing the necessary planning consents. These issues are discussed further below.

Regarding the attributes required of the modern storage and distribution warehouse, Drury and Brebner (2007: 15.2) suggest that the minimum economic clear internal height must be at least 7.5 metres, although the norm is to provide a 12 metre clear internal height, sometimes referred to as haunch height. For the new generation of very large super-sheds, which utilize computer controlled automated order picking and stacking systems, the clear internal height may be anything from 15 metres up to 30 metres. Given that the racking systems may extend up to these sorts of heights, the load bearing capacity of the ground floor slab in these buildings will normally need to be at least 50 kN per m². The office element will tend to be around 5 per cent of the overall floorspace and it will tend to be provided as an external extension to the building so that the storage box in the main building is left entirely unencumbered.

A company which has specialized in developing and managing large distribution warehouses as ongoing investments on a global basis is ProLogis. In the UK the company has a portfolio of invested property of around 2 million m² of floorspace, the bulk of which comprises modern warehouses of various sizes including some 'big box' units with over 90,000 m² of floorspace. This newer and larger generation of storage and distribution warehouses will normally have multiple dock-levellers built into the flank walls and in a larger warehouse there could be over 70 such bays provided. A dock-leveller is essentially a weather-tight and height adjustable loading bay designed to enable tailboard-high loading and unloading of HGV containers.

The service yard surrounding these large warehouses must enable easy HGV manoeuvrability so that trucks can reverse up against the dock-levellers without impinging upon other HGV parking spaces (there may be a fleet operating from the building) bays and staff car parking spaces which might number several hundred for very large units. To accommodate this separation and vehicle manoeuvrability the service yard depth should be a minimum of 50 metres reducing to 35 metres on non-loading sides. The significant parking and circulation space together with a very large building footprint will necessitate a site easily in excess of 15 hectares for a unit containing around 50,000 m² of floorspace and thus a distribution park containing several such buildings will require a considerable area of land. These types of sites are therefore seldom random or windfall occurrences and they will need to be brought forward as part of the local planning process. Thus some expertise is required on the part of the developer to choose the right sites both from an economic and planning perspective.

Given the HGV access requirements and size of sites required; this type of development has naturally gravitated to motorway junctions and intersections on the outskirts of regional centres. Indeed one of the criteria for developing a distribution park is to assess the one hour and two hour drive-time isochrones for a HGV to establish the scale of the market which may be serviced from the particular location. For example, there are large distribution parks on the outskirts of Bristol where the M4 and M5 intersect and from where a vast hinterland including the South West, South Wales and the West Midlands can be reached within acceptable HGV outward and return drive times. Proximity to Avonmouth Docks and Bristol Airport also strengthen the decision to develop and invest in this type of property in this type of location.

Given that even in depressed property market conditions a large modern distribution warehouse of say 30,000 m² which is strategically located on the motorway network can still attract annual rental values in excess of £50 per m². Thus from an investor's perspective a unit like this will be generating at least a gross annual income of around £1.5 million and if an initial yield of say 8 per cent is assumed the capital value will be of the order of £18.75 million.

4.8 Leisure properties

The range of leisure related property investment opportunities is very diverse and includes pubs, wine bars, hotels, theatres, nightclubs, cinemas and restaurants. There are also more specialized properties such as casinos, golf courses, indoor bowling centres, theme parks, marinas, private sports, health and fitness centres. The scale of investment varies considerably across the sector from the purchase of an individual pub up to the multimillion pound investment required to develop a Centre Parcs style holiday centre as undertaken by one of the major leisure groups. It is not possible in this book to explore the investment characteristics of all of these properties as each warrants their own specialist discussion. For example, those interested in the investment qualities of hotels could examine Harper (2008) and those interested in pubs could look at Crocker (2008) while Gimmy and Johnson (2003) have explored the valuation of golf courses and country clubs albeit from an American perspective.

While it is not possible to discuss leisure property investment in any depth here, it is possible to provide a least some general comments regarding the characteristics which distinguish leisure properties from other types of property investment. The first feature is that leisure properties provide the space for businesses which are trading against peoples' leisure time and the budgets that they have to spend on leisure activity. The time and money spent on leisure is not a necessity of life when compared with spending time at work and spending money on food shopping or meeting mortgage repayments. Thus expenditure in the leisure sector will tend to come after the main bills have been paid and for this reason that part of a household's budget which may be spent on leisure is sometimes referred to as disposable income.

Spending on different leisure sectors is also subject to the 'lifestyle choices' which people make and which are in turn influenced by changes in fashion, social mores' and even advances in home entertainments. Thus there are a number of interacting variables which for the investor make this sector appear capricious and quite risky.

The propensity of individuals to spend on leisure is also determined by how well the economy is performing which in turn affects consumer confidence and the so called 'feel good factor'. Thus when there is low inflation, low unemployment, business expansion and job security, spending on leisure will tend to increase. Conversely when there is job insecurity, high unemployment, rising prices and general uncertainty, expenditure in the leisure sector will tend to fall sharply. Thus when the economy is strong and individuals are secure in well paid jobs they will not look upon paying an annual gym membership fee as a particular problem. However when jobs and prospects are threatened, perhaps because stringent public spending cuts are necessary to reduce national debt, the renewal of an individual's annual gym membership might then be seen as an unaffordable luxury. Leisure businesses are therefore among the first to feel the effects of economic downturns or government imposed austerity measures.

For the reasons discussed above there is always a degree of risk that leisure businesses, and particularly those which are not well diversified, will struggle to consistently maintain operating margins. Thus the value of invested leisure properties is assessed using what is sometimes referred to as the 'profits method' and which entails an examination of the audited accounts of a business going back at least three years. The value of the property is ultimately determined by the average profitability of the occupying business and therefore variations in profit will have a major effect on investment value.

Despite the risks, developers and investors still choose to become involved in well located leisure schemes particularly where they form part of a mixed use development where there is the potential for synergy. An obvious example is the leisure element provided in a regional out of town shopping centre which will typically include a multiplex cinema and food court and which blurs the demarcation between what is a leisure trip and what is a shopping trip. From an investment perspective the leisure element could be seen to diversify the risk as the income profile will vary from the rental income arising from the retail units. Leisure uses may also work well where the local authority has taken a deliberate policy to create a leisure zone where the night time economy is encouraged to flourish in a managed way.

Because of the dynamism and volatility associated with leisure businesses, the sector was one of the first to come into conflict with the set of assumptions around the traditional institutional lease under which landlords expected long-term lease commitments with upwards only rent reviews. The response to this 'culture clash' was a greater preparedness on the part of more enlightened landlords to explore the use of both shorter lease terms and turnover rents, so that the return on the property was harmonized with the performance of occupying leisure businesses. This flexibility helps the longer-term survival of a leisure business and in the end that must be preferable for a property investor to the prospect of a bankrupt tenant and a void unit.

4.9 Residential investments

As discussed in previous chapters the private rented sector was once a major tenure category but as local authorities took greater responsibility for housing and legislation introduced controls in the private rented sector, the latter diminished considerably. As Havard (2008: 35) points out the introduction of assured short-hold tenancies which enabled properties to be let for short terms at market rents gave investors some encouragement to re-enter this sector. The real stimulus however was a change in attitudes on the part of mortgage lenders who brought forward more flexible financial products which helped fuel a minor revival of the private rented sector under the buy-to-let badge. Despite the newfound enthusiasm for the private rented sector on the part of investors, realistically it will remain a minor housing sector in comparison to the 70 per cent of homes which are owner-occupied in the UK.

Although a relatively small housing sub-sector, the private rented sector still boasts over 3 million homes. These properties, which are owned by private residential landlords, are very diverse. At the high-value end of the market there are luxury penthouses, apartments and townhouses in prestigious locations and/or with waterside settings. It is in the middle of the market that smaller buy-to-let investors have been most active in the last decade by purchasing semi-detached and terraced houses and purpose built apartments, typically located in suburban settings close to commuter railway stations. At the budget end of the market there are large Victorian and inter-war houses which have been subdivided to form basic flatted accommodation and where gardens have often been paved over to provide off-street parking spaces. At the lower value and more rudimentary end of the market there are properties let to those reliant on government provided housing benefits. The private rented sector also contains hybrid properties such as loft apartments, live-work units, studios of various types and sizes and even suburban bungalows.

Because of the expansion in higher education provision in the UK in recent years, the student housing market has also expanded and is now quite diverse. There are still the basic student 'digs' which are typically older terraced houses in inner city locations which are let in multiple occupation. At the other end of the student lettings market there are the modern halls of residence which have been developed collaboratively between a landowning university and a private sector partner under a PFI scheme. Companies such as UNITE have seen the potential in the student housing market and have developed stand alone schemes as well as working collaboratively with universities in order to build up a sizeable investment portfolio of managed student housing blocks.

Wilcox (2009: 24) confirms statistically that there is no such thing as the standard private rented property, as 18 per cent of the private rented stock comprises one bedroom properties, 38 per cent have two bedrooms, and 33 per cent have three bedrooms with the balance made up of properties with four bedrooms or more. While housing types in the private rented sector are quite diverse Ball (2007: 14) points out that there is some geographic concentration with 48 per cent of the total stock found in London and the South East of England. There are other high concentrations of private rented properties in the major cities of Birmingham, Manchester and Leeds.

While in the commercial property investment market large corporate investors exert considerable leverage over the specification and types of buildings which developers produce, the same is less true in the residential sector. The average residential landlord will tend to be competing with owner-occupiers by purchasing second-hand stock from the housing market either through an estate agent or at auction. Investors also purchase new build properties as they roll off the volume house builders' production lines.

Stewart (2007: 9) advises that private residential landlords should try to build a picture of their ideal tenant type and then to look at the functionality of dwellings from the notional tenant's perspective. Location is therefore very important with regards to proximity to railway stations, shops and other services. Invested property should ideally be located in streets and districts where properties have been maintained and where the streetscape does not generate a sense of decline. The property should be adequately decorated, double glazed, centrally heated and easy to maintain and there should be adequate internal space standards so that the property has the widest possible appeal in the lettings market. Investors should probably avoid properties with large gardens or trees as tenants are less likely to take ownership of regular pruning and gardening duties than might an owner-occupier.

In an urban setting the criteria discussed above will often lead to the conclusion that the best investment vehicle might be a purpose built two bedroom flat with off street parking and which is within walking distance of the nearest commuter station and local shops. Even here landlords might want to avoid ground floor flats which are sometimes overexposed to street noise and, depending on the characteristics of the area, are statistically more prone to break-ins and burglary. Potential tenants will be sensitive to these issues, making letting just that little bit more challenging particularly at times when there is plenty of choice in the lettings market. Similar principles apply on resale, and most estate agents will confirm that the capital value of ground floor flats will not be as high as comparable flats on the floors above.

While some flats are commonhold, the majority are leasehold with terms of either 99 years or 125 years. Where a property investor buys a new flat and then holds it for say 10 years before selling it, there would still be a considerable unexpired term on the lease. However where a flat is purchased in the second-hand market with say 85 years remaining on the lease and the property is held for 10 years, then on resale there is a question mark against the diminished term relative to a full term which could be obtained on a new flat. This will be an obvious disincentive for most purchasers and it will have a detrimental effect on the capital value achieved on resale. The concept of a lease as a wasting asset does have some relevance in this context. While there are conditional provisions to extend the term of a residential lease, this will require legal fees and costs which a property investor would need to be aware of at the outset. Where a lease has 80 years or less, its extension will require a payment of a share of the marriage value to the landlord.

At a more prosaic management level, the owners of leasehold flats will normally have to pay an annual ground rent of perhaps £150 and a service charge of around £1,000 per annum. These outgoings will be the responsibility of the landlord and so will be a deduction from the rental income. While the budgeting issue is of course manageable (some buy-to-let financial appraisals are considered in Chapter 8) there is also some loss of control to a third-party regarding the standard of ongoing maintenance of the common areas, the timing and extent of repairs and maintenance to the external fabric of the building. There is therefore a degree of hassle involved in the purchase of leasehold flats which may be sufficient to deter less experienced residential buy-to-let investors. The latter may prefer to develop their residential property investment experience by acquiring standard freehold houses where there is more control over the timing, cost and standard of repairs and maintenance.

As Wilcox (2007: 25) explains tenants in the private rented sector are relatively youthful and more mobile than the rest of the population and there is thus a higher churn rate in the sector than for other housing tenures. From a landlord's perspective this necessitates periodic marketing and reletting of properties. Thus a property that is well located and can be relet fairly quickly will provide more continuity of income in comparison to a property which is not very well located and has a number of other snags which put off potential tenants. Residential property investors should therefore be focused in their property acquisitions by identifying a particular tenant market and the type of property that could easily be let in that market. Stewart (2007: 27) advises that investors should identify particular streets on the basis of a visual survey. Once the strategy has been decided upon, investors should resist being pulled offline by an estate agent trying to promote a property which might appear to be a bargain but which did not conform to the strategy. The residential investment market is not a place for impulse buys and if the desired property type is not available on the market at a particular time, then it is better to wait than to compromise on the investment strategy.

Code for Sustainable Homes

Beyond a cursory examination of a property's Energy Performance Certificate, private landlords and indeed most home purchasers do not put the issue of sustainability at the top of their housing search agenda. They will however look at the basic qualities of a property to establish whether it is properly insulated, has double glazing and a central heating system. Where any or all of these are missing, then purchasers might subjectively put aside a budget for improvements or seek to negotiate a reduction in the asking price to compensate for the absence of what are now seen as reasonable expectations in a dwelling.

A growing minority of home owners are installing renewable energy, often in the form of roof mounted solar panels with some financial support from the government on condition that an approved installer is used. Thus the issue of housing sustainability is gradually gaining momentum in the housing market and in the background there is a direction of travel towards higher standards of sustainability in the new housing development. Regarding the latter, the government's ultimate ambition is set out in the Code for Sustainable Homes which anticipates that by 2016 all new homes will be zero carbon.

While the new housing produced each year only represents a tiny proportion of the existing stock of dwellings, year on year the presence of an increasing number properties which have higher environmental standards and lower energy requirements (and lower heating bills) will gradually influence the housing market. Owners of existing properties will thus find it a little harder to sell or let a property which is not 'keeping up with the Joneses' in terms of adequate sound and thermal insulation, double glazing and an energy efficient hot water and heating system. There is probably a long way to go before the sustainability of a home begins to rank anywhere near as high as location and price in a purchaser's decision-making hierarchy. However the following summary is provided to illustrate where the sustainability journey has reached and how it might ultimately begin to impact upon the investment activity of the private residential landlord.

The Code for Sustainable Homes was introduced in 2007 and is the recognized standard for establishing the sustainability of housing projects. To date, the Code has had most impact in the affordable housing sector where the government requires developing social landlords to build to ever increasing Code levels if they wish to receive grant support for projects.

The Code, which replaced the EcoHomes scheme, was initially a voluntary rating system; however it was made mandatory in 2008 so that all new housing must be rated against the Code. Privately developed housing does not currently (2010) have to achieve a specific level in the Code and thus the rating could be zero for the least sustainable private housing developments. The point of requiring new housing to record a Code level is that it tells potential purchasers something about how sustainable (or unsustainable) a new dwelling is. The government (Communities 2009b) acknowledges that the Code is as much about a learning curve and establishing a direction of travel towards zero carbon housing by 2016. It is acknowledged that the Code will be periodically updated as understanding develops around how to build a cost efficient sustainable home.

Trained independent assessors use the Code to measure the sustainability of a new home as a complete package against the following design categories:

- energy and CO_2 emissions;
- water;
- materials;
- surface water run-off;
- waste;
- pollution;
- health and well-being;
- management; and
- ecology.

A Code assessor uses 'stars' to communicate the overall sustainability perform-ance of a home. The award of 1 star: ★ signifies entry level which is 10 per cent better that the Building Regulations while the award of 6 stars: ★★★★★★ is the highest Code level and which is deemed to be a zero carbon home.

There are as yet no proposals to enforce the Code retrospectively against the existing stock of dwellings and thus advances made in case study schemes (Communities 2009c) are more about leading by example. For the average buy-to-let investor the presence of the Code does not at present have an impact beyond signifying that the environmental performance of housing is set to improve gradually and that in time the resale value of less sustainable stock will be affected.

4.10 Summary

This chapter has examined the characteristics of properties in the three main sub-sectors in the commercial property market which have attracted large-scale invest-ment and which are retail, offices and industrial. It was noted that the term 'industrial' also subsumes within it a sizeable investment market in storage and distribution warehouses. There was some commentary on leisure property but this was mainly to distinguish it from the main property investment markets and to signpost the fact that more in-depth and specialized texts would need to be exam-ined to do justice to this sub-sector. The chapter has also considered the qualities of different types of residential properties from an investment perspective.

One of the themes in the chapter concerned the need for arms length special-ist legal advice, particularly when considering the purchase of commercial prop-erty. There may be legal or planning restrictions on the use of property which may not be immediately apparent but which may significantly affect the value of a property asset when reletting and resale is contemplated.

Another issue discussed in the chapter was the growing awareness of sustain-ability. In the commercial property sector the 'green badge' that is increasingly sought by corporate property investors is a BREEAM rating. There is some evidence from the United States that green buildings which have a recognized certification will attract a marginal rental and capital value premium. In the resi-dential sector sustainability is firmly established for new affordable housing development supported by public money, which will normally be require to meet a specific level in the Code for Sustainable Homes. However beyond that controlled environment progress towards sustainability in the wider housing market is patchy and it is unlikely at present that the average buy-to-let investor will place sustainability very high on their purchasing agenda. However what might be said is that progress towards the development of genuinely sustainable property in the residential and commercial sector is likely to gain momentum. Investors will need to keep a watching brief on the gradually improving standards of new property and to review whether the costs of retro-fitting property to improve sustainability might be worthwhile in terms of enhancing quality and therefore the value of their investments.

References

Baiche, B. and Walliman, N. (eds) (2000) *Neufert Architects' Data*, 3rd edn (Oxford: Blackwell).

Ball, M. (2007) *Large-scale Investor Opportunities in Residential Property: An Overview* (London: Investment Property Forum).

British Council for Offices (2009) *Guide to Specification* (London: British Council for Offices).

Crocker, S. (2008) 'Public Houses', in Hayward, R. (ed.), *Valuation Principles into Practice*, 6th edn (London: EG Books).

Department for Communities (2009a) *Planning Policy Statement 4: Planning for Sustainable Economic Growth* (London: Stationery Office). Available in e-format at: www.communities.gov.uk

Department for Communities (2009b) *Sustainable New Homes – The Road to Zero Carbon* (London: The Stationery Office). Available in e-format at: www.communities.gov.uk

Department for Communities (2009c) *The Code for Sustainable Homes – Case Studies* (London: Department for Communities and Local Government). Available in e-format at: www.communities.gov.uk

Dixon, T., Thompson, B., McAllister, P., Marston, A. and Snow, J. (2005) *Real Estate and the New Economy: The Impact of Information and Communications Technology* (Oxford: Blackwell).

Drury, J. and Brebner, I. (2007) 'Industrial facilities', in Littlefield, D. (ed.), *Metric Handbook: Planning and Design Data*, 3rd edn (Oxford: Architectural Press).

Eichholtz, P., Kok, N. and Quigley, J. M. (2009) *Doing Well by Doing Good? An Analysis of the Financial Performance of Green Office Buildings in the USA* (London: RICS).

Gimmy, A. E. and Johnson, B. A. (2003) *Analysis and Valuation of Golf Courses and Country Clubs* (Illinois: Appraisal Institute).

Gunne-Jones, A. (2009) *Town Planning: A Practical Guide* (London: RICS).

Harper, D. (2008) *Valuation of Hotels for Investors* (London: EG Books).

Havard, T. (2008) *Contemporary Property Development*, 2nd edn (London: RIBA Publishing).

Isaac, D., O'Leary, J. and Daley, M. (2010) *Property Development, Appraisal and Finance*, 2nd edn (Basingstoke: Palgrave Macmillan).

Lawson, F. (2007) 'Retail shops and stores', in Littlefield, D. (ed.), *Metric Handbook: Planning and Design Data*, 3rd edn (Oxford: Architectural Press).

London Borough of Greenwich (2006) *Unitary Development Plan* (London: Greenwich Council). Available in e-format at: www.greenwich.gov.uk

Ratcliffe, J., Stubbs, M. and Keeping, M. (2009) *Urban Planning and Real Estate Development*, 3rd edn (Abingdon: Routledge).

Stewart, M. (2007) *The New Landlord's Guide to Letting*, 4th edn (Oxford: How To Books).

Wilcox, S. (2008) *UK Housing Review 2008/2009* (Coventry: Chartered Institute of Housing; London: Building Societies Association).

5

Property appraisal techniques

Aims

This chapter aims to summarize the valuation toolkit available to property valuers before focusing on the traditional and modern methods of investment valuation. The chapter explains where the search for more robust and explicit methods of valuation has led in terms of discounted cash flow approaches. The chapter also explores how valuation formulas are used in different circumstances and it attempts to explain why there can be differences between the market value placed on a property by a valuer and the worth attributed to it by a specific investor.

Key terms

>> **Implicit method** – a way of describing the traditional method of investment valuation in which a valuer selects an all risks yield in order to capitalize an income. The yield adopted is said to imply future rental and capital growth.

>> **Explicit method** – a way of describing methods of investment valuation which lay out future income and expenditure and any growth likely to occur in those elements over time. The approach does not guarantee that the future will conform to the assumptions made but it does enable a critique of the data in a way that is not possible with the traditional method.

>> **Worth and investment value** – the RICS Red Book explains that this is a particular type of valuation which explicitly takes into account the specific criteria of the organization or individual requesting the valuation. For example the valuer would take account the client's specific target rate of return when valuing an asset so that the client was clear about what the asset

was worth on those criteria. Sometimes the evaluation of worth to a specific client will accord with market value and sometimes it will not, depending upon the client's specific requirements.

>> **Market rent** – is the term that should really be used when valuers or writers refer to *rack rent* or *estimated rental value* (ERV). A summary of the RICS *Red Book* definition of market rent is the estimated amount for which a property could be let to a willing lessor by a willing lessee after proper marketing had taken place and that both parties had acted prudently.

>> **Net rent** – the sum which the landlord receives after allowance has been made for any outgoings for insurance or repairs which are the responsibility of the landlord. Where a full repairing and insuring lease is in place those outgoings will be the responsibility of the tenant and so the rent received by the landlord is deemed to the be the net rent for valuation purposes.

5.1 Introduction

This chapter begins by looking at the various methods available to valuers when they are faced with the challenge of putting a value on a property asset. The circumstances and purpose of the valuation will have a bearing upon which method is used by a valuer. Given that this book is about property investment there will naturally be more consideration of the investment method of valuation, although even that method relies upon the comparative method for the calibration of variables which feed into the valuation.

It will be seen that there are in fact two types of investment method. The first is the so called *traditional method* which relies on a valuer's judgement to select an appropriate all risks yield, which is then used to capitalize a rental income to arrive at a capital value. The traditional method has supporters on the grounds that it is straightforward. However the traditional method has also attracted criticism because the growth implied in the yield adopted by the valuer is a little mysterious and that a more explicit or transparent method such as discounted cash flow is felt to be a superior 'modern method'.

The chapter includes a brief summary of Parry's Valuation Tables as they form part of the property valuer's toolkit. There are also worked examples to illustrate the principles of both the traditional and discounted cash flow approaches to determining the capital values of investment properties. This chapter therefore sets out some basic valuation principles and the chapter which follows looks in more depth at the techniques introduced here.

5.2 Property valuation methods

There are said to be five methods of valuation available to valuers of real property and these are:

1 the comparison method;
2 the investment method;
3 the residual method;
4 the profits method; and
5 the contractor's method.

The professional body which represents and regulates valuers in the UK is the RICS and it confirms that valuers must use their experience and professional judgement to decide on which method of valuation to use in which particular set of circumstances. A golfing analogy applies in that the golfer must choose the most appropriate club for the particular shot required.

It is not the central aim of this book to systematically assess the advantages and disadvantages of each valuation method; however it is relevant at this point to provide a brief summary of each method so that a distinction and focus can be made on those methods which are most relevant to the property investor. Those readers who are interested to learn more about all five methods could examine specialist books on the subject such as Scarrett (2008) or Blackledge (2009).

The comparison method of valuation

As the name implies this method compares the capital values and rents of commercial properties which have recently been sold or let with the subject property, in order to try to determine its capital or rental value. The comparison method of course applies equally to the residential property market, where buy-to-let investors or those looking for a home will consult estate agent's property particulars and then negotiate in the light of the values recently achieved for the sale or letting of similar dwellings in a locality.

The comparison method is the simplest of the valuation methods but it does require adjustments to be made by the valuer as no two properties are exactly the same. For example even within the same block of flats, the value of two flats can vary enormously despite the fact that they may be in similar decorative condition and have identical floor areas and number of bedrooms. The value differential and the judgement made about its magnitude could simply arise because one of the flats is on the ground floor while the other is on the fifth floor and benefits from views and distance from a noisy street environment. Similarly no two commercial properties are exactly the same and so the recent sale or letting of one property can only be a guide to the value of the next similar property to become available on the market.

Whenever the courts have considered disputes involving property valuations, the maxim 'simplest first' has usually emerged which suggests that wherever possible, direct comparison is the preferred method of valuation. The RICS takes a more conditional position in recognition of the fact that the comparison approach has limitations particularly when the variation in property types begins to widen and comparable data becomes scarce. For example, where land for development is being valued, the RICS (2008) acknowledge that comparison may have a role to play. This could arise for example in a rural context where there are similar development and infrastructure costs and where development density will be very similar. Thus the recent sale of a 1 hectare site which has planning consent for housing at 50 units per hectare on the edge of a large rural town, will provide a good indication for the value, on a hectare for hectare basis, of other sites nearby with similar planning consents. However the RICS advise that:

> Generally, high density or complex developments, urban sites and existing buildings with development potential, do not easily lend themselves to

valuation by comparison. The differences from site to site (for example in terms of development potential or construction cost) may be sufficient to make the analysis of transactions problematical. The higher the number of variables and adjustments for assumptions the less useful the comparison. (2008: 7)

While comparison has its limits and may legitimately be rejected as the principle method of valuation in some situations, comparison will continue to play a role in calibrating the variables which feed into the chosen method. This will become more apparent over the next three chapters where those valuation methods which have most relevance to property investment will be discussed and illustrated.

The investment method of valuation

Given the subject of this book this method of valuation will be discussed later in the chapter as it is fundamentally about valuing capital investment in property. In fact the investment method subdivides into traditional and discounted cash flow approaches. The traditional approach has already been touched upon in Chapter 1, however as a reminder, it is a form of valuation which uses the years' purchase (which is the reciprocal of the yield) as a multiplier to capitalize rental income. The discounted cash flow approach to the investment method of valuing is sometimes referred to as a 'modern method' or an 'explicit method' because it lays out all assumptions about future income and costs and discounts them back to a capital value. As this approach is central to property investment, a number of worked examples are included in this chapter so that the versatility and potential of this method can be fully understood.

The residual method of valuation

The residual method is used in development situations and is based on a calculation of value less cost and profit to provide a residual capital sum which is available to purchase the land. The residual method can also be adapted to isolate the profit where the land cost and other construction related costs are already known. This method does have some relevance to particularly large corporate property investors as they sometimes instigate the development process in order to create a real estate asset which meets their particular investment specification. Although not considered further in this chapter, there will be worked examples of the residual valuation method in Chapter 7 where the topic is revisited.

The profits method

The profits method works on the assumption that the value of a property is based on the profit produced by the business occupying the premises. This method is used to value specialized properties such as hotels, pubs, cinemas or casinos. Inspection and interpretation of the accounts arising from these businesses over a period of say three years is an important element in this valuation process. One of the distinguishing features of these types of property is that they may benefit from a licence which enables them to attract a particular clientele or market and therefore a degree of monopoly is enjoyed in the particular location. Thus it is not possible to value these properties accurately by comparison.

The contractor's method

The contractors approach is more formally referred to by the RICS (2010) in the Red Book and in Valuation Information Papers (2007) as the *Depreciated Replacement Cost* (DRC) method of valuation. However some authors still prefer to refer to this method as either the contractor's method or the contractor's test and the terms are used interchangeably in this book. The method is based on the cost of construction and as the RICS confirms:

> DRC is only to be used where there is no active market for the asset being valued: that is where there is no useful or relevant evidence of recent sales transactions due to the specialised nature of the asset. (2007: 3)

Thus the contractors method is used where there is no market in the type of property being valued and nor are there business accounts which are specific to the premises to inspect. For example, a pumping station owned by a water company may require a valuation, however these types of property are seldom if ever the subject of market transactions and they do not easily fit in to the other valuation scenarios described above. The valuer thus has to break down the asset and might begin by trying to assess the depreciated value of the building on the site with a further adjustment to allow for any obsolescence. This is not an easy task, particularly if, for example, the pumping station was Victorian but was still in perfectly good working order. When that task is resolved the valuer adds in the land value by trying to deduce what a similar plot of land might cost in the event that an identical pumping station needed to be built. Because of the number of assumptions and judgements required to weight variables to generate a valuation, this is perhaps the valuation method of last resort. However because expensive assets such as buildings do depreciate valuers sometimes have to try to reflect that loss of value when valuing property assets held by public or private sector clients. The topic of how to assess depreciation will be revisited in Chapter 7 where specialized valuation related topics are discussed.

Having briefly summarized the five methods of valuation, it is apparent that they have different bases as shown in Table 5.1.

Table 5.1 The bases for valuation methods

Valuations based on sales or rental values	*Valuations based on construction costs*	*Valuations based on the profitability of the business*
Applicable methods: Comparison method Investment method Residual method	*Applicable method:* Contractors method	*Applicable method:* Profits method

Of the five methods of valuation considered above it is probably evident by now that the profits method and contractors method are somewhat specialized and are perhaps less relevant to the concerns of this book. Little more will therefore be said about those methods and the emphasis going forward in this chapter will be upon the investment method and how it is relies upon the comparison method for market evidence on rents and yields. The residual method will be revisited in Chapter 7, as it deals with development which could be seen as an applied form of investment. After all, large corporate investors will engage in commercial property development so that investment grade buildings which precisely meet their investment requirements are produced.

5.3 The traditional investment method

It was suggested earlier that the investment method subdivides into traditional and modern approaches and thus the traditional approach is considered here first while the later part of the chapter looks at modern or explicit approaches which use discounted cash flows.

Whether a modern or traditional approach is taken to an investment valuation, there are some preliminary common factors which need to be considered. First, even in owner-occupied property, a notional rent is assumed to be passing, thus a rental value is still assumed even if it is not actually passing. Second, the market rent is the variable that is used and while it is sometimes referred to as the rack rent or the estimated rental value (ERV) the term *market rent* is really the correct term, a definition of which is provided in the RICS's *Red Book* as follows:

> The estimated amount for which a property, or space within a property, should lease (let) on the date of valuation between a willing lessor and a willing lessee on appropriate lease terms in an arm's-length transaction after proper marketing wherein the parties had acted knowledgeably, prudently and without compulsion. Whenever Market Rent is provided the 'appropriate lease terms' which it reflects should also be stated. (2010: 50)

The lease terms are an important consideration because, for example, if the tenant is responsible for all repairs and insurance then the rent will be less than if the landlord is responsible for those outgoings. The usual situation is that the tenant enters into a lease under which they have an obligation arising under the covenants in the lease to pay for repairs and insurance. So the tenant in that case would meet all outgoings and this is called a fully repairing and insuring (FRI) lease. The landlord therefore does not have any outgoings and the market rent on FRI terms is therefore strictly the *net* market rent.

The comparison method provides the market rent and the investment method converts that income into a capital sum as follows:

Income × years' purchase (YP) = capital value

The above arrangement can be transposed to become:

Income/capital value = yield

And to complete the circle:

$$YP = capital\ value/income$$

The specific calculation used in the traditional investment method of valuation depends on whether the income is perpetual, variable or deferred. A perpetual income occurs where a freehold property is let at the market rent. For example consider a freehold shop let on FRI terms at an annual market rent of £50,000. The calculation assumes that the income is received in perpetuity and by comparison a yield of 7 per cent is felt appropriate for this asset class in the particular location. The lease would typically contain provision for rent reviews but given that a market rent is passing, the yield allows for the growth that is expected to take place at those reviews. This is one of the debatable aspects of the traditional investment method, as the yield 'implies' growth but is not explicit about it.

Net annual income	£50,000
YP in perpetuity @ 7%	14.286
Capital value	£714,300

As illustrated above the valuer needs to identify an appropriate yield from market comparison so that it can be converted into a year's purchase in order to multiply the net rent to produce a capital value. Because markets fluctuate and property is of widely different quality and represents different risks, the valuer has to exercise judgement and make adjustments when assessing comparable evidence on initial yields arising from property transactions. However as Shapiro *et al.* (2009: 96–101) suggests there are at least some parameters which valuers can use as a guide.

	Suggested yields
Houses, ordinary quality:	10% to 15%
Houses, good quality:	5% to 10%
Flats, ordinary quality:	8% to 10%
Factories/warehouses:	8% to 15%
Offices:	6% to 12%
Shops:	4% to 6% for prime, going out to 15% for secondary.
Ground rents:	6% to 15%

Letting terms

A summary of the financial terms arising from an FRI lease might look as follows.

Annual rent:	£100,000
Annual internal and external repairs allowance @ 15% of annual rent:	£15,000
Annual insurance @ 2.5% of annual rent:	£2,500
Tenant's annual outgoings under the lease:	£117,500

From the tenant's property outgoings of £117,500 the landlord receives £100,000. Other outgoings are business rates, water rates and other bills for which the tenant is usually responsible except in multiple letting situations where the landlord pays and recovers costs from the tenants through an apportionment.

The figures below assume that the lease terms are now internal repairing only, so the landlord has now become responsible for external repairs and insurance and the management of these responsibilities. To put the landlord back in the position under FRI terms above the rent would have to increase, as now the landlord has some outgoings and management responsibilities to contend with.

Net annual rent:	£100,000
Landlord now paying for external repairs @ 10% of annual net rent:	£10,000
Landlord now paying for insurance @ 2.5% of annual net rent:	£2,500
Management fee @ 10% of rent, repairs and insurance:	£11,250
Expected gross annual rent therefore:	£123,750

Thus in the internal repairing lease scenario the investor/landlord will collect an annual gross rent of £123,750 but will pay out management fees, insurance and repairs costs amounting to 23,750 leaving a net rent of £100,000. Thus the landlord is no better or worse off than if an FRI lease existed.

Rental value

At regular stages during a commercial property lease, the rent will be reviewed. Commercial leases and their review periods have been shortening in recent years, although 20-year leases containing provision for five-year rent reviews are still committed to by some business tenants. The situation in the residential buy-to-let sector is entirely different, as there are short-hold tenancies of six months or one year which normally form the basis of the landlord and tenant relationship. The rent in that situation is normally revised at the expiration of these shorter leases.

When rent reviews occur under commercial property leases the rental value is determined by comparison. The unit of comparison for most commercial properties is per square metre of net lettable floorspace, although very unusually for shops it could be per metre frontage. In the rent review process the net rental value is used after deductions have been made for any outgoings under the lease as described in the example above. Thus, rent less outgoings equals net income.

Repairs

Most commercial landlords will try to negotiate an FRI lease under which the tenant will be responsible for the annual repairs and insurance. If the landlord is responsible, this is usually limited to structural or external repairs. A detailed repairs estimate could be worked up however valuers become familiar with the

Table 5.2 Standard allowances for repairs to commercial properties

Property type	External repairs costs as a % of rent	Internal repairs costs as a % of rent
Offices and commercial	10	5
Shops	5	5
Residential	30	10

tone of repairs costs from building to building and so can normally gauge repairs costs at a percentage of the rent as shown above in Table 5.2.

Insurance

Properties will require fire insurance which is based on the reinstatement costs which are calculated by multiplying the area of the building by the cost of construction per m^2. The annual insurance premium payable approximates to 2.5 per cent of the rent.

Business rates

These are usually the liability of the tenant and landlords only become liable when the building is un-let. Thus one of the incentives for a landlord to offer a rent free period to entice a tenant to take a lease on a building in a difficult lettings market, is that a tenant in occupation will normally be liable for the business rates. In general terms business rates are a product of the assessed rateable value of the property multiplied by the tax rate. For large commercial buildings this can be a considerable bill and it is not surprising therefore, that firms of chartered surveyors employ rating specialists who on behalf of clients can assess and if necessary challenge the rateable value assigned to commercial properties.

Management charges

These occur when there is a need to set up a system for rent collection and to check that the tenant is in occupation and abiding by the terms of the lease. If a net income is being received by the landlord under an FRI lease, a deduction for management is not always necessary. Where a management fee is to be levied, it is normally benchmarked at 10 per cent of the rack rent but this may be reduced for properties which are easy to manage.

Having considered some of the typical outgoings related to lease terms and how market rents are capitalized it is worth at this point examining some traditional investment valuation examples to consolidate the principles discussed so far

Example 5.1: A traditional investment valuation

Value the freehold interest in a vacant office unit on a business park which has 2,000 m^2 of net lettable floorspace, assuming a yield of 7.5 per cent and a lease on FRI terms. Nearby on the business park, a unit with 3,000 m² of net lettable space and with a similar specification to the subject property, has just been let at an annual rent of £450,000 on internal repairing terms. For that unit therefore the landlord is responsible for external repairs and insurance.

A valuer would probably take a number of steps as follows:

Step 1: given that capital value equals net income multiplied by the YP, the valuer would use the known yield for this type of investment to generate the YP which is 1/yield.

Step 2: the net income is required but as the office unit is not let, some analysis of the letting of the office unit nearby is required.

Step 3: the analysis of the letting of the comparable property will need to establish the rent per m² on an FRI basis, which is the net income.

Step 4: complete valuation.

So, step 1 is simply 1/0.075 = YP 13.333

Steps 2 and 3 require the analysis of the comparable as follows:

Gross annual rent received:		£450,000
Less:		
External repairs @ 10% of rent:	£45,000	
Insurance @ 2.5% of rent:	£11,250	
Management fee @ 5% of rent:	£22,500	
Total outgoings:	£78,750	
Net annual rent:		£371,250
Net income per m² therefore: £371,250/3,000 =		£123.75

Step 4 is the valuation of the subject property as follows:

Net income per m² £123.75 × floorspace of 2,000 m²:	247,500
YP in perpetuity @ 7.5%:	13.333
Capital value:	£3,299,918
Rounded up to:	£3,300,000

If however the comparable property had subsequently been sold for £5,303,678 to a property investor after a proper period of marketing then this would cause the valuer to rethink the approach on the subject property as follows:

Net income on comparable:	£371,250
YP in perpetuity:	X
Capital value of comparable:	£5,303,678

YP (X) = £5,303,678/£371,250 = 14.286

Yield = 1/14.286 = 7% (rounded up)

The valuation on the subject property would then be redone at a 7% yield.

5.4 The valuation tables

The examples and discussion so far in the chapter have included the present value of £1 per annum which is more commonly known as the years' purchase in perpetuity (abbreviated to YP in perp.) the

$$\text{formula for which is: } \frac{1}{i}$$

The formula applies to incomes assumed to be receivable in perpetuity from freehold properties let at market rent. The situation is not always that straightforward and investors sometimes wish to know the value of incomes which will be received for shorter periods. In those circumstances a YP formula for a given term is used which is as follows:

$$\text{YP for } n \text{ years} = \frac{1 - (1 + i)^{-n}}{i}$$

To overcome the problem of repetition when calculating this and other valuation formulas to accommodate different interest rates and terms *Parry's Valuation and Investment Tables* edited by Davidson (2002) contains tables of constants reflecting all of the likely permutations. Thus to save time and to provide a check against the possibility of errors in calculations, Parry's Tables are often referred to by valuers. Indeed Parry's Tables contains not only a whole range of constants but also conversion tables which are useful to those working in the various fields of property.

In order to understand the basis of the traditional investment method and the formulas used for compounding and discounting in investment calculations, there is a need to briefly consider the tables which underpin the appraisals. The essence of investment appraisal is the consideration of the purchase of an asset which promises to generate an income stream over a period of time and then to convert the value of the income stream in the future to an equivalent capital sum in the present. *Parry's Tables* deals with the process of discounting these sums to present value and for example, the Amount of £1 table will add compound interest to an initial sum to give a future capital sum. The six main options of conversion in Parry's Tables are:

- Capital to income and vice-versa.
- Present sums to future sums and vice-versa.
- The compounding of sums into the future, and discounting them back to the present.

A summary of Parry's Valuation Tables

Amount of £1

This table provides the amount that £1 will accumulate to over *n* years at any given annual interest rate denoted by *i*. The table thus compounds up from a present capital sum and the formula which is referred to in its abbreviated form as A (for Amount of £1) = $(1 + i)^n$

Present value (PV) of £1

The present value of £1 gives the sum which needs to be invested at the interest rate i to accumulate to £1 in n years. i discounts a future capital sum to a present capital sum; it is the process of the Amount of £1 in reverse and the formula is:

$$\frac{1}{A}$$

For example the present value of the right to receive £100 in 10 years @ 10% could be found from Parry's Tables (or formula) which will give the constant for £1 which is: 0.3855. That constant would then be multiplied by the actual capital sum, which is this example is £100, to give the present value of the investment as: £38.55

Amount of £1 per annum

This is the amount to which £1 invested annually will accumulate to in n years. It is thus compounding a present income stream to a future capital sum and the formula is:

$$\frac{(A - 1)}{i}$$

Annual sinking fund (ASF) to produce £1

This is the amount which needs to be invested annually to accumulate to £1 in n years at an interest rate represented by i. It thus discounts back the future capital sum to a present income stream. This particular table enables the estimation of the sum which will need to be saved each year at a given interest rate so that it compounds into a known future sum. This facility is useful in property where a large repairs bill to say a block of offices or a managed block of flats is anticipated to surface at a later date and a sinking fund has to be established to meet the cost. For example refurbishment costs of £100,000 are estimated to arise on a property investment in 10 years' time:

Future refurbishment costs estimated at:	£100,000
ASF 10 years @ 10% from Parry's Tables (or use of formula):	0.0627
Annual sinking fund (ASF) required:	£6,270

Annuity £1 will purchase

This is the income stream that will be generated over n years by an original investment of £1. The income produced will be consumed as part capital and part interest on capital. Assuming the rates of consumption are the same, a single rate approach gives an equation:

$$\frac{i}{(1 - PV)}$$

If the rates differ, then the formula (i + s) needs to be used, where s is the annual sinking fund formula above at a different interest rate from i. This is the way a mortgage is calculated by a building society which provides the initial capital sum and expects repayments of equal amounts throughout the loan period (assuming fixed-rate money) which consist of interest and capital elements (that is, the sinking fund). The mortgage instalment tables in Parry's are therefore based upon the annuity £1 will purchase. Although amortization schedules are available in electronic form on the internet from providers of mortgage finance, it is useful to know that Parry's Tables can provide a check on the figures if required.

For example a buy-to-let investor is considering the purchase of flat as an investment property but requires a top up mortgage of £50,000 from a building society to add to existing funds to purchase the property. The investor plans to pay off the 7.5 per cent fixed-rate loan within eight years and so could check in Parry's Tables to establish what the monthly repayments would be in order to gauge whether the anticipated net monthly rental income will be sufficient to meet repayments. The mortgage instalment tables in Parry's Tables works on a lending multiple of £100 enabling this to be factored up to represent the actual sum borrowed. So for the above example of a 7.5 per cent loan over 8 years, the monthly repayments required to redeem a £100 loan would be would £1.4227. Because £50,000 is actually being borrowed, the monthly repayments would actually be 1.4227 × 500 = £711.35

Present value (PV) of £1 per annum

The present value of £1 per annum is the present value of the right to receive £1 each year over n years. The future income stream is discounted back to the

Table 5.3 A summary of the valuation tables

Option	Cash flow		Formula
	Now	Future	
Amount of £1 (A)	Capital sum	Capital Sum *Compounding* ⟶	$A = (1 + i)^n$
PV of £1 (PV)	Capital sum	Capital Sum ⟵ *Discounting*	$PV = \dfrac{1}{A}$
Amount of £1 pa	Income	Capital Sum *Compounding* ⟶	$\dfrac{A - 1}{i}$
ASF to produce £1 (ASF)	Income	Capital Sum ⟵ *Discounting*	$ASF = \dfrac{i}{A - 1}$
Annuity £1 will purchase	Capital sum	Income *Compounding* ⟶	$\dfrac{i}{(1 - PV)}$
PV of £1 pa (YP)	Capital sum	Income ⟵ *Discounting*	$YP = \dfrac{(1 - PV)}{i}$

present value and is the opposite of the annuity calculation. Thus the formulation for a single rate is $(1 - PV) / i$ or for the dual rate, $1/ (i + s)$, where s is the annual sinking fund at the sinking fund rate. This approach is commonly known as the years' purchase and gives the present value of a future stream of rental income. For instance, the present value of £100,000 receivable over 10 years with a 10 per cent rate would be as follows.

Income $\times$ YP = Capital value
£100,000 $\times$ YP for 10 years @ 10% (obtainable from Parry's tables = 6.1446)
        = capital value
£100,000 $\times$ 6.1446 = £614,460

5.5 The debate on valuation methods, price value and worth

It is perhaps not surprising that as far back as the property crash in the early 1970s, which saw sharp rises and then steep falls in property values over a relatively short time-span, that attention has been drawn to the property valuation methods being used. Like any body of professionals, valuers are naturally keen to improve the rigour of valuation methodology which in turn should improve the quality of the valuations produced for clients. There is also more awareness of the duty of care which professionals owe to their clients. A general consensus has thus arisen that the property professional should not just act as an agent during the exchange process but should also provide a view on how a property investment is likely to perform.

In parallel the large-scale property investment overseen by advisers acting for the financial institutions has seen increasing scrutiny and analysis taking place on the issues which underpin property values. Because actual returns on property investments have not always reflected target returns which influenced the price paid, there has been a degree of scepticism regarding valuation techniques and whether they are entirely fit for purpose.

As far back as 1994, the Mallinson Report carried out for the RICS on commercial property valuation, suggested that the valuer should obtain clearer instructions from the client and in return should add clarity and qualification to the valuations provided on property in company accounts. In addition, the report suggested that there should be more comment on valuation risk factors, price trends and economic factors and that discounted cash flow techniques should be used more regularly.

The observations made in the Mallinson Report helped to fuel a professional and academic debate which among other things explored differences in the *price, value and worth* of property assets. Fine distinctions were drawn between these three concepts which in essence were that:

- *Price* is an observable phenomena arising from transactions in a market, i.e. it is the actual price that one party paid another for an asset. Comparable market evidence is a series of prices paid and helps build a picture of what is happening in a market.
- *Value* is a monetary sum placed on an asset at a specific point in time by a valuer who has assessed all the relevant factors before ascribing a value which it is believed the asset would change hands for if it were sold.

- *Worth* is more of a subjective individual or corporate appraisal, in that participants in a market will have differing views on what an asset is worth to them. For example an individual or company might have their own specific target rate of return and this will influence the worth that they place on assets.

By 2010 this exercise in semantics had led the RICS to distinguish in its *Red Book* between *market value* and *worth and investment value* which the RICS define as:

The value of a property to a particular owner, investor, or class of investors for identified investment or operational objectives.

The RICS confirm that an assessment of worth could well be different from market value, as a company or individual may simply use different internal assessment criteria or target rates than are prevalent in the market. This may cause them to place a higher, lower or similar worth on an asset than is suggested by its market valuation. Valuers should clarify in their valuation reports that in arriving at an assessment of worth for a specific client they are not producing a market valuation.

5.6 Alternatives to the traditional investment method of valuation

It is probably clear from the above 'soul-searching' debate that despite the apparent simplicity of the investment method of valuation its use of an all risks yield and reliance on a valuer's judgement seem to leave a lot of questions unanswered. There has thus been a search to find more explicit and perhaps robust methods of arriving at capital values and some of the leading candidates are now considered.

Capital appraisal techniques

Appraisal techniques require clear criteria on which to measure investment opportunities. Given that investment usually involves money it is not surprising that these techniques have evolved to express their outcomes in monetary terms. There are of course other decision-making techniques such as the SWOT analysis discussed in Chapter 1 which can deal with qualitative issues, but here the focus is upon quantitative techniques which measure the performance if investment in money terms. To aid decision-making these quantitative methods should also allow comparison between alternative investment projects. In this section of the book capital appraisal techniques from the business sector are thus considered.

It was noted earlier that in the property field there are traditional and modern methods of valuation and capital appraisal techniques from the business world mirror this distinction. The traditional methods in business, however, are more basic than those in the property field. Property valuation methods discount income and costs in the future back to present value so that the time value of money is accounted for in the sense that a £1 available today is worth more than a £1 in a year's time. This is because if £1 is immediately consumed, the benefit is obtained a year earlier or that £1 now can be invested to earn interest over the year. In property valuation the traditional years' purchase approach takes into account the time value of money, whereas in business, traditional methods ignore this. The two basic approaches discussed first are the payback period method and the rate of return on investment method.

Payback period method

This method involves the calculation of the number of years that it takes to pay back the original investment in a project. The important criterion is therefore the length of the payback period implying that the shorter the period the better the project. On this basis either project A or B in Table 5.4 below could be chosen, as there are no other criteria to distinguish between them. Time in this analysis is used in a crude way as it does not take into account the precise timing of the cash flows over future years. For instance the high cash flows in the first year for projects B and C compared to A. The analysis is also silent about the strengthening cash flow in years 3 and 4 for project C leaving it with the largest overall nominal income.

The advantages of the approach lie in its simplicity, as it enables perhaps a more short term and risk averse investor to see how long competing and perhaps volatile investments are exposed to risk. However because the approach ignores what might be strengthening cash flows which occur after the payback cut-off point, a clearer picture of overall profitability is not provided.

Table 5.4 A payback comparison for three competing projects

	Project		
	A	B	C
Investment (£)	10,000	10,000	10,000
Cash Flow (£)			
Year 1	1,000	7,000	7,000
Year 2	9,000	3,000	0
Year 3	2,000	2,000	3,000
Year 4	0	0	7,000
Total cash inflow	12,000	12,000	17,000
Payback period	2 years	2 years	3 years
Ranking	Equal 1st place	Equal 1st place	3rd place

Rate of return method

This approach expresses a rate of profit as a percentage of the cost of an investment:

$$\frac{\text{Profit}}{\text{Cost}} \times 100\%$$

The cost figure is calculated by the capital employed in the project. A target rate of return is set and if the profitability exceeds this figure then the project is acceptable. This is a replica of the basic traditional all risks yield in perpetuity:

$$\frac{\text{Net income}}{\text{Capital Value}} \times 100\%$$

Note, however, that the capital value in this context is the price paid and the yield is an initial yield, this appraisal is thus a form of a market valuation rather than an analysis of the investment. In business finance the calculation can be done on various bases including profit before interest and tax (PBIT) or after tax. Profit figures can be for the first year, the maximum annual figure over the project life or the average figure over the project life. The latter is usually considered the most suitable. An allowance is usually made for any interest outstanding on debt raised by the company. The capital employed may be shown gross or as an average figure over the life of the asset with an annual deduction for depreciation. Depreciation is calculated on a straight-line basis with an equal amount of the total depreciated each year.

Assuming there is no resale or scrap value for the investment shown in Table 5.5 below, then the original £8,000 is lost at the end of the investment period and the depreciation on the investment is therefore £8,000.

Table 5.5 Rate of return method

Year 0 Investment = £8,000	Cash inflows (£)
Year 1	4,000
Year 2	6,000
Year 3	4,000
Year 4	2,000
Total cash inflow	16,000

$$\text{Average profit is:} \frac{£16,000 - £8,000}{4 \text{ years}} = £2,000$$

Return on the investment before tax and any interest payment is:

$$\frac{£2,000}{£8,000} \times 100\% = 25\%$$

The advantage of this method is that it uses the same criterion related to profitability both for projects and the overall business. The choice of target rate for a project could therefore be the same rate as the firm sets for overall profitability. The disadvantage of using this method is that it again ignores the time value of money. The use of a straight-line approach to depreciation may not realistically reflect the actual decline in the value of an asset.

In answer to the deficiencies of the traditional approaches in respect of their inability to take into account the time value of money, business has adopted the discounted cash flow techniques outlined in the following section.

5.7 Discounted cash flow techniques

Discounted cash flow (DCF) techniques have become an important tool in the evaluation of business and property investment opportunities largely because analysts found the traditional approach of surveyors to be unacceptable on its own. A DCF approach is versatile because it can accommodate varying costs and revenues over different time periods such as, yearly, quarterly or monthly. Another key advantage of the DCF technique is that it recognizes the time value of money by adopting a discount rate which enables appraisers to assess the overall profitability of a project. DCF therefore has the potential to be a more accurate evaluation technique than those approaches which use the traditional methods of payback period and return on investment. However like other evaluation methods, a DCF analysis is only as good as the data that are put into the calculation.

The evaluation of any capital investment opportunity poses two difficulties. First, costs and revenues arise at different times and this means that they are not directly comparable. This problem is handled by discounted cash flow analysis. The second problem is that the future is uncertain and that forecasted cash flows may not arise as predicted. The DCF approach cannot solve the problem of future uncertainty but it does at least make explicit expectations regarding the quantity and timing of future cash flows.

A DCF appraisal does provide a clear accept/reject decision for a project and this works well when there is only one project being considered in isolation. In reality, projects will face competition arising from the fact that investors will seldom have sufficient funds to accept all projects indicated as acceptable under the analysis. This is a problem of capital rationing and reflects an inevitable restriction of choice when resources are limited. The second problem is where two competing projects fulfil the same objective and only one is required. These problems can be analysed by DCF which is capable of generating outcomes in terms of a net present value (NPV) and internal rate of return (IRR) (considered below). This analysis concerns individual projects but it may also be necessary to consider investment opportunities as part of a portfolio of investments and this is dealt with later in the book.

As stated above, the DCF technique is based on calculating the present worth of anticipated income or expenditure. This technique is not unknown to valuers who are familiar with using present value of £1 and present value of £1 per annum from *Parry's Tables*. Indeed the traditional investment method estimates the present value of future periodic incomes and therefore in many senses DCF could be thought of as just a more explicit version of what valuers have been doing for years.

The arguments for using DCF approaches in place of the traditional years' purchase investment method are however convincing. It is true that the traditional and DCF methods both arrive at the net present value of an investment; however, the important difference lies in the processes involved and in the greater versatility of DCF in being able to model changes in variables at different points in time. A DCF approach also appears to be a logical way of dealing with over-rented property where existing contractual rents under a lease which have been agreed in the past are now higher than those generally evident in the market for equivalent properties. It is also difficult to defend the use of the traditional capitalization technique in recessionary markets when there are lengthy rent free periods, reverse premiums and other tenant incentives which give rise to uneven income streams over the short, medium or long term.

To produce a DCF, the valuer has at least three forms of discount rate to choose from:

- The rate which has to be paid for borrowing capital – the borrowing rate.
- The rate which could be earned if the capital was invested elsewhere – the opportunity rate.
- The rate of return which the investor requires to compensate for the risk involved, the loss of immediate consumption and inflation – the target rate.

In investment appraisal and analysis it is the target rate which is most commonly used and it is sometimes referred to as the 'hurdle rate', i.e. the investment has to jump over this corporately imposed rate.

DCF to net present value (NPV)

This form of DCF produces a capital sum: the net present value (NPV) which may be positive or negative. Where the NPV is a positive sum then the investment has met and exceeded its target rate. Conversely where the NPV is negative the investment has not met its target rate.

For single sums receivable in the future, the present value of £1 Table can be used, or it can be calculated by using the formula:

$$\frac{1}{(1 + i)^n}$$

This is the inverse of the Amount of £1, or compound interest formula discussed earlier.

Where the same amount is being received or spent for a series of years, then the present value of £1 per annum can be used. The latter is more familiarly known as the years' purchase (YP) and it is simply the sum of a series of individual present values. For example, an investor who required an 8 per cent return and was wondering what should be paid for the right to receive £1 per annum for 4 years could work out the present value of each of the 4 years and add them together to discover that the present value was £3.31 (rounded up) as shown below.

PV £1	1 year	@ 8%	0.9259
PV £1	2 years	@ 8%	0.8573
PV £1	3 years	@ 8%	0.7938
PV £1	4 years	@ 8%	0.7350
YP 4 years		@ 8%	= 3.3120

Alternatively the investor could avoid four calculations and use the YP formula to achieve the same answer as follows:

$$\text{YP for } n \text{ years} = \frac{1 - (1 + i)^{-n}}{i}$$

$$= \frac{1 - (1 + 0.08)^{-4}}{0.08} = 3.312$$

Of course the investor would not bother with the calculation for such trifling sums but the point is that once the concept is understood for £1 it can be multiplied for whatever constant sum is actually offered. For example the actual annual sum available may have been £75,000 reflecting the rent passing under the remaining four years of a lease. Thus the investor would take the above answer of 3.3120 and multiply it by 75,000 to discover that no more than £248,400 should be paid for this investment in order to preserve an 8 per cent return.

However DCF really comes into its own when the flows of income and expenditure over time are irregular as the following example illustrates.

The NPV of a project whose purchase price is £10,000 is sought relative to the projected cash flows set out below. Assuming a discount rate of 10 per cent the NPV can be calculated using a DCF as follows in Table 5.6.

Table 5.6 DCF to evaluate varying income to NPV

Year	Cash flow (£)	PV £1 @ 10%	Present value (£)
1	2,000	0.9091	1,818
2	5,000	0.8264	4,132
3	4,000	0.7513	3,005
4	2,000	0.6830	1,366
			10,321
		Less outlay	10,000
		NPV =	321

Some interim points on DCF can be made at this stage of the discussion. The first point is that because the future cash flows are set out explicitly, they are sometimes taken too literally in that it can become too easy to assume that there is no risk. Of course this is not the case as the cash flows are best estimates of what will happen. Should the decision-maker decide to investigate an investment in a little more depth, then some modelling of best-case and worst-case scenarios around future cash flows would always be prudent.

A DCF presentation is usually presented gross of tax because individuals and organizations have different tax status, although it is quite possible to model net of tax if required. As discussed earlier the discount rate is a target rate, so if the NPV is positive, the target rate has been reached and the anticipated profit is therefore made. The target rate may be based on the cost of borrowing, the rate of return on other projects or it may be benchmarked against the prevailing rate obtainable on government stock. However, some organizations will have in-house periodically reviewed target rates so that they will not invest in assets unless it can be demonstrated that they will earn a minimum rate of X%.

If there are a number of competing investment opportunities the one with the highest NPV is normally chosen by the rational investor assuming the capital outlay on these competing projects is in the same ball park. If the capital outlay differs then the deciding factor might be to look at the benefit: cost ratio which can be found by dividing the discounted PV of total benefits by the discounted PV of total costs. The project with the highest ratio is then chosen.

In Table 5.7 below, an investment is purchased for £20,000 on the basis that it is expected to generate the following incomes: year 1, £3,000; year 2, £5,000; year 3, £6,000; year 4, £3,000; year 5, £6,500; year 6, £5,750; year 7, £3,000. In year 4, £1,000 of maintenance costs will arise and at the end of year 7 the asset will be disposed of for £1,500, so that the total income for that year becomes £4,500. If the investor's target rate were 10 per cent per annum, the discounted cash flow would look as follows.

Table 5.7 DCF to NPV which evaluates varying income and expenditure

Year	Expenditure (£)	Income (£)	Net cash flow	Present value of £1 @ 10%	Discounted cash flow (£)
0	20,000	0	−20,000	1	− 20,000
1	0	3,000	3,000	0.9091	2,727
2	0	5,000	5,000	0.8264	4,132
3	0	6,000	6,000	0.7513	4,508
4	1,000	3,000	2,000	0.6830	1,366
5	0	6,500	6,500	0.6209	4,036
6	0	5,750	5,750	0.5645	3,246
7	0	4,500	4,500	0.5132	2,309
			Net present value @ 10% =		**2,324**

The DCF appraisal generates a positive NPV and this signifies that the purchase of the asset would be worthwhile as it earns the 10 per cent target rate and in addition a 'bonus' of £2,324 which can be added to profit.

To consolidate the discussion so far, the discount rate adopted can be: (a) the borrowing rate; (b) the opportunity rate; or (c) the target rate. Whichever form of rate is used, when a positive NPV is obtained then the project will have met the investor's expectations. The out-turn figures are very helpful in clarifying the likely financial performance of an investment however in themselves the figures do not make the decision, as there will always be other factors to consider such as the quality, availability and likely performance of other investment opportunities.

DCF to internal rate of return (IRR)

NPV is most frequently used in investment appraisal for acquisition purposes, but it can also be used for analysis on a trial-and-error basis. Analysts will also be interested in the actual return on capital to be obtained from an investment. This is the rate generated internally from the income and expenditure incurred, and therefore it is known as the internal rate of return (IRR). It is the discount rate at which the NPV of income equals the NPV of expenditure, or in other words the rate which produces a nil NPV.

In the DCF example above, the target rate was 10 per cent and the positive NPV signified that the asset was generating returns above that target rate. A negative NPV would have indicated that the target rate would not be achieved. An analogy could be made with raising the bar in a high-jump competition, because as successively higher target rates are used to test the same pattern of income and expenditure there will come a point when the NPV turns negative (the bar has not been cleared). Thus the higher the target rate set, the more stringent the test of the investment.

There is an IRR function in Microsoft Excel which makes the evaluation of cash flows in spreadsheets very easy and rapid. However for those who prefer conventional methods and to fully understand what they are doing the IRR can be calculated using a formula provided below or from Parry's Tables. Mathematicians will also confirm that the IRR can be calculated using a graph but for those working in a property investment context this is unlikely to be a practical option. For those who do prefer to work through a formula there is a requirement to select two discount rates. This requires a little judgement to select a trial rate which will generate a positive NPV and another which will generate a negative NPV. The formula then enables interpolation between the two trials rates to identify the IRR. The following example in Table 5.8 illustrates the principle by using the expenditure and income characteristics of the asset in Table 5.7 above.

As the NPV value generated at the lower trial rate of 10 per cent is positive and at the higher trial rate of 14 per cent it is negative, the IRR (which is the rate at which NPV is zero) will lie somewhere between 10 and 14 per cent. The IRR can be calculated by interpolation using the following formula:

$$ R_1 + \left[(R_2 - R_1) \times \frac{NPV\ R_1}{NPV\ R_1 - NPV\ R_2} \right] $$

Where R_1 is the lower trial rate (10 per cent in the above example) and R_2 is the higher trial rate (14 per cent in the example). NPV R_1 is the value generated by

Table 5.8 DCF containing two trial rates

Year	Expenditure (£)	Income (£)	Net cash flow	PV £1 @ 10%	DCF	PV £1 @ 14%	DCF
0	20,000	0	−20,000	1	− 20,000	1	− 20,000
1	0	3,000	3,000	0.9091	2,727	0.8772	2,632
2	0	5,000	5,000	0.8264	4,132	0.7695	3,848
3	0	6,000	6,000	0.7513	4,508	0.675	4,050
4	1,000	3,000	2,000	0.6830	1,366	0.5921	1,184
5	0	6,500	6,500	0.6209	4,036	0.5194	3,376
6	0	5,750	5,750	0.5645	3,246	0.4556	2,620
7	0	4,500	4,500	0.5132	2,309	0.3996	1,798
				NPV @ 10% =	2,324	NPV @ 14% =	− 492

using the lower trial rate (which in the example above is 2,324) and NPV R_2 is the value generated by the higher trial rate (which in the example above is −492). In the equation the negative value of the NPV R_2 is deducted from the positive value of NPV R_1 and this creates an addition of both values, as the deduction of a minus value in algebraic terms creates a plus. So if the above variables are used the outcome in that part of the equation will be 2,324 − 492 = 2,816.

The workings of the formula will probably become clearer when the data from the above example are inserted as follows:

$$10 + \left[(14 - 10) \times \frac{2,324}{2,324 - -492} \right] \quad 13.3\%$$

Further examples of discounted cash flow approaches applied to property investments are set out below.

Using the cash flow from Table 5.6 above, the internal rate of return (IRR) can be calculated as follows.

Table 5.9 DCF to produce an IRR

Year	Cash flow (£)	PV £1 @ 11%	Present value (£)	PV £1 @ 12%	Present value (£)
1	2,000	0.9009	1,802	0.8929	1,786
2	5,000	0.8116	4,058	0.7972	3,986
3	4,000	0.7312	2,925	0.7118	2,847
4	2,000	0.6587	1,317	0.6355	1,271
			10,102		9,890
		Less outlay	10,000		10,000
		NPV	102		− 110

At 11 per cent a positive NPV is produced but at 12 per cent a negative NPV is generated, whereas the IRR is that rate which produces a NPV of zero. In this case, the IRR will lie somewhere between the narrow range of 11 and 12 per cent. The precise value of the IRR may be found using the formula previously shown and by inserting the variables from above to give:

$$11 + \left[(12 - 11) \times \frac{102}{102 - -110} \right] \quad 11.48\%$$

DCF techniques facilitate comparisons and can be used to generate a percentage outcome in IRR terms and/or a NPV which expresses the monetary value of a property investment. DCFs can also be very explicit about the growth assumptions being made regarding capital or income or both over time. To illustrate this point the DCF example below contains an explicit assumption regarding the capital growth which is anticipated to take place over the four year holding period. Purchase and exit costs are also factored in.

In the example shown below in Table 5.10 an investor has the opportunity to purchase an asset which is on the market for £100,000 but which promises to generate an annual income of £11,000. The investor plans to sell the investment after 4 years by which time the value of the investment is expected to have grown to £140,000. The investor decides to factor in some purchase and sales costs to see if the investment will reach a target rate of 12 per cent as follows.

Table 5.10 DCF to NPV with an explicit capital growth assumption, discounted at 12 per cent

Year	Particulars	Outflow	Inflow	Net flow	PV of £1 @ 12%	DCF
0	Purchase price	100,000				
	Purchase costs	8,000		−108,000	1	−108,000
1	Rent		11,000	11,000	0.8929	9,822
2	Rent		11,000	11,000	0.7972	8,769
3	Rent		11,000	11,000	0.7118	7,830
4	Rent		11,000			
	Sale proceeds		140,000			
	Sale costs	6,000		145,000	0.6355	92,148
					NPV @ 12% =	**10,568**

In the example above the investment has more than met the investor's desired rate of return and in effect it has sailed over the bar by earning an additional £10,568 on top of expectations. Clearly if the investor's assumptions regarding capital growth as set out in the DCF actually materialize, then this investment will obviously be a strong performer. The investor could then decide to raise the bar by testing the investment at a higher discount rate of say 15 per cent to see if it earns that rate of return. The calculation would look as shown in Table 5.11.

Table 5.11 DCF to NPV with an explicit capital growth assumption discounted at 15 per cent

Year	Particulars	Outflow	Inflow	Net flow	PV of £1 @ 15%	DCF
0	Purchase price	100,000				
	Purchase costs	8,000		−108,000	1	−108,000
1	Rent		11,000	11,000	0.8696	9,566
2	Rent		11,000	11,000	0.7561	8,317
3	Rent		11,000	11,000	0.6575	7,233
4	Rent		11,000			
	Sale proceeds		140,000			
	Sale costs	6,000		145,000	0.5718	82,911
					NPV @ 15% =	**26**

Because the NPV at £26 is very close to zero in the context of the scale of investment, there is no need to go further by calculating the IRR, as it is for all practical purposes demonstrated to be 15 per cent.

Table 5.12 below depicts the purchase by a large corporate investor of a multimillion pound property investment which has the following characteristics. Assuming that rental income is received annually in arrears the DCF would look as shown below in Table 5.13.

Table 5.12 Investment valuation using DCF:

Purchase price £	50,000,000	Sale price £	60,060,306
Net annual rent passing £	4,000,000	Estimated rent on sale	5,105,126
Initial yield	8%	Exit yield	8.50%
Fees on purchase	2.75%	Fees on sale	2.75%
Expected rental growth	5%	Discount rate	10%
Expected holding period	5 years	Next rent review	5 years' time

Table 5.13 DCF to NPV and IRR

Year	Income (£)	Capital (£)	Fees (£)	Cash flow	PV £1 @ 10%	DCF
0	0	−50,000,000	−1,375,000	−51,375,000	1	−51,375,000
1	4,000,000			4,000,000	0.9091	3,636,400
2	4,000,000			4,000,000	0.8264	3,305,600
3	4,000,000			4,000,000	0.7513	3,005,200
4	4,000,000			4,000,000	0.6830	2,732,000
5	4,000,000	60,060,306	−1,651,658	62,408,648	0.6209	38,749,530
					NPV =	**53,730**
					IRR =	**10.03%**

5.8 Summary

This chapter has introduced the valuation toolkit used by property valuers in different circumstances. There has been a focus upon the traditional or implicit method of investment valuation and the modern or explicit approach. The latter involves the use of discounted cash flows which lay out future expectations on income and expenditure and then discounts these back to present value.

There are two types of outcomes from DCFs. The first is the net present value (NPV) which provides a capital sum which, if it is positive, confirms that the investor's target rate has been reached. If the NPV is negative then the investor's target rate has not been reached. A large positive NPV signifies that an investment opportunity has easily exceeded the investor's target rate and this raises the question of what rate has actually been achieved. The answer can be found by calculating the internal rate of return (IRR) as shown in this chapter. Financial functions such as NPV and IRR are available in Microsoft Excel but it is important for those using these functions to have some grounding in the principles, so that they can fully grasp the significance of the process and its outcomes.

It will have become apparent that one of the drawbacks with setting out discounted cash flows is that they can take time to construct and then check and so academics and practitioners have sought formula-based 'short cuts' to generate the same answer. The so-called short-cut methods will be explored in the chapter which follows along with some variations on the theme of discounting future cash flows.

References

Blackledge, M. (2009) *Introducing Property Valuation* (Abingdon: Routledge).

Davidson, A. W. (ed.) (2002) *Parry's Valuation and Investment Tables*, 12th edn (London: Estates Gazette).

RICS (2007) *Valuation Information Paper 10: The Depreciated Replacement Cost Method of Valuation for Financial Reporting* (London: RICS).

RICS (2008) *Valuation Information Paper 12: Valuation of Development Land* (London: RICS).

RICS (2010) *RICS Valuation Standards*, 6th edn (London: RICS).

Scarrett, D. (2008) *Property Valuation: The Five Methods*, 2nd edn (Abingdon: Routledge).

Shapiro, E., Davies, K. and Mackmin, D. (2009) *Modern Methods of Valuation*, 10th edn (London: EG Books).

6

The application of property investment appraisal techniques

6.1 Introduction	6.4 Appraising over-rented properties
6.2 Reversionary property	6.5 Explicit assumptions about rental
6.3 Leasehold property, dual rate	growth
and tax	6.6 Summary

Aims

This chapter includes worked examples to explore traditional investment valuation approaches to providing a capital value for reversionary properties which have a term income which is ultimately replaced by a reversionary income. The chapter discusses some of the criticisms of these approaches, which imply rental growth but are not explicit about how that has affected judgements made by the valuer. The latter part of the chapter contains examples to support the discussion around more explicit approaches which employ DCF and which promise a more logical and transparent approach to property investment appraisal.

Key terms

>> **Reversionary property** – an investment property where the rent passing is lower than the current market rent and there is thus an expectation that at the next rent review or on lease expiry, the rent will revert to a higher level benchmarked by the market rent.
>> **Term and reversion** – describes the stepped pattern of income from a reversionary property. A term and reversion valuation would thus capitalize the rent passing on a property for the term, which is the number of years remaining until the reversion, and then add it to the value of the property on reversion. Because the reversionary income and its capitalization are realizable at a future date determined by the lease, that part of the value is said to be deferred and is it is therefore discounted for the relevant number of years to reflect this fact.
>> **Over-rented property** – because the property market experiences long periods during which rents and capital values tend to increase at or above

the rate of inflation followed by shorter periods when values fall quite sharply, it is not uncommon to find over-rented properties. This is because of the periods between rent reviews (normally five years) on a commercial lease and during which the rent will not change. The most recent property recession in the UK began in early 2008 so if a rent review had taken place prior to that, the rent passing for the ensuing five years would probably be higher than the market rent. The valuation methodology to deal with this situation is discussed in this chapter.

>> **Equated yield** – is the return expected on a property investment based upon explicit judgements about rental growth. The equated yield is the same as the internal rate of return (IRR) discussed in the previous chapter. The equated yield can also be induced into a valuation to reflect the client's target rate of return in order to see if rental and/or capital growth in a property investment is likely to achieve the target rate.

6.1 Introduction

In the previous chapter a distinction was drawn between traditional investment valuation methods which require a valuer to select a yield to capitalize an income, and more explicit techniques which use a discounted cash flow (DCF) to set out future income and expenditure. This chapter builds on this distinction by looking at how both approaches can be used to deal with stepped income which commonly arises when the rent on investment properties is periodically reviewed. Normally the step will be upwards to reflect a rise in the market rent which ordinarily would keep pace with inflation. However this will not always be the case and because there are periodic downturns in the property market, a rent agreed at one point in time might begin to look over priced relative to the market rent at a later stage. This chapter therefore looks at valuing reversionary property and those that are over-rented and in doing so, some of the shortcomings of the traditional investment method surface relative to more explicit DCF-based approaches.

6.2 Reversionary property

Reversionary properties are those which have a business tenant in occupation on a lease. The freeholds of these properties are bought and sold by investors who are interested in the income stream that is currently passing under the lease and the future income when the rent is reviewed or when the lease expires and a new letting occurs. The income which is passing during the term up until rent review or lease expiry is a known quantity and it is therefore considered to be less risky than the promise of future income at reversion which is less certain and therefore more risky. Traditional valuation methods used to identify a capital value for these investment properties have therefore concerned themselves with capitalizing the known rent which is passing and then adding that to the capitalized value of the expected rent which will occur at reversion. The discussion below will reveal that there are at least three ways that this can be done using traditional methods.

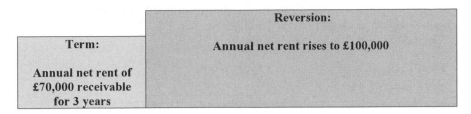

Figure 6.1 Term and reversion

Example 6.1: Traditional approaches to valuing stepped rental income

A freehold shop is let at an annual rent of £70,000 on FRI terms. The estimated market rent is however £100,000. The capitalization rate at full rental value is 5.5 per cent. There are three years left on the lease to run. There are three options for calculating the capital value of this investment property using the traditional valuation method. The first option is the term and reversion approach as shown in Figure 6.1 above, where the rent is assumed to follow a stepped pattern which is separated vertically into two slices.

The calculation would look as follows:

Term annual rent £	70,000	
YP 3 years @ 5%	2.7232	
		190,624
Reversion to annual market rent £	100,000	
YP in perp. @ 6%	16.6667	
PV in 3 years at 6%	0.8396	
		1,399,336
Capital value £		1,589,960

Note that the 5 per cent yield on the term is adjusted below the capitalization rate of 5.5 per cent for properties let at market rent to reflect the security of the income. The reversionary rent, which is three years away, is not yet a certainty and it is therefore relatively more risky than the term rent. For that reason the 6 per cent yield on the reversion is adjusted above the current market capitalization rate of 5.5 per cent for market rented properties.

The second option shown in Figure 6.2 is called the hardcore or layer

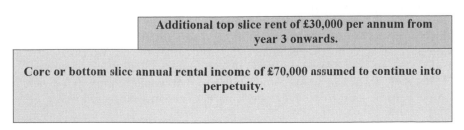

Figure 6.2 The layer approach

approach in which the rental income stream is assumed to be split horizontally when the uplift to market rent takes place at year 3.

The calculation would look as follows:

Core annual rent £	70,000		
YP in perp. @ 5%	20		
		1,400,000	
Reversion to annual market rent £	100,000		
Less term rent £	70,000		
Top slice rent therefore £	30,000		
YP in perp. @ 6%	16.6667		
PV £1 in 3 years @ 6%	0.8396		
		419,801	
Capital value £			1,819,801

In a similar manner to the term and reversion method, the less risky bottom slice or core income in the horizontal slicing method is capitalized at a 5 per cent yield while the slightly riskier top slice income is capitalized at the higher rate of 6 per cent.

Although credible adjustments may have been made to the yield to reflect the relative risk and security of the income during the term and reversion, the difference in capital values generated by the two methods is considerable at £230,000. Isaac and Steley (2000: 74–5) synthesize some of the advantages and disadvantages arising from the layer method and note that the use of a lower yield for the core income in perpetuity may have the effect of overvaluing this element. Thus, as the example above suggests, it is quite possible for the layer method to generate a significantly higher overall valuation than is achieved by the term and reversion method, particularly where there is a significant gap between the term and reversionary income. Given that the use of these two methods can generate quite wide discrepancies in the out-turn valuation, perhaps a more robust valuation can be achieved using the third method which is the equivalent yield.

In equivalent yield model the rental income stream may be split vertically as in the term and reversion method or horizontally as in the layer method, as the yield applied to both tranches of income, however divided, will be the same. The question is how to decide upon the yield to apply. Market comparison might suggest that for properties let at market rent, the yield is 5.5 per cent. As a starting point therefore, the yield to apply here should be somewhere close to that, because there is only three years of relatively low-risk income (suggesting a lower than 5.5 per cent yield) but a lengthy reversion which is not certain but which promises at least the market rent (and so a slightly higher yield than 5.5 per cent may apply to that element). The outcomes of the two previous runs could also be considered in that the average capital value generated is £1,704,881. To obtain an outcome similar to that would require that a yield of 5.6 per cent be used to capitalize both parts of the income as follows:

Core annual rent £	70,000		
YP in perp. @ 5.6%	17.8571		
		1,249,997	
Reversion to market rent £	100,000		
Less hardcore rent	70,000		
Top slice rent therefore £	30,000		
YP in perp. @ 5.6%	17.8571		
PV £1 in 3 years @ 5.6%	0.8492		
		454,927	
Capital value £			1,704,924

Having explored the three options for valuing stepped income under the umbrella of the traditional method, it is clear that quite wide variations are possible in the capital value generated. The variation stems from both the view taken by the valuer on how to partition the income and the extent of the variation in the yield to reflect the relative risk or security of the particular part of the income. It may be that in the hands of a skilled and experienced valuer who is conversant with the workings of a local property market, a degree of consistency could develop. However there also appears to be a lack of science, justification and transparency in these methods, which as the examples show, are capable of generating wide variations in capital value from the same set of income assumptions.

Baum and Crosby (2008: 7) identify the contradiction that despite the lack of science and transparency associated with the traditional investment valuation methods, they still dominate valuation practice. Baum and Crosby suggest that inertia may be playing a part because historically valuers in the UK were faced with long leases on properties which were relatively simple to value by way of comparison. There was also sufficient turnover in the stock of properties for comparable data to become available sooner or later. Thus if the initial yield used to capitalize the rent on a standard high street shop unit let on a long lease with FRI terms was X per cent then a valuer was not motivated to go beyond that methodology to value a similar shop let on similar terms in the same part of the high street. However, particularly in recessions when there are rent-free periods, break clauses in leases, shorter overall lease lengths against a backdrop of falling market rents, the use of traditional valuation methods begins to look a little suspect. Baum and Crosby who advocate more logical and explicit DCF-based approaches state that:

> We believe that investment value can be identified by a rational analysis of market transactions, and we do not believe that having a relatively transparent, high turnover market, as in the UK, gives valuers an excuse to develop simplistic rules of thumb to make up for the heterogeneous nature of the asset ... [and that] ... It should be the aim of an appraisal to achieve accuracy by rational techniques. (2008: 7)

The RICS position at least informally, does not discourage valuers from using traditional methods such as term and reversion. However there is tacit encouragement, where large values and complexity is involved, for valuers to use discounted cash flow techniques in which assumptions and attitudes to risk are made explicit:

Such an approach tends to be more applicable to complex investments and/or to markets in which sophisticated investors operate. (2010: 11)

It is difficult to conceive of major global real estate investors being entirely convinced by what might appear to be arbitrary judgements by valuers using traditional investment valuation methods such as term and reversion. Thus while discussion on these traditional methods will not cease at this point, as the chapter develops there will be a shift towards methods which promise a little more transparency and rationality around the judgements being made.

6.3 Leasehold property, dual rate and tax

In traditional leasehold valuations the leasehold yield reflects a margin above the freehold yield and adjusted for tax and a sinking fund to replace the asset on expiration of the lease. There has been much debate about the relevance of both the sinking fund and the tax adjustment and critics have suggested that an appropriate approach would be to value without the sinking fund adjustment or even without both. This section shows the conventional approach and a valuation without adjustment.

Example 6.2: Dual rate, with sinking fund tax adjusted

A leasehold interest in a shop is subject to an annual head rent of £70,000 net. The market rent however is £100,000. The capitalization rate at market rent is 5 per cent. There are three years left on the lease to run. Calculate the capital value of the leasehold interest.

Annual market rent £	100,000	
Less head rent £	70,000	
Profit rent £	30,000	
YP 3 years @ 6% + 3% (40p tax)	1.6688	
Capital value £		50,064

The criticisms of this approach relate to how the leasehold rate is assessed from the freehold, the tax rate is an individual calculation and not a market one and the remuneration rate used at 3 per cent is low.

Single rate

Annual market rent £	100,000	
Less head rent £	70,000	
Profit rent £	30,000	
YP 3 years @ 6%	2.6730	
Capital value £		80,190

Of course the yield in the above calculation could be increased to provide a similar answer to that achieved from the dual rate calculation.

6.4 Appraising over-rented properties

The layer approach discussed earlier in this chapter, has also been used to value properties which are over-rented. That is where the property is let at an annual rent which is higher than the market rent and thus in the absence of an upwards-only rent review clause the rental will fall at the next review. Conversely where there is an upwards-only rent review clause then this will prevent the rent passing from falling back to the prevailing market rent. This distortion of market forces is why the government considered legislation to outlaw this restrictive practice, but suspended the proposal in return for a commitment from the property industry to use a code of practice to achieve the same effect. However there is a continuing legacy of commercial leases in the market which pre-date the code of practice which contain upwards-only clauses and which therefore valuers have to deal with.

Where an over-rented layer exists, it is sometimes referred to as the overage and in valuation terms it is treated differently to the core rental income represented by the market rent. As Grenville-Mathers and Taylor (2008: 121) suggest the overage is at some risk and will depend on how financially robust the tenant is. That market rents have fallen is one indicator that the business climate generally has become more challenging and in such circumstances firms do go bankrupt. Thus the income from particularly over-rented properties is at more risk than for those let at market rents. Different yields are therefore applied to the core and upper slice of the income to reflect the risk differential as illustrated in the example which follows.

Example 6.3: Valuing over-rented property

A freehold shop is let at an existing annual rent of £100,000 on FRI terms with upward only rent reviews. The market rent however is £80,000. The capitalization rate at the market rent is 6 per cent. The lease has eight years to run with the final upwards-only rent review in three years' time. Calculate the capital value of the freehold.

Layer approach

Core rent		
Annual market rent £	80,000	
YP in perp. @ 6%	16.6667	
		1,333,336
Top slice		
Annual rent passing £	100,000	
Less market rent £	80,000	
Overage	20,000	
YP 8 years @ 10%	5.3349	
		106,698
Capital value		1,440,034

The calculation makes the perhaps unrealistic assumption that the market rent will be less than the rent passing for the eight-year duration of the lease and beyond. However by applying a realistic growth rate to the market rent, a convergence point could be predicted when the market rent had grown to the same level as the rent passing. Forecasting like this is not strictly part of the traditional investment method which relies on current market evidence.

However adopting the same scenario but factoring in an assumed rental growth rate of 5 per cent per annum by using the Amount of £1 formula, it could be established whether the growth in market rent was sufficient to converge with or exceed the current rent passing at or before the next rent review in three years' time.

Current market rent: $£80,000 \times (1 + i)^n$ in which i = 5% and n = 3 years
$$= £80,000 \times 1.05^3 = £92,610$$

So, even with a healthy assumed annual growth rate of 5 per cent the market rent has not caught up with the rent passing by the rent review in three years time. Because of the upwards-only rent clause in the lease, the passing rent of £100,000 would therefore continue to the expiration of the lease in 8 years time. At that stage, the rental growth assumption of 5 per cent would have seen the market rent exceed the passing rent of £100,000 as follows:

$$= £80,000 \times 1.05^8 = £118,196$$

The valuation for this scenario could be simplified as shown in the example below.

Example 6.4: An over-rented property valued into perpetuity

Rent in perpetuity	100,000	
YP in perp. @ 7%	14.2857	
Capital value		1,428,570

In Example 6.4 above the all risks yield of 7% has been selected by the valuer to reflect some risk to the term rent but also the assumption that the reversionary will be at least £100,000.

Of course forecasting growth rates in rental value is not an easy task as rental performance will be affected by the interplay of many factors. For example the quality of the building and its environmental credentials will have a bearing on its ability to attract a competitive rental value. There is also a regional dimension which will typically see rents increase faster in locations where the economy is particularly strong and where there are restrictions on the supply pipeline of new floorspace. Grenville-Mathers and Taylor (2008: 121) suggest that when in doubt, a proxy for rental growth forecasts which could be used are the economic forecasts produced by the Treasury.

The valuation considered above and in which there is an implicit assumption about rental growth, is a short step away from what is known as a short-cut DCF valuation, the key features of which are:

Term rent $\times$ YP n years @ e%

plus

Reversion to market rent $\times$ amount of £1 for n years @ g%

$\times$ YP in perp. @ k%

$\times$ PV for n years @ e%

Where n = number of years to rent review

e% = equated yield

k% = all risks yield of comparable

g% = the implied rental growth per annum

The equated yield is used to capitalize the rent passing over the term and also to discount the capital values over this period. This is because the rent passing is fixed and does not reflect market conditions. The market rent is inflated to the time of the reversion at the adopted growth rate and then capitalized at the all risks yield. The short-cut DCF does not inflate the rent through the reversion period thus the discount rate for the all risks yield is used on the reversion.

To consolidate understanding of the short cut DCF approach, an example follows which explores how it may be applied to the challenge of valuing an over-rented property.

Example 6.5: An over-rented property and the short-cut DCF method

A prime central London office block with 3,800 m² of net lettable space has become available on the property investment market. The annual rent passing under the FRI lease is £2,200,000 although the current market rent is £2,000,000. The lease has only two years to run until expiry although there is every indication that the tenant wants to negotiate a new long lease. A pension fund is interested in acquiring the property and therefore undertakes the following calculation to identify the maximum bid that could be made net of 5.5 per cent purchase costs and while maintaining the corporate target rate of 10 per cent for this type of investment.

Stage 1: Analyse market comparables and from them calculate the implied rental growth using the following formula (which will be discussed again later in the chapter):

$$(1 + g)^t = \frac{\text{YP perp. @ } k - \text{YP } t \text{ years @ } e}{\text{YP perp. @ } k \times \text{PV } t \text{ years @ } e}$$

where g = implied annual rental growth rate %

e = equated yield (target rate) = 10%

t = rent review pattern of the comparable = 5 years

k = all risks yield of the comparable = 5.5%

$$(1 + g)^t = \frac{18.1818 - 3.7908}{18.1818 \times 0.6209} = \frac{14.391}{11.2891}$$

$$(1 + g)^t = 1.2748$$
$$1 + g = 1.2748^{(1/5)}$$
$$g = 0.0498 = 4.98\%$$

Stage 2: Complete the valuation:

Rent passing £	2,200,000	
Market rent £	2,000,000	
Rent review period (years)	5	
Term to reversion	2	
All risk yield at market rent £	5.5%	
Equated yield	10%	

Term: Rent passing £		2,200,000
YP 2 years @ 10%		1.7355
		3,818,100
Reversion to market rent £:	2,000,000	
Amount of £1 in 2 years @ 4.98%	1.1021	
	2,204,200	
YP in perp. @ 5.5%	18.1818	
PV of £1 in 2 years @ 10%	0.8264	
	15.0254	
		33,118,987

Capital value of the investment inclusive of purchase costs		36,937,087
Purchase costs @ 5.5% of net value =	1,925,630	
Maximum price to be paid by fund net of purchase costs		35,011,457

6.5 Explicit assumptions about rental growth

One of the criticisms levelled at the traditional methods of valuation such as those considered earlier in the chapter, is that the yield adopted implies growth but is not transparent about the actual rate of growth anticipated. In contrast, growth can be explicitly built into DCF cash flows so that the NPV which arises will have taken into account the expected rental and/or capital growth. As explored in the previous chapter, DCF can also be used to generate an IRR which is also known as the equated yield. The equated yield would therefore reflect explicit assumptions about growth, as illustrated below.

Equated yield

The main steps in identifying the equated yield are as follows.

1 Assume an annual growth rate for the rent and apply this to the original income using the Amount of £1 formula.
2 Insert the income with growth into the DCF and then calculate the IRR which is the equated yield.

Example 6.6: Using DCF to indentify the equated yield

A freehold investment which has been purchased for £600,000 has an annual market rent of £30,000. It is let on a lease for 25 years with five-year rent reviews. Assuming rental growth of 10 per cent per annum the calculation to determine the equated yield would look as follows.

Capital value £	600,000	
Initial annual rent £	30,000	
Initial yield	5%	
Trial equated yields	14%	15%
Rent review periods	5 years	
Rental growth rate	10%	
YP for the review period at the two trial rates	3.4331	3.3522

The IRR arising from the above by interpolation = $14 + (1 \times (19,301/89,548))$ = 14.22% rounded up.

In the above equation the frequency of rent reviews is five years and therefore the cash flow represents this with five-year slices of income which cannot

Table 6.1 Tabular representation of Example 6.6: Using DCF to indentify the equated yield

Period (years)	Amount £1 @ 10%	Cash flow	PV £1 @ 14%	Deferred YP	PV of slice
0	n/a	−600,000	1	n/a	− 600,000
1–5	n/a	30,000	n/a	3.4331	102,993
6–10	1.6105	48,315	0.5194	1.7832	86,155
11–15	2.5937	77,811	0.2697	0.9259	72,045
16–20	4.1772	125,316	0.1401	0.4810	60,277
21–25	6.7275	201,825	0.0728	0.2499	50,436
26–30	10.8347	325,041	0.0378	0.1298	42,190
31–perp	17.4494	523,482	0.0196	0.3920	205,205
				NPV =	19,301

Period (years)	Amount £1 @ 10%	Cash flow	PV £1 @ 15%	Deferred YP	PV of slice
0	n/a	−600,000	1	n/a	600,000
1–5	n/a	30,000	n/a	3.3522	100,566
6–10	1.6105	48,315	0.4972	1.6667	80,527
11–15	2.5937	77,811	0.2472	0.8287	64,482
16–20	4.1772	125,316	0.1229	0.4120	51,630
21–25	6.7275	201,825	0.0611	0.2048	41,334
26–30	10.8347	325,041	0.0304	0.1019	33,122
31–perp	17.4494	523,482	0.0151	0.3020	158,092
				NPV =	− 70,247

change within the five-year period. The cash flows for each period have been inflated by the amount of £1 at the growth rate of 10 per cent to the beginning of each period, showing the rent with growth at each review.

The deferral rate is calculated for each cash flow period for each trial rate (PV of £1 for deferred period at 14 and 15 per cent). This is multiplied by the PV of £1 column to give the deferred YP. The period cash flow is valued by capitalizing at the trial rates for the 5 year period (YP 5 years at 14 and 15 per cent). This is multiplied by the PV of £1 column to give the deferred YP. The deferred YP at the trial rates is multiplied by the inflated cash flow to give the value of the deferred slice. The values of the deferred slices are added together to give the Net Present Value. To calculate the equated yield which is the same as the IRR, a positive and negative NPV are required for interpolation to obtain the point where the NPV = 0.

The calculation could go on indefinitely but because of the deferral factor, cash flows after 30 years make much less difference to the calculation; after this, no growth is added to the income and thus the initial yield is used for the trial rates. In this case the initial yield is 5 per cent and the final deferred YP is YP in perpetuity @ 5 per cent deferred 30 years. In view of the problems of predicting growth over the longer period it may be more desirable to restrict the analysis to 20 years.

The formula which links the equated yield and the assumptions about future rental growth is:

$$k = e - (SF \times P)$$

In the above equation the variables are:

k which is the initial yield and which is the net rent divided by the capital value.
e which is the equate yield.
SF which is the sinking fund, the formula for which is:

$$\frac{i}{(1 + i)^n - 1}$$

and which uses e above and n which is the applicable rent review period.
P which is the percentage growth rate in the market rent over the rent review period.

The formula can be transposed depending on whether the target rate is given (in which case the rate of rental growth would be the unknown variable to discover) or alternatively if the rate of rental growth is assumed then the target rate becomes the unknown variable to identify.

Where the rental growth rate is not known, then the formula can be transposed to a formula which was considered earlier in the chapter and which is:

$$(1 + g)^t = \frac{\text{YP perp. @ } k - \text{YP } t \text{ years @ } e}{\text{YP perp. @ } k \times \text{PV } t \text{ years @ } e}$$

A reminder that the additional variables which appear in the above configuration of the equation are:

g which is the implied annual rental growth rate, and
t which is the rent review period.

The example which follows will illustrate the principle.

Example 6.7: The implied growth rate

A prime freehold shop is let on a 25 year FRI lease with five-year reviews at the market rent of £40,000 per annum. The freehold of the property is being offered for sale to investors at £800,000. An investor is considering whether to match the asking price, but first wishes to ascertain the rate of rental growth which would be needed to achieve the investor's target rate of return of 15 per cent. The calculation would look as follows.

$$\text{Capitalization rate } (k) = \frac{£40,000}{£800,000} = 0.05 = 5\%$$

Target rate of return (e) = 15%
Rent review period (t) = 5 years

The implied annual growth rate for the rent (g) can be calculated by using the formula set out above and by inserting the known variables as follows:

$$(1 + g)^5 = \frac{20 - 3.3522}{20 \times 0.4972}$$

$$(1 + g)^5 = \frac{16.6478}{9.9440} = 1.6742$$

$$1 + g = 1.6742^{(1/5)} = 1.10860$$

$$g = 0.10860 = 10.86\%$$

As confirmed by Baum *et al.* (2006: 96) the alternative version of the formula discussed above: $k = e - (SF \times P)$ can be used where the unknown variable is the target rate of return (e). For example if the investor was fairly confident that an annual rate of rental growth of 10.86% was realistic in the context of the other variables in Example 6.7 above, the calculation to find the target rate or equated yield would look as follows:

$$k = e - (SF \times P) \text{ in which } P = (1 + g)^5 - 1$$
$$e = k + (SF \times P) = 5\% + (0.1483 \times 0.6742)$$
$$e = 15\% \text{ (rounded up)}$$

To prove the integrity of the formulas, the variables could be inserted into a DCF as shown in Table 6.2 and into which the rate of rental growth identified by formula: 10.86 per cent has been inserted.

Table 6.2 Tabular representation of Example 6.7: implied growth rate

Period (years)	Amount of £1 @ 10.86%	Cash flow	PV £1 @ 15%	Deferred YP	PV of slice
0–5	1	40,000	1	3.3522	134,088
6–10	1.6745	66,980	0.4972	1.6667	111,636
11–15	2.8038	112,152	0.2472	0.8287	92,940
16–20	4.6949	187,796	0.1229	0.4120	77,372
21–25	7.8614	314,456	0.0611	0.2048	64,401
26–30	13.1635	526,540	0.0304	0.1019	53,654
31–perp	22.0418	881,672	0.0151	0.3020	266,265
				Capital value =	800,356

It should be noted that a consistent annual growth rate in the shop rent of 10.86 per cent is a substantial and possibly unrealistic expectation (depending on the specific location of the shop and how well the economy was functioning). This might cause the investor to re-evaluate either the amount offered to purchase the investment or the target rate of 15 per cent. Readers might like to practice the technique by assuming a scenario in which the investor made a lower offer of say £727,000 and which was accepted by the vendor to reflect an initial yield of 5.5 per cent. What then might be the rental growth rate required to achieve the investor's target rate of return of 15 per cent?

Rounding the figures

In the above example there is a difference in the capital value generated (which is the NPV arising from the DCF) of £356 due to the rounding up of the numerous variables in the cash flow. This raises the issue of when it may be appropriate to round up figures and to what extent decimal places should be rounded up in valuations. Armatys *et al.* (2009: 112) usefully summarizes the key principles which emerged from a rare case on this issue (*Abrahams* v. *Ramji*) heard by the Valuation Tribunal in 2007. The Tribunal agreed that there was no necessity at any point in the valuation to use pence and so when monetary values are used they can be rounded up to the nearest pound. However in the body of the valuation considered by the Tribunal, the years' purchase (YP) had been rounded up to two decimal places and the present value of £1 (PV) to four decimal places. The Tribunal felt that this amounted to 'over-rounding' which had distorted the outcome. The Tribunal would have preferred an approach which was consistent with Parry's Tables and in which the YP tables are reproduced to four decimal places and the PV to seven decimal places. The Tribunal felt that these full figures should be used in the body of a valuation and that the only appropriate place for rounding up was then in the final financial sum generated. For example the above NPV of £800,356 might wrongly suggest that a process containing numerous variables over a time frame of 30 years was capable of a degree of valuation accuracy down to the last six pounds. Of course this is not the case and in the Valuation

Tribunal's view it was reasonable to round up such sums; and which in this case would be to £800,000.

Given that valuations will usually be undertaken using Microsoft Excel spreadsheets or a proprietary software package such as those provided by the KEL group the full range of decimal places can be entered into cells. However this can lead to anomalies in academic discussions like this where the headline figures need to surface and be clear relative to the variables shown in the examples. It is also not very conducive to publishing formats where the full range of underlying decimals which have generated an answer in an Excel spreadsheet may fail to appear on the printed page and this can lead to confusion in how an answer was achieved. So a degree of rounding up is appropriate in this context to enable readers to conduct their own audit trails to see how answers were generated and in this book the general approach is not to go beyond four decimal places for any variable. For example there is no academic purpose in setting out the full range of decimals for something like YP nine years @ 7% multiplied by the PV of £1 in five years at 10% which in full would look as follows:

$$6.5152 \times 0.6209213 = 4.04542645376$$

Equated rents

The valuation of equated rents or constant rents relate to the adjustment of comparables for non-regular rent review patterns. K, the constant rent factor is based on the formula:

$$K = \frac{A - B}{A - 1} \times \frac{C - 1}{C - D}$$

The variables in the above are:

A which is the Amount of £1 @ R% (the equated yield) for L years (the actual abnormal review period);
B which is the Amount of £1 @ G% (the growth rate for property of this type) for L years;
C which is the Amount of £1 @ R% for Z years (normal rent review pattern);
D which is the Amount of £1 @ G% for Z years.

Example 6.8: Non-regular rent review patterns

Calculate the rent appropriate on rent review for a lease with 21-year rent reviews. The lessor's required return on capital is 15% (equated yield) and the growth rate anticipated is 8%. The annual market rental is £10,000 on a normal rent review pattern of five years.

$$K = \frac{\text{Amount of £1 @ 15\% for 21 years} - \text{Amount of £1 @ 8\% for 21 years}}{\text{Amount of £1 @ 15\% for 21 years} - 1}$$

$$\times \frac{\text{Amount of £1 @ 15\% for 5 years} - 1}{\text{Amount of £1 @ 15\% for 5 years} - \text{Amount of £1 @ 8\% for 5 years}}$$

$$K = \frac{18.8215 - 5.0338}{18.8215 - 1} \times \frac{2.0114 - 1}{2.0114 - 1.4693}$$

$$K = 0.7737 \times 1.8657$$

$$K = 1.4435$$

Thus the rent appropriate on review is:

$$K \times \text{rent on normal review} = 1.4435 \times £10,000 \text{ per annum} = £14,435 \text{ per annum}$$

6.6 Summary

This chapter began by considering traditional approaches to valuing stepped rental incomes which typically arise from reversionary investment properties let to businesses on commercial leases. These properties typically generate a term rent followed by the promise of a reversionary rent, when ordinarily the rent increases. It was seen that there are different approaches to these traditional ways of valuing reversionary property, including term and reversion and the horizontal layer method. In each case the valuer is required to make a judgement on which yield to adopt to capitalize the different tranches of income. The judgement on calibrating the yield is expected to balance the perceived risks to the income and implicitly the anticipation of growth.

Because faith needs to be placed in the judgement of the valuer and because these methods are capable of generating quite different capital valuations given the same set of variables, it is perhaps not surprising that these methods have attracted academic criticism from authors such as Baum and Crosby (2008). The latter would prefer to see more explicit DCF-based appraisals used because within these methods the valuer's assumptions and judgements are made more transparent. Thus the latter half of the chapter began to explore DCF approaches and how these might be used to evaluate properties which were over-rented. There were necessary forays into valuation vocabulary and formulas, for example to identify implied rental growth rates from comparable market transactions. It is hoped that if readers work through the examples included in the chapter they will strengthen their understanding of the terminology and the valuation processes followed.

References

Armatys, J. Askham, P. and Green, M. (2009) *Principles of Valuation* (London: EG Books).

Baum, A. and Crosby, N. (2008) *Property Investment Appraisal*, 3rd edn (Oxford: Blackwell).

Baum, A., Nunnington, N. and Mackmin, D. (2006) *The Income Approach to Property Valuation*, 5th edn (London: EG Books).

Grenville-Mathers, L. and Taylor, A. (2008) 'Offices', ch. 6 in Hayward, R. (ed.), *Valuation: Principles into Practice*, 6th edn (London: EG Books).

Isaac, D. and Steley, T. (2000) *Property Valuation Techniques*, 2nd edn (Basingstoke: Macmillan).

RICS (2010) *Property Investment Valuation in the UK: A Brief Guide for Users of Valuations* (London: RICS). Available in e-format at: www.rics.org/valuation

7

Specialized aspects of property investment appraisal

Aims

This chapter considers some of the more specialized aspects of property investment appraisal which it was not possible or appropriate to consider in the preceding two chapters where more fundamental issues were being explored. This chapter will consider the role played by the residual valuation for the property investor and how that type of appraisal can be linked to and strengthened by different types of cash flow appraisals. There are worked examples of this type of appraisal along with examples of quarterly in advance appraisals. Specialist issues such as depreciation are considered and the chapter concludes by discussing expectations around valuation accuracy.

Key terms

>> **Gross development value** – an estimate usually made in the context of a property appraisal which seeks to establish the market value of an envisaged property development. Thus it is a valuation of an asset which does not yet exist and uses current market data to value an asset which may only be ready for the market in several years' time.

>> **Quarterly in advance** – a valuation which reflects the normal requirement under a commercial lease for business tenants to pay the annual rent in four instalments at the beginning of each quarter.

>> **Depreciation** – The loss in value which real property is prone to as it ages due to deterioration in the fabric and/or obsolescence which might arise because

the building's original function is no longer economically viable. Different types of building will experience different rates of depreciation and maintenance, refurbishment and adaptation can arrest or even reverse the effects of depreciation. Depending on the use and location the rise in land value can counteract any loss in value cause by depreciation of the building.

>> **Inducements** – sometimes referred to as tenants' incentives and which usually comprise rent-free periods at the beginning of a commercial lease. The length of any rent-free periods will vary depending on the location, property type and the relative bargaining strength in the market between landlords and business tenants. Where rent-free periods are granted, property investors would normally factor in this loss of income in their appraisals by establishing the equivalent rent.

>> **Equivalent rent** – sometimes referred to as the net effective rent which is an adjustment of the headline rent to allow for any rent-free periods or other tenant inducements such as reverse premiums. The equivalent rent is a more reliable basis for assessing the true value of a rental income stream for a term than is provided by the headline rent.

7.1 Introduction

Having looked at the principles and practices which have evolved regarding traditional and modern methods of investment valuation, this chapter rounds up on the theme of appraisal methods by looking at more specialized techniques and applications. Given that by the end of this chapter there will have been discussion and examples of valuations over three chapters, it is appropriate at that point to consider the debate regarding the accuracy expected of the valuation process. The chapter begins however by looking at development appraisal as property development creates property investment assets. Rather than buy property investments 'off the shelf' in the property market, large property investors will sometimes undertake property developments in order to create investment-grade property from scratch.

7.2 Development, a specialized form of investment

It was mentioned in Chapter 5 that large corporate property investors, which include pension funds and insurance companies, will sometimes play the role of developer so that they have complete control over the type of building that emerges and which will entirely meet their investment specification. Indeed some of these funds have established development departments whose role it is to seek out development opportunities and undertake development appraisals. Even where the fund takes a more passive role and provides funds to an established developer to produce an investment-grade building, the fund will still look at development viability to ensure that it is getting value for money and is not exposing itself to a venture that is too risky. This section will therefore look at development as a specialized form of investment and in doing so the residual valuation method will come into focus because it is the development appraisal method most commonly used in these situations.

The basic principle underpinning a residual valuation is that it works backwards from establishing the finished value of a development and then deducts all of the costs (including a profit margin) needed to get to that position. If a scheme is viable a residual sum will be left which is the total amount that could be paid for the site. The approach can be transposed if the land value is already known (perhaps because it is being sold at a fixed price) and so the land cost is added to the other costs (excluding profit) which are then deducted from the final value of the scheme. This version of the residual is used to identify the profit. Despite methodological criticisms of the residual method, it has stood the test of time and is particularly useful at the outset where broad viability can be assessed before a more detailed commitment to a scheme is made. The following is a simplified example of a residual to illustrate the principle.

Example 7.1: A simplified residual valuation of an office development

Annual rental income £		600,000	
YP in perp. @ 8%		12.5	
Gross Development Value (GDV)			7,500,000
Less costs			
Building costs and fees £	4,000,000		
Finance @ 10% over ½ of the			
2 year construction period	400,000		
		4,400,000	
Return for risk and profit @ 18% of GDV		1,350,000	
Total costs therefore:			5,750,000
Site value in 2 years' time: GDV − total costs =			1,750,000
PV of £1 in 2 years @ 10%		0.8264	
Site value today including purchase costs £			1,446,200

Even a cursory examination of the above simplified example reveals a number of things. Firstly that there is an investment valuation included at the start to establish the gross development value (GDV) of the scheme. A criticism here is that the value of the scheme is being assessed two years ahead of its completion based upon current market data on all risks yields and the rental value. It is very likely that either one or both of these is likely to change over the two years while the scheme is being built. Traditionally developers would take the view that the change over two years would be positive so that a scheme more valuable than £7.5 million would be realized. However as the credit crunch has illustrated, there are considerable risks in assuming that property values will continue to rise inexorably year on year.

Given that there is more risk involved in property development than purchasing a readymade investment property, there is conventionally a higher profit expectation which is normally benchmarked at between 15 and 20 per cent of GDV. The precise fixing of the profit margin will depend on the specific project risk and also upon rates of return available on other media. Some residuals express the profit as a percentage of costs; however this approach is counter-intuitive as it implies that being inefficient and allowing cost to spiral out of control will reward the developer with a higher profit.

A second criticism that could be levelled at the residual method illustrated above, relates to the crude calculation of the project finance over two years. The method assumes that by the end of the first year roughly half of the funds will have been drawn down from the bank with the remainder being drawn down over the second year. The approach therefore summarizes the situation as if the whole sum of money has been borrowed for half of the development period, i.e. one year over which the 10 per cent interest rate has been applied.

However the draw-down of a development loan facility from a bank is seldom that linear, as it tends to start with relatively modest withdrawals and accelerates at later stages of the construction process when more labour and capital equipment are required on a site. This is because during the early groundbreaking stage of a development there is only room on site for a set number of contractors who might (for example) be carrying out piling work. Thus the developer's spend at that stage will typically be less than at the later stages of the development when there may be a multi-storey superstructure in place. At that stage, the site will have become a warren of activity as numerous subcontractors will be at work simultaneously in different parts of the building. Some of the subcontractors will be installing very expensive capital equipment such as lifts, telecommunications cabling, fire sprinkler systems, heating systems and possibly air conditioning. Thus towards the middle and end of the development process, the project will tend to consume money faster than at the beginning. If this acceleration of the spend rate were applied to the £4 million of construction costs in the above example by quarter, the figures might look as follows. In the example only 30 per cent of the costs have been consumed by the halfway stage (the fourth quarter).

Of course all projects will have different S-curve profiles and projects requiring land decontamination, highways and flood defence works will generate considerable front end loading of costs. One of the value-adding capabilities of a competent developer or project manager is to be able to map out the specific costs and revenues profile over the time line of a project. A bank providing the loan will want to see a cash flow as part of the loan application and for subsequent project monitoring.

Example 7.2: The principle of the S curve illustrated

Quarter	Monthly spend %	Amount (£)	Cumulative construction spend (£)	Cumulative %
1	7.5	300,000	300,000	8
2	5.0	200,000	500,000	13
3	7.5	300,000	800,000	20
4	10.0	400,000	1,200,000	30
5	15.0	600,000	1,800,000	45
6	17.5	700,000	2,500,000	63
7	20.0	800,000	3,300,000	83
8	17.5	700,000	4,000,000	100

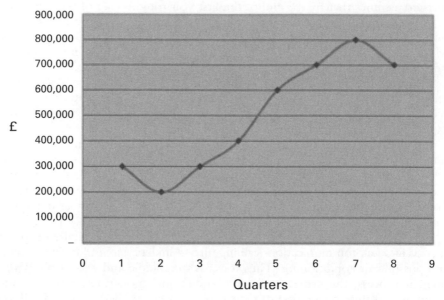

Figure 7.1 'S' curve of building costs

The S-curve depicting this pattern of spending across the two years is illustrated in Figure 7.1.

7.3 Using cash flows in development appraisal

To try to address the criticisms levelled at the residual method, valuers have linked cash flows to it in order to bolster its transparency, particularly in the way that it deals with the accumulation of costs and interest charges over the development period. A cash flow approach enables the division of the development period into periods during which interest charges can be calculated more precisely. Cash flows also enable more explicit assumptions to be put into the appraisal such as changes to costs or irregular inflows or outflows of funds. These changes cannot be accommodated in the 'snapshot' residual valuation.

In a period of inflation, a suitable adjustment can be made to revenue and costs in the calculation so that growth assumptions can be made explicit. A cash flow can make allowance for the timing of possible one-off payments or tax deductions and capital allowances. There are therefore a number of persuasive arguments in favour of supplementing a residual valuation with cash flows and it is not surprising therefore that commercial development appraisal software packages such as Prodev have adopted this belt and braces principle.

Example 7.3: Cash flow methods compared

The following examples show how the residual method can be supplemented by three types of cash flow, those being the period-by-period cash flow, the discounted cash flow and the net terminal value approach. Rather than try to explain each of the three options they are now set out in turn followed by a summing up of the advantages and disadvantages associated with each approach. The residual valuation set out in Example 7.1 above is used to provide the base data and readers might like to compare the site value that each approach generates. Before considering the data, it should be noted that the conversion of an annual rate of interest such as 10 per cent into a quarterly equivalent is not as straightforward as simply dividing 10 by 4 to generate 2.5 per cent. This is because what is needed is the quarterly rate which if compounded over four quarters will equate with 10 per cent. The conversion formula will be familiar to some readers but just in case this is not known it is:

$$((1 + i)^{0.25}) - 1 \text{ in which } i \text{ is the annual interest rate.}$$

Given that the example includes an annual interest rate of 10 per cent and the quarterly equivalent is required, the calculation would be: $((1 + 0.1)^{0.25}) - 1 = 0.0241$ (rounded up) = 2.41%.

Period-by-period cash flow

Quarter	Costs £	Income £	Net cash flow £	Capital outstanding from previous quarter	Interest @ 2.41% (on *d*)	Capital outstanding
	a	*b*	*c = b − a*	*d*	*e*	*f = c + d + e*
1	300,000	0	−300,000	0	0	−300,000
2	200,000	0	−200,000	−300,000	− 7,230	−507,230
3	300,000	0	−300,000	−507,230	− 12,224	−819,454
4	400,000	0	−400,000	−819,454	− 19,749	−1,239,203
5	600,000	0	−600,000	−1,239,203	− 29,865	−1,869,068
6	700,000	0	−700,000	−1,869,068	− 45,045	2,611,113
7	800,000	0	−800,000	−2,614,113	− 63,000	−3,477,113
8	700,000	0	−700,000	−3,477,113	83,798	−4,260,911

GDV		7,500,000
Less outstanding debt	4,260,911	
Plus return for risk and profit @ 18% of GDV	1,350,000	
Total costs therefore:		5,610,911
Site value in 2 years' time: GDV − total costs =		1,889,089
PV of £1 in 2 years @ 10%		0.8264
Site value today including purchase costs £		1,561,143

Discounted cash flow

Quarter	Cash flow	PV of £1 @ 2.41%	PV of cash flow
1	−300,000	0.9765	− 292,950
2	−200,000	0.9535	− 190,700
3	−300,000	0.9310	− 279,300
4	−400,000	0.9091	− 363,640
5	−600,000	0.8877	− 532,620
6	−700,000	0.8669	− 606,830
7	−800,000	0.8465	− 677,200
8	−700,000	0.8265	− 578,550
Total cost			− 3,521,790
− Profit	−1,350,000	0.8265	− 1,115,775
+ GDV	7,500,000	0.8265	6,198,750
Site value today including purchase costs £			1,561,185

Net terminal value

Quarter	Cash flow	Interest until completion @ 2.41%	
1	−300,000	1.1814	− 354,420
2	−200,000	1.1536	− 230,720
3	−300,000	1.1264	− 337,920
4	−400,000	1.0999	− 439,960
5	−600,000	1.0741	− 644,460
6	−700,000	1.0488	− 734,160
7	−800,000	1.0241	− 819,280
8	−700,000	1	− 700,000
			− 4,260,920

GDV   7,500,000
Less outstanding debt: 4,260,920
Plus return for risk and profit @ 18% of GDV 1,350,000
Total costs therefore: 5,610,920
Site value in 2 years' time: GDV − total costs =   1,889,080
PV of £1 in 2 years @ 10%   0.8264
Site value today including purchase costs £   1,561,136

Having looked at how the three cash flow approaches might be used to bring more rigour to the output from a residual valuation some summary points can now be considered.

For the period-by-period cash flow the interest is assessed quarterly on the outstanding amount from the previous quarter and this enables a more accurate statement of cost plus interest. The total cost is then deducted from the GDV to generate a more competitive site value of £1,561,143 than is possible by using the residual method in which interest is over calculated with the effect of depressing the residual sum for the site to £1,446,200. Essentially a developer could therefore bid an extra £115,000 if necessary to acquire a site for which there was competition. The discounted cash flow and net terminal value approaches are also versatile enough to deal with the quarterly cash flow although most will be familiar with the DCF approach while the NTV approach is less commonly used. Both approaches however generate credible and competitive outcomes relative to the residual approach, again enabling a stronger bid to be made for a site if that is necessary.

Period-by-period cash flow	Discounted cash flow	Net terminal value
Characteristics: Interest accrues quarterly according to how the bank charges or monthly for payments to the building contractor. Interest on the previous quarter is added to the next.	*Characteristics:* It converts the period payments to present day value.	*Characteristics:* Like the residual valuation, it adds interest on the outstanding amount to the end of the construction period.
Advantages: The debt is shown for each period and interest rate changes can easily be made.	*Advantages:* Quickest approach, the internal rate of return is calculated.	*Advantages:* Quicker, logical extension to the traditional residual.
Disadvantages: Can be laborious to construct.	*Disadvantages:* Not related to how costs evolve. Does not show the total debt.	*Disadvantages:* Not flexible nor particularly user friendly.

At a broader perspective, cash flows are a necessity for certain developments, for instance residential estates with phased disposal or for complex central area shopping schemes with phasing and funding related to the phases. The cash flow approach is also essential for appraisal of industrial estates or business parks with a program of disposal of sites and completed buildings to minimize cash outlay. Cash flows are also essential where significant expenditure may be required under a section 106 agreement so that infrastructure and social provision is provided to match the phased implementation of a large development. Discounted cash flow techniques can be useful if a scheme is to be retained and financed by mortgage and leaseback as the net return can be seen. Cash flows also offer the following benefits for a developer or a property investor playing that role:

- the effects of inflation on rents and building costs can be modelled over time;
- sensitivity analyses can be conducted to examine the effect of changes on the elements of cost;
- the effects and timing of tax can be explored;
- the effects of phased acquisition or development and partial disposal can be modelled;
- the amount of debt outstanding at any point can be identified; and
- the point of maximum cash outlay (risk exposure) can be identified.

7.4 Using predicted values and costs in development appraisal

One of the alleged benefits of using a cash flow approach mentioned above is that it may be possible to model the effects of forecast changes to variables. Thus the effects of inflation (or deflation) can be explored. Current estimates of costs and values can easily be overtaken by time, particularly where markets are moving rapidly.

Of course the use of predicted values in a valuation by the application of inflation to the variables is subject to the risk of errors in forecasting the magnitude and direction of change. However the dilemma is that the risk may be less than the equivalent risk of using current figures. Property developments as with other major investment projects have a long time scale over which the market will change and the danger will be that the estimates will be inaccurate. But consider the danger of taking no action, many business and personal decisions involve the need to take decisions and to review those decisions periodically in what is really an iterative process. Some would say not to engage in this process of review is an abdication of responsibility, which in rapidly changing environments will probably lead to a loss. The explicit approach of looking to the future and making adjustments accordingly may be flawed but is likely to be the only option.

To some extent the shortcomings associated with the problems of forecasting can be alleviated by the application of statistical techniques. However if a market rate of interest is used to discount and compound the elements within a valuation, then this builds in a degree of comfort as a market discount rate will include an inflation element. Approaches to determining the discount rate will be looked at in the following chapter where there is a fuller discussion of risk.

An approach to building in predicted costs and values into the cash flow would involve the cash flow being broken down into its elements of cost and appropriate inflation rates applied. These total costs can then be increased by the interest charges to completion. Finally, the building and finance costs can be incorporated into a residual valuation with a rental figure in which a growth rate has been applied. This approach is shown in the simplified example which follows.

Example 7.4: Cash flow with inflated costs and rents

The project has the following characteristics and a development period of 1 year which is divided into four quarters.

Net annual rental value £	250,000	
YP in perp. @ 5%	20	
Gross Development Value (GDV)		5,000,000

Quarter	Building costs	Fees
1	250,000	
2	450,000	60,000
3	650,000	80,000
4	500,000	100,000

Growth rate for rent	0.75%	per quarter
Inflation for building costs	1%	per quarter
Inflation for fees	1.5%	per quarter
Interest rate	2.5%	per quarter

Step 1: Apply inflation to costs

Quarter	Current estimate of building costs	Building cost inflation @ 1% per quarter	Inflated building costs	Current estimate of fees	Fees inflation @ 1.5% per quarter	Inflated fees	Total costs
1	250,000	1	250,000				250,000
2	450,000	1.01	454,500	60,000	1.015	60,900	515,400
3	650,000	1.0201	663,065	80,000	1.0302	82,416	745,481
4	500,000	1.0303	515,150	100,000	1.0457	104,570	619,720

Step 2: Include interest

Quarter	Total costs	Interest @ 2.5% per quarter	Cost to completion
1	250,000	1.0769	269,225
2	515,400	1.0506	541,492
3	745,481	1.025	764,118
4	619,720	1	619,720
		Total	2,194,555

Step 3: Valuation with growth rate applied to rent

Present estimated rental income £		250,000
Rental growth 4 quarters @	0.75%	1.0303
Future estimated rental income £		257,575
YP in perp. @ 5%	20	
Revised GDV =		5,151,500
Less cost and finance	2,194,555	
Risk and profit @ 20% of GDV	1,030,300	
Total costs therefore		3,224,855
Site value in 1 year's time (GDV – total costs)		1,926,645
PV £1 in 4 quarters @	2.5%	0.9060
Site value today including acquisition costs		1,745,540

7.5 Quarterly in advance valuation

Thus far the examples of valuations have tended to take a conventional annual in arrears approach to rental income. However this is at odds with reality, where most commercial leases require rent to be paid by the tenant quarterly in advance. Thus in a strict sense, the income stream is worth a little more in present value terms given that some of the money becomes available at an earlier stage and could be reinvested to earn interest. This is perhaps an area where practice and academic books have tended to suffer from a degree of inertia in that they have been slow to abandon the assumption that rent is available annually in arrears. If there is a defence for academic books, then it is that splicing in the added complication of quarterly in advance will sometimes act to obscure the fundamental principle of discounting being explored. However more recent editions of Parry's Tables include tables which provide the YP in perpetuity and for a given number of years on a quarterly in advance basis. If readers have made it this far with the core principles then perhaps now is the time to introduce the principle of quarterly in advance valuation.

A very simple comparative example will show to what extent there is a difference between accounting for quarterly in advance and annually in arrears. Imagine a shop rent of £60,000 per annum which is available for 3 years. An investor has a target rate of 8 per cent for this opportunity and discounts it firstly by the conventional annual in arrears method to ascertain what its present value is. The NPV arising below suggests that the investor should pay no more than £154,620 for the right to receive that income stream while maintaining the target rate of return of 8 per cent.

Example 7.5: Annual in arrears compared with quarterly in advance rental income

DCF annually in arrears			
Year	Income £	PV of £1 @ 8%	Discounted cash flow £
1	60,000	0.9259	55,554
2	60,000	0.8573	51,438
3	60,000	0.7938	47,628
		NPV =	154,620

Aware that the income was available quarterly in advance, the investor could also discount the income by the quarterly equivalent of the 8% discount rate using the formula:

$$((1 + i)^{0.25}) - 1 = (1.08^{0.25}) - 1 = 1.94\% \text{ rounded}$$

Once the quarterly equivalent interest rate is ascertained it can be used to generate the PV of £1 for any quarter by using the formula: $1/(1 + i)^n$ where i becomes the quarterly rate and n the particular quarter. So for example the present value of £1 in 7 quarters in the example below where the quarterly rate is 1.94% would be $1/1.0194^7 = 0.8742$ (rounded). Note that the cash flow begins with a zero in the quarter column to denote the position in the present when the investor is considering purchasing the asset and in doing so would be entitled to the first quarter's income in advance. Thus the first tranche of income is not discounted as it is already at present value.

DCF quarterly in advance			
Quarter	Income £	PV of £1 @ 1.94%	Discounted cash flow £
0	15,000	1	15,000
1	15,000	0.9810	14,715
2	15,000	0.9623	14,435
3	15,000	0.9440	14,160
4	15,000	0.9260	13,890
5	15,000	0.9084	13,626
6	15,000	0.8911	13,367
7	15,000	0.8742	13,113
8	15,000	0.8575	12,863
9	15,000	0.8412	12,618
10	15,000	0.8252	12,378
11	15,000	0.8095	12,143
		NPV =	162,308

Because more of the income is available earlier in the quarterly in advance model, it is a slightly more valuable income stream than the annually in arrears model, although nominally £60,000 is changing hands each year in both cases. At a practical level the investor could pay marginally more (£7,688 in this case) for the quarterly in advance income while still maintaining the target rate of 10 per cent.

For readers who prefer to use Parry's Tables, the year's purchase single rate quarterly in advance tables should be consulted and in which the YP for three years at 8 per cent is 2.7047. That constant would then be multiplied by the annual income which in this case is £60,000 to give £162,282. The difference (of £16) with the £162,308 NPV shown above is that there has been rounding in the DCF table to suit the publication format. Parry's YP single rate quarterly in advance tables is based upon the following formula in which r is the investor's annual target rate and n is the number of years. The formula therefore provides a further check and when used for the above example the figures would look as follows.

$$\frac{1 - (1 + r)^{-n}}{4\,[1 - (1 + r)^{-1/4}]} = \frac{0.206168}{0.076225} = 2.7047 \text{ (rounded)}$$

Again the resulting value would be multiplied by the actual annual income of £60,000 to give £162,282 which is the present value of the investment when the target rate is 8 per cent.

Having established the quarterly in advance principle the following example explores how it might be applied to the evaluation of a significant commercial property investment opportunity.

Example 7.6: DCF quarterly in advance with explicit rental growth assumptions

A pension fund has become aware of a property investment opportunity in the form of a 2,500 m^2 B1 unit on a well connected business park in an area where the economy is buoyant. The property was fully let to a well established business tenant 2½ years ago on a 20-year FRI lease with five-year rent reviews at a then market rent of £210 per m^2. Rental growth on this particular business park for this type of property seems to have followed a consistent trend over the last 10 years of RPI + 1%. The pension fund has a target rate of 9 per cent for this type of investment and is interested in purchasing the unit and holding it until the second rent review. Initial enquiries suggest that the vendor's agent is expecting bids from investors to reflect an initial yield of around 6.5 per cent. Assuming that there will be competition from other funds to acquire this unit, the fund sets about evaluating what its maximum bid might be while preserving the corporate target rate of 9 per cent.

Valuers acting for the fund ascertain from available measurements that the gross to net ratio in this relatively new building is 85 per cent and so the gross floorspace converts to 2,125 m^2 net lettable space. Given that the unit was let at £210 m^2, the annual rent passing is therefore £446,250 which is paid quarterly in advance instalments of £111,563. Valuers have indentified that the building has no special sustainability accreditation such as a BREEAM rating and therefore over the envisaged holding period of 7½ years its attractiveness will inevitably decline relative to newer buildings which will appear on the business park and which will probably have a sustainability rating of one kind or another. Valuers therefore allow for this loss of competitiveness by assuming that at the point of sale the exit yield will slacken to 7.5 per cent in comparison to the initial yield of 6.5 per cent. This is a judgement based upon how similar buildings have performed in the past.

Although there is a FRI lease in place and the income is therefore net of significant outgoings, the fund's valuers decide to make an allowance of 1.5 per cent against the rent to cover management costs. Valuers identify that the inflation rate as measured by RPI has averaged 2.62 per cent over the last 10 years and so they decide to use that figure plus 1 per cent to project the growth in rent as follows.

The market rent which was agreed when the lease commenced 2½ years ago was £446,250 and this will continue for another 2½ years until the first rent review. The valuers working for the fund are assuming a growth rate of RPI + 1% = 3.62% per annum. The market rent which could therefore be expected to apply following the first rent review would therefore be $1.0362^5 \times £446,250 = £533,084$. Assuming that this growth rate continues to the second rent review, the market rent would then be $1.0362^5 \times £533,084 = £636,815$. It is this rental value which would be capitalized to establish the sales value, as it is the fund's intention to take the investment to the second rent review and then dispose of it. The fund's valuers are assuming that the developer who currently owns the property (the vendor) will absorb the purchaser's costs as this is the established practice when funds purchase tenanted investment properties from developers.

The fund however are anticipating some exit costs at say 3 per cent of the capital value achieved on a sale at that stage. One way to calculate the discount rate applicable in any quarter is to use the PV of £1 formula: $1/(1 + i)^n$ and to insert into it the annual rate (9 per cent in this case) and n which can be a whole or part of the relevant year. So for example the discount rate applicable for the fourth quarter in the third project year below can be calculated by $1/1.09^{2.25}$ = 0.8237. Given the above assumptions and figures, the DCF evaluation of this investment prospect might look as follows.

Year	Beginning of:	Time in years	Expenditure (£)	Income (£)	Net Cash flow (£)	PV of £1 @ 9%	Discounted Cash flow (£)
1	3rd quarter	0	6,867,058	111,563	−6,755,495	1	−6,755,495
	4th quarter	0.25	1,673	111,563	109,890	0.9787	107,549
2	1st quarter	0.5	1,673	111,563	109,890	0.9578	105,253
	2nd quarter	0.75	1,673	111,563	109,890	0.9374	103,011
	3rd quarter	1	1,673	111,563	109,890	0.9174	100,813
	4th quarter	1.25	1,673	111,563	109,890	0.8979	98,670
3	1st quarter	1.5	1,673	111,563	109,890	0.8787	96,560
	2nd quarter	1.75	1,673	111,563	109,890	0.8600	94,505
	3rd quarter	2	1,673	111,563	109,890	0.8417	92,494
	4th quarter	2.25	1,673	111,563	109,890	0.8237	90,516

Year	Beginning of:	Time in years	Expenditure (£)	Income (£)	Net Cash flow (£)	PV of £1 @ 9%	Discounted Cash flow (£)
4	1st quarter	2.5	1,999	133,271	131,272	0.8062	105,831
	2nd quarter	2.75	1,999	133,271	131,272	0.7890	103,574
	3rd quarter	3	1,999	133,271	131,272	0.7722	101,368
	4th quarter	3.25	1,999	133,271	131,272	0.7557	99,202
5	1st quarter	3.5	1,999	133,271	131,272	0.7396	97,089
	2nd quarter	3.75	1,999	133,271	131,272	0.7239	95,028
	3rd quarter	4	1,999	133,271	131,272	0.7084	92,993
	4th quarter	4.25	1,999	133,271	131,272	0.6933	91,011
6	1st quarter	4.5	1,999	133,271	131,272	0.6785	89,068
	2nd quarter	4.75	1,999	133,271	131,272	0.6641	87,178
	3rd quarter	5	1,999	133,271	131,272	0.6499	85,314
	4th quarter	5.25	1,999	133,271	131,272	0.6361	83,502
7	1st quarter	5.5	1,999	133,271	131,272	0.6225	81,717
	2nd quarter	5.75	1,999	133,271	131,272	0.6093	79,984
	3rd quarter	6	1,999	133,271	131,272	0.5963	78,277
	4th quarter	6.25	1,999	133,271	131,272	0.5836	76,610
8	1st quarter	6.5	1,999	133,271	131,272	0.5711	74,969
	2nd quarter	6.75	1,999	133,271	131,272	0.5589	73,368
	3rd quarter	7	1,999	133,271	131,272	0.5470	71,806
	4th quarter	7.25	1,999	133,271	131,272	0.5354	70,283
9	1st quarter	7.5	254,726	8,490,867	8,236,141	0.524	4,315,738
						NPV =	187,786
						IRR =	9.50%

Although the investment looks as if it will exceed the target rate of 9 per cent even if the vendor's asking price is met in full, a valuer would not simply adopt the figures arising from the first run of the DCF. It is very likely that the fund's valuer would explore changes in the variables in order to generate best-case and worst-case scenarios. For example a judgement has been made about what the exit yield will be and variations around this assumption would be explored to see how they alter the outcome. Assumptions have also been made about a constant rate of rental growth based upon historic trends in inflation and this is where a competent analyst would model variations in assumed growth rates. Given that most investors are risk averse, a combination of changes which would constitute a worst-case scenario would be looked at and some sort of probability modelling would take place around that. This type of modelling helps to provide a frame for decision-making and there will be further discussion on some of the techniques that may be used later in the book.

7.6 Adjusting for inflation

A conceptual weakness of the traditional term and reversion valuation method relates to the marginal adjustments made to the capitalization rates for the term and reversion income tranches to reflect their relative security in money terms. It is not explicit in the margin of adjustment how inflation has been taken into account.

Isaac and Steley (2000) discuss the calculation of the inflation risk-free yield (IRFY) which is the real interest rate and which is simply the market rate of interest with inflation taken out. The formula used to identify the IRFY is:

$$(1 + e) = (1 + g)\,(1 + i)$$

where $g\%$ is the growth rate %
   e is the equated yield %
   i is the IRFY %

Transposing the formula the IRFY or $i = \dfrac{(1 + e)}{(1 + g)} - 1$

Once the IRFY is identified it can be used in what has become known as the real value/equated yield hybrid approach, the formula for which is as follows:

YP of the whole (n) = $YP\ t\ @\ e \times \dfrac{YP\ n\ @\ i}{YP\ t\ @\ i}$

e = equated yield
t = rent review period
n = valuation term
i = IRFY

The practical application of this formula is illustrated as follows.

Example 7.7: Real value/equated yield hybrid approach

An investment property was recently let at £100,000 per annum on a five year rent review pattern. Assuming a rental growth rate of 3 per cent per annum and that the equated yield is 10 per cent the value of the freehold could be calculated as follows using the variables e = 10 per cent, g = 3 per cent, n is in perpetuity and t = 5.

Calculate $i = \dfrac{1 + 0.10}{1 + 0.03} - 1 = 0.06796 = 6.796\%$

Calculate YP in perp. = YP 5 years @ 10% $\times \dfrac{\text{YP in perp.@ } 6.796\%}{\text{YP 5 yrs @ } 6.796\%}$

$$= 3.7908 \times \frac{14.7145}{4.1227}$$

$$3.7908 \times 3.5691 = 13.5297$$

Valuation: Market rent per annum: £100,000
                  YP in perp.   13.5297
                  Capital value: £1,352,970

The calculation of a leasehold interest using the real value/equated yield hybrid approach is in two parts, the valuation of the right to receive the rent from the sub-lessee is found and the capital value of the liability to pay the ground rent is deducted. This head lessee's valuation is calculated at the risk rate for the head lessee's net income. The valuation is thus:

Calculate IRFY: $i = \dfrac{1 + e}{1 + g}$

where i = IRFY
      e = equated yield of head lessee's interest
      g = growth rate p.a.

Valuation:

Value of rent received = rent received $\times$ YP t years @ e% $\times \dfrac{\text{YP } n \text{ years @ } i\%}{\text{YP } t \text{ years @ } e\%}$

less
value of rent paid = rent paid $\times$ YP n years @ e%

where: i = inflation risk-free yield
       e = equated yield of head lessee
       n = length of lease
       t = rent review period

7.7 Inducements

Inducements tend to arise in markets when there is a larger supply of commercial floorspace available than there is demand from businesses to occupy that space. Periodic imbalances like this will occur either because businesses are downsizing or are not able or willing to take leases on buildings and/or because of the lag effect in the property pipeline which will sometimes see a glut of new buildings arriving on the market just at a time when demand from business tenants has dried up. The laws of supply and demand will dictate that in these circumstances the landlords of commercial properties will have to take a longer term view by offering rent-free periods of perhaps of 1, 2 or 3 years in order to commit a business tenant to sign a lease of say 10 years. There can also be reverse premiums which are tantamount to rent-free periods in that while the rent is assumed to start passing from day 1 the landlord effectively pays a premium to the tenant as a multiple of the rent and effectively writes off the rent for the agreed period.

The RICS (2006: 5) confirms that it is customary at the beginning of a commercial lease to allow for a tenant's fit-out period, which would normally be three months during which there would be no rent payable by the tenant. This period would not normally be considered as an inducement because it is normal practice. For example, if the rent did not pass between the parties for the first two years, it could be assumed that the rent-free inducement was really 1¾ years, i.e. 2 years less a 3-month fit-out period. The examples below will illustrate how such a transaction might be analysed.

Where market conditions dictate that inducements need to be offered then some jargon comes into play as follows:

Headline rent: the rent payable after the inducements have expired.
Equivalent rent: the adjusted rent which takes account of the inducements offered and which is more formally known as the *net effective rent.*

Inducements such as rent-free periods reduce the value of the rental stream over the term below what the headline rent might suggest and this raises two challenges for valuers in that:

1 the capital valuation of a property subject to a rent-free period will have to take account of the detrimental effect that this will have on capital value; and
2 the transaction may be used by other valuers as a comparison to value a similar property and they will therefore need to calculate the equivalent rent by making an allowance for the rent-free period.

As Shapiro *et al.* (2009: 407–8) explain there are two principal ways that these related problems can be tackled and the example below illustrates the principles involved.

Example 7.8: Identifying the equivalent rent for valuation purposes

A business tenant has signed a 10 year lease to take several floors of offices in a large multi-let office tower in a city centre. The headline rent agreed was £90,000 per annum on FRI terms with a rent review in year 5. Market comparison suggests a capitalization rate of 7 per cent for this type of investment. The landlord has agreed a rent-free period so that the rent will only begin to pass from the beginning of year 3.

A valuer who was analysing this transaction would quite legitimately assume that the first two years during which no rent was passing included a 3-month fit-out period and thus the true length of the rent-free period (the incentive) was in fact 21 months. The valuer could then calculate the total of the headline rent which would nominally pass during the first five-year term less the rent-free incentive and then divide that figure by the actual length of the term. The result of the calculation would then be capitalized at 7 per cent. The calculation on a quarterly in advance basis would thus look as follows.

Headline rent assumed to pass for 3.25 years × £90,000 =   £292,500
Divide by the actual term of 5 years =   £58,500
Capitalize with YP for 5 years (quarterly in advance) @ 7% = 4.2781
Capital value therefore: £250,269

The capital value of the first 5 years to rent review of £250,269 could then be added to the value of the second five-year term using the term and reversion method described in Chapter 6. The discussion here is on the first five-year term, as it is within this period that the rent-free period takes effect.

The second approach to valuing the term up to the first rent review is described by authors such as Jayne (2008: 342) and is perhaps more conceptually robust. However this method generates a lower equivalent rent and capital value as follows.

Headline rent: £90,000
YP 3.25 years @ 7% quarterly in advance =   2.9422
x PV £1 in 1.75 years @ 7%   0.8881
Capital value: £235,167
Divide by YP 5 years @ 7% quarterly in advance   4.2781
Annual equivalent rent therefore: £54,970

The above approach can be checked if necessary by setting out the variables in a quarterly in advance discounted cash flow as follows.

Beginning of quarter:	Headline rent per quarter £	Equivalent rent per quarter £	PV £1 @ 7% per annum (1.71% per quarter)	Discounted cash flow of headline rent £	Discounted cash flow of equivalent rent £
1		13,743	1		13,743
2		13,743	0.9832		13,512
3		13,743	0.9667		13,285
4		13,743	0.9504		13,061
5		13,743	0.9344		12,841
6		13,743	0.9187		12,626
7		13,743	0.9033		12,414
8	22,500	13,743	0.8881	19,982	12,205
9	22,500	13,743	0.8732	19,647	12,000
10	22,500	13,743	0.8585	19,316	11,798
11	22,500	13,743	0.8440	18,990	11,599
12	22,500	13,743	0.8299	18,673	11,405
13	22,500	13,743	0.8159	18,358	11,213
14	22,500	13,743	0.8022	18,050	11,025
15	22,500	13,743	0.7887	17,746	10,839
16	22,500	13,743	0.7754	17,447	10,656
17	22,500	13,743	0.7624	17,154	10,478

Beginning of quarter:	Headline rent per quarter £	Equivalent rent per quarter £	PV £1 @ 7% per annum (1.71% per quarter)	Discounted cash flow of headline rent £	Discounted cash flow of equivalent rent £
18	22,500	13,743	0.7496	16,866	10,302
19	22,500	13,743	0.7370	16,583	10,129
20	22,500	13,743	0.7246	16,304	9,958
			NPV =	235,116	235,089

The differences in the capital values arrived at are due to rounding at various points for publication purposes.

Despite the theoretical superiority of the second method above Shapiro *et al.* (2009) report that in practice valuers prefer to use the first method, perhaps because it is more straightforward. The RICS (2006: 11) takes a pragmatic approach acknowledging that it may be appropriate to use the more sophisticated second method where properties of significant value are being evaluated for large corporate investors. Conversely where the rent-free period relative to the term is relatively short and the properties involved are not in the multimillion pound bracket, then a simple averaging approach set out in the first method above may be appropriate. As RICS comments:

> The choice of method adopted and assumptions behind the analysis undertaken is a matter for the valuer in the light of all of the circumstances regarding the problem to be assessed. (2006: 11)

7.8 Investment appraisal and strategic decision-making

The discussion on inducements above stems from periods when there is too much supply of a particular type of property relative to the demand for it. If the property involved is a new development and is being let for the first time there is probably little alternative but for the owner to offer a rent-free period consistent with what the market dictates at the particular time and location. However if the property is second-hand stock and the lease is nearing an end there may be other alternatives for the landlord to consider rather than just offering inducements in order to relet the building to existing or other tenants. Thus an interlude of one or two years when there will be no income from the building should cause the owner to think more strategically and to evaluate the alternatives. The history of trends in the property market suggests that after about two years of recession the market tends to recover, so if refurbishment work was undertaken during a downturn there is the possibility of reletting a refurbished building on a rising market two or so years later. Depending on the particular type of property, its age and location, the alternatives might include:

- Seeking a change of use from the local planning authority, converting and marketing the building for use by a different business sector. Location specific market research would be needed in this scenario.

- Refurbishing and retro-fitting the building so that it attracted a sustainability accreditation (such as a BREEAM rating) enabling it to achieve a stronger rental performance on reletting.
- Redeveloping the site in order to increase both the quality and quantity of lettable floorspace.
- Selling the site to a developer with the benefit of a planning consent for redevelopment.

Of course there would be added complications if the building was listed (as discussed in Chapter 1 of this book) although even then, there are plenty of successful examples of the creative and valuable reuse of listed buildings.

When the need to take strategic decisions like those posed above arises, the following example illustrates how discounted cash flows can aid decision-making.

Example 7.9: DCF as an aid to strategic decision-making

This example assumes a 20-year-old office unit set within its own plot on a business park. The occupier's lease has one year remaining at the passing rent of £70,000 per annum. That rent reflects the market rent achieved at review four years ago but since then, the market has gone into recession and the current market rent for a second-hand building like this one would be £65,000. The building is a no-frills business unit built to a tight budget and in quality terms it is not particularly competitive when compared to some of the newer buildings which have appeared recently on the business park. There is some doubt that the unit would easily relet in the current market and there might be an extended void period when the landlord would have to meet outgoings such as insurance premiums, business rates and water rates which are currently met by the tenant under the FRI lease.

Current office lettings in the vicinity have also reflected the market in that rent-free periods have been needed in order to induce tenants to commit to leases of any length. Aware that the balance of power in the market has shifted towards tenants and away from landlords, the current tenant has indicated that if a two year rent-free period were offered then they would sign a new 10-year lease based upon the current market rent. The modelling of that scenario is reflected in *Scenario A* below which envisages that the tenant's requests are met and the landlord takes the income up to the first rent review but then disposes of the building at an exit yield of 8.5 per cent to reflect what would then be a dated building in business park terms. The scenario also assumes a fairly conservative rental growth rate of 2 per cent per annum between the signing of the new lease in year 2 and the first rent review five years later. The landlord has a target rate of return for property assets held in its property portfolio of 10 per cent and thus the discount rate corresponds to that expectation.

Scenario A – Agree to a new lease with two years' rent free and a reduced rent

Annual rent passing £70,000   Exit yield: 8.50%
Market rent: £65,000   Landlord's target rate of return: 10%
Assumed annual rental growth years two to six: 2%

Year	Income £	Expenditure £	Net cash flow £	PV of £1 @ 10%	Discounted cash flow £	Event
1	70,000	0	70,000	0.9091	63,637	Final rent payment
2	0	0	0	0.8264	0	Rent-free period
3	0	0	0	0.7513	0	Rent-free period
4	65,000	0	65,000	0.6830	44,395	New rent for 3 years
5	65,000	0	65,000	0.6209	40,359	
6	65,000	0	65,000	0.5645	36,693	
7	71,765	0	71,765	0.5132	36,830	Rent review
7	844,294	25,329	818,965	0.5132	420,293	End of year sale
				NPV =	£642,206	

Scenario B: Refurbish, retro fit and relet the building

This scenario envisages that the terms required by the existing tenant are not met and a new lease is not agreed but that the landlord takes advantage of the ensuing void to refurbish the building. Refurbishment in this scenario includes retrofitting the building with renewable energy technology, such as photo-voltaic panels, in order to raise the building's sustainability credentials thereby enabling it to attract a BREEAM rating. The strategy would then be to market the enhanced quality of the building to new tenants and to include a one year rent-free period incorporating a 3-month fit-out period as an inducement.

Given that the building now has added sustainability advantages, its market rent would be comparable to newer and more energy efficient buildings on the business park and this is reflected in the £70,000 rental income shown below from year 4 onwards. Again a conservative annual growth rate in that rent is assumed at 2 per cent to reflect a gradually recovering market. A firmer exit yield of 7.5 per cent is assumed in contrast to *Scenario A* above, to reflect a more competitive building at the time of disposal following the first rent review.

Year	Income £	Expenditure £	Net cash flow £	PV of £1 @ 10%	Discounted cash flow £	Event
1	70,000	0	70,000	0.9091	63,637	Final rent payment
2	0	250,000	−250,000	0.8264	−206,600	Refurbishment
3	0	0	0	0.7513	0	Rent-free period
4	70,000	0	70,000	0.6830	47,810	New rent for 4 years
5	70,000	0	70,000	0.6209	43,463	
6	70,000	0	70,000	0.5645	39,515	
7	70,000	0	70,000	0.5132	35,924	Rent review
8	77,286	0	77,286	0.4665	36,054	
9	1,030,480	30,914	999,566	0.4665	512,977	End of year sale
				NPV =	£572,780	

Scenario C: Redevelop the site to increase the quality and quantity of floorspace

Because the unit sits in its own plot and the landlord owns the freehold title, this scenario assumes that the landlord can achieve planning consent to increase the floorspace on the plot by adding a storey and improving overall site coverage. Thus redevelopment takes place over two years which while obviously the most expensive option will result in a considerable increase in lettable floorspace and a qualitative improvement overall, assuming that the new building is designed to qualify for a BREEAM rating. The income of £120,000 reflects this below following an inducement of a one year rent-free period including a 3-month fit-out period. Again the strategy for the landlord is to retain the property up to the first rent review and then dispose of it at a competitive capitalization rate of 6.5 per cent to reflect a state of the art building.

Year	Income £	Expenditure £	Net cash flow £	PV of £1 @ 10%	Discounted cash flow £	Event
1	70,000	0	70,000	0.9091	63,637	Final rent payment
2	0	275,000	−275,000	0.8264	−227,260	Redevelopment
3	0	425,000	−425,000	0.7513	−319,303	Redevelopment
4	0	14,000	−14,000	0.6830	−9,562	Rent-free period
5	120,000	0	120,000	0.6209	74,508	New rent
5	1,846,154	55,385	1,790,769	0.6209	1,111,888	End of year sale
				NPV =	£ 693,909	

Of course a mechanical approach to comparing the NPVs arising under each scenario and choosing that which generates the highest value is not advocated. However the modelling of the financial implications of the options available is a valid part of the strategic decision-making process for the corporate property investor. Thus regarding scenarios A, B and C above, other factors would also feature in the decision-making process such as market research for new sustainable office space relative to the demand for cheaper second-hand space in the locality and the overall picture provided by the landlord's property portfolio. For example if relatively risky redevelopment was already being carried out on another property owned by the investor then the safer option provided by *Scenario A* might be appropriate at that time and which would mean a deferral of the redevelopment of this particular site for the time being.

7.9 Depreciation

The RICS Valuation Standards (the Red Book) (2010: 178) adopts the definition of depreciation set out by the Accountancy Standards Board in its Financial Reporting Standards 15 'Tangible Fixed Assets' and which is:

> The measure of the cost, or revalued amount, of the economic benefits of a tangible fixed asset that have been consumed during the period. Consumption includes the wearing out, the using up or other reduction in the useful economic life of the tangible fixed asset whether from use, effluxion of time or

obsolescence through either changes in technology or demand for goods and services produced by the asset.

When dealing with straightforward capital assets accountants will normally assess depreciation by looking at the purchase price and the sale price or scrap value, to calculate depreciation over the useful life of the asset in a straight line as follows.

Example 7.10: Straight-line depreciation

A small fleet of company cars is purchased for £100,000. It is estimated that they will have an operational life with the company of 5 years before being sold on for an estimated £20,000. The cars can be written down in accounting terms using the straight line method as follows:

Purchase price:	£100,000
Less resale price:	£20,000
Amount to be written off:	£80,000
Life of the assets is 5 years	
Depreciation per year is therefore:	£16,000

Example 7.11: Reducing balance approach to depreciation

Assets such as cars above are more likely to depreciate at a proportion of their value each year which means that there is a higher fall off in value in the earlier years of the asset's life. Thus taking the example of the company cars above an accountant might take a view that this type of asset depreciates at 25 per cent of value each year and could set out the schedule below.

Year	Capital value £	Annual depreciation rate %	Annual depreciation £
0	100,000	25	25,000
1	75,000	25	18,750
2	56,250	25	14,063
3	42,188	25	10,547
4	31,641	25	7,910
5	23,730		

However the long-hand version is not necessary as the following formula will achieve the same result.

Depreciated value = Original capital value $\times (1 - r)^n$
in which r is the depreciation rate and n the number of years.
Depreciated value = £100,000 $\times (1 - 25\%)^5$
= £100,000 $\times 0.75^5$
= £100,000 $\times 0.2373 = $ £23,730

Capital assets such as IT equipment will have even higher rates of annual depreciation as rapid advances in the technology renders equipment obsolete and valueless only several years after it has been purchased.

There is even a third alternative of modelling depreciation which is referred to as the S-curve. This method requires the accountant to model specific rates of depreciation each year to replicate either a faster or slower rate of depreciation in the earlier years relative to the rest of the life of the asset. Discussion on this method would stray beyond what is necessary for this book and those who are particularly interested in this topic should consult a specialized accountancy text.

Depreciation and real property

When considering depreciation and real property, the situation becomes more complicated than for capital assets such as cars discussed above. This is because while buildings clearly do depreciate the land that they sit upon will normally appreciate and so it is difficult to disentangle the two effects. Buildings in different asset classes will also depreciate at different rates depending on the interplay of a number of factors such as location, design and obsolescence caused by changes in the demand for the commodity being made in or sold from the buildings.

For example an integrated iron and steel works built in an industrial area in the 1960s will have depreciated because the technology will have moved on, there will have been physical deterioration of the buildings and the global markets for iron and steel will have shifted so that the location may have become redundant for iron and steel making. The rate of depreciation experienced for the iron and steel plant will differ considerably from a standard shop unit in a prime high street location which is not threatened by out of town retail competition. The shop unit may have been built long before the iron and steel plant but despite some modest wear and tear the rate of depreciation on the shop will probably be slight compared to the steel works.

In the residential sector readers will be aware of perfectly habitable and depending on the location, very valuable Victorian terraced housing which might be 130 years old. These properties have existed well beyond what might have been expected by the original developers as they have benefitted from maintenance and improvement by successive owners. Periodic reinvestment has therefore reduced the effects of depreciation and (depending on location) the land value has risen to offset any measurable building depreciation.

Baum (2009) reports upon examples where depreciation has markedly affected the ability of office blocks in the City of London to command comparable rental values. This relates to the fact that (assuming a prime location) when new, office buildings will tend to be state of the art and will therefore command a market rent commensurate with their designation as prime office space. Thus the leading rents in the City of London might be found in the Swiss Re building designed by Norman Foster and otherwise known as the Gherkin. Its rental value per m^2 will be significantly higher than for 30-year-old office blocks in the same street. As time passes newer office buildings such as the office tower on Bishopsgate dubbed the Cheese Grater and the Shard of Glass at London Bridge will appear on the city skyline and these buildings will in turn become the new prime property. Gradually the generation of buildings completed in the early 2000s such as the Gherkin, will merge into the second-hand stock of properties. The phenomenon is of course not unique to the London office market but there is a universal difficulty in predicting the rate at which rental value will gradually depreciate relative to the new stock and how that affects capital value in the longer term. To complicate matters further there will be maintenance expenditure and periodic refurbishment which together will slow down or temporarily halt the rate at which a commercial building becomes less competitive in rental terms against its newer neighbours.

One of the difficulties is in predicting the rate at which the rental value will diminish and the cross over point at which buildings like the Gherkin cease to be considered as prime but become secondary in rental terms. To some extent the issue of declining value is acknowledged in the choice of exit yield used by a valuer in that it is assumed that the lack of competitiveness will affect the end value as reflected in a slacker exit yield in contrast to the initial yield. However that is only part of the equation and DCF cash flows can contribute here by setting out the likely rental pattern going forward, so that as a building ages it is shown not to be able to capture the prime rents it achieved when it was new. The examples considered by Baum suggest that depreciation occurs in both dimensions in that there is both a slacker exit yield and reduced rental performance over time.

An example follows which tries to illustrate the principle of depreciation on just the rental income over time. Simplifications have been made in order to focus upon the principles at work and so for example there is no allowance for quarterly in advance income and nor are there allowances for purchase, exit and management costs which would probably arise.

Example 7.12: The effects on value of depreciating rental performance

A new state of the art sustainable office building has just been let at an initial rent reflecting the market rent for prime offices of £400 per m^2 in the particular location. The building has 3,000 m^2 of net lettable floorspace and from market comparison the initial yield for the investment is 7 per cent. The appraiser recognizes that there will be some loss of competitiveness over the envisaged 10-year holding period and thus subjectively adjusts the exit yield to 8 per cent. The first run through of the DCF below assumes that there will be no loss of rental performance and that the building will continue to attract the market rent for prime property at the rent reviews in years 5 and 10. Historic data suggests that prime office rents in this location have grown on average by 3.5 per cent per annum over the longer term and so that growth rate is projected forward in the appraisal below. Thus at the first rent review the calculation would be £1,200,000 × 1.035^5 = £1,425,224. The same process takes place at the second rent review in year 10 where the reviewed rent is capitalized by the exit yield to generate the sale value shown.

The second run of the DCF assumes that there will be some loss of rental performance and so the rent reviews at years 5 and 10 are depreciated by 1 per cent per annum. Thus what might have been the prime rent in year 5 of £1,425,224 is multiplied by $(1 - 1\%)^5$ to generate a depreciated rent of £1,355,373. The overall comparison is shown in the NPVs generated by each

DCF and which signifies the difference between achieving the corporate target rate of return of 9 per cent and not achieving it by a considerable margin.

Initial market rent of £400 per m²
Assumed annual rental growth for prime property: 3.5%

Initial yield: 7%
Exit yield: 8%

Year	Income £	Expenditure £	Net cash flow £	PV of £1 @ 9%	Discounted cash flow £	Event
0	0	17,142,857	–17,142,857	1	–17,142,857	Purchase building
1	1,200,000	0	1,200,000	0.9174	1,100,880	5 years of income begins
2	1,200,000	0	1,200,000	0.8417	1,010,040	
3	1,200,000	0	1,200,000	0.7722	926,640	
4	1,200,000	0	1,200,000	0.7084	850,080	
5	1,200,000	0	1,200,000	0.6499	779,880	
6	1,425,224	0	1,425,224	0.5963	849,861	New rent begins
7	1,425,224	0	1,425,224	0.5470	779,598	
8	1,425,224	0	1,425,224	0.5019	715,320	
9	1,425,224	0	1,425,224	0.4604	656,173	
10	1,425,224	0	1,425,224	0.4224	602,015	
10	21,158,988	0	21,158,988	0.4224	8,937,557	Capital sale on reviewed rent
				NPV =	65,186	

Rental depreciation applied at a rate of 1% rate per annum:

Year	Income £	Expenditure £	Net cash flow £	PV of £1 @ 9%	Discounted cash flow £	Event
0	0	17,142,857	–17,142,857	1	–17,142,857	Purchase building
1	1,200,000	0	1,200,000	0.9174	1,100,880	5 years of income begins
2	1,200,000	0	1,200,000	0.8417	1,010,040	
3	1,200,000	0	1,200,000	0.7722	926,640	
4	1,200,000	0	1,200,000	0.7084	850,080	
5	1,200,000	0	1,200,000	0.6499	779,880	
6	1,355,373	0	1,355,373	0.5963	808,209	New rent begins
7	1,355,373	0	1,355,373	0.5470	741,389	
8	1,355,373	0	1,355,373	0.5019	680,262	
9	1,355,373	0	1,355,373	0.4604	624,014	
10	1,355,373	0	1,355,373	0.4224	572,510	
10	19,135,797	0	19,135,797	0.4224	8,082,961	Capital sale on reviewed rent
				NPV =	–965,993	

The above DCF comparisons have only looked at one dimension of depreciation by focusing on the effects of depreciating rental performance. A fuller picture would emerge if more were known about how depreciation affects the exit yield which reflects the capital value achievable on resale. While a very modest widening has been made between the initial and exit yields in the example above to reflect some depreciation in capital value, the figures adopted are hypothetical. In all probability the gap between the initial and exit yields would be wider than is suggested above to reflect the capital depreciation which was likely to take place over 10 years on say a prime city centre office block. Looking forward, the gap may widen particularly between those buildings which have a sustainability accreditation and those that do not.

Even if sustainability characteristics are taken out of the equation, examples mentioned by Baum (2009: 8) illustrate why in business districts such as the City of London, capital depreciation will trigger either major refurbishment of office towers or sites will be completely redeveloped every 20 years or so. The refurbishment or redevelopment cycle could be extended where the building is of the highest quality and is a prestigious landmark development designed by a leading architect. Otherwise, less distinguished buildings in these settings will tend to depreciate very quickly relative to the new competition, so that complete redevelopment is often the only way to stay abreast of the pace of change driven by business occupiers' expectations. Knowledge on how to precisely depreciate capitalization rates 10 years ahead of time in a modelling process is yet another agenda for further research. In the interim period reliance must be placed on valuers to make the best possible judgements in the light of how similar buildings may have depreciated over time in a particular locality. The issue of depreciation and capitalization rates is however revisited in Chapter 9 where risk is explored.

The loss of rental performance in commercial buildings as they age, which is illustrated above, was explored in a research project undertaken by the Investment Property Forum (IPF) in 2005 which generated the following indicative rates of rental depreciation.

Rental depreciation rates % per year		
Property type	Rate of depreciation 19 year sample 1984 to 2003	Rate of depreciation 10-year sample 1993 to 2003
Standard shops	0.1	0.3
Offices	1.0	0.8
Industrial	0.6	0.5
All property	1.0	0.7

The IPF pointed out that the depreciation rates identified were time specific and based upon a particular sample of commercial properties and therefore those rates should not be used mechanically to project into the future. Appraisers will still have to consider the specific circumstances and characteristics of the particular property asset before deciding whether to adopt a particular depreciation rate in their modelling exercises. The IPF research raised as many questions as it answered confirming that this is an agenda for further research. Baum sums up the situation with the comment that:

> depreciation is an unavoidable and understated problem in real estate investment. (2009: 10)

The issue of depreciation and how it affects property investment values going forward is therefore a 'wicked problem' in that there are no quick fixes to apply to any given situation and judgements will need to be made by experienced valuers supported by assumptions. Partly because of these sorts of difficulties, valuers are encouraged to adopt market comparison in their appraisals wherever they can, since it is assumed that at prudent purchaser who bought a 20-year-old office building was doing so in the full knowledge that the 20-year-old building was not quite as competitive as a brand new equivalent building. Thus instead of trying to disaggregate the effects of depreciation it is assumed that depreciation has been taken into account in the overall capital value paid for the property. The valuation of a comparable 20-year-old building is thus made easier and more transparent by using market comparison.

There are however particular circumstances when valuers will have no market evidence to go on and nor is there an income stream to assess. In those circumstances the depreciated replacement cost (DRC) method or contractor's method (as outlined in Chapter 5) comes into play. As Thorne (2008: 432) confirms the DRC method is typically used for public sector buildings such as town halls, museums, schools, hospitals, prisons and swimming pools which are seldom if ever subject to market transactions. Similarly in the private sector there are manufacturing complexes, refineries, ports and power stations which are seldom bought and sold but which require periodic valuations for company accounts.

As the RICS (2007) explain, the substitution principle underpins DRC in that the value of a hypothetical modern equivalent building is used to benchmark the value of the asset being assessed. The gross value of the modern equivalent is then depreciated to reflect the actual age and degree of obsolescence in the asset being valued. Functionality also comes into the equation in that if the modern equivalent building could provide an environment for the same functions to be carried out more efficiently by utilizing less space and on a smaller site then those parameters should be adopted as the modern equivalent building. Example 7.13 illustrates the principles involved in which there are fundamentally three steps. The first step is to calculate how much it would cost to replace the current building with a new one inclusive of all costs and finance charges. The next step is then to depreciate this hypothetical new building to reflect the degree of obsolescence found in the real building. The third step is to add in the value of a plot of land needed to accommodate the new building and which is not necessarily the same size as the exiting plot. The total then reflects the depreciated replacement value of the asset being valued.

Example 7.13: The DRC method used to value a water company's pumping station

A water company requires a valuation for accounts purposes of a Victorian water pumping station which it owns and which has 500 m² of internal space on a site of 0.5 hectares of land. It has an estimated 15 years of life remaining. Because of technological improvements a modern equivalent building would not need to be so large and a valuer concludes that the same service could be provided within a building of 350 m² on a smaller site of 0.35 hectares. A summary of the valuer's calculation might look as follows.

Step 1: Calculate the cost of a modern equivalent building

350 m² of floorspace of @ £1,100 m²:		£385,000
Professional fees and planning costs associated with developing a new building:		£77,000
Contingency allowance:		£23,100
Finance costs over a 2 year development process:		£43,659
Total building cost of new pumping station:		**£528,759**

Step 2: Depreciate to reflect the age and obsolescence of the actual building

Life in years of modern equivalent pumping station:	60	
Remaining life in years of actual building:	15	
Depreciation therefore 45/60:	75%	
Depreciated value to reflect age and obsolescence therefore 25% of value of the replacement modern building:		£132,190

Step 3: Add in land value of a plot to accommodate a modern building

Land cost for a 0.35 hectare site based on industrial land values in the vicinity of £500,000 per hectare:	175,000	
Land acquisition costs and finance over 2 years:	26,250	
Total land costs therefore:	201,250	
Depreciated replacement cost therefore:		**£333,440**

Of course the above is a summary of what would be a more involved process and which would become more complicated if the building were listed or had any peculiarities which required a further depreciation allowance for loss of efficiency.

The use of the DRC method assumes that the building being assessed still fulfils the role required of it by the owner. Thus in the example above the pumping station continues to fulfil an important function for the water company. However it is often the case that the buildings and the site may have a higher value if it were to be disposed of for a change of use or complete redevelopment. As the RICS explains (2007) the Red Book requires the valuer to report upon this higher value as well as conducting the DRC valuation. The client would therefore have a book value for the asset as part of the ongoing enterprise and a comparison of what the asset might be worth if it were sold for

(a)   (b)

Figure 7.2 The old Middlesex hospital in Fitzrovia (a) and its modern replacement on the Euston Road (b)

development. This is obviously helpful for large organizations such as health authorities who have some flexibility in the precise location of facilities and who are constantly juggling their estate to maximize its operational efficiency. This typically involves disposals of older inefficient buildings which may be scattered across disparate sites and which may no longer have an optimal relationship with population centres. Strategic facilities management based upon knowledge of asset values enables organizations such as health authorities to pool resources arising from disposals of older less efficient buildings and sites in order to fund state-of-the-art health facilities.

The images above illustrate where a health authority in London (the UCL Hospital Trust) was able to dispose of the old Middlesex Hospital in Fitzrovia (along with some smaller annexes) to property developer Candy & Candy who are redeveloping the site for a mixed use scheme predominantly containing luxury housing. The revenue arising from disposals like this enabled the development of a much more accessible service in a multi-storey building on a smaller site on the Euston Road (second image above right) and which represents efficient estate management by the health authority.

For those who are particularly interested in the specialized topic of DRC valuation, it is discussed at more length than is possible here by Blackledge (2009: 308–18) Shapiro *et al.* (2009: 446–51) and Scarrett (2008: 159–84).

7.10 Valuation accuracy

As Anderson (2009) confirms, the issue of valuation accuracy tends to resurface particularly during falling markets when some clients of valuers who have seen large reductions in the value of their property try to seek redress by suing the valuer for negligence. The market downturn between 2008 and 2009 in the wake of the credit crunch was one such period when the spotlight turned on property valuers. However as far back as the 1980s there has been research on whether valuers were producing valuations which were a good proxy for prices. For example Hager and Lord (1985) conducted a limited experiment involving the valuation of two properties by a team of valuers. The authors wished to test the hypothesis that the range of valuations for any particular property would be about 5 per cent either side of the average. When results of the test failed to confirm the hypothesis, the authors proceeded to counsel caution about the accuracy of property valuations.

In 1993 controversy arose regarding the valuation for accounts purposes of a portfolio of hotels owned by the Queens Moat Houses plc. The portfolio was valued independently by two leading firms of chartered surveyors referred to as Firm A and Firm B in the quote below (the names of the firms are in the public domain but it is not the purpose here to discuss company reputations). The two valuations of the same portfolio at the same valuation date differed by a massive £537 million. A subsequent Department of Trade and Industry investigation into the running of the Queens Moat Houses plc considered the variation in the valuations and reached a surprisingly benevolent conclusion:

> we consider and compare [Firm A's] final valuation in the gross amount of £1,398.2m with [Firm B's] final valuation of £860.8m. In the extraordinary financial climate which existed during 1993 with very few willing sellers and not many buyers the normal relatively narrow range within which one would expect all competent valuers' reasonable valuations to fall did not apply. Our conclusion was that the [Firm A] final valuation was at the higher end of the permissible range, but we could not say was above it, and the revised [Firm B] valuation was at the lower end of the permissible range but we could not say below it. In saying this, we are stating a conclusion we have reached on the overall valuations, not on any, or each, valuation of an individual hotel. (2004: 348)

Although there were special circumstances in the above case, the news must not have been easy reading for valuers, their clients and the relevant professional body, the RICS. In 1996 the RICS sponsored research by teams from the Universities of Aberdeen and Ulster who sought to identify the margin of variation in commercial property valuations undertaken by professional valuers. The researchers asked local and national firms of surveyors to value hypothetical properties in 14 UK locations and then calculated the variation from the mean valuation. For rack-rented property only 57 per cent of office and industrial valuations and 70 per cent of retail valuations showed a variation of less than 10 per cent. For reversionary property 60 per cent of industrial valuations, 73 per cent of retail and 74 per cent of office valuations were in the 10 per cent band.

These results were based on prime property only, and so presumably the variation would have been higher had secondary property been included in the study. The main reason for the divergence appeared to be accounted for by a lack of data. However the methods of valuation used also caused some concern, with only one of the 446 valuations submitted being based on DCF techniques (Jenkins 1996). However over 80 per cent of the total valuations produced a variation from the mean of less than 20 per cent and in the case of reversionary investments over 90 per cent were in that range, however Hutchinson concluded at that time:

> The results of this research do not inspire confidence that valuers would produce accurate valuations in stable conditions. (1996: 41)

In the early 2000s as Grenfell (2003) reported, there was further research undertaken jointly by Nottingham Trent University and the University of Reading which explored valuers' attitudes and behaviour when undertaking valuation work. Some of the opinions which surfaced (and which were anonymized) revealed a less than objective approach to the work and in some cases there was an absence of any methodology or rationale for changes made to valuations. The Enron accountancy scandal surfaced at about the same time and the RICS therefore felt that the time was right to commission an independent report to investigate whether improvements needed to be made to make the property valuation process more transparent and rigorous. What has become known as the Carsberg Report (2002) made 18 recommendations to the RICS with a view to strengthening the rigour of valuations.

One of the Carsberg recommendations led to the establishment of annual monitoring by the RICS drawing upon data collected by the Investment Property Databank (IPD) so that the degree of correlation between the valuations produced for clients and the price subsequently achieved on a sale could be reported. This type of monitoring would be expected to indentify whether valuers were improving the accuracy of their work or whether there appeared to be shortcomings which needed to be addressed.

An example of this annual monitoring is provided by the RICS's 2009 *Valuation and Sale Price Report* which examined the data arising for 2008. The latter was a particularly challenging year for valuers, as the credit crunch induced recession and the global banking crises saw the IPD index record a 26 per cent drop in the value of the IPD sample of commercial properties. Given such a turbulent year it might be expected that a gap might open up between the values placed on commercial property by valuers and the subsequent selling price. However the RICS report revealed as shown in Figure 7.3 that there had been no significant change from previous years and that 60 per cent of properties sold for a price that was within +/− 10 per cent of the preceding valuation.

There was also a stout defence of the role of the valuer by the RICS in the report:

> It is the nature of markets that values rise and fall with the passage of time. The property market is not isolated from this cycle. Indeed, due to the inelasticity of supply and demand, the rises and falls are often more dramatic than for other asset classes. (2009: 4)

And further that:

> Those who have questioned rapidly downward valuations over the last year must remember that valuers must track the market as it is, not as they would like it to be. Some commentators have sought to blame valuers and valuations for the bubble and the bust. However, it is important not to blame the heart monitor for the heart attack and despite the pain that has been experienced in recent times, realistic valuation provides part of the essential transparency that a robust global economy relies upon.

Given the often considerable sums of money involved in property transactions it is inevitable that there have been court cases which have explored what might

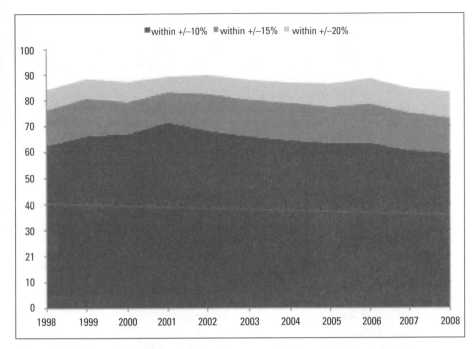

Figure 7.3 Proportion of transactions between 10, 15 and 20% bands

Based on: RICS (2009; reproduced courtesy of the RICS)

be a reasonable tolerance between a valuation and the price subsequently achieved on a sale. This is not quite as straightforward as it might at first seem and one complicating factor is the 'lag effect' which arises because valuations tend to be based, at least in part, upon sales which have previously taken place. Thus some of the inputs into valuations, however carefully calibrated, will inevitably be a historic reflection of how the market was rather than how it actually is. Once the valuation has been produced it is fixed for that moment in time (it is not a forecast) and the sale might then take place several months later. The timeline involved may therefore be extended and so in turbulent market conditions the odds are stacked heavily against the price being exactly the same as the preceding valuation.

Valuers will also be faced with gaps in the data and they will have to rely on the best judgements and assumptions that they can make in order to bridge those gaps. Thus despite the presence of a toolkit of techniques property valuation is still more an art than a science.

The presence of mitigating factors like those described above, has not stopped the courts from seeking to give an opinion on what an acceptable tolerance (sometimes referred to as *the bracket*) might be for a valuation relative to a sale price. Scarrett (2008: 110–13) and Murdoch (2009: 577–96) have helpfully reviewed the case law arising from disputes over valuation accuracy and the principles which have arisen are of some interest. Perhaps not surprisingly, the cases reveal that the acceptable valuation tolerance will vary depending on the complexity of the valuer's task. Where properties are very similar, relatively straightforward to value and where there is plenty of comparable evidence, then the courts will expect the sale price achieved to be within 5 per cent either side of the valuation. However those idyllic circumstances seldom exist and so as the degree of complexity increases the courts have accepted that the bracket within which the valuation will be deemed to be acceptable may widen.

A summary table below captures the outcome of the leading cases such as *Merivale Moore plc* v. *Strutt & Parker* in 1999 and *Arab Bank plc* v. *John D Wood (Commercial) Ltd* in 2000, although it must be stressed that these figures should only be considered as guidelines, as each case and the circumstance surrounding it will be different. Perhaps the essential point is that the courts have shown a willingness not to apply arbitrary parameters but rather to consider the specific circumstances in a case and then to make an allowance for the degree of complexity faced by the valuer. Given that it is neither possible nor necessary to delve into each case in this book, readers who wish to learn more about this subject are referred to the Scarrett and Murdoch references cited above.

Valuation brackets arising from court cases	
Permissible tolerance between the valuation and the subsequent price achieved on a sale	Circumstance
+/− 5%	Valuation for sale of standard estate housing.
+/− 10%	General tone of decisions for the valuation of commercial or residential properties which are a little more complicated than the above but are not development properties as below.
+/− 15%	Development sites with complexity, such as a proposed mixed use development for which there are no direct comparables.
+/− 20%	For a franking valuation where a valuer is asked to provide a second opinion on the value of a complex development proposal or property portfolio but is required to use the same assumptions and work to the facts ascertained by the first valuer.

One of the problems valuers sometimes face is that some of their clients see a valuation as 'good for all time' in that some assume because a Red Book valuation was put on a property at a particular point in time that it will never fall below that value. This is of course not the case and a brief consideration of other investments confirms that although a share price might have been £X at one point or that an oil painting achieved £Y at an auction it does not mean that these prices will remain static or will never fall. A property valuation like a quoted share price or the auction price achieved for a piece of art reflects the market value at one point in time. The valuation may be based on assumptions as to what will happen in the future but it is not a forecast. A forecast will be concerned entirely with the future and while forecasting is sometimes used in property its use is not widespread because of the acknowledged limitations regarding historic data sets, problems of future uncertainty and reliance upon forecasters' assumptions.

As would be expected of a professional body, the RICS has promoted an ongoing process of quality enhancement regarding the service that valuers provide to their clients. This process is underscored by periodic updates of the Red Book and through the issue of specialized *Valuation Information Papers* to guide valuers on good practice when they become involved in specialized valuation work. The RICS is also proposing to introduce in 2011 the mandatory registration of valuers with a view to raising standards and to protect the status of valuers. There is therefore no complacency on the part of the professional body regarding the need to constantly improve the quality of valuations produced by practitioners.

7.11 Summary

This chapter has explored a number of specialized areas of property investment valuation one of which was how quarterly in advance appraisals might be a more accurate way to evaluate the present value of an income stream arising from a commercial lease. Despite the logic of the approach, practice and academic texts have both been slow to abandon valuation principles based upon annual in arrears income, illustrating that as with other branches of industry, property is not immune from inertia.

Property development was also explored as it is felt to be a particular type of investment decision, particularly when a financial institution instigates the development process in order to produce what it sees as an investment-grade building. In the recent past such buildings have been criticized for their aesthetic blandness as they have tended to be buildings which would have the most adaptability and which would raise the least management or maintenance issues and which would have widest possible appeal to the widest range of business occupiers. However going forward, the design of such buildings will have to pay more cognizance to the sustainability agenda as more firms will adopt corporate social responsibility policies and will look for these principles to be embedded in the properties they purchase or lease.

The depreciation of real property was considered and while it is a fact that buildings will tend to depreciate for either physical reasons or because of obsolescence, there is no universal formula which can be applied to accurately assess either the decline in rental performance as a building ages nor in how depreciation might affect capital values when assets are finally sold. Where there is no alternative but to value by the depreciated replacement cost method (DRC) which is also known as the contractor's method, considerable reliance must be placed on the ability of a valuer to make credible and defensible assumptions. This is perhaps one reason why valuers will first investigate whether there are any market comparisons against which to assess value, as embedded in the value realized in a market exchange is an allowance for depreciation along with all the other positive and negative attributes which a property may have. While periodic investment in maintenance and refurbishment may reduce or even arrest depreciation, the whole topic of how to convincingly model the effects of depreciation on major investment properties is for further research.

On the subject of valuation accuracy it could be the case that some clients wrongly conceive of a Red Book valuation produced by a professional as a form of insurance policy that the value of the property will never fall below that datum. In the event that some properties do fall in value it seems that some of these clients feel entitled to sue the valuer for negligence. While the courts have found that in certain circumstances there are acceptable brackets within which a value might fall relative to an actual sale, the difficulty of the task and the time lags involved are also recognized by the courts as mitigating factors. Thus the knee-jerk reaction to try to sue a valuer just because the market has fallen will not automatically succeed unless there are other circumstances which suggest negligent practice.

Perhaps some of the clients of valuers who have resorted to the courts have misunderstood that a Red Book valuation is essentially about establishing the market value at a moment in time and it is not a research project on whether the market will change in future. Perhaps some clients might otherwise have commissioned some forecasting work which looked at a range of different scenarios going forward and which could form one input into the decision-making process. As with all other investments, there are risks that property values may fall in response to external factors such as the state of the global and national economy. Another perspective is to consider whether a court would entertain an attempt by an investor to sue a stock broker because the value of some shares which had been purchased had fallen.

References

Anderson, A. (2009) 'Defend against negligence claims', *Estates Gazette*, 28 November, p. 125.

Baum, A. (2009) *Commercial Real Estate Investment – A Strategic Approach*, 2nd edn (London: EG Books).

Blackledge, M. (2009) *Introducing Property Valuation* (Abingdon: Routledge).

Carsberg, B. (2002) *Property Valuation – The Carsberg Report* (London: RICS).

Department of Trade and Industry (2004) *Queens Moat Houses plc – Investigation under Section 432(2) of the Companies Act 1985* (London: Stationery Office).

Grenfell, W. (2003) 'Perfect pricing', *Estates Gazette*, 29 November, pp. 122–3.

Hager, D. P. and Lord, D. J. (1985) The Property Market, Property Valuations and Property Performance Measurement (London: Institute of Actuaries).

Hutchinson, N. (1996) 'Variations in the capital values of UK commercial property', *Chartered Surveyor Monthly*, April, pp. 40–1.

Investment Property Forum (2005) *Depreciation in Commercial Property Markets: Findings and Recommendations* (London: Investment Property Forum). Available in e-format at: www.ipf.org.uk

Isaac, D. and Steley, T. (2000) *Property Valuation Techniques*, 2nd edn (Basingstoke: Macmillan Press).

Jayne, M. R. (2008) 'Rating', in R. Hayward (ed.), *Valuation: Principles into Practice*, 6th edn (London: EG Books).

Jenkins, S. (1996) 'Valuations still highly variable', *Estates Times*, 15 March, p. 2.

Murdoch, J. (2008) 'Negligence and valuations', ch. 23 in R. Hayward (ed.), *Valuation: Principles into Practice*, 6th edn (London: EG Books).

RICS (2006) *Valuation Information Paper No. 8: The Analysis of Commercial Lease Transactions* (London: RICS).

RICS (2007) *Valuation Information Paper No. 10: The Depreciated Replacement Cost Method of Valuation for Financial Reporting* (London: RICS).

RICS (2009) *Valuation and Sale Price Report 2009* (London: RICS). Available in e-format at: www.rics.org

RICS (2010) RICS *Valuation Standards*, 6th edn (London: RICS).

Scarrett, D. (2008) *Property Valuation: The Five Methods*, 2nd edn (Abingdon: Routledge).

Shapiro, E., Davies, K. and Mackmin, D. (2009) *Modern Methods of Valuation*, 10th edn (London: EG Books).

Thorne, C. (2008) 'Valuation for financial statements', in Hayward, R. (ed.), *Valuation: Principles into Practice*, 6th edn (London: EG Books).

8

Residential property investment appraisal

8.1 Introduction
8.2 Background to residential property investment
8.3 Gearing and loan-to-value ratios
8.4 Purchase costs and stamp duty land tax
8.5 Letting and tax on income

8.6 Capital gains tax
8.7 Funding and viability of buy-to-let investments
8.8 Funding options and viability compared
8.9 Summary

Aims

This chapter considers the financial appraisal of residential property investment which is perhaps better known by its modern name: buy-to-let. The chapter aims to highlight the specialised nature of this particular property investment sector with regards to tax, management responsibilities and funding options. The chapter takes a small investor perspective in contrast to the corporate perspective which has been taken in the preceding chapters where commercial property investment was the focus. The discussion and examples in this chapter aim to show that there is no reason why the appraisal techniques such as DCF, which featured in previous chapters, cannot be adapted and used to ascertain the viability of residential buy-to-let opportunities.

Key terms

>> **Gearing** – the use of a smaller equity stake (such as 25 per cent of an asset's value) by an investor to supplement a larger loan (of 75 per cent of an asset's value) which in combination enable the purchase of an investment such as a buy-to-let property. So long as the rate of return on the investment outstrips the interest rate payable on the loan it is likely that the investor will be able to profit. Gearing can enable a small investor to simultaneously gain exposure to a number of investments by spreading available equity to supplement a number of different loans. There are of course considerable risks in taking on multiple or large loans and those

contemplating gearing for investment purchases will need to appraise the situation very carefully and obtain professional advice.

>> **Amortization** – the process of making regular repayments in order to pay off a mortgage loan over an agreed term. An amortization schedule (an example of which is included in this chapter) is helpful where a capital and interest repayment loan is sought by a longer-term borrower. This is because a schedule can show the scale of monthly repayments required and how the early repayments are dominated by interest payments before the capital is gradually eroded. An amortization schedule also shows the balance of debt remaining at any interim point during the term.

>> **Rent cover** – lenders of buy-to-let mortgages will look at loan applications from property investors to ensure that the envisaged gross monthly rental income from a property would represent at least 125 per cent of the loan repayments each month.

>> **Loan-to-value ratio** – lenders such as building societies and banks who offer buy-to-let mortgages will have a loan-to-value ceiling normally at around 75 per cent of the capital value of a property. Thus the borrower will have to provide an equity stake in the investment equivalent to 25 per cent of its value. Some buy-to-let mortgage providers have a lower LTV ceiling at 60 per cent because of their perception of the risks involved in lending in this specialized market.

8.1 Introduction

This chapter considers private residential property investment which is perhaps better known as buy-to-let, where private landlords acquire flats and houses in order to lease them to tenants. Investors in this market obviously hope to profit from both the rental income and the capital growth which might be expected from holding housing over the medium to long term. After a long period of decline in this sector, the last decade has seen a resurgence of interest in the buy-to-let market particularly from smaller investors. This interest has been stimulated by factors including changes in housing legislation which created assured short-hold tenancies. There has also been an expansion in the range of buy-to-let mortgage products offered by lenders and a mushrooming of residential letting and management agencies. The government has also played its part by acknowledging that while private renting is a small housing sector, it has a role to play in maintaining a spectrum of choice in the housing market. This chapter will focus not upon the merits of this policy but on the financial appraisal of this special type of investment from an investor's perspective.

8.2 Background to residential property investment

Residential property investment has a long history in the UK and in the Victorian era the private rented sector (as it is formally known) was the dominant housing tenure. However during the twentieth century there was a long decline in the private rented sector as home ownership came within the purview of an increasing proportion of households. There was also a considerable investment in public sector housebuilding from the 1950s through to the 1970s. Although the latter programme was effectively discontinued in the 1980s, there has since been an expansion in affordable housing provision by housing associations which are also known as registered social landlords or registered providers.

There has therefore been a widening of housing alternatives to private renting over the long term. It is also fair to say that private renting does not have a very positive reputation amongst the general public and most would not see private renting as their tenure of choice. This is partly because private renting has a chequered history involving some infamous cases where some landlords have exploited tenants. The sector also has a mixed reputation in terms of the quality and state of repair of the housing which it provides. For example Wilcox (2008: 24) reports that there is a higher proportion of housing in the private rented sector which does not meet the government's Decent Homes Standard than in any other housing sector. There are also thought to be wide variations in the responsiveness of landlords in the private sector regarding repairs and maintenance. On the landlord side, some claim that there are insufficient rewards for the management responsibilities and risks involved in letting residential property.

It is not the purpose of this book to explore housing policy in any depth, as there are a number of excellent sources for those who wish to learn more about this topic such as Balchin and Rhoden (2002) or Mullins and Murie (2006). The focus of this book is on investment and this chapter explores residential investment appraisal. This brief introductory section aims to put the topic into perspective by providing a brief reminder of the discussion in Chapter 2 where the historical background and scale of the residential investment sector was identified. Department for Communities (2010) data summarized below in Table 8.1, confirm that private renting only represents 12.4 per cent of the UK's overall housing stock of nearly 26.7 million dwellings.

While in relative terms the scale of the private rented sector may seem modest, it still accounts for over 3.3 million dwellings. The long-term decline in the private rented sector described above has now stabilized and recently there has been a marginal increase in the stock of dwellings in the sector due partly to its popularity with buy-to-let investors.

The private rented sector continues to fulfil an important housing role by providing short-term accommodation for new arrivals in a locality. These households will ultimately move out of the private rented sector to purchase their own homes but in the interim period they may need time to orientate themselves and to learn about the local housing market before making a commitment. The sector is also useful for more transient groups such as

Table 8.1 A summary of UK housing tenure

UK housing stock by tenure in 2007			
Owner occupied	Private rented	Rented from a housing association (registered social landlord)	Rented from a local authority
69.5%	12.4%	8.4%	9.7%

students or those on temporary employment contracts or those who are simply saving up a deposit in order to purchase a property at a later stage with a mortgage. Regarding the latter group, Wilcox (2008: 26) confirms that the average private rent represents around 75 per cent of the average costs of purchasing a house with a mortgage. Thus the private rented sector does provide a stepping stone for those moving on to other perhaps more permanent housing solutions.

8.3 Gearing and loan-to-value ratios

Gearing is a term which is applicable to both residential and commercial property investment. To use a cycling analogy, the use of gears enables more output to be achieved from a limited input. In property investment, gearing is used to describe the relationship between the investor's equity input which is usually the smaller portion of the purchase price of an asset, and a loan which makes up the larger part of the purchase price. The basic premise is that if an investor can use an equity stake to lever in a much larger loan, the combined sum will give the investor access to an investment which could not otherwise have been considered. If for example a fixed-rate loan can be obtained at 6 per cent and an asset promises to generate an income of 8 per cent then the investor is effectively using somebody else's money to make a 2 per cent return.

In recent years small investors in particular have used gearing as a way of gaining exposure to the buy-to-let investments and by the middle of 2010 the Council of Mortgage Lenders (CoML) confirmed that there were 1.26 million buy-to-let mortgages in the UK with a combined value of £149 billion. Kemp (2010: 132) explains that in 1998 there were only 28,700 buy-to-let mortgages and that the dramatic increase was due to a grass-roots initiative from the Association of Residential Letting Agents (ARLA) and a panel of mortgage lenders in 1996. The concept of buy-to-let soon took off with the relatively affluent middle class who had some spare capital to invest. Mortgage lenders also began to realize the potential scale of the buy-to-let market and so began to relax what had previously been prohibitive lending criteria for this specialized type of mortgage. What began as a small-scale investment experiment has mushroomed into a multibillion pound market and which as seen a reversal of the decline in the private rented sector.

When investing in real property the process is not quite as straightforward as comparing loan interest rates against rates of return on properties as there are both rental income and capital value dimensions for the investor to consider. While gearing can generate attractive rewards for the prudent investor, it is also very risky because if an asset underperforms then it might not be possible for the borrower to service the loan. Once arrears begin to accumulate they will compound and the situation can spiral out of control. The CoML (2010) confirms that the rate of possessions by lenders of buy-to-let properties is significantly higher than the rate of repossessions for properties being purchased for owner occupation using conventional mortgages. Thus not all investors who have ventured into the buy-to-let market have been successful.

There are also limits put in place by lenders on what can be borrowed and therefore on the extent to which gearing can be exploited by buy-to-let investors. The most obvious limitation is the loan to value ratio (LTV) required by lenders. In the buy-to-let mortgage market, lenders will typically offer loans of between 60 and 75 per cent of the capital value of a property. Thus the borrower will have to contribute between 25 and 40 per cent of the value of a property depending on the particular circumstances and lender's perception of risk. Lenders will also look at rent cover to ensure that the gross rental income from the buy-to-let property will represent at least 125 per cent of the loan repayments each month. However where these parameters can be made to work by the buy-to-let investor, gearing is a good way to maximize returns even where a 100 per cent cash purchase is an option for the investor. The following simple example explores the basic concept of gearing.

Example 8.1: The advantages of gearing in a buy-to-let scenario

A property investor is considering the acquisition of a buy-to-let apartment which is available on the market for £200,000. The investor plans to let the property for five years before disposing of it. The investor calculates that the income will be £10,000 per annum and the outgoings will be £1,000 excluding any loan repayments. The investor is in the fortunate position to consider either a 100 per cent cash purchase or to borrow 75 per cent of the value of the property and to contribute a 25 per cent equity stake. If the loan option is chosen then interest-only repayments at 6 per cent will add £9,000 per annum to the expenditure. Because the investor is at the early stage of establishing the basic principles, no assumptions are made about future rental growth but a growth rate of 4 per cent per annum is adopted to calculate what the property's value might be when it is disposed of in five years' time. The investor has a target rate of return of 8 per cent for these types of investments and the figures for both funding options are as follows.

DCF appraisal of a buy-to-let property on the basis of a 100% cash purchase

Initial purchase price of a property £ 200,000
Capital value after 5 years assuming an annual growth rate of 4% £ 243,331
Annual costs: £ 1,000   Annual income: £10,000

Year	Expenditure £	Income £	Net cash flow £	PV £1 @ 8%	Discounted cash flow £
0	200,000	0	–200,000	1	–200,000
1	1,000	10,000	9,000	0.9259	8,333
2	1,000	10,000	9,000	0.8573	7,716
3	1,000	10,000	9,000	0.7938	7,144
4	1,000	10,000	9,000	0.7350	6,615
5	1,000	253,331	252,331	0.6806	171,736
				NPV =	1,544
				IRR =	8.18%

Thus on these basic assumptions it looks as if a 100 per cent cash purchase would just about earn the investor's target rate of return. For comparison, the investor then models the gearing option by assuming an interest-only loan as follows.

DCF appraisal of a buy-to-let property on the basis of an interest-only mortgage

Equity contribution by the investor at 25% of the property value: £ 50,000
An interest-only loan to make up the balance of 75%:   £ 150,000
Annual interest-only repayments at a 6% borrowing rate therefore: £   9,000
Capital value after 5 years assuming an annual growth rate of 4%   £ 243,331
Difference between the exit value and the loan therefore: £ 93,331

Year	Expenditure £	Income £	Net cash flow £	PV £1 @ 8%	Discounted cash flow £
0	50,000	0	−50,000	1	−50,000
1	10,000	10,000	0	0.9259	0
2	10,000	10,000	0	0.8573	0
3	10,000	10,000	0	0.7938	0
4	10,000	10,000	0	0.7350	0
5	10,000	103,331	93,331	0.6806	63,521
				NPV =	£13,521
				IRR =	13.30%

The gearing option thus produces a much higher rate of return of over 13 per cent per annum albeit on a smaller capital sum i.e. £50,000. However the investor could of course invest £50,000 in four properties on the above basis and would thus be earning a higher rate of return on the £200,000 which is available for investments. This is very much how the smaller buy-to-let investor uses gearing to gradually build up an investment portfolio.

ARLA produce an index of returns on buy-to-let property investment and for the second quarter of 2010 the figures compare the rate of return over a five-year period for residential property in different regions. The figures reveal the stark differential between the returns possible on geared investments and those purchased by cash.

Region	Annual rate of return over 5 years for buy-to-let investments purchased using 100% cash	Annual rate of return over 5 years for buy-to-let investments purchased on a geared basis using 25% equity and 75% loan
Prime Central London	8.12%	19.70%
Rest of London	8.59%	20.86%
Rest of South East	8.29%	20.11%
South-West	8.52%	20.70%
Midlands	8.44%	20.49%
North-West	8.42%	20.44%
North-East	8.76%	21.27%
Scotland, Wales and Northern Ireland	8.71%	21.15%

Of course as with any statistical exercise like this, data are inevitably averaged across regions and there are specific assumptions being made. Budding investors should not therefore jump to the conclusion that the purchase of any buy-to-let property on a geared basis in (for example) the South-West will provide an average annual return of 20.7 per cent. Investors would always be advised to carry out a property-specific appraisal. Experienced investors will also recognize that the figures are silent regarding the risks and management responsibilities which come with this form of investment.

8.4 Purchase costs and stamp duty land tax

For a modest buy-to-let acquisition of say a two-bedroom Victorian terraced house in a suburban location at say £150,000 the purchaser would be facing solicitor's fees for conveyancing (including title and local authority searches and land registration fees) of around £1,000 to which is added fees for a building survey at around £600 including VAT. Stamp duty land tax (SDLT) at 1 per cent would also arise for the above property at £1,500. In 2010 the SDLT rates for residential property in the UK were as follows.

Property value	SDLT	Exemptions
Up to £124,999	Zero rated	Not applicable
£125,000–£249,999	1%	First-time buyers
£250,000–£499,999	3%	None
£500,000 or over	4%	None

Thus far the entry costs for the aspirant buy-to-let investor would be of the order of £3,100. If a mortgage is involved there will be arrangement fees plus the lender's survey fees which might add perhaps another £1,000 raising the total to £4,100. Of course the property is unlikely to be in a state of repair that it can be let immediately and so there would need to be a contingency fund to deal with partial or complete redecoration, part or full furnishing/carpeting, replacement of faulty or high maintenance equipment such as obsolete gas boilers or even faulty central heating systems. It is difficult to be prescriptive on what these costs might amount to because a lot will depend on the type and age of the property purchased.

Experienced investors tend to target new or recently built standard apartments in urban areas as these will pose the least problems in terms of equipping and then letting. Large Victorian houses which require modernization and have been poorly maintained with unkempt gardens will obviously feature at the costly end of the spectrum. However assuming some sort of median property it would not be unreasonable to add another £5,000 as an entry level contingency fund. The total entry costs for the investor are now around £9,100 and this is before an equity contribution of say 25 per cent of the purchase price to supplement a buy-to-let mortgage loan at say 75 per cent of the purchase price. In the example of the £150,000 house the equity required from the investor would therefore be £37,500 bringing the total entry costs to £46,600 before the letting process can begin.

8.5 Letting and tax on income

Most buy-to-let investors will operate through a residential letting and management agent whose fees will represent between 10 and 18 per cent of rental income. Given the range and potential costs involved investors would obviously shop around in this particular market. The agents can advise on what a realistic monthly rental value might be for a particular property type in a particular location. Agents will then market the property and carry out tenant vetting through a credit referencing agency before obtaining signatures from the landlord and tenant on the tenancy agreement.

There are standard forms of assured short-hold tenancy agreement and for those who are particularly interested in this aspect the Residential Landlords Association (RLA) at: www.rla.org.uk is a valuable source of advice. Indeed membership of this organization would be sensible for those contemplating a move into this sector, as the RLA can provide practical advice on a range of issues which typically arise in this specialist investment market. Experienced residential landlords will be aware of the requirements for annual gas safety checks, electrical safety checks and Energy Performance Certificates. Regulatory obligations will increase where flats and/or dwellings are in multiple occupation. New investors might not have a comprehensive overview of what is required and therefore the collective learning which has gone on and which is disseminated by an organization like the RLA will be a valuable resource.

Regarding tax on income arising from residential investment property, the general principle is that the buy-to-let investors are treated as if they were businesses where tax is liable on the net profit after operational cost are deducted. HM Revenue & Customs sets out the legitimate operating costs and Booth

(2006: 21) confirms that these include letting agency fees, legal fees for arranging a lease, accountancy fees, interest payments on property loans (but not capital repayments) allowance for maintenance and repair costs, utility bills (during voids) ground rent and service charges (where the property is a leasehold flat) council tax (during voids) services such as gardening and cleaning (during voids between tenancies), building insurance and associated administration costs such as phone calls and sundry expenses.

Once the net profit is identified it can be offset against any losses made on other properties for tax purposes. Assuming the investor is operating successfully, a tax return is required and the net profit will be taxed taking into account the investor's other income sources. Above the tax-free allowance of £6,475 income up to £37,400 will be taxed at the basic rate of 20 per cent. Income above £37,400 and up to £150,000 per annum would be taxed at the higher rate of 40 per cent and over £150,000 at 50 per cent. Thus the tax which the investor faces on buy-to-let income will depend on the investor's overall income profile and indeed whether a net profit has been achieved from the particular buy-to-let asset(s).

8.6 Capital gains tax

Although capital gains tax (CGT) is not liable on the sale of an individual's or family's home, CGT would be liable on the sale of an investment property by a buy-to-let investor. This assumes the capital value of the property increased by more than the tax-free threshold of £10,100 after deductable allowances had been made. Deductable allowances include the costs of buying and selling the property which would ordinarily include solicitor's, estate agent's and building surveyor's fees, stamp duty (to avoid double taxation) and the capital cost of any improvements made to the dwelling. The following example illustrates how CGT might apply on the sale of an investment property which had been held for eight years.

Example 8.2: A CGT calculation for a residential investment property

A two-bedroom house was purchased in 2003 for £85,000 when the combined costs of purchase were £2,000. A small rear extension and new bathroom were then added at a cost of £10,000 to improve the property to a point where it could be let. In 2011 the property is sold for £120,000 when the combined costs of sale were £2,000.

The gross gain before allowances are deducted would therefore be £120,000 − £85,000 = £35,000. The total allowances are the costs of purchase and disposal plus the improvements made to the property, which in this example total £14,000 and which would reduce the taxable capital gain to £21,000. Applying the tax exemption threshold of £10,100 leaves a net gain for taxation purposes of £10,900. This figure is then taxed at the current rate of 18 per cent so the investor would face a tax bill on this transaction of £1,962 assuming that it could not be offset against losses on other similar transactions. If the investor decided to gift or sell the property at a significant discount to a member of the family or a friend, the tax would not be avoided as recourse would then be made by the tax office to the true market value.

Figure 8.1 Berkeley Homes' Royal Arsenal development, south-east London, also popular with buy-to-let investors

Figure 8.1 shows the new apartments at Berkeley Homes' Royal Arsenal development in south-east London, which have proved popular with buy-to-let investors. This particular scheme is a large regeneration project on the site of the former Woolwich Arsenal. Although the credit crunch from 2008 onwards inevitably dampened returns on buy-to-let properties, investors who are able to take a longer-term view will probably see capital values on sites like this benefit from local infrastructure improvements such as the Docklands Light Railway extension and the Crossrail project. It is likely therefore that longer-term investors in buy-to-let properties on sites like this will be facing CGT when they ultimately dispose of what will probably be very valuable assets.

8.7 Funding and viability of buy-to-let investments

Having explored some of the basic financial principles of buy-to-let property, more detailed examples can now be considered in which account is taken of entry and operating costs which would typically arise. In Examples 8.3 to 8.5 which follow, three different ways to fund the same investment are explored. The first two funding methods involve gearing; that is the contribution of an equity stake by the investor to supplement a mortgage loan. The third method of funding is a cash only option, as the investor is in the fortunate position to consider this alternative. Following each example there are some evaluative comments on the merits of using the particular funding option in the scenario. It will become apparent why fixed-rate interest-only mortgages have become a popular funding method for investors seeking some medium-term exposure to the buy-to-let market.

Example 8.3: Appraising a residential buy-to-let investment using a fixed-rate capital and interest repayment mortgage

A buy-to-let investor is considering the purchase of a two-bedroom flat in an urban area. The flat benefits from off street parking and is on sale for £170,000.

The investor intends to let the property over an 8 year period and then to dispose of it in the hope of making a capital gain. Based on comparable evidence from the locality, a realistic rental value for the property is felt to be £800 per month.

Because the economy has been going through a difficult period the investor decides to take a cautious rather than optimistic view when factoring in anticipated rental and capital growth rates. The Association of Residential Letting Agents (ARLA) quite reasonably suggests that capital growth in such appraisals could reflect average annual growth in house prices over the last 20 years which was 5.21 per cent. The investor however decides to take a more pessimistic view by assuming that the value of the flat will grow over the 8 year holding period at a rate of 3.5 per cent per annum. ARLA (2010) benchmark rental growth to the prevailing inflation rate measured by RPI, which is the second quarter of 2010, was 5.1 per cent. This is a legitimate approach but the investor believes that inflation might average out at below this rate over the 8 year holding period and so adopts a more cautious rental growth rate of 3 per cent.

The investor assumes that furnishing, white goods and carpets which form part of the initial entry costs will last for the holding period of eight years but will have depreciated to negligible value by the end of the period. The investor decides to set the investment a 9 per cent target rate of return.

The first step in the appraisal below is to establish the loan repayment obligations and other outgoings which will arise over the envisaged holding period. While in reality the investor might remortgage during the eight-year term in order to obtain the best mortgage deals available, the appraisal assumes a conventional fixed-rate capital and interest repayment mortgage so that the core principles of amortization can be appreciated. This helps to establish not only how much the repayments would be using this type of mortgage but also how much capital would still be outstanding on the loan and would need to be repaid to the lender out of receipts arising on the sale of the property at the end of year 8. Step 2 of the appraisal involves a DCF which is shown beneath the amortization schedule. The DCF takes an annually in arrears approach to income and expenditure and seeks to identify the rate of return possible using this funding method.

Step 1: Consider the loan repayment implications along with other costs

Amortization of a mortgage to support the purchase of a two-bed buy-to-let flat

Market value of a 2-bed flat with parking	£170,000
Amount of loan at 75% loan-to-value ratio	£127,500
Equity (deposit) required therefore	£42,500
Term of loan in years	25
Loan interest rate	5.5%
Amortize to	0

Year	Opening balance £	Annual payment £	Interest element £	Capital element £	End balance £
1	127,500	9,505	7,013	2,493	125,007
2	125,007	9,505	6,875	2,630	122,378
3	122,378	9,505	6,731	2,774	119,604
4	119,604	9,505	6,578	2,927	116,677
5	116,677	9,505	6,417	3,088	113,589
6	113,589	9,505	6,247	3,258	110,331
7	110,331	9,505	6,068	3,437	106,894
8	106,894	9,505	5,879	3,626	103,269
9	103,269	9,505	5,680	3,825	99,443
10	99,443	9,505	5,469	4,036	95,408
11	95,408	9,505	5,247	4,258	91,150
12	91,150	9,505	5,013	4,492	86,658
13	86,658	9,505	4,766	4,739	81,919
14	81,919	9,505	4,506	4,999	76,920
15	76,920	9,505	4,231	5,274	71,645
16	71,645	9,505	3,940	5,565	66,081
17	66,081	9,505	3,634	5,871	60,210
18	60,210	9,505	3,312	6,193	54,017
19	54,017	9,505	2,971	6,534	47,483
20	47,483	9,505	2,612	6,893	40,589
21	40,589	9,505	2,232	7,273	33,317
22	33,317	9,505	1,832	7,673	25,644
23	25,644	9,505	1,410	8,095	17,549
24	17,549	9,505	965	8,540	9,010
25	9,010	9,505	496	9,010	0

Costs	Monthly	Yearly
Mortgage loan repayments:	£ 792	£ 9,505
Service charge and ground rent:	£ 80	£ 960
Management and letting fees:	£ 80	£ 960
Insurance:	£ 35	£ 420

Costs	Monthly	Yearly
Allowance for repairs:	£ 50	£ 600
Legal and accountancy fees:	£ 30	£ 360
Total expenditure =	£ 1,067	£ 12,805

Step 2: Frame assumptions and input variables into a DCF appraisal to identify the rate of return

Equity contribution to purchase price (25% of market value)	£42,500
Add stamp duty land tax @ 1% of market value	£1,700
Add solicitors and other fees plus other set up costs say:	£4,000
Equity required for entry therefore:	£48,200
Property value at end of year 8 assuming 3.5% annual growth	£223,858
Deduct balance owing on the mortgage at that stage	
(see schedule above)	£103,269
Balance	£120,589
Market rent of property is £800 per month, so gross annual income is	£9,600
Allowance of one month void per year when there will be no rent	£800
Allowance for property's outgoings during 1 month void	£150
Net rental income per annum therefore	£8,650
Exit costs at end of year 8 say:	£3,500

The rent is assumed to grow at 3 per cent per annum and the costs apart from the fixed-rate mortgage repayments are also assumed to grow at 3 per cent per annum. For example in the second year the expenditure is £12,904. The mortgage repayment element within that figure is £9,505 and this element is fixed throughout the term. However the balance of £3,399 is costs which will rise with inflation assumed to be 3 per cent. This is reflected in the following year's total costs which are £13,006.

Year	Expenditure £	Income £	Net cash flow £	PV £1 @ 9%	Discounted cash flow	Event
0	48,200	0	−48,200	1	− 48,200	Purchase property
1	12,805	8,650	−4,155	0.9174	− 3,812	1st year's letting
2	12,904	8,910	−3,995	0.8417	− 3,362	2nd year's letting
3	13,006	9,177	−3,829	0.7722	− 2,957	3rd year's letting
4	13,111	9,452	−3,659	0.7084	− 2,592	4th year's letting
5	13,219	9,736	−3,484	0.6499	− 2,264	5th year's letting
6	13,331	10,028	−3,303	0.5963	− 1,970	6th year's letting
7	13,445	10,329	−3,117	0.5470	− 1,705	7th year's letting
8	17,064	131,227	114,164	0.5019	57,299	8th year's letting and year end sale
			Net Present Value (NPV) =		−£ 9,562	
			Internal Rate of Return (IRR) =		6.62%	

Summary of the capital and interest mortgage funding method

Given that the rent cover expectations of the average buy-to-let lender will be 125 per cent, the monthly rent in the above example would need to be 1.25 × £792 = £990. The investor's market research has revealed that a rent of £800 per month is the maximum that could be achieved in the particular locality for this type of property. On this test therefore, it would be unlikely that this funding option would work, as a loan at a competitive interest rate would not be obtainable from lenders to support this venture on these terms.

The cash flow also shows a continuing debt scenario each year which is only redeemed on the basis of an anticipated capital sale at the end of year 8. This is a high-risk strategy which relies entirely on the capital growth assumed for the property. Were that expectation not to be realized the investor would be in serious financial difficulty by year 8. It is also unlikely that bank would support the ongoing debt scenario unless there were other assets whose performance was able to compensate the poor interim performance of this asset. The investor would also probably be racking up considerable fees associated with the condition of indebtedness and this would probably compound the situation. The overall annual rate of return of 6.62 per cent also falls below the investor's target rate of 9 per cent.

Given that there is an income loss, the investor might be able to use this to offset income gains on other investments to avoid or reduce the tax burden. However it is likely that there would be a capital gains tax bill at the end. Most readers would by now have concluded that a capital and interest repayment mortgage has a number of shortcomings which make it an unlikely funding method in the scenario. The next funding option looks at an interest-only mortgage.

Example 8.4: Funding using an interest-only fixed-rate mortgage

As in example 8.3 above there are two steps in the process.

Step 1 consider the costs arising

Funding on an interest-only mortgage basis

Market value of a 2-bed flat with parking	£ 170,000
Amount of loan at 75% loan-to value ratio	£ 127,500
Equity (deposit) required therefore	£ 42,500
Loan interest rate	5.5%

Costs	Monthly	Yearly
Interest-only mortgage repayments	£ 584	£ 7,013
Service charge and ground rent:	£ 80	£ 960
Management and letting fees:	£ 80	£ 960
Insurance:	£ 35	£ 420
Allowance for repairs:	£ 50	£ 600
Legal and accountancy fees	£ 30	£ 360
Total expenditure =	£ 859	£ 10,313

Equity contribution to purchase price (25% of market value)		£42,500
Stamp duty @ 1% of market value		£1,700
Solicitors and other fees plus other set up costs say:		£4,000
Equity required for entry therefore:		£48,200

Assume property value to grow at 3.5% per annum

Value at end of year 8 =	£223,858
Deduct original loan amount	£127,500
Balance remaining	£96,358

Market rent of property is £800 per month, which annually is:	£9,600
Allowance of one month void per year when there will be no rent:	£800
Allowance for property's outgoings during 1 month void:	£150
Income per annum therefore:	£8,650
The rent is assumed to grow at 3% per annum.	
Exit costs at end of year 8 say:	£3,500

As before, the costs apart from mortgage interest payments have been inflated annually at 3 per cent.

Step 2: Insert the variables into a DCF to identify the rate of return

Year	Expenditure £	Income £	Net cash flow £	PV of £1 @ 9%	Discounted cash flow	Event
0	48,200	0	−48,200	1	− 48,200	Purchase property
1	10,313	8,650	−1,663	0.9174	− 1,526	1st year's letting
2	10,412	8,910	−1,503	0.8417	− 1,265	2nd year's letting
3	10,514	9,177	−1,337	0.7722	− 1,033	3rd year's letting
4	10,619	9,452	−1,167	0.7084	− 827	4th year's letting
5	10,727	9,736	−992	0.6499	− 644	5th year's letting
6	10,839	10,028	−811	0.5963	− 484	6th year's letting
7	10,953	10,329	−625	0.5470	− 342	7th year's letting
8	14,572	106,996	92,424	0.5019	46,388	8th year's letting and year end sale
			Net Present Value (NPV) =		−£ 7,931	
			Internal Rate of Return (IRR) =		6.77%	

Summary of funding using an interest-only fixed-rate mortgage

This method of funding appears to succeed on the rent cover test, as monthly repayments on an interest-only basis are £584 so that the 125 per cent cover test necessitates a rent of $1.25 \times £584 = £730$. The realistic rental value of the property is £800 per month and so this would satisfy a lender. However there is still the problem of ongoing indebtedness during the interim years, which is redeemed by capital growth realized in the final sale. The overall annual rate of return falls below what the investor was seeking, although is positive at 6.77 per cent. The interest-only loan method is therefore a possibility if the investor is willing to accept the possibility of a marginally lower rate of return or if costs could be reduced so that the rate of return increased closer to the target level. The investor might also take the view that because a pessimistic weighting has been taken on the rate of rental and capital growth, the rate of return might signify the worst possible outcome. If growth rates turn out to be stronger than expected then a higher rate of return will materialize from the investment. The final funding option to consider is a 100 per cent cash purchase as follows.

Example 8.5: Funding using 100 per cent cash

As in Examples 8.3 and 8.4 above this is a two step process beginning with a confirmation of the costs as follows.

Property price (assumes 100% cash purchase)	£170,000
Stamp duty @ 1% of market value	£1,700
Solicitors and other fees plus other set up costs say:	£4,000
Investment required for entry therefore:	£175,700
Assume property value to grow at 3.5% per annum	
Value at end of year 8 =	£223,858
Market rent of property is £800 per month, which annually is:	£9,600
Allowance of one month void per year when there will be no rent:	£800
Allowance for property's outgoings during 1 month void:	£150
Income per annum therefore:	£8,650
The rent is assumed to grow @ 3% per annum	
Exit costs at end of year 8 say:	£3,500

Costs	Monthly	Yearly
Service charge and ground rent:	£ 80	£ 960
Management and letting fees:	£ 80	£ 960
Insurance:	£ 35	£ 420
Allowance for repairs:	£ 50	£ 600
Legal and accountancy fees	£ 30	£ 360
Total expenditure =	£ 275	£ 3,300

Step 2: Insert the variables into a DCF to identify the rate of return

Year	Expenditure £	Income f.	Net cash flow £	PV of £1 @ 9%	Discounted cash flow	Event
0	175,700	0	-175,700	1	-175,700	Purchase property
1	3,300	8,650	5,350	0.9174	4,908	1st year's letting
2	3,399	8,910	5,511	0.8417	4,638	2nd year's letting
3	3,501	9,177	5,676	0.7722	4,383	3rd year's letting

Year	Expenditure £	Income £	Net cash flow £	PV of £1 @ 9%	Discounted cash flow	Event
4	3,606	9,452	5,846	0.7084	4,141	4th year's letting
5	3,714	9,736	6,021	0.6499	3,913	5th year's letting
6	3,826	10,028	6,202	0.5963	3,698	6th year's letting
7	3,940	10,329	6,388	0.5470	3,494	7th year's letting
8	7,559	234,496	226,938	0.5019	113,900	8th year's letting and year end sale
			Net present value (NPV) =		–£ 32,623	
			Internal rate of return (IRR) =		5.93%	

A summary of the 100 per cent cash funding option

Because there is no borrower involved the investor does not have to worry about meeting rent cover tests or loan-to-value ratios. Because there are no loan repayments, the balance between costs and income in the interim years is positive, providing a nominal income yield. For example in year 1 the net cash flow is positive at £5,350 which when divided by the total capital investment of £175,700 is producing an income yield of just over 3 per cent. There might be some income tax implications depending on the investor's overall income profile and tax status. It is also likely that there will be capital gains tax on the projected increase in capital value of just under £54,000 which is above the current tax-free allowance. However the size of the tax bill will be contingent on whether there are losses on other investments which the investor's accountant could use to offset the tax bill on this asset. Setting aside the tax issue, when the increase in capital value of the property is factored into the DCF above the overall annual rate of return is 5.93 per cent over the holding period. The return is therefore lower than for the two geared funding options considered above and is therefore consistent with the concept of gearing discussed earlier in the chapter.

8.8 Funding options and viability compared

The rates of return indentified in Examples 8.3 to 8.5 above are not as attractive as the ARLA figures cited earlier in this chapter which suggested a rate of return on cash only buy-to-let purchases at around 8 per cent and up to 20 per cent on a geared basis. The differences between the ARLA figures and the worked examples above where rates of return were around 7 per cent primarily stem from the fact that the ARLA figures were produced at a time when annual inflation was 5.1 per cent per annum and that figure was used to calibrate future rental growth. The average annual rise in house prices over the last 20 years of 5.21 per cent was also used in the ARLA figures to calculate future capital value. This combination could be thought of as modelling an optimistic scenario, while a more pessimistic view is taken on rental and capital growth rates in the worked examples above. Similarly a pessimistic view was taken in the worked examples that there would be a one month void period when no income was generated, while the ARLA figures are based upon survey data which suggest that the annual void period would be slightly less at 22 days per year.

Examples 8.3 to 8.5 also take a 'fuller' view of the likely scale and range of costs which a residential landlord is likely to face than is taken in the ARLA figures. This does not suggest that the ARLA forecast rates of return are incorrect or that the returns in the above worked examples are wrong, but that the two sets of figures are probably revealing optimistic and pessimistic ends of a continuum. A risk averse investor might be more interested in the pessimistic scenario, which perhaps reflects hard experiences during the credit crunch which set in during 2008. A risk seeking investor might however be more persuaded by the ARLA figures which suggest recovery in a post-credit crunch world. Perhaps the risk neutral investor would be interested in the average which lies between the two positions and this would bear some relationship to the annualized returns for residential property investment recorded in the Investment Property Databank index for 2009 as shown below.

IPD Index: annualized total returns for residential property investment		
Over 3 years up to 2009	**Over 5 years up to 2009**	**Over 9 years up to 2009**
3.1%	6.8%	10.0%

The chapter which follows will be exploring different perceptions of risk and it will look at various risk assessment techniques which have evolved to help investors identify the range of possible outcomes and the attendant financial risks involved.

8.9 Summary

After a long period of decline, residential property investment experienced something of a revival over the last 10 years under its new marketing badge: buy-to-let. Although the private rented sector is a small housing tenure sector in the UK it still accounts for over 3.3 million homes. The sector plays an important stepping-stone role in providing short-term accommodation for more mobile households and those who may be saving up a deposit to purchase a property.

While there are a wide variety of investors in the sector, it is particularly popular with the smaller investor who can access the market using a buy-to-let mortgage. Residential investment however involves significant management responsibilities and risks and while some of the management responsibilities can be delegated to letting and managing agents the risks cannot be delegated. Some buy-to-let investors who may have selected the wrong properties in the wrong location have been left exposed by the downturn in the housing market in the wake of the credit crunch. This partly explains why lenders' repossession rates on buy-to-let properties are higher than for conventional house purchases. As with all investments there are risks and careful research and appraisal are sensible precautions which can help identify the risks before a purchase is undertaken. There are also useful sources of information and advice available for would be buy-to-let investors from organizations such as the RLA and the ARLA. The chapter which follows takes up the theme of risk and how it might be appraised in the context of property investment.

References

Association of Residential Letting Agents (2010) *The ARLA Review and Index for Residential Investment, 2nd Quarter 2010* (Warwick: Association of Residential Letting Agents).

Balchin, P. and Rhoden, M. (2002) *Housing Policy: An Introduction*, 4th edn (London: Routledge).

Booth, T. (2006) *The Buy to Let Handbook* (Oxford: How To Books).

Council of Mortgage Lenders (2010) various press releases at: www.cml.org.uk

Department for Communities and Local Government (2010) *Statistical Table 101: Dwelling Stock: By Tenure, United Kingdom (Historical Series)*. Available at: www.communities.gov.uk

Investment Property Databank (2010) *IPD UK Residential Investment Index* (for 2009). Available in e-format at: www.ipd.com

Kemp, P. (2010) 'The transformation of private renting', in P. Malpass and R. Rowlands (eds), *Housing, Markets and Policy* (Abingdon: Routledge).

Mullins, D. and Murie, A. (2006) *Housing Policy in the UK* (Basingstoke: Palgrave).

Wilcox, S. (2008) 'Where next for private renting?', in S. Wilcox (ed.), *UK Housing Review 2008/2009* (Coventry: Chartered Institute of Housing; London: Building Societies Association).

9

Risk appraisal

Aims

This chapter first explores how risk is considered at a theoretical level as the potential variance from expected outcomes. From the abstract level the aim is then to look at the types of risks that are posed to the financial performance of assets held by property investors. The chapter then examines some common risk assessment techniques and how they may be used to assess the risks associated with property investment opportunities.

Key terms

>> **Sensitivity analysis** – explores changes to the variables which form the inputs into a property investment appraisal such as a discounted cash flow. Where the acquisition of a large value investment is contemplated, it would be prudent for the investor to model change in the more sensitive variables which in property investment are the rental income, the initial yield and the exit yield. A sensitivity analysis would explore marginal change in these variables to assess the effect on the outcome.

>> **Scenario testing** – property investors might look at the downside risk posed to an investment by modelling a worst-case scenario to see if the target rate of return could still be met even if the worst-case scenario were to become reality during the envisaged holding period for an asset.

>> **Probability analysis** – sensitivity analyses and scenario testing both involve making marginal changes to variables to ascertain the effect on the target rate of return. A probability analysis supplements this by attributing subjective

probabilities to the range of choices being made, so that a most likely outcome can be identified.

>> **Covenant strength** – refers to the reliability of a business which is or proposing to lease property. A business which is diversified and financially robust would have a strong corporate credit rating and would therefore be a strong covenant from a property investor's perspective. All property investors would like business tenants with these characteristics but in reality compromises will be required as companies vary in terms of the risks they present as tenants. If a commercial landlord is in the fortunate position where several businesses are vying to lease space, the landlord may look at the financial security offered by each company before deciding who to negotiate with.

>> **Simulation** – the use of software which through iteration and the use of random numbers produces a distribution of the range of possible values for a variable in a property appraisal such as the rental growth or the exit yield. Simulation models combine the distributions for each variable selected for analysis to produce an overall distribution for the outcome of the appraisal. The latter might be expressed in the range of possible IRRs or NPVs. An investor could therefore look at the outside probability at the end of the distribution range, to see whether such an outcome could be tolerated.

9.1 Introduction

A rational property investor is somebody who invests in property because it suggests income and capital growth. The more sophisticated investors who operate at the high-value end of the market will normally have corporate target rates of return which are benchmarked above the rates of return available on so called safe investments such as government stock. However property investment tends to be a long-term activity in which the investor hopes that the future performance of a property will bear some relationship to an appraisal normally undertaken at the point of acquisition. Given that many years may pass between the initial appraisal and the disposal of an asset it is very likely that the actual financial performance will be at some variance to that predicted several years earlier in the appraisal. This variation is risk. Given that much of the variance is driven by change in the wider economy, a degree of risk must always be accepted in property investment.

There appears to be two fundamental ways to assess and respond to risks in property investment. One way is to model change in the variables so that ultimately the downside risk is identified. If the investment still achieves the investor's expectations in that scenario, then the investment would appear to be robust and worthy of further investigation. The second way is to adjust the discount rate in an appraisal so that it already has an embodied risk allowance against which an investment can be appraised. For instance, if a risk-free rate is 5 per cent and the risk premium is 2 per cent then this premium is added to the risk-free rate to give a discount rate of 7 per cent to reflect the risk taken. If the project succeeds at the risk-adjusted discount rate it could be said to have withstood a rigorous test against the investor's expectations and was therefore a robust investment.

Hargitay and Yu (1993: 155) have considered risk analysis in some depth and suggest that discounting at a risk-adjusted rate combined with some probability analysis could be the most practical approach. While this advice has validity, there are limits to this, as to use both a risk-adjusted discount rate and then to model worst-case scenarios by adjusting variables could lead an investor into 'double counting' for risk. In that position an investor would probably perceive of every investment opportunity as being unviable unless large and possibly unrealistic reductions were made in the asking price by the vendor. Thus to apply too much sophistication and belief to risk analysis courts the danger that an investor will become too risk averse relative to the investor's peer group. This would result in an investor failing to acquire any assets because they all appeared to be too risky. A degree of risk must be accepted by investors, as this is the trade-off for the potential rewards. To put it another way, without any risk-taking there is unlikely to be any rewards.

Risks posed to property investments are often derived from factors beyond the investor's control and thus some time spent at the outset assessing the extent of the risk before an acquisition takes place is probably time well spent. Once a property asset has been acquired there are only so many things that can be done to mitigate ongoing risks. This chapter will try to steer a practical way through the debate about risk as it has developed in the context of property investment.

9.2 The theory of risk

In a world where the future is uncertain, all decisions involve a degree of risk. Investments offer the expectation of returns for the investor as a reward for taking the risks involved in acquiring and managing an asset. In the capital markets the rate of return offered on an investment reflects the degree of risk that an asset may or may not perform to expectations. Thus in the markets there is no single interest rate but a continuum of interest rates depending on market sentiment on the riskiness of a particular investment. The challenge for the investor is to weigh the degree of risk involved against the returns offered and to decide whether there is an acceptable trade-off.

With regards to property investment, risk relates to the degree of probability that a required return, measured in capital value and income will be achieved. Over time, the variance of actual return from expected return (the volatility) can be measured and used to help determine probability levels.

While assets exhibit different degrees of volatility in the returns they provide, on the other side of the equation individuals and corporations also have different tolerances to risk taking. It is possible to characterize individuals' or corporations' perceptions of risk at an abstract level by first assuming that investors will tend to make decisions which they believe will maximize their utility.

Risk-averse investors have utility curves which are concave to the origin (point 0) in Figure 9.1, signifying that as the risks rise, increasingly higher rates of return are required to tempt this type of investor to invest further. If an investor has a degree of certainty about a project's expected value they may continue to invest in it so long as the returns continue to increase as an incentive. A simple example of this is the increasingly attractive interest rates offered on savings accounts or bonds related to the scale and duration of investment made. Thus investors who commit significant funds over an extended period will be offered better rates of interest than will smaller short-term investors. The risk-and-reward trade-off

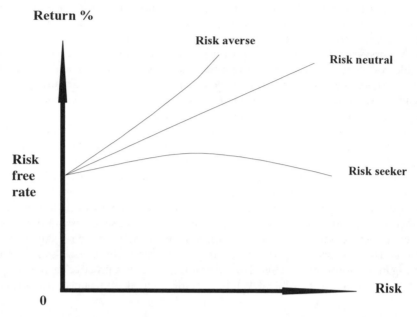

Figure 9.1 The risk-and-return trade-off

could be mapped in a straight line and the investor could be said to be 'risk neutral'.

If an investor commits funds to a venture which at first appears to offer low rates of return they may be looking at longer-term but as yet unspecified performance. The curve mapped for those investors in the risk-and-return trade-off diagram (Figure 9.1) is convex to the origin and it represents risk-seeking investors.

Essentially the risk-averse investor will require more reward for bearing more risk than the risk neutral investor and much more that the risk-seeking investor. These curves all represent risk avoidance in the sense that all require more reward for more risk but the classification is determined by the extent of the additional return required. Generally most investors are considered to be risk averse and there is evidence to suggest that all investors are risk averse when making important large value investment decisions.

There are also differences related to the scale of investment available. For example an investor who has £1 million to invest may seek some risk exposure on say 5 per cent of that sum while putting 95 per cent of the funds into less risky but modestly rewarding investments. Thus higher risks than might usually be borne can be taken on £50,000 of the total sum. In that guise the investor might play the role of a venture capitalist by investing the £50,000 in a small but developing company where there will be little if any return in the short term and even the potential for a total loss. However the investor will have seen some potential for longer-term growth which could be substantial if the company develops and its products capture market share. An investor who only had £50,000 in total to invest would be unwise to put all of it at such risk and would be better off with perhaps a combination of tax efficient savings products, premium bonds, gilt edged stock and some shares in leading companies. The investor would therefore be characterized as risk averse but probably very sensible given the limited funds available.

Lumby and Jones (2006) have considered the theoretical dimension of the risk-and-reward trade-off in investments and they use the expression 'utility function' to indicate how an investor chooses between alternative risky projects. Lumby and Jones assume that investors are rational and that their utility maximizing choices are informed by four basic axioms which are as follows:

1 Investors are able to choose between alternatives by ranking them in some order of merit, so that they are able to reach a decision.
2 The ranking of alternative projects is 'transitive' so that if project A is preferred to project B and project B to C, then project A must be preferred to C.
3 Investors do not differentiate between alternative projects which have the same degree of risk; their choice is dispassionate in that it is based solely upon consideration of the risk involved rather than on the nature of alternatives available.
4 Investors are able to specify for any investment whose returns are uncertain, an exactly equivalent alternative which would be just as preferable but would involve a certain return, so for a decision involving risk an investor would be able to specify a certainty equivalent.

These axioms can be used to construct a utility function which can act as a model of the investor's risk attitudes. This utility function is shown in Figure 9.2 below and while it is possible to calibrate the axes to show comparison between alternative risky projects the purpose here is to appreciate the shape of the function as representative of attitudes to risk.

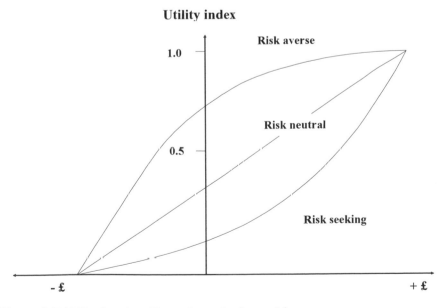

Figure 9.2 Utility functions illustrating attitudes to risk

Data from: Lumby and Jones (2006)

9.3 Definitions of risk

Property investments all carry a degree of risk because no matter how thorough the initial appraisal, there will still be a degree of uncertainty regarding the actual return which will arise from an investment over the holding period. Hargitay and Yu (1993: 35) have considered the spectrum of risk which extends from the present when values are certain to the immediate future where there are risks. Beyond that position there is partial uncertainty and beyond that total uncertainty. Thus every step or assumption taken beyond the present embodies additional uncertainty and therefore additional risk. Forecasters face the same dilemma as the further a forecast extends into the future the more uncertain it becomes.

Certainty represents precise knowledge of the outcome; risk is a situation where alternative outcomes are identified together with a statement of the probability of such outcomes. Partial uncertainty is where alternative outcomes can be identified but without the knowledge of the probabilities of such outcomes. Total uncertainty is where even the alternative outcomes cannot be identified.

If risk is regarded as the extent to which the actual outcome of an action or decision may diverge from the expected outcome, an action or decision is risk-free when the consequences are known with certainty. For a rational investor, the possibility of a lower than expected return has more importance than the possibility of a higher than expected return. The former case is sometimes referred to as the downside risk and it is perhaps not surprising that the risk appraisal techniques which are explored later in this chapter focus primarily on this aspect of risk.

Discussions on the topic of risk tend to include some definitions which are perhaps of more interest in an academic than practical context. While it is not necessary to delve too deeply into that vocabulary, there are some descriptors that identify the sources of risk and these terms are used in the context of framing the discount rate to reflect the degree of risk posed to a particular investment. There are also analytical definitions which essentially look at the probability that an investment will not generate the expected rate of return. Both of these branches of risk vocabulary will be explored later in the chapter but before moving on some of the key concepts are set out below where a distinction is drawn between systematic and unsystematic risks.

Systematic risk	Unsystematic risk
Caused by extrinsic factors which affect all investments and over which the property investor has no control.	Risks affecting particular investments and over which the investor has some control.
Examples include changes in the economic, political, or social environment and which for example may trigger changes in legislation, regulation or interest rates. Property investors might undertake a SWOT or PEST analysis to identify what these risks are likely to be over the project timeline.	*Examples include* the way a project has been financed in that highly geared investments are more risky. The investor has some control here and might for example look at alternative funding options. Tenant selection may also be managed to reduce the risk of exposure to a flagging market sector. Property selection and location can also be chosen by the investor to reduce risk.

Having considered the vocabulary and theoretical perspectives on risk, the focus of the chapter now turns to more practical considerations regarding the causative factors which give rise to risks for the property investor.

9.4 Risk and property investments

The types of risk which may be encountered by an investor are summarized in the following paragraphs which discuss the risks to the income flow and capital value as well as the risk that there might be unexpected future outgoings required to sustain the value of an investment. The risks considered here relate to the single asset, i.e. a property investment because given the sheer scale of investment required for direct involvement in property, not all investors can spread these risks across a portfolio of properties.

Risks to income flow

Apart from government stock, any investment carries the risk of default. For example with equities, there is no certainty regarding whether dividends will actually be paid to shareholders, as it will depend on company performance. With property, the risk of default on market rented investments will depend on the strength of the covenant, which in essence is the reliability of the business tenant to meet rental payment obligations. This is characterized in the expression: tenant risk.

Large corporate landlords will usually investigate the financial standing of businesses who are seeking to lease space in their properties. Leases might not be granted where a company has begun to show signs of financial frailty or significant loss of market share. However that is not always easy to detect, as complete and reliable data are seldom available and a sharp economic downturn can sometimes see hitherto reliable business tenants suddenly go into receivership. The propensity for this to happen will increase or decrease depending on which industrial sector the tenant is operating in. For example during economic downturns when there is reduced consumer expenditure on leisure, it is known that companies in that sector will suffer more than companies operating in sectors which provide necessities. From a landlord's perspective there are therefore differential sector risks which can threaten income streams.

In the case of reversionary property, risk is attached to the projected income flow, potential voids and possible depreciation. With leasehold properties, there may be problems associated with dilapidation claims. Many appraisals of property, especially during buoyant market periods, tend to build in explicit expectations of rental growth. The order of magnitude of the predicted growth will relate to the age and type of property, projected demand and historical growth trends. Growth assumptions can be built into the capitalization rate where a lower yield signifies high expectations of capital growth but with a higher risk that these expectations may not be met in full.

Future outgoings

The risk that there will be unexpected expenditure required by a property investor applies even if the property is new and let on full repairing and insuring

(FRI) terms to a reliable tenant. This is because there is a strong possibility that technology and expectations around sustainability can affect a property so that premature obsolescence can set in. This might necessitate significant and unforeseen expenditure to retro-fit a building so that it can attract a sustainability rating. Similarly, a town centre shopping centre which is showing its age and is losing shoppers to more recent out of town competition may need an expensive upgrade to remain competitive.

This type of expenditure may be significant and while a sinking fund may have been put in place by a prudent investor the scale of expenditure required often outstrips any reserves built up for future refurbishment. Other unexpected outgoings which might arise could stem from changes in legislation which require improved means of escape on fire safety grounds or improved access arrangements beyond the current regulations for those with disabilities or even unexpected legal costs arising from a court case. These are quite apart from changes in the taxation regime which can obviously have effects for the net income received by a property investor.

Capital value

The capital value depends on the expected income flow, which in turn is affected by the likely level of outgoings. Even where this dimension is known and thought to be stable, the capital value can vary with the yield. Capital value predictions may prove inaccurate because of general imperfections in market knowledge, lack of comparable transactions and sometimes the secrecy surrounding deals. There may also be some uncertainty regarding valuations as there is an accepted margin of tolerance of ±10 per cent which can have significant consequences for high-value properties.

Because property valuations are not tested through transactions in the market with the same frequency as gilt or equity prices, property valuations can remain notional for long periods before the process of market correction takes practical effect in a sale. While in rapidly moving markets there is increased frequency with which property assets held in investment portfolios are revalued, the price that a property actually realizes on a sale may sometimes be very different from its book valuation. This could be because of the volatility of the market at the time of the sale or due to prevailing market sentiment which is reacting to wider market information. The pressure in some institutions to realize their assets may at particular moments mean that the price achieved in transactions may be less than the theoretical value.

For some new developments such as out of town retail warehouse developments, the rental value can be hard to predict and the appropriate capitalization rate yet more difficult, as there simply may be no direct comparisons in the particular locality. The difficulties can be compounded because there is no clear leasing pattern and it is not clear how well the park is likely to trade as the full retail offer is not yet apparent.

Large high-value office towers (see Figure 9.3) are bought and sold by large corporate property investors. These investments will always come with a bundle of risks which the investor has to assess relative to the returns.

Figure 9.3 The Canary Wharf office cluster in East London

9.5 The risk assessment toolkit

Given that there are different types of risk which the property investor has to be aware of, the following discussion considers the range of techniques which have evolved as attempts to quantify risk. These techniques aim to put the decision-maker in a better position to form a response to the identified risks. It will not be possible to do justice to all of the techniques shown in the risk assessment toolbox set out below, however the principles underpinning the main candidates will be discussed.

Methods of risk analysis	
Methods which attempt to describe the riskiness of a project	Methods which attempt to incorporate the perceived risk in appraisal models
Sensitivity analysis Scenario testing Simulations The mean variance method Beta analysis	Risk-adjusted discount rate (RADR) Certainty equivalent method Sliced income approach

Before looking at some of these techniques it should be borne in mind that the traditional investment method of valuation considered earlier in the book and which uses an all risks yield (ARY) is to some extent an implied risk assessment technique. That is because the ARY adopted by a valuer is thought to reflect implicitly the bundle of risks posed to a property investment relative to the potential rewards. However the criticism of this approach is based upon the subjectivity used in its determination as it leaves a lot unsaid about how the particular rate was arrived at.

9.6 Sensitivity analysis

The aim of sensitivity testing is to examine the effects on the final outcome of making marginal changes to the variables. As Baum and Crosby (2008: 231) note it enables the question 'what if?' to be asked of a property investment. The basic method involves changing one variable at a time and then comparing the percentage change in the variable against the percentage change in the final value. If a small percentage change in a variable produces a large percentage change in the final value then the variable is said to be very sensitive.

Sayce *et al.* (2006: 161) comment that sensitivity analysis has operational value in the overall risk assessment process as among other things, it helps the decision-maker to think more clearly about the probable degree of change that is likely to take place in variables and the likely consequences of these changes.

Baum *et al.* (2006: 245) also note that while sensitivity analysis and other risk appraisal techniques are well known there is a degree of scepticism in practice surrounding their practical value. This standpoint has to do with the potential complexity which can arise by deciding upon a discount rate, which is theoretically taking risk into account, and then adjusting variables to also explore risk. There is therefore the danger that the decision-maker becomes too embroiled in the risk assessment process and begins to 'double count for risk'. Baum *et al.* (2006: 245) note that there is also a danger that the more the decision-maker becomes involved in these complex processes the further they may be divorcing themselves from reality, as at each stage in a risk assessment process different assumptions are being layered in. Ultimately the out-turn results may be at variance with the reality of the situation.

Accepting that there are some legitimate criticisms associated with risk identification and appraisal techniques the following example looks at a simple application of sensitivity analysis.

Example 9.1: Simple sensitivity testing

In this scenario a developer has let a retail unit on a long lease with five-year rent reviews of an annual rent of £188,000. The first year of the lease was rent free and this was absorbed by the developer who is now marketing the unit to property investors at an asking price of £2,570,000. The developer is offering to cover the purchaser's costs so if the asking price were met in full the initial yield from a purchaser's perspective would be around 7.3 per cent.

Based on historic data, an investor who is interested in acquiring the building, assumes that the annual rental growth will be of the order of 3 per cent. The investor plans to purchase the building and hold it for the remaining four years until the first rent review and then dispose of it based upon the capitalized value of the reviewed rent at that time, which will be a product of $1.03^5 \times$ £188,000. The exit yield is assumed to widen only very slightly relative to the initial yield because this is a new building and given the short holding period the effects of depreciation are assumed to be negligible. The investor has a target rate of return of 9 per cent for these types of acquisitions. Based upon the above assumptions the DCF below suggests that the investment would meet the target rate with a margin to spare as the internal rate of return (IRR) is 10.1 per cent.

Annual rent passing: £188,000   Assumed annual rental growth: 3%
Exit costs @ 2% of exit value   Exit yield: 7.5%

Year	Quarter	Income £	Expenditure £	Net cash flow £	PV £1 @ 9% (2.18% per quarter)	Discounted cash flow £
1	0	47,000	2,570,000	−2,523,000	1	−2,523,000
	1	47,000	0	47,000	0.9787	45,999
	2	47,000	0	47,000	0.9578	45,017
	3	47,000	0	47,000	0.9374	44,058
2	4	47,000	0	47,000	0.9174	43,118
	5	47,000	0	47,000	0.8979	42,201
	6	47,000	0	47,000	0.8787	41,299
	7	47,000	0	47,000	0.8600	40,420
3	8	47,000	0	47,000	0.8417	39,560
	9	47,000	0	47,000	0.8237	38,714
	10	47,000	0	47,000	0.8062	37,891
	11	47,000	0	47,000	0.7890	37,083
4	12	47,000	0	47,000	0.7722	36,293
	13	47,000	0	47,000	0.7557	35,518
	14	47,000	0	47,000	0.7396	34,761
	15	47,000	0	47,000	0.7239	34,023
	16	2,905,914	58,118	2,847,796	0.7084	2,017,379
			IRR =	10.10%	NPV =	90,334

However the investor decides to conduct a sensitivity analysis by modelling stepped changes in two of the key variables which are the assumed rental growth rate and the exit yield to ascertain the effects on the rate of return. The results of this test set out below show the variance in the cells surrounding the core outcome which is an IRR or 10.1 per cent when the rental growth rate is 3 per cent and the exit yield 7.5 per cent.

		Annual rental growth range						
		3.75%	3.50%	3.25%	3%	2.75%	2.50%	2.25%
Exit	6.9%	13.03%	12.73%	12.43%	12.13%	11.83%	11.53%	11.23%
yield	7.1%	12.32%	12.02%	11.73%	11.43%	11.13%	10.83%	10.54%
range	7.3%	11.64%	11.34%	11.05%	10.75%	10.46%	10.16%	9.87%
	7.5%	10.98%	10.68%	10.39%	10.10%	9.80%	9.51%	9.22%
	7.7%	10.34%	10.05%	9.76%	9.47%	9.18%	8.89%	8.60%
	7.9%	9.72%	9.43%	9.14%	8.85%	8.57%	8.28%	7.99%
	8.1%	9.12%	8.84%	8.55%	8.26%	7.98%	7.69%	7.41%

The cells shaded dark grey in the bottom right-hand corner indicate where the investor's target rate is not met due to a combination of changes in the rental growth and exit yield assumptions. There are a number of points which arise from this analysis one of which is that if the exit yield remained unchanged at 7.5 per cent the investor's target rate would be met even if the annual rental growth rate fell to 2.25 per cent. However the more sensitive variable is the exit yield as it only has to move out by 40 basis points to 7.9 per cent with the rental growth rate remaining at 3 per cent for the rate of return to fall beneath the investor's target rate of 9 per cent. This type of analysis also enables a degree of comparison with other similar investment opportunities so that the relative riskiness of each could be compared.

However there are criticisms of this approach which include the fact that the decision-maker is not presented with an easy to interpret nor definitive answer. Baum and Crosby (2008: 233) add that there remain unanswered questions regarding the probable direction and order of magnitude of change which is likely for each variable. Thus at this elementary level of analysis the stepped adjustment of variables may be logical but it is silent on which scenario is most realistic and likely to happen.

9.7 Scenario testing and probability analysis

This involves changing a combination of a number of inputs and the output is then calculated in the light of those changes. Various combinations of variables can be used, although key variables for the commercial property investor will tend to be rental growth, the initial and exit yield. This is because these three variables reflect how much could reasonably be paid to acquire the asset, what level of income will be achieved over the holding period and how much will the asset be worth when it is sold. Other candidates for analyses are the outgoings and length of void periods. These variables can be modelled on a core or realistic scenario, an optimistic and a pessimistic scenario as suggested in the table below.

Example 9.2: Scenario testing

		Scenario		
		Optimistic	Realistic	Pessimistic
Variable	Annual rental growth	3.5%	2.5%	1.5%
	Initial yield	7.5%	7%	6.5%
	Exit yield	7.5%	8%	8.5%
Results	Income	*A*	*B*	*C*
	Capital value	*X*	*Y*	*Z*

As the scenario testing table above suggests, appraisal models will usually contain several uncertain variables and this makes the predicted output subject to a range of different outcomes rather than a single value. One way to reduce this complexity to manageable proportions is to induce some probability around the variables achieving particular values. Subjective weightings are therefore assigned to the variables as in the example below where the probability of rental growth achieving specific values in a simplified annual in arrears scenario is explored.

Example 9.3: Probability analysis of rental growth

A property investment opportunity has become available and is being marketed to investors at £1,231,000 exclusive of purchase costs. The property is fully let to a reliable business tenant who 3 years ago signed a 20 year FRI lease with five-year rent reviews. The market rent agreed at that time was £80,000 per annum and there is thus two years of that rent remaining until the first rent review. If the vendor's asking price were met this would reflect an initial yield of 6.5 per cent which bears some comparison with similar investment properties recently sold in the locality. An investor is interested in purchasing the investment on the basis that it will be held until the second rent review and then disposed of based on the value of the reviewed rent at that time. One of the uncertain issues is the value that the rent will achieve at the two rent reviews as this will obviously have implications both for the rental income over the holding period and the capital value on disposal.

The investor decides to look at rental growth statistics for this type of property over the previous 10 years and notices that the rental growth rate correlates very closely with the average inflation rate as measure by the Retail Price Index (RPI) over that period and which was 2.5 per cent per annum.

	Probability of rental growth			
	As average RPI over 10 years: 2.5%	RPI +1%	RPI − 1%	Expected outcome
Rental growth	2.50%	3.50%	1.50%	
Subjective weighting	60%	15%	25%	100%
Probability	1.5%	0.525%	0.375%	2.4%

In the above table, the investor is assumed to have made some subjective judgements about which scenario is most likely to materialize. Thus the investor has placed a 60 per cent weighting on the probability that rental growth will conform to the average RPI rate over the last 10 years. A 25 per cent weighting is placed on a pessimistic scenario in which rental growth will be less than RPI over the last 10 years and there is only a 15 per cent weighting placed upon the probability rental growth will exceed the average rate of inflation over the last 10 years. The probability adjusted rental growth rate which arises is therefore 2.4 per cent.

This growth rate can be fed into a DCF appraisal as follows to determine whether, on those assumptions, the investor's target rate of 8 per cent will be achieved if the vendor's asking price is met in full.

Rent passing: £80,000   Initial yield: 6.50%   Acquisition costs: 5.75%
Exit yield: 7.50%   Exit costs: 3%   Management costs: 5%
Probability adjusted rental growth rate: 2.4%

Year	Expenditure £	Income £	Net cash flow £	PV £1 @ 8%	Discounted cash flow £	Event
0	1,301,538	0	−1,301,538	1	−1,301,538	Purchase investment
1	4,000	80,000	76,000	0.9259	70,368	Year 1 income
2	4,000	80,000	76,000	0.8573	65,155	Year 2 income
3	4,504	90,072	85,568	0.7938	67,924	Reviewed rent
4	4,504	90,072	85,568	0.7350	62,893	Year 4 income
5	4,504	90,072	85,568	0.6806	58,238	Year 5 income
6	4,504	90,072	85,568	0.6302	53,925	Year 6 income
7	4,504	90,072	85,568	0.5835	49,929	Year 7 income
7	40,565	1,352,161	1,311,596	0.5835	765,316	Disposal based on the value of reviewed rent
				NPV	−107,790	

If the investor were confident about the rental growth rate adopted, it is clear that on this test the investment does not meet the target rate of return signified by the negative NPV of £107,790. However the use of the Goal Seek function in Excel would enable the investor to quickly identify what the initial purchase price would need to be in order to deliver a zero NPV, i.e. exactly 8 per cent return. That figure would be £1,193,748 and would be the investor's maximum bid reflecting an initial yield of 7.09 per cent.

Considerable sums are invested by corporate landlords in acquiring commercial property investments in the City of London (such as those shown in Figure 9.4).

Figure 9.4 Corporate landlords are allured by commercial property investments in the City of London

Given the potential for change in key variables such as rental growth, it would seem reasonable that investors and their analysts would spend some time looking at the best-case and worst-case scenarios. Investors will be particularly interested in the downside risk to see whether the investment would be palatable in that eventuality. The discussion which follows on simulation suggests the direction in which this evaluative process might be heading.

9.8 Simulation

As explained by Sayce *et al.* (2006: 167) advances in software applications have opened up the potential for property investors and analysts to engage in arguably a more sophisticated level of modelling than is possible by changing variables in the slightly mechanistic and potentially laborious manner required in sensitivity and scenario testing described earlier. However with sophistication there is complexity and even more scope for the analyst to become detached from reality or for a gap to open up between the statistical expert and the property expert. There is also the added danger that the more sophisticated the modelling exercise, the more chance it becomes an end in itself and that there is insufficient attention paid to the quality of the data inputs. 'Snow-blindness' can also occur in that operators become seduced by the process and cannot spot fundamental logic or omission errors in an appraisal. However, so long as there is some practical arm's-length quality control process in place, authors such as Baum *et al.* (2006: 245) feel that simulation models can potentially provide more confidence for the decision-maker when faced with investment risk.

The Monte Carlo model is the most commonly referred to in discussions regarding simulation in property investment analysis and a version of this model can be run on Excel spreadsheets using @RISK software marketed by the Palisade company. Oracle's Crystal Ball software is an alternative, although the focus in the design of that software is perhaps broader by enabling exploration of risk in business decision-making.

The key feature of a Monte Carlo simulation is that because the degree of variance in key variables like rental growth, void periods or yields cannot be stated with certainty they are treated as distributions. When the simulation is run, parameters for change in each variable are selected by the operator and within those parameters the model uses random numbers to provide a distribution of outcomes. Through a process of iteration this is repeated thousands of times to generate a distribution of the possible outcomes for the selected variables. The distributions for each variable are then combined to generate an overall distribution for the NPV or IRR which is likely to arise for the property investment being analysed. The mean and standard deviation for the distribution is provided and assuming that the range of results is a normal distribution, there is a 95 per cent likelihood that the actual NPV or IRR will fall in the range of ± 2 standard deviations either side of the mean.

The standard deviation is an indication of the variability of the results and therefore represents risk. A very risk-averse investor will tend to concentrate on the downside risk represented by that part of the distribution falling beyond one standard deviation to the left of the mean. This part of the distribution will contain the lowest values i.e. the worst possible outcomes for the investor and for which there will be approximately a 16 per cent chance that they will occur. Thus if an investor could tolerate the outcome even in the unlikely event that the worst-case scenario were to be realized, then the analysis was suggesting that the investment was robust and worthy of further consideration.

Investors could cut into the distribution to superimpose their own minimum expectation line and then look at the probability surrounding that choice or they could adopt the cut-off point at the boundary of two standard deviations left of the mean and beyond which there is only a $2\frac{1}{2}$ per cent probability of those results occurring. Because the results are presented as a distribution they are versatile and enable interpretation. For example risk-averse and risk-seeking investors will take different perspectives on where the boundary for their own specific downside risk begins.

For those readers who want to learn more about the role that simulation might play in property investment decision-making, Sayce *et al.* (2006: 169–88) provide a good briefing of the subject with illustrative examples. It is not necessary in this book to explore the mechanics or statistical principles underpinning these models any further. However what could be said in conclusion on this topic is that the decision-making surrounding very high-value commercial property investments might well see the increased use of simulation in future, if only as one element in the overall corporate decision-making process.

9.9 Risk-adjusted discount rate

Above and in preceding chapters, there are a number of discounted cash flows which illustrate how these modelling exercises attempt to discount future income streams to identify if an investor's target rate can be achieved. The discount rate adopted in the examples represents the investor's target rate which is sometimes referred to as a hurdle rate, the analogy being that the hurdle is set at a particular height in order to see if the investment can get over it. Perhaps a better analogy is the high jump bar being raised to a point sufficient to see if the jumper (the investment) can perform to or exceed that level. If the NPV outcome of a DCF is positive it signifies that the investor's target has been achieved with a margin to spare. Returning to the high-jump analogy, the size of the NPV reflects the margin by which the bar has been cleared. While corporate investors may have discount rates which represent their minimum target rates of return, the question which obviously arises is how are those discount rates derived?

Theoretically the discount rate comprises two fundamental elements the first of which is the risk-free rate of return available to the investor and the second element is an allowance for the risks posed by the specific property investment. Baum (2009: 139) suggests that the first element: the risk-free rate, could be thought of as the redemption yield on gilts for the matched life of the investment. Thus if an investor is considering investing in a property for 10 years, the risk-free alternative is deemed to be the purchase of gilt edged stock which will be redeemable in 10 years' time and could notionally be invested in and held for that length of time. However investing in a building is a riskier option and the discount rate will need to exceed the risk-free rate and hence the second element needs to be added to the discount rate. The latter should therefore be adjusted to reflect the specific risks posed by the property investment contemplated and when that premium is added to the risk-free rate, the outcome is a risk-adjusted discount rate (RADR) which is encapsulated in the simple formula:

> The investor's RADR = RFR + r
>
> in which RFR = the rate of return available on a risk-free alternative investment; and
>
> r = a premium to reflect the specific risks posed by the property investment being evaluated.

While it is quite easy to go to the markets to identify the RFR part of the equation, the challenge lies in calculating the risk premium or uplift represented by r. There is unfortunately no easy solution for deducing what r might be in any particular set of circumstances and judgement is required on the part of the investor or analyst. However Baum (2009: 143) helpfully suggests how it might be done by disaggregating r into its constituent parts. The discussion earlier in the chapter identified some of the specific risks posed to property investments and this is similar to what Baum has in mind and which is illustrated in the following example.

Example 9.4: Scenario exploring the calculation of the risk-adjusted discount rate

A property investment opportunity has become available in the form of a retail warehouse on an edge of town retail park. The unit is occupied by a business tenant who has been trading reasonably well for two years of a 10-year lease. The lease contains a break clause at year 5, although if the break clause is not exercised there is provision for a rent review at that time. The tenant is a sports and leisurewear retailer although not a recognized high street name and the company only has two other outlets elsewhere in the country. The rent passing reflects the market rent at the time the lease was signed and there was no rent-free period granted beyond the three months allowed as a fitting out period.

Recently the economy has shown signs of deterioration and the government has announced stringent spending cuts which could result in public sector redundancies. The knock on effects are likely to be felt in the leisure, package holidays and retail sectors where it is likely that consumer spending will drop. The investor recognizes that this investment obviously poses some risks and sets about constructing a property specific risk-adjusted discount rate for use in a discounted cash flow to see if the investment could withstand that viability test.

Risk-adjusted discount rate		
Risk-free rate (RFR) available on gilts		3.5%
Add risk premium comprising		
Base premium for all property investments	3.5%	
Tenant risk	1.5%	
Lease length and terms including break clause option	1%	
Depreciation	1.5%	
Location risk	1%	
Risk premium: r therefore		8.5%
Risk-adjusted discount rate therefore (RFR + r) =		12%

The resulting RADR would set a stiff test for the investment depending on the asking price sought by the vendor relative to the rental income. As Baum and Crosby (2008: 234) comment, the use of the RADR implies that more return is required to compensate for greater risk. Criticism could obviously be levelled at the weightings given to the individual components in the RADR, but at least those weightings are explicit and available for scrutiny and comparison with other appraisals which the investor might be undertaking. The investor might also have longer-term ambitions for the property or the site and these would not surface in this type of assessment.

9.10 Certainty equivalent techniques

This approach uses the statistical techniques of the mean and standard deviation to indicate the position where a risk-averse investor would be able to avoid the downside risk. Taking a normal statistical distribution as shown in Figure 9.5, ± 1 standard deviation of the distribution from the mean will incorporate 68 per cent of the range of outcomes. The downside risk is defined as the area below the curve, more than 1 standard deviation less than the mean. This area will incorporate only 16 per cent (half the balance) of the distribution. Using this position the distribution tells us that the investor has an 84 per cent chance of bettering the position.

The downside risk is the 16 per cent of outcomes on the left side of the diagram below the curve. The calculation which is the counterpart to this is in five steps as illustrated in the following example.

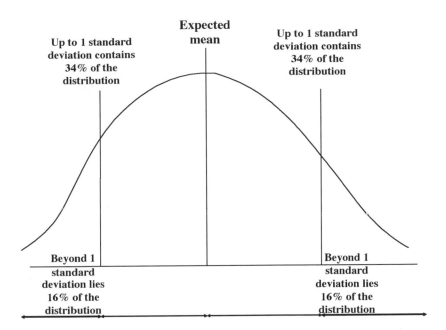

Figure 9.5 Distribution under a normal curve

Example 9.5: The certainty equivalent approach

Investment valuation				
Annual rental income			£200,000	
YP perp. @ 8%		12.5		
Capital Value				£2,500,000
Step 1: Calculate the expected value				
The two variables are income and yield				

Income:	Outcome	Probability –		sample outcome
	$\hat{r}$	p		$(p \times \hat{r})$
	180,000	0.3		54,000
	200,000	0.6		120,000
	220,000	0.1		22,000
Expected value $(\bar{r}) = \Sigma\,(p \times \hat{r})$			Total	196,000

Yield:	outcome	probability =		sample outcome	
	$\hat{r}$	p		$(p \times \hat{r})$	
	0.07	0.1		0.007	
	0.08	0.5		0.04	
	0.09	0.4		0.036	
Expected value $(\overline{r}) = \Sigma\,(p \times \hat{r})$			Total	0.083	

Step 2: Calculate the variance

Income:

Outcome	Expected value			Probability	
$(\hat{r})$	$(\overline{r})$	$(\hat{r} - \overline{r})$	$(\hat{r} - \overline{r})^2$	p	$p(\hat{r} - \overline{r})^2$
180,000	196,000	−16,000	256,000,000	0.3	76,800,000
200,000	196,000	4,000	16,000,000	0.6	9,600,000
220,000	196,000	24,000	576,000,000	0.1	57,600,000
Variance$(\sigma^2) = \Sigma(p)\,(\hat{r} - \overline{r})^2$					144,000,000

Yield:

Outcome	Expected	$(\hat{r} - \overline{r})$	$(\hat{r} - \overline{r})^2$	Probability P	$p(\hat{r} - \overline{r})^2$
0.07	0.083	−0.013	0.000169	0.1	0.0000169
0.08	0.083	−0.003	0.000009	0.5	0.0000045
0.09	0.083	0.007	0.000049	0.4	0.0000196
Variance $(\sigma^2) = \Sigma(p)\,(\hat{r} - \overline{r})^2$					0.000041

Step 3: Calculate the standard deviation (sd)

Income: sd = $\sqrt{\text{variance}}$ = σ	12,000	
Yield: sd = $\sqrt{\text{variance}}$ = σ	0.006403	

Step 4: Calculate certainty equivalents			
= expected value – standard deviation			
Income:	196,000 –12,000 =	184,000	
Yield:	0.083 + 0.006403 =	0.089403	
For the yield the risk is of a higher yield/lower YP/less value so it is the upper end of the range that is discarded = expected value + standard deviation.			
Step 5: Reinsert values in calculation			
Investment valuation (certainty equivalent)			
Income		£184,000	
YP perp. @ 8.9403%	11.19		
Capital value		£2,058,960	

9.11 The sliced income approach

This approach which Baum and Crosby (2008: 238) first aired in the late 1980s develops the risk-adjusted discount rate and certainty equivalent techniques to provide a hybrid method. Like the layer approach discussed in Chapter 6 and in Isaac and Steley (2000: 69–77) the sliced income approach distinguishes between layers of income which are less risky (core income) and more risky (top slice income). The less risky core income could thus be discounted at or close to a risk-free rate, while the top slice income or overage, would be discounted at a higher risk-adjusted rate. The justification for the latter is that this part of the income is more risky given that it might (but might not) become available as an addition to the core income at a later date following a rent review (see Figure 9.6).

Developing the example of the retail warehouse unit discussed above in Example 9.4 the corresponding DCF which follows has been simplified to illustrate the slicing principle. Thus there are no allowances made for entry, exit and ongoing management costs which would probably arise in reality. In the DCF a

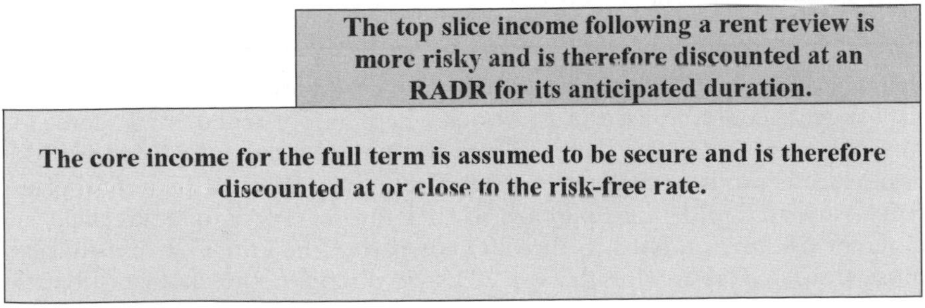

> **The top slice income following a rent review is more risky and is therefore discounted at an RADR for its anticipated duration.**

> **The core income for the full term is assumed to be secure and is therefore discounted at or close to the risk-free rate.**

Figure 9.6 Diagrammatic representation of the sliced income approach

2.5 per cent annual rental growth rate has been assumed so that at the first rent review after three years an additional top slice income of £9,856 is generated. That income stream has been discounted at a risk-adjusted rate of 12 per cent. The continuing core income has been discounted at a rate to reflect the investor's risk-free rate of 3.5 per cent plus a base premium which the investor applies to all property investments of 3.5 per cent, producing a discount rate of 7 per cent.

The investor is assumed to sell the investment at the end of year 8 when the combined rental income at that point is assumed to have grown by the annual rate and is capitalized at the exit yield shown. It is debatable whether that capital should be discounted at the lower or higher discount rate, although in the example it has been discounted at 12 per cent to reflect the overall riskiness of this particular venture. On this test there is a considerable negative NPV and thus the investor would probably explore other investment opportunities or seek to negotiate a reduced asking price from the vendor.

Annual rent passing: £75,000
Initial yield: 7%   Exit yield: 8%
Assumed annual rental growth rate: 2.5%
Discount rate for core income: 7%
Risk-adjusted discount rate for top slice: 12%

Year	Expenditure £	Core income £	Top slice income £	PV £1 @ 7%	PV £1 @ 12%	Discounted cash flow £
0	1,071,429	0	0	1	1	−1,071,429
1		75,000	0	0.9346	0.8929	70,095
2		75,000	0	0.8734	0.7972	65,505
3		75,000	0	0.8163	0.7118	61,223
4		75,000	9,856	0.7629	0.6355	63,481
5		75,000	9,856	0.7130	0.5674	59,067
6		75,000	9,856	0.6663	0.5066	54,965
7		75,000	9,856	0.6227	0.4523	51,160
8		75,000	9,856	0.5820	0.4039	47,631
8			1,200,079	0.5820	0.4039	484,712
					NPV	−113,590

Baum and Crosby (2008: 240) also illustrate examples of this approach which they suggest could be used in situations where a core rental is guaranteed or with turnover rents where there is a core element with the potential for an addition which is profit or turnover related. There is a degree of theoretical plausibility associated with this approach in that the income is disaggregated and different risk rates applied to the different parts. The criticisms are similar to those discussed above for the risk-adjusted discount rate in that subjective weightings are required on the part of the analyst or investor to generate the swing between the two discount rates used.

9.12 Summary

In order to earn rewards from property investment investor's will inevitably have to bear some risks. The question of course is what is a reasonable degree of risk relative to the potential rewards from investing in property? The answer is different for different investors as some investors may only have limited funds and cannot afford to take risks or they may be operating as trustees or under standing orders which prevent risk exposure. Other investors may have most of a fund in secure investments and may be at liberty to take more risks with a small proportion of the funds in order to seek higher rewards. There is also a temporal dimension in that the benchmark for what is considered a safe 'no risk' rate of return is seldom static for very long.

Given that property investment is a future-oriented activity and that there will always be some risks that the financial return will vary from the expected return, it is not surprising that a number of risk assessment techniques have emerged to try to help investors make wiser decisions. Most of these techniques have an origin in a wider business/project decision-making context and have evolved from that generic setting to deal with property specific risk scenarios. Thus the property investor now has a limited but specialized toolkit of risk appraisal techniques which could be used to assess property investment opportunities. While not all of those tools were discussed in this chapter there was a focus upon those techniques which are most likely to surface in a practice setting.

Risk assessment techniques considered included sensitivity analysis which looks at 'what–if?' adjustments to key variables and the out-turn effect on the bottom line. Scenario testing and probability analysis were discussed as evolutions from sensitivity testing in that best-case, worst-case and core positions could be looked at in terms of how probable they might be. Risk assessment techniques also include the adjustment of the discount rate to account for risk, for instance, an increase of three per cent on top of the risk-free rate could be used to compile a discount rate which reflected the risk. In certainty equivalent techniques, probabilities are assigned to alternative capital values and costs.

Statistical techniques which use standard deviations within normal distributions can also provide the investor with a view on the downside risk, i.e. what would the outcome be if the unlikely but possible worst-case scenario materialized. Probability and normal distributions also provide the basis for simulation testing using the Monte Carlo model which requires iteration and random numbers to explore change in variables within set parameters. The outcome can be expressed in a distribution showing the range of possible NPVs or IRRs. While rapid improvements have been made in software and the processing power of personal computers, it is difficult to conceive of the practical application of simulation models extending beyond the decision-making around high-value commercial property investments.

The sliced income approach was also considered and it was found that it adopts different interest rates for the different layers of income that a property investment is likely to generate going forward. The less risky bottom slice of income could be discounted at closer to a risk-free rate of return, whereas the top slice income (sometimes referred to as overage) is more risky and would therefore be discounted at a higher rate. The sum of what are two discounted cash flows would then reflect the present value of the investment.

The use of risk assessment techniques like those discussed in this chapter, improve the learning curve and intuitive feel around the specific risks posed to a property investment. Risk assessment techniques also allow a degree of comparison between competing projects. However none of the techniques can provide any value to the decision-making process without credible up-to-date data inputs and the exercise of a considerable degree of judgement by those with experience and knowledge of the field of property investment. It is also easy to become over-fixated with risk assessment techniques when there are wider and more significant issues which will affect property values more fundamentally.

Despite the refinement available in some of the risk assessment tools discussed in this chapter, very few analysts accurately forecast the recent global recession which saw residential and commercial property values plummet in most countries around the world. Even seemingly invincible financial centres such as Dubai ultimately succumbed to the effects of the downturn. At first this phenomenon was perceived to be a minor problem caused by some imprudent lending on residential mortgages in parts of the United States. However it is easy in hindsight to see that this was the tip of the iceberg and that banking practices across the world have become far too blasé regarding risk and lending policy and this in turn had inflated asset values including property, way beyond their true worth. Markets will in the end correct these aberrations. Cynics would say that after a period of recovery and growth all the good financial habits and prudence which had been rediscovered will again be forgotten, until the next financial crisis occurs.

References

Baum, A. (2009) *Commercial Real Estate Investment: A Strategic Approach*, 2nd edn (Oxford: EG Books).

Baum, A., Nunnington, N. and Mackmin, D. (2006) *The Income Approach to Property Valuation*, 5th edn (London: EG Books).

Baum, A. and Crosby, N. (2008) *Property Investment Appraisal*, 3rd edn (Oxford: Blackwell).

Hargitay, S. E. and Yu, S. M. (1993) *Property Investment Decisions: A Quantitative Approach* (London: Spon).

Isaac, D. and Steley, T. (2000) *Property Valuation Techniques*, 2nd edn (Basingstoke: Macmillan).

Lumby, S. and Jones, C. (2006) *Fundamentals of Investment Appraisal* (London: Thomson Learning).

Sayce, S., Smith, J., Cooper, R. and Venmore-Rowland, P. (2006) *Real Estate Appraisal From Value to Worth* (Oxford: Blackwell).

10

Financial management

Aims

This chapter examines the role played by annual company reports in the management of publicly listed commercial property companies and Real Estate Investment Trusts which customarily rely on a combination of debt and equity to fund their activities. The chapter explores key aspects contained in the financial statements which form part of the annual reports and which reveal the extent of borrowing, the ability to service debt from income and the returns to shareholders. The chapter also looks at profitability and liquidity and how these characteristics are measured within a corporate entity.

Key terms

>> **Gearing ratio** – reflects the balance between debt and equity in the compilation of the total assets held by a company. Prudent borrowing by a property company makes business sense in that it can enable growth through development and/or property acquisitions as well as increasing returns to shareholders. A board of directors will however ensure that the extent of borrowing does not expose the company to unacceptable risks in the event that income reduces to the point where loan repayments cannot be met. Thus when considering current debt levels and whether there is capacity to borrow more, boards will also look at the loan cover ratio. A company's gearing ratio will fluctuate as company boards respond to development and acquisition opportunities as well as instructing that some assets be disposed of to reduce debts. There is no single rate of gearing which would suit all companies although most boards will have target parameters which they try to stay within.

>> **Liquidity ratio** – represents the relationship between a company's short term financial liabilities and its liquid assets, which are essentially cash or

assets which can be turned into cash very quickly. A company could survive for short periods on an overdraft facility if its liquidity ratio dropped below 1:1.

>> **Profitability** – a concept which is not as simple as it might first appear, as there are a number of different ways that company profitability can be measured. For a property company or REIT one of the key measures of profitability is the relationship between annual income and the total capital employed expressed as a percentage. There is no prescribed rate of return and company profitability will vary from year to year in response to macro-economic events and the position reached in the business cycle. Between 2007 and 2009 property companies typically reported losses, as the property market felt the full effects of the global credit squeeze. During more stable economic periods shareholders would expect that the added risk of investing in a property company was rewarded with a rate of return at a margin above that achievable on safe, low risk investments, such as high street savings accounts which are a proxy for the risk-free rate.

10.1 Introduction

Particularly for commercial property investment appraisal, knowledge of the principles of company accounting is desirable, as annual reports provide data which can be assessed to determine the financial health of a company. The annual reports contain financial statements which are examined by a number of different groups holding different perspectives. Thus in deciding whether to grant a commercial lease to a business tenant such as a retailer, a commercial property landlord might wish to examine the trading position of the retailer. Companies considering forming joint ventures might wish to assess the capacity of potential partners to contribute to a partnership. Financial advisors and stockbrokers might want to obtain a picture of the financial prospects of share ownership in a particular company. Thus a company's annual reports speak to a wide range of existing and potential stakeholders. This chapter provides an outline of some of the key elements contained in company annual reports.

10.2 Company reports

A publicly listed company's financial statements are contained in its annual report which is made available to shareholders and the general public most of who will peruse e-versions lodged on company websites on the internet. The reports provide details of the operations of a company as well as a chairman's statement which looks at the preceding year and prospects for the future. There is also a chief executive's report which comments on such matters as company profits, dividends per share, fixed assets and the balance between debt and equity invested in those assets. The company's overall strategy is outlined and property companies will explain the rationale for key property acquisitions and disposals and how these fit within the overall portfolio of properties held. The reports will normally contain risk assessments and there will be an independent auditors report on the financial position of a company.

As pointed out by Westwick (1980), a company's annual report and accounts will be of interest to a number of different audiences including:

- *Equity investors*, which includes domestic and international corporate and individual shareholders, potential shareholders and holders of convertible securities, options or warrants.
- *Company creditors*, including existing and potential holders of debentures and loan stock, and providers of short-term secured and unsecured loans and finance.
- *Company employees*, including existing, potential and past employees.
- *Investment analysts*, including financial advisors, journalists, economists, statisticians, researchers, trade unions, stockbrokers and other providers of advisory services such as credit rating agencies.
- *Business contacts*, including customers, trade creditors and suppliers and in a different sense business rivals and those interested in mergers and takeovers.
- *The government*, including tax authorities, departments and agencies concerned with the promotion and regulation of commerce and industry and local authorities.
- *The public* in their various guises as taxpayers, consumers, community and special interest groups such as political parties, environmental protection societies and pressure groups.

The various groups above will be interested in a company's annual report for different reasons. However, those who are interested in a company's financial prospects will focus on the financial statements contained in annual reports. There are a number of different financial statements but the core documents which perhaps reveal most about the financial status of a company are the:

- balance sheet;
- income statement;
- cash flow; and
- notes to the accounts.

The following discussion will focus upon the balance sheet and the income statement because in combination these two financial statements say a lot about the financial health of a company.

10.3 The balance sheet

The balance sheet would normally be produced for an individual company but if it were part of a group, then group statements may also be included. As its name suggests, the balance sheet sets out the balance reached between the assets and liabilities of a company at the accounting date. The balance reached one year previously is also shown for comparative purposes.

A company balance sheet is essentially made up from three categories of entry which are: assets, liabilities and shareholders' funds. From a company's perspective, the total assets are equal to the sum of the shareholders' funds plus liabilities. However from a shareholder's perspective, the difference between the total assets and total liabilities of the company is the shareholders' funds. In summary therefore the basic relationships in the balance sheet are:

Company perspective:	Assets = Shareholders' funds + Liabilities
Shareholder perspective:	Assets – Liabilities = Shareholders' funds

A simplified example of a balance sheet is shown in Table 10.1 so that the key elements can be identified and their significance discussed beneath the balance sheet.

Non-current assets are also referred to as fixed assets and where these are investment properties, there is the need for annual revaluations by an external firm of valuation surveyors. The appointed firm of surveyors will follow the procedures set out in the RICS Valuation Standards (otherwise known as the Red Book) so that the total market value of the property portfolio can be reported in the accounts. For a property which is in the course of development but will ultimately become an investment property, the surveyors will report the current realizable value of the project. The value of the company's plant and

Table 10.1 Balance sheet for a fictitious property company reporting at the end of 2010

	2010 £ Millions	2009 £ Millions
Non-current assets		
Investment properties	2,400	2,100
Plant and equipment	15	16
Investments in joint ventures	500	350
Loan investments	50	40
Current assets		
Trading properties	1,800	1,600
Trade and other receivables	350	400
Money held in deposit accounts	95	80
Cash and cash equivalents	180	230
Total assets	**5,390**	**4,816**
Current liabilities		
Short-term borrowing and overdrafts	200	120
Trade and other payables	300	350
Tax liabilities	75	80
Non-current liabilities		
Borrowing	2,100	2,300
Total liabilities	**2,675**	**2,850**
Net assets (Total assets less total liabilities)	**2,715**	**1,966**
Equity		
Ordinary share capital	725	725
Revenue reserves	250	150
Capital reserves	75	68
Shareholders' interest	1,665	1,023
Total equity	**2,715**	**1,966**

equipment shown in a balance sheet represents the cost less straight line depreciation.

Non-current assets are intended to be permanent company assets in contrast to current assets which are turned into cash usually within one year. For a property company, properties to be traded within a year will be valued at their market value less costs including expenses and interest paid out on a property since purchase.

Current liabilities reflect amounts due to be paid to creditors within one year. The balance of current assets less current liabilities is called the net working capital. Non-current liabilities reflect amounts owed by the company but which will require repayment beyond one year and could, for example, be commercial mortgages being used to refinance investment properties held by the company.

Under the heading of *Equity* in the balance sheet, ordinary share capital is the amount paid by the shareholders to the company when its shares were first issued. This figure will remain unchanged unless the board decides to raise additional capital by issuing more shares, which is referred to as a rights issue. Reserves arise because profits are not distributed to shareholders but retained by the company, although there is a distinction between revenue and capital reserves. Revenue reserves reflect a board's decision to retain earnings in the face of what might be difficult times ahead. Capital reserves arise on the revaluation of assets which can give rise to a surplus. This is a common occurrence in property company accounts when investment properties can attract a higher valuation year on year, generating an accounting surplus which is distinct from profits arising from rents or trading.

When these accounting principles are applied to large and well established property companies such as Hammerson plc which is a leading Real Estate Investment Trust in the UK, the variables are measured in billions of pounds. For example in Hammerson's 2009 annual report, the balance sheet showed that at the end of that year the company had total assets valued at £5,666,400,000 while total liabilities were £2,643,300,000 leaving net assets at £3,023,100,000. The latter is the same as the total equity of the company. After a deduction to minority interests of £73,400,000 the equity shareholders fund was £2,949,700,000 which when divided by the 702,800,000 Hammerson shares in circulation, provided a net asset value per share of £4.20.

It is however unlikely that Hammerson shares will trade on the stock market at £4.20 for the whole of the ensuing year because, as discussed earlier in the book, the stock market has tended to take a pessimistic view regarding the liquidity of property companies' assets. The consequence is that there is a tendency for shares in property companies like Hammerson to trade at a discount to net asset value and between 1990 and 2009 Reita (2009) has recorded this discount to fluctuate around an average of 18 per cent. However large property companies such as Hammerson are also FTSE 100 companies and positive market movements generally, might see Hammerson shares trade occasionally at a premium above the reported net asset value per share. For example at the end of 2010 shares in Hammerson were trading at £4.25 and during the year the share price had fluctuated between a low of £3.32 up to a high of £4.38.

For companies like Hammerson to grow, there will need to be an increase in the assets owned. The balance sheet shows that assets equal liabilities plus shareholders' funds, so that the ways open to a board to grow a company would be to increase liabilities (borrow more) or increase shareholders' funds. There are two ways of increasing the shareholders' funds, the first is to issue more shares and the second is to plough back profits and of course a combination of the two could be tried. Ploughing back profits is not necessarily the cheapest source of long-term funds for the company and it also restricts the payment of dividends to shareholders. When faced with the dilemma of how best to expand a company, a board of directors will be very conscious of a company's current trading performance as revealed in the company's income statement, the principles of which will now be discussed.

10.4 The income statement

While the balance sheet reflects the balance between assets and liabilities at the accounting date, the income statement (sometimes referred to as a profit and loss account) shows the relationship between a company's revenue and costs over the year ending on the accounting date. The income statement therefore shows the results of a year's business activity by the company with the previous year's figures shown for comparative purposes. The profit is shown before and after tax and any profit attributable to minority interests arising from investment in other companies will also be consolidated into the income statement. A simplified income statement is shown below in Table 10.2 where it can be seen that it fulfils number of functions, such as confirming the earnings per share achieved across the accounting year.

The income statement shows how much net cash has been generated by activities over the accounting period by deducting the expenditure incurred

Table 10.2 Income statement for a fictitious property company reporting at the end of 2010

	2010 £ Millions	2009 £ Millions
Revenue	450	430
Costs	175	170
Gross profit	275	260
Less indirect costs		
Interest payments on loans	45	50
Costs of disposals	30	20
Administration costs	15	14
Profit/loss before tax therefore	185	176
Tax	65	62
Profit/loss for the financial year	120	114
Transfer to reserves	12	10
Dividends to shareholders	108	104
Earnings per share in pence (assuming 50 million shares)	216	208

over the year from the revenue. For a property company, the cost of sales in the income statement includes the staff costs and associated overheads of running the company. Sometimes an income statement will feature an extraordinary item which is unusual in terms of its size and frequency of occurrence. From an analyst's perspective, these items need to be omitted when considering profit trends over a number of years. Thus a large profit from the disposal of part of the business and which is unlikely to occur again, should not distort an interpretation of the underlying profit generated during that year.

A company's income statements are assessed by various stakeholders including its own board of directors who will be interested in whether the company is making a satisfactory profit relative to its peer group. Analysts will also determine whether a company is short of cash or cash rich and whether there is scope to improve the relationship between long-term debt and equity. These characteristics relate to profitability, liquidity and capital structure and are as applicable to individual property development projects as they as are to managing property companies such as REITs who hold large portfolios of commercial investment properties. The evaluative techniques used to assess company performance are relatively simple and based upon the relationships between variables in the financial statements.

10.5 Assessing profitability

Regarding profitability there are some well-established ratios which are used to analyse the profitability of an enterprise and theses are:

- Trading profit as a percentage of turnover.
- Profit before interest and tax as a percentage of average capital employed.
- Earnings per share either basic (based on issued share capital) or fully diluted (based on authorized share capital, which is the total share capital that can be issued). For example Land Securities which is a major REIT, reported in 2010 that total earnings per share that year were 34p.
- Dividend per share. In 2010 Land Securities dividend per share payable to shareholders was 28p.
- Number of times covered – that is, the number of times a share dividend is covered by total earnings per share, thus for Land Securities it was 0.8 in 2010.
- Assets per share which is the value of the net assets of the company divided by the number of shares. Land Securities had over 823 million shares in circulation at the end of 2010 and the net asset value per share for the company was reported to be £6.91. Thus the total net assets owned by Land Securities shareholders at that accounting date was £5.69 billion (rounded up).

As Scarrett (2008. 152) points out, investors who purchase shares in a company are taking on a higher risk than if they were to deposit their money in a relatively safe bank or building society savings account. Thus shareholders will be aware of a notional safe rate of return which acts as a benchmark against which they can assess returns on their shares. Given that the share price will fluctuate on the markets over a year and that dividends may be payable on a three or six month cycle and that on some of those events the board may retain dividends, it is not straightforward to predict what the actual returns to each shareholder will be. Thus a proxy for assessing the return to shareholders is to look at a company's net asset value in relation to the annual return which was generated from those assets. This is commonly referred to as the return on capital employed and is represented by the following relationship:

$$\text{Return on capital employed} = \frac{\text{Profit before tax, interest and dividends}}{\text{Total net assets}}$$

For Land Securities at the end of the 2010 the pre-tax revenue profit for the year was £251.8 million which when divided by the company's total net assets of £5.69 billion produced a return on capital of 4.4 per cent. This is very similar to dividing the annual dividend per share of 28p by the net asset value per share which was £6.91 which produces just over 4 per cent. Thus when deciding the dividends to be paid to shareholders, the board of directors were probably taking account of the current revenue generating capacity of the company's assets. The dividend return to shareholders was thus kept within what the board felt to be sustainable limits for the prevailing market conditions. While a nominal rate of return of around 4 per cent is fairly modest, the base rate at the time was a historically low 0.5 per cent and that the best a savings account could offer was around 1 per cent, thus the safe investment benchmark principle was at least being met.

The modest rate of return also reflected a gradual climb out of a period of a recession which had seen the value of most property companies' portfolios devalued significantly. There had also been business failures which had a knock on effect of reducing rental income to property companies. For example Land Securities' revenue profit cited above was 20 per cent down on the previous year, while the company's asset value had risen, principally because the revaluation of its property portfolio reflected a gradual economic recovery. Thus while the figure on the bottom half of the equation had grown on the back of strengthening asset values, the income on the top half of the equation had reduced, resulting in a modest nominal rate of return on capital employed.

Of course the rate of return on capital will may vary between industries and between different companies within the same sector depending on the point of development that they may have reached. Thus for property companies the losses or low rates of return reported around 2009 and 2010 were reflecting a period when there were asset disposals, rights issues and rebalancing of portfolios in the face of very challenging market conditions. Although the annual returns might not have appeared to be very exciting for shareholders, property companies such as Land Securities had taken strategic decisions, the outcome of which might take several years to materialize in the form of strengthening returns. During difficult economic periods one of the functions of comparing property company profitability ratios is to provide a gauge how well a company is faring given adverse trading conditions. Profitability is also a reflection on how robust a company's business strategy is and the quality of the property in the portfolio.

10.6 Liquidity

As well as being profitable, it is also important that a company should remain sufficiently liquid. A profitable and fast expanding company could fall into the trap of tying up too much of its capital in fixed assets, stocks and debtors only to find that it then has difficulty paying its debts when they fall due. There are two main ratios used to examine the liquidity of a company and they are the *liquidity ratio* and the *current ratio*.

The liquidity ratio is also called the acid test because it is a critical measure of whether a business can remain viable in the short term. As mentioned above, organizations may be rich in assets but can still fail because they have insufficient cash flow to meet short-term obligations. The minimum safe ratio of liquid assets to current liabilities is considered to be 1:1, as this signifies that a company has sufficient cash to pay its immediate debts. Liquid assets are defined as current assets excluding stocks of goods which cannot be quickly converted into cash. In effect liquid assets are debtors, cash and any short-term investments or government securities which can readily be turned into cash. The relationship is therefore:

Liquidity ratio = Liquid assets: Current liabilities

A company could survive for short periods if the liquidity ratio fell below 1:1 so long as there was an unused bank overdraft facility.

The other test of a company's liquidity is the *current ratio* where the definition of current assets is expanded to include stocks and work in progress on the grounds that these resources will soon convert into their cash equivalent. The current ratio is therefore the relationship between all current assets and current liabilities as follows:

Current ratio = Current assets : Current liabilities

A ratio of 2:1 is regarded as being satisfactory for most businesses.

10.7 Gearing

Another important measure of financial performance of a company is the gearing ratio. Gearing was discussed in Chapter 8 where buy-to-let appraisals revealed that judicious borrowing in the form of a mortgage could be seen as a creative use of debt to increase the return on equity invested. The same principle is applicable at the corporate level when applied to property developments and/or long-term investment properties. However, in each case, a lot will depend on the rates of interest which the debt can be secured at. When interest rates are low and loans can be secured on a fixed-rate basis, prudent borrowing when combined with equity is a credible method to expand a business. Those acting for large corporate borrowers with good credit ratings are aware of this and thus negotiate competitive terms and conditions for loans used for business expansion. For example, British Land which is a successful REIT reported (2010) that 80 per cent of its debt was either fixed interest or capped.

The gearing (or leverage) ratio represents the relationship between a company's debt and equity and is used to compare levels of debt between companies. The gearing ratio is as follows:

$$\text{Gearing ratio} = \frac{\text{Debt (borrowings)}}{\text{Equity (shareholders' funds)}}$$

Related to the gearing ratio is the ability of companies to service their debt from income, as the greater the reliance on debt the higher the interest payments and the larger the drain on company income. To prevent companies from becoming overburdened by debt, company directors will ensure that there is more than sufficient annual income to meet interest charges, so that even if annual income fell, there would still be a sufficient safety margin remaining. For example British Land (2010) reported that its income cover was 2.3 times, i.e. the company's annual income before interest payments and tax deductions could meet interest payments on its debt 2.3 times over, suggesting that the company was within safe borrowing limits. Interest cover is therefore calculated from:

$$\text{Interest cover} = \frac{\text{profit before interest and tax}}{\text{net interest}}$$

Gearing ratios and interest cover are scrutinized by stakeholders such as banks who might wish to determine whether a property company's borrowings are at a reasonable level and whether it is prudent to provide further loans to the company. Potential investors consider whether a highly geared company is exposed to the risks of interest rate rises or loss of income, either of which could threaten the returns to shareholders as a greater proportion of income will be needed to service debt. In that scenario there could be a loss of market confidence, leading to share price devaluation plus loss of share earnings.

Experienced investors will look to see if a company has sufficient capacity to absorb reduced profits without having to sell assets in possibly unfavourable market conditions. The gearing ratio is also therefore a measure of the potential to finance further expansion without recourse to the shareholders which would depress the share price. If a company requires additional debt to fund a new project the resultant gearing ratio might depress the share price and restrict flexibility to respond to future opportunities. Thus company boards of directors will try to keep gearing within optimal parameters so that debt is used to maximize returns to shareholders but does not place the company in a risky position nor fetter the ability to borrow if a relevant business opportunity presents itself.

As confirmed by Sayce *et al.* (2006: 220) companies which are highly geared, require a higher level of revenue to break even and in that scenario there is likely to be greater volatility regarding profitability. To explore the related concepts of interest cover and gearing a little further, the summary accounts of two fictitious property companies are now compared in Table 10.3 to illustrate the effects of different degrees of gearing. Both companies have the same asset value and operating profits but Company A relies mainly on equity with very little borrowing, while Company B relies heavily on borrowing and is thus highly geared.

Table 10.3 Accounts for companies A and B compared

Balance sheet	Company A	Company B
	£ Million	£ Million
Net assets	400	400
Financed by:		
Debt	80	320
Shareholders' equity	320	80
	400	400
Income statement		
Operating Profit	60	60
Less loan interest at 10%	8	32
Profit before tax therefore:	52	28
Tax @ 35%	18.2	9.8
Profit after tax therefore:	33.8	18.2
Gearing ratio (debt/equity)	25%	400%
Interest cover (operating profit/ interest payments)	7.50	1.88
Earnings per share £ (profit after tax/ number of shares)	0.11	0.23

One interpretation of the above accounts is that the directors of Company A should consider increasing the use of debt to expand the company, because at present the company is too deep within the 'comfort zone' with interest cover at 7.5 and a comparatively poor return to equity shareholders relative to Company B. Indeed market forces would see shareholders sell shares in Company A and buy those in Company B although the prices that the respective shares traded at would tend to reduce the margin of return between the two companies.

In reality leading property companies and REITs such as Land Securities (2010: 24) report a target rate of gearing of between 35 per cent and 45 per cent although their competitors tend to rely more heavily on borrowing so that their respective gearing ratios are consequently higher. For example SEGRO's gearing ratio was 91 per cent in 2009 and in the same year Hammerson's gearing was 72 per cent while Derwent London's gearing was 62 per cent. Great Portland Estates (2010: 28) reported that following a spate of property disposals its gearing had fallen from 65 per cent in 2009 to 26 per cent in 2010 but with the anticipation that this would be rise to between 50 per cent and 70 per cent when programmed developments had begun.

For a highly geared company such as Company B above, a relatively small percentage increase in operating profits will generate a larger percentage increase in the profits remaining to be distributed to shareholders. Thus in the adjusted accounts shown in Table 10.4 the operating profit has been increased by 10 per cent to £66 million for both companies is illustrated the effects of gearing in the context of rising incomes.

Table 10.4 Accounts for companies A and B given a 10 per cent increase in operating profits

Balance sheet	Company A	Company B
	£ Million	£ Million
Net assets	400	400
Financed by:		
Debt	80	320
Shareholders' equity	320	80
	400	400
Income statement		
Operating profit	66	66
Less loan interest at 10%	8	32
Profit before tax therefore:	58	34
Tax @ 35%	20.3	11.9
Profit after tax therefore:	37.7	22.1
Gearing ratio (debt/equity)	25%	400%
Interest cover (operating profit/ interest payments)	8.25	2.06
Earnings per share £ (profit after tax/ number of shares)	0.12	0.28

Table 10.5 Accounts for companies A and B given a 10 per cent decrease in operating profits

Balance sheet	Company A	Company B
	£ Million	£ Million
Net assets	400	400
Financed by:		
Debt	80	320
Shareholders' equity	320	80
	400	400
Income statement		
Operating profit	54	54
Less loan interest at 10%	8	32
Profit before tax therefore:	46	22
Tax @ 35%	16.1	7.7
Profit after tax therefore:	29.9	14.3
Gearing ratio (debt/equity)	25%	400%
Interest cover (operating profit/6.75 interest payments)	1.69	
Earnings per share £ (profit after tax/ number of shares)	0.09	0.18

The adjusted accounts above show that a 10 per cent increase in operating profits has increased the return to Company A shareholders from 11p to 12p per share, which is a 9.1 per cent increase in earnings per share (assuming a £1 share price). Meanwhile the shareholders of Company B have seen their earnings increase from 23p to 28p per share or an increase of 21.7 per cent in earnings per share. Conversely a 10 per cent decrease in revenue can have a disproportionately large effect in reducing the profit remaining to be distributed to shareholders. These swings are illustrated below where the operating profit has fallen 10 per cent from £60 million £54 million.

Given an understanding of the dynamics of gearing a company's board of directors are in a better position to assess the consequences of further borrowing for acquisitions or to undertake developments. It is also possible to run scenario tests to gauge the effects of reduced operating profits on earnings.

10.8 Summary

Those contemplating indirect investment in commercial property by purchasing shares in listed property companies and REITs should examine annual company reports. The latter contain company financial statements such as the balance sheet and income statements, which together show the relationship between the value of investment properties held and income generation.

Between 2007 and 2009 property companies and REITs went through a turbulent period in which the capital value of their assets was written down and the rental income from property investments fell as some business tenants failed leaving rental voids. Given those circumstances, boards of directors had to make some difficult decisions which typically involved the disposal of some assets to reduce debt, share rights issues to raise equity and retention of some earnings by either reducing or withholding dividends on shares. During what were challenging market conditions, equity investors had to take a longer-term view by looking at the overall strategy and positioning of a property company and how that might in the longer-term see share values rise and shareholder dividends increase.

The chapter confirmed that measured borrowing is a credible way for a property company or REIT to expand its business and to optimize returns to shareholders. However it is important that company directors keep the gearing ratio and loan cover ratios under review as the history of the property cycle shows that the most vulnerable property companies during a downturn are those which are highly geared. Considerable learning has been done by property companies and their boards, so that the proportion of debt to equity is kept under review in order to prevent debt from becoming a corporate problem. Where debt is used to fund acquisitions or developments, boards seek to ensure that the majority of loans are either fixed rate or capped rather than variable or floating rate. A company which is heavily indebted with floating rate loans will find its share price suffering especially in a period of volatile interest rates. Such a company will see its corporate credit rating eroded and ultimately it could find itself taken over by a better resourced competitor.

References

British Land Company plc (2010) *Annual Report and Accounts 2010* (London: British Land Company plc).

Derwent London plc (2009) *Report & Accounts 2009* (London: Derwent London plc).

Great Portland Estates (2010) *Annual Report 2010* (London: Great Portland Estates).

Hammerson plc (2009) *Annual Report 2009* (London: Hammerson plc).

Land Securities Group plc (2010) *Annual Report 2010* (London: Land Securities Group plc).

Reita (2009) *Understanding Commercial Property Investment*, available in e-format at: www.reita.org

Sayce, S., Smith, J., Cooper, R. and Venmore-Rowland, P. (2006) *Real Estate Appraisal from Value to Worth* (Oxford: Blackwell).

Scarrett, D. (2008) *Property Valuation: The Five Methods*, 2nd edn (Abingdon: Routledge).

SEGRO (2009) *SEGRO plc Annual Report* (Slough: Slough Estates Group plc).

Westwick, C. A. (1980) *Property Valuation and Accounts* (London: Institute of Chartered Accountants).

11

Portfolio theory and strategy

Aims

This chapter explores key contributions made by a number of writers on portfolio theory and how those ideas seek to reduce investment risk while optimizing returns. The chapter also examines portfolio strategy and the degree to which it is practically possible for portfolio managers to implement theory. The chapter will explain why there are greater possibilities in applying the theory to multi-asset investment portfolios than to portfolios comprising only investment property.

Key terms

>> **Beta** (β) – is used when discussing the degree of financial volatility that a property investment has relative to its peer group. Thus if a widely based commercial property index revealed that capital values had risen 10% in one year but that office values (a sub group in the index) had risen by 20% then offices could be seen as more volatile with a *beta* of $20/10 = 2$. Thus if the index for all property were to fall 10%, then office values might fall 20% and thus offices with their high *beta*, would be seen as a risky investment. Alternatively if shop values only rose by 8% over the same period the *Beta* would be: $8/10 = 0.8$ signifying lower volatility relative to the asset class.

>> **Systematic risks** – are those posed to a property investment (or portfolio of investments) by factors beyond the control of a single investor. Thus changes in market sentiment regarding the value of a class of properties will affect property values, but changing market perceptions of value cannot be controlled by individual investors. These changes in market behaviour are categorized as a systematic risk.

>> **Unsystematic risks** – apply to individual properties or locations. In theory, individual investors have at least some ability to reduce or mitigate these risks through prudent stock selection and portfolio diversification.

>> **Correlation coefficient** – a statistical term which describes the degree to which variables change in relation to one another over time. Thus if time-series data showed that retail rents in a city always moved in the same direction and order of magnitude as changes in average income, then the two variables could be said to have a perfect correlation coefficient represent by 1 (or 100%). It is virtually impossible to fund such a pure relationship in reality and anything over 0.6 (or 60%) would suggest a high correlation coefficient. Conversely those wishing to diversify the risk in an investment portfolio might be looking for low or negative correlations between investment assets.

>> **Modern portfolio theory** – in essence suggests that unsystematic risk can be reduced and returns optimized when investment assets which have negative or low correlations are selected for inclusion in an investment portfolio. The ideas were suggested by Markowitz in the 1950s in the context of share dealing. The concepts have some applicability to commercial property portfolios because it is possible to find properties with a low correlation of returns, although it is more difficult to find those with negative correlations. There are also practical difficulties in constantly reviewing a property portfolio to achieve risk reduction given the costs of property transfer and general issues regarding the availability of stock and illiquidity.

11.1 Introduction

As discussed in earlier chapters, property poses some particular challenges when viewed as an investment, and there is therefore an ongoing need to manage it effectively. Given the scale of investment flowing into property from financial institutions, property companies and unit trusts, there is a need for both transparency and accountability in the way that the money is invested. Objective management decisions are required to ensure that investment in property is justified in comparison to alternative investment opportunities.

The annual reports of corporate property investors such as REITs reveal ambitions to maximize returns for shareholders while reducing risks, which is perhaps the goal of any rational investor. These organizations take an active role in managing their property investments, some of which require refurbishment or even partial or complete redevelopment. Thus these companies seldom treat even their fully let prime investment properties as if they were paper investments requiring no asset management.

The main challenges posed by commercial property as an investment relate to the size and indivisibility of lots, complexity of funding and the need for strategic management decisions on whether to acquire, upgrade or dispose of properties in a portfolio. Sayce *et al.* (2006: 287) refer to the ability to pick winners and discard losers, which they acknowledge is far from straightforward. Decisions on these issues are taken against the backdrop of the scale and type of property which has been assembled in a portfolio.

For a multi-asset portfolio such as that held by a financial institution, managers have to take a view on the balance to be struck between gilts, equities, property and other investments. Within the property element, further decisions are needed on the proportions of investment to be placed in retail, offices, industrial or leisure property. Property companies who only hold property investments also face the same challenge on what might be the optimal mix from different property sectors in different locations in order to maximize returns to the investors.

This chapter will initially explore some of the theory which has emerged to try to assist portfolio managers responsible for these types of allocation decision. It will become apparent that some of the subtlety and intent in the theory cannot always be implemented at a practical level. What might be said is that at least some of the theoretical concepts help portfolio managers reflect upon their decisions and the results arising from those decisions. The discussion is focused upon commercial property as it in that sector where most of the theorizing, data gathering and learning has taken place regarding the building and management of property portfolios. This is not to say that some of the generic concepts and vocabulary could not also be applied in the context of a portfolio of resi dential investment properties.

11.2 Modern portfolio theory

Early work by Markowitz (1952, 1959 and 1991) regarding share portfolios led to Modern Portfolio Theory which in common with all theoretical models is based upon some reasoned assumptions. Thus it is assumed that investors are risk averse in that they rationally expect a higher rate of return to compensate them for taking greater risks. It was also assumed that risk can be measured by analysing the likely divergence between the returns from a portfolio and its expected return. When considering whether or not to buy an asset, investors were also assumed to be concerned about the effect of the decision on their overall portfolio and thus would not consider the risk of the asset in isolation from other assets held. Markowitz suggested that investors should select assets for inclusion in their investment portfolios on the basis of mean variance or alternatively mean and semi-variance. Semi-variance seemed the more plausible measure of risk but posed greater computational difficulties.

Markowitz suggested that assets in a portfolio can be combined to provide an efficient portfolio that will give the highest possible level of return for any level of portfolio risk as measured by the variance or standard deviation. The risk-and-return trade-off for investments in a portfolio can be described graphically as an 'efficient frontier' as shown in Figure 11.1.

Investments which have a combination below this efficient frontier will not be achieving an efficient trade-off in the light of an investor's preference. Given an efficient frontier, investors have to choose where their preferences lie on the frontier and that choice will depend on attitudes to risk. Some investors will wish to minimize risk at the expense of return, while others will be prepared to take a higher risk to potentially achieve a higher return. Institutional investors have tended to be characterized as risk averse while private or specialist investors may be able to accept higher risk on some of their investment activities. The trade-offs that an investor makes between risk and return can be depicted in the form of indifference curves as shown in Figure 11.2.

Each curve represents a frontier of the highest acceptable level of risk for a given return. The indifference curves can be superimposed on the efficient frontier and the optimal choice will be that point at which the indifference curve touches the efficient frontier as shown by point X in Figure 11.3.

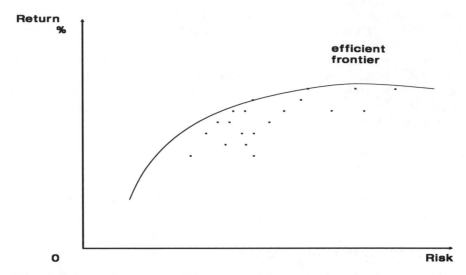

Figure 11.1 The efficient frontier

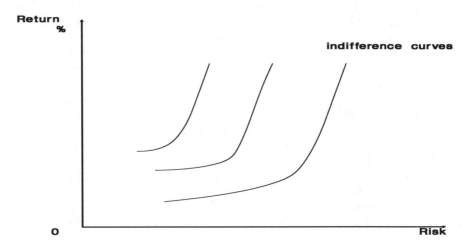

Figure 11.2 Indifference curves

In reality plotting the efficient frontier is very complex as it requires a forecast of future expected returns and the likely variance from those returns as well as the calculation of the correlation between investments. Although the mathematics is complex it is now possible to use a spreadsheet optimizer using matrix methods for the portfolio calculation.

The expected return is found from a weighted average of investments that make up the portfolio, the risk of the portfolio is however less than the weighted average risk of its constituent parts. This reduction of risk can be seen from the following portfolio consisting of two investments A and B with a total investment assumed to be 1 with x being invested in A. Thus in a two asset portfolio, the expected return is given by:

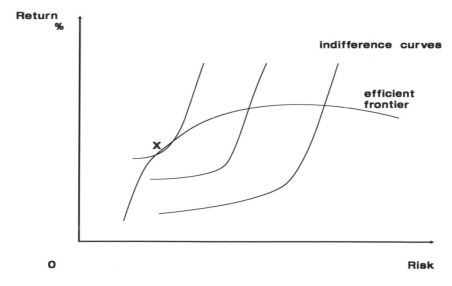

Figure 11.3 Indifference curves and the efficient frontier

$$E(r_p) = xE(r_A) + (1 - x) E (r_B)$$

The risk is given by:

$$\text{Variance } \sigma^2_p = x^2 \, \sigma^2_A + (1 - x)^2 \, \sigma^2_B + 2x(1 - x)\text{Cov}(r_A, r_B)$$

Cov is the covariance of the returns between investment A and investment B and it measures the degree to which the variability of returns tend to move in the same way. Covariance can be positive or negative, positive covariance indicating that the returns are moving in the same way and negative covariance in the opposite direction. The range is from +1 to −1 as with coefficients of correlation on which it is based, the nearer the covariance is to ±1 the stronger the positive–negative covariance.

The reduction in risk in the portfolio is the effect of the third term in the equation above, so the further from +1 (i.e. toward −1) the smaller will be this term's contribution to the risk of the portfolio. When this third term = +1 (perfect positive correlation between the two investments) then the portfolio risk is the weighted average of the component investments' risks and reduces as the value of this term reduces. The effect of risk and return and the composition of the portfolio can be seen from Figure 11.4.

When perfectly negatively correlated the graph appears as a dogleg, when positively correlated as a single line, variations between appear as a nonlinear function between the lines. Positions higher on the graph allowing greater return for the same risk are preferred. For instance take the case of two perfectly negative correlated investments. Investment combinations AB are preferred to AC because along AB increased returns are obtained for the same levels of risk. Options along the portfolio boundary AB are said to dominate AC. If we take

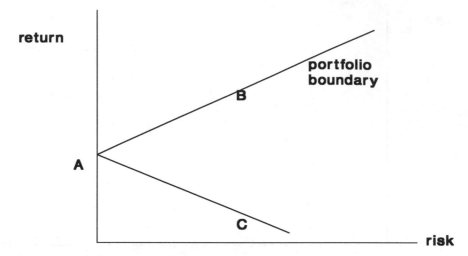

Figure 11.4 Two asset portfolio, assets negatively correlated

a case between the perfect correlations, then the portfolio will be a nonlinear curve increasing in value from the origin. The number of options in a two investment portfolio will be represented by the umbrella shape as in Figure 11.5.

The boundary to the north west will be the efficient boundary here, the analysis shows that at the point where the utility curves of the investor touch the efficient frontier then the investor's utility will be maximized. The addition of a risk-free investment such as government bonds or stocks produces a linear relationship identifying the risk–riskless efficiency boundary which is shown in Figure 11.5. The addition of borrowing and lending facilities extends the frontier, the borrowing rate will determine the position of the capital market line, the relationship between risk and reward. As the number of investments in the portfolio increases, so risk reduces but only to a defined limit. This remaining risk is called non-diversifiable risk whereas the rest is diversifiable risk.

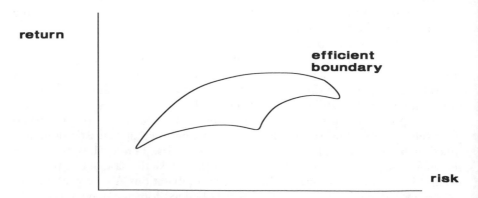

Figure 11.5 Two asset portfolio, general case

Risk is analysed in the market by the capital market line (CML). The slope of the CML is:

$$\frac{[E(r_M) - r_F]}{\sigma_M}$$

Where:

$$E(r_M), \sigma_M, r_F$$

are the expected return of the market portfolio, the risk of the market portfolio and the risk-free return respectively. The slope of the CML is the risk–return relationship in the market. So if:

$E(r_M) = 16\%$
$\sigma_M = 3\%$
$r_F = 10\%$
Market price of risk = $(16\% - 10\%)/3\% = 2\%$

Thus the CML would have a slope of +2 and thus for every percentage point of risk taken, the investor can expect a premium return of 2% above the risk-free rate. An investor taking on 4% of risk in a portfolio will receive 10% + (4 × 2%) = 18%.

The return to a portfolio will consist of the risk-free return plus the risk premium and the risk premium is the product of the portfolio risk and the market price of risk. This approach is only applicable to efficient portfolios lying along the CML. The market price of risk compensates the investor for additional non-diversifiable risk as no reward is paid for diversifiable risk.

Institutional and well-resourced investors aim to hold diversified portfolios and will be aware of the risk of acquiring new and particularly large assets which might bring additional risks to the entire portfolio. In this case, it is preferable to measure the asset's covariance with those of the other assets in the portfolio. For example, if a stock has high returns when the overall return of the portfolio is low and vice-versa, the stock has a negative correlation with the portfolio. It acts as a hedge against risk, reducing the risk of the portfolio. If the stock has a high positive correlation, there is a high risk for the investor.

Investors will only hold a risky investment if its expected return is high enough to compensate for its risk. There is a trade-off between risk–reward. The expected return on a security should be positively related to the asset's beta. Expected return on an asset =

Risk-free rate + (beta × (Expected return on market portfolio – Risk-free rate))

The term in brackets is positive so the equation relates the expected return on an investment as a positive function of its beta. This equation is the basis of the Capital Asset Pricing Model (CAPM) which will be discussed below and whose formula is expressed a follows:

$$\bar{R} = R_F + \beta(\bar{R}_M - R_F)$$

Where $\bar{R}_M$ is the expected return on the market, $\bar{R}$ is the expected return on the security, R_F is the risk-free rate and beta is the measure of risk. Beta is a measure of the security's sensitivity to movements in an underlying factor, a measure of systematic risk. Systematic risk affects a large number of assets and is also called market, portfolio or common risk. Diversifiable risk is a risk that affects a single asset or small group of assets, this is also called unique or unsystematic risk. The total risk for an individual security held in a portfolio can thus be broken down:

Total risk of individual security = portfolio risk + unsystematic or diversifiable risk.

Total risk is the risk borne if only one security is held. Portfolio risk is the risk still borne after achieving full diversification. Portfolio risk is often called systematic or market risk. Diversifiable, unique or unsystematic risk is that risk which can be diversified away in a large portfolio.

11.3 Capital Asset Pricing Model

The Capital Asset Pricing Model (CAPM) pioneered by Sharpe (1964) is a further development of modern portfolio theory. The CAPM is applicable to a wide range of investment choices including selecting investment properties for inclusion in a property portfolio. The CAPM is a tool which can be used to identify assets which have a value different to the current market value; that is they are underpriced relative to their returns. These assets are therefore desirable for portfolio managers should they be able to identify them from among the wider market.

The model is based upon the precept that the market only rewards investors for taking on that part of risk which cannot be diversified away, that is the systematic or market risk. The purpose of the analysis is to identify the potential to make abnormal returns before the event and some texts use the Latin phrase *ex ante* to denote this. Thus the ability to identify underpriced properties using the model depends on effective analysis, assumption building and forecasting. The approach uses comparables and the estimated beta for properties. By using a riskless rate of return, if the slope of the security market line is known then it is possible to work out underpriced and overpriced property as shown in Figure 11.6.

Brown and Matysiak (2000: 176–80) explain that for CAPM to have practical value at a stock selection level, investors must articulate their expected rates of return. So for example, an investor is assumed to have an expected rate of 10% return on portfolio assets and an asset becomes available in the market at £1,000 including acquisition costs. The assumption here is that the investor is going to hold the asset for one year before selling it. In order for it to meet expectations the asset must realize £1,100 at that point in time as when discounted at 10% to present value this will equal £1,000. If one year later the sale actually achieves £1,200, then this equates to a present value of £1,091 when discounted at the investor's target rate. According to Brown and Matysiak the asset will therefore have achieved an abnormal return and is thus underpriced relative to its returns. The asset would on this performance appear above

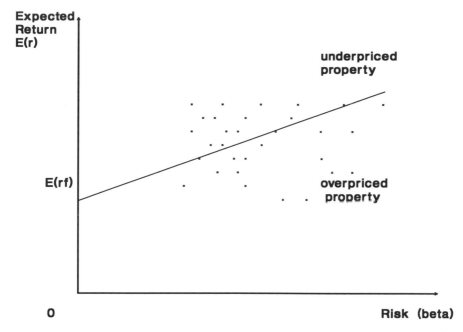

Figure 11.6 The CAPM and underpriced and overpriced property

the line in Figure 11.6. Abnormal returns can of course also be negative where an investor's target rate is not met when a sale is achieved, and those assets might be thought of as overpriced relative to their returns. These assets would therefore appear below the line in Figure 11.6.

To apply the CAPM to practice would require a degree of statistical analysis and the selection of a relevant sample of properties to work on. The valuation used is the equated yield model, assuming property is valued part way through the rent review period. This is a sophisticated analysis and due to the number of assumptions involved can be error prone, and thus some expertise is obviously necessary.

Assuming there are sufficient resources available to carry out this type of analysis, properties which appear above the trend line are those which might be targeted by a fund manager on the basis that they are underpriced relative to their potential returns. This also assumes that the underpriced assets identified are in fact available to be acquired. If market information is available then prices have already impounded values. There is also doubt that there is a sufficient quantity and quality of market data to operate these techniques to good effect and that if underpriced properties are to be discovered it is more likely to be from chance than analysis. Thus there are a number of practical difficulties faced when trying to implement these rather delicate analytical processes.

11.4 Portfolios and risk quantification

Quantitative measures can be allocated to concepts of risk and return. Returns are measured by expected cash flow returns but risks are measure by standard

Table 11.1 Portfolio risk and return

		Opportunity A	Opportunity B
Return %		Between 3 and 7	Between 1 and 9
Expected return	x	5	5
Probability of each return	$\bar{x}$	0.5	0.5
Variance %	σ^2	4	16
Standard deviation %	σ	2	4

deviation and variance, the standard deviation is not actually risk but a surrogate for risk. An example of risk diversification is explored Table 11.1.

Variance = σ^2 and is the sum of the differences between the return and the expected returns squared and divided by the number of returns:

$$\sigma^2 = \frac{\Sigma(x - \bar{x})^2}{n}$$

For opportunity A:

$$\sigma^2 = \frac{(3-5)^2 + (7-5)^2}{2} = 4, \quad \text{thus } \sigma = 2.$$

For opportunity B:

$$\sigma^2 = \frac{(1-5)^2 + (9-5)^2}{2} = 16, \quad \text{thus } \sigma = 4.$$

Both opportunities have the same expected return but differ in risk. Opportunity B has a greater variance than A and is therefore more risky. Rational decision-makers faced with two projects of the same return will take one with less risk and in this case they would invest in Opportunity A. However an investor could invest in both. For example it is now assumed that the two opportunities are inversely correlated and that an investor has decided to invest 2/3 of available funds in Opportunity A and 1/3 of funds in Opportunity B. The expected return on the portfolio is the weighted average of the returns on the individual opportunities, using the fraction of the funds invested in each as the weighting factor in the following formula:

$$ER_p = \Sigma x_i (E_i)$$

In the above formula ER_p is the return on the portfolio, x_i is the proportion invested in opportunity i and E_i is the expected return on opportunity i. ER_p = 2/3(5) + 1/3(5) = 5. The expected return is the same as if one had directly invested in A or B. However the risk of the portfolio is reduced if A and B are inversely correlated. When A is a high return, then B is low and vice-versa:

A high: ER_p = 2/3(7) + 1/3(1) = 5
B high: ER_p = 2/3(3) + 1/3(9) = 5
The risk of the portfolio is 0 (σ=0)

Combining two risky opportunities, the decision-maker has achieved a risk-free return. The situation has arisen because the two investment opportunities are perfectly inversely correlated and thus they have a coefficient of correlation of −1. The effect is based on diversification and illustrates the theory of how risk can be reduced through diversification.

Portfolio analysis assumes that an investor's assets are a collection of different property assets. The key criterion is the relationship between one property asset and another in the portfolio not the consideration of risk in respect of a single property. Although the future is uncertain, investment decisions need to be forward looking and thus have to consider expectations of return and risk and these two elements have to be quantified. Thus quantitative analysis uses the concept of expected returns and standard deviation (σ) or variance (σ^2) for risk.

The concept that diversification leads to risk reduction is the basis of modern portfolio theory discussed earlier. This reduction occurs when the investment returns are not perfectly correlated. Perfect positive correlation of investments would appear as shown in Figure 11.7. However in reality it would be very difficult if not impossible to find two investments whose returns were as harmonized over time as this theoretical construct suggests.

Perfect negative correlation will thus smooth out the variations in returns as shown in Figure 11.8. Again it would in practice be very difficult to find two investments whose returns were perfectly negatively correlated. Indeed it is quite challenging to find any two investments which are negatively correlated, as despite their diverse nature, investments tend to respond in a similar way to external influences, either macroeconomic or related to the investment class

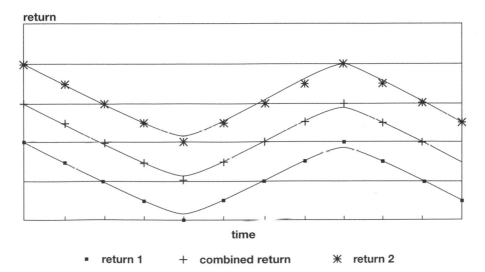

Figure 11.7 Positive correlation of investment returns

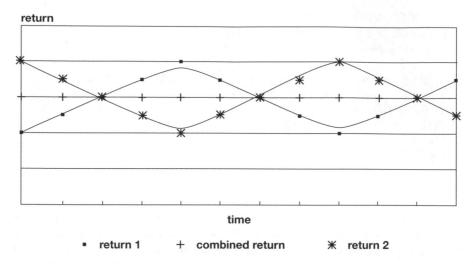

return

time

- **return 1** + **combined return** ✳ **return 2**

Figure 11.8 Perfect negative correlation of investment returns

more directly. Thus it is practically difficult to diversify away all unsystematic risk, simply because it is difficult to source different investment assets which have a negative correlation with each other. However proponents of portfolio theory acknowledge that while risk can never be entirely diversified away it might at least be *reduced* through asset diversification.

Brown and Matysiak (2000: 248–54) have explored the theoretical risk reduction benefits of portfolio diversification. The following example shown in Table 11.2 and Figure 11.9 draws inspiration from those ideas but uses actual change in the average value of semi-detached houses in London between 1995 and 2009 correlated against a fictitious portfolio of company shares. The assumption is that an investor is aware of the risk reduction potential of diversification and has chosen to invest equally in these two assets, which as Table 11.2 shows, have a negative correlation of –0.61.

A risk-averse investor would probably choose to invest only in the company shares as there is far less volatility reflected in a standard deviation of 2.31% when compared to investing in housing whose price changes over the 15 years are far more volatile, reflected in a standard deviation of 8.09%. However in choosing the risk-averse option, the investor will have to accept lower average annual returns at 4.38% than if all of the money had been invested in housing, where the average annual rate of return is 9.43%. In this example the investor has chosen to combine the two investments in a portfolio and thus the returns are the average of the returns for each investment at 6.91%.

The average return will remain unchanged by any combination across the two assets but the risk is less than the average risk. Thus a higher rate of return is possible with only a moderate increase in risk above investing only in shares. An alternative way to express this is that portfolio theory suggests a way to reduce risks relative to returns. The reason why it was possible to reduce risk in the above example was because the two investments were negatively correlated. If the investments had been positively correlated, then diversification would not have reduced risk to anything like the same degree, but there would

Table 11.2 Diversification in a two asset portfolio

Year	Housing	Company shares	Portfolio return
1	1.09%	8.95%	5.02%
2	−0.35%	7.75%	3.70%
3	16.70%	6.35%	11.53%
4	11.90%	4.88%	8.39%
5	20.11%	2.24%	11.18%
6	17.76%	−0.77%	8.50%
7	11.18%	1.88%	6.53%
8	14.54%	2.45%	8.50%
9	20.94%	3.68%	12.31%
10	11.11%	4.20%	7.66%
11	2.45%	5.25%	3.85%
12	3.77%	4.75%	4.26%
13	13.79%	3.99%	8.89%
14	3.70%	4.87%	4.29%
15	−7.20%	5.29%	−0.96%
Average	9.43%	4.38%	6.91%
Standard Deviation	8.09%	2.31%	3.46%

Correlation between Housing and Company Shares = −0.61

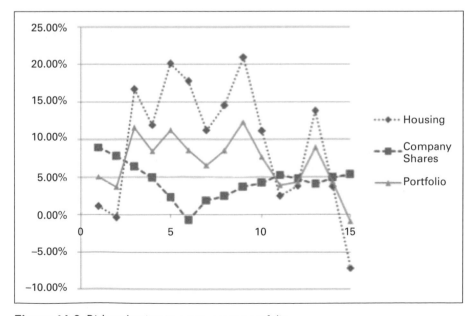

Figure 11.9 Risk reduction in a two asset portfolio

have been some marginal risk reduction where investments were not perfectly correlated.

At a practical level fund managers in charge of multi-asset portfolios containing shares, gilts, property and sundry other investments, will have a better chance of finding at least some negative or at least very low correlations between assets in the portfolio. It will be much harder for those managing investments on behalf of a REIT where the portfolio will be comprised entirely of different types of commercial property. Perhaps the best that could be sought in those circumstances would be to choose different property types which have a low or only moderate correlation. However Baum and Crosby (2008: 55) doubt that even this modest ambition could in reality be achieved, as there are both large lots sizes to contend with and a number of facets of unsystematic risk to mitigate, as they state:

> Given the current minimum level of investment necessary to purchase prime investment property, few, if any, funds can diversify internationally, regionally, by city and by property type in order to diversify away tenant risk, sector risk, planning risk, legal risk and some structural risk. Even the largest insurance companies may not be in this position. The analyst's strategy must therefore be to identify the most likely purchaser, the relevant conception of risk and its effect upon the likely selling price or return to that purchaser. (ibid.)

The approach implied in the quote above requires a number of 'bread and butter' practical steps to be taken which will be very familiar to those dealing in commercial investment properties. This involves a number of investigations regarding the title of the property, its use class, the lease structure, highways considerations allied to commissioned market research. These steps have been discussed in earlier chapters and are also covered by authors such as Baum *et al.* (2006: 246–53).

In line with these more prosaic observations, Brown and Matysiak (2000: 251) suggest that in a commercial property investment context, diversification might simply mean that a portfolio manager selects a spread of offices and retail property. The justification is that rises in interest rates and/or VAT will have a fairly rapid and negative effect on consumer high street spending and thus retail rents and capital values might be affected adversely in the short term. However the feed through of those changes to office based companies could be expected to be less dramatic and less immediate and thus there would not be a perfect correlation between movements in the values of the two property types. Geographical spread will also help diversification and reduce any tendency towards correlation between commercial property types. Thus some judicious mixed use investments in regeneration areas where values could be expected to grow quite steeply in the near future could be contrasted with some office investments in mature central business districts.

These risk reduction principles partly explain why REITs in the UK manage quite diverse mixes of properties in their investment portfolios. For example British Land (2010) has developed and retained BREEAM Excellent office developments in central London (such as Ropemaker Place) large out of town retail warehouse developments in the north of England (such as Teesside shopping park) and French shopping centres (such as Bon Accord in Paris). Clearly while the company has an obligation to manage commercial investment property, not all of its investment eggs are in one basket.

11.5 Portfolio strategy

Property portfolios are held for a number of different objectives, which may include revenue generation for charitable purposes, maximizing shareholder returns or to generate income and capital growth needed to match long-term liabilities. Thus a REIT might focus upon adding value for shareholders while pension funds might seek longer-term but more predictable performance to meet pension obligations. As the theory discussed above suggests, at a fundamental level a property investment strategy should ideally try to achieve a spread between types of property and location, the overall policy being to avoid too many eggs in too few baskets.

Risk reduction is therefore a key principle which will help a portfolio achieve its objectives, but there also needs to be performance targets, as a fund which merely exists to avoid risks will probably achieve very little in the way of real growth. However the setting of arbitrary profit targets is not entirely compatible with the strategic objectives set for investment portfolios. It is perhaps more realistic to compare the performance of a property portfolio with what could realistically have been achieved by investing in other media. Thus returns have tended to be measured as the relative performance against a benchmark of the average performance of related or other investment media.

In financial markets around the world investors in company stock have long used indices such as the FTSE 100, Dow Jones or the NASDAQ 100 as a benchmark to compare the performance of individual shares or more likely a portfolio of shares. In the UK, property portfolio managers use the Investment Property Databank (IPD) index as their performance benchmark. If it were possible to create a portfolio which tracks such an index, then all unsystematic risk would have been eliminated through diversification and thus the returns would be in line with those suggested by the index.

In this context the expression 'buying the index' has emerged to reflect a property portfolio which is so diverse that it performs in the same manner as a large representative sample of the whole commercial property investment market. As mentioned above, the index in this case is that produced by IPD which in the UK monitors the performance of 11,214 commercial properties contained within 293 property investment portfolios. IPD (2009) estimates that this sample represents almost 54% of the total commercial property investment market by value. The composition of the IPD databank of properties shows a geographic spread and in terms of broad property category it comprises 37.1% retail property, 28.6% offices and 27.6% industrial property. The balance is made up of 'other' investment properties such as leisure property.

Because the IPD index is broadly based it is widely agreed to be representative of the performance of whole property investment market. Managers who control investment property portfolios therefore commonly cite the IPD index as the benchmark against which they monitor the performance of the portfolios under their control. Thus performing as well as or outperforming the index, is not surprisingly viewed as a measure of success in the property investment industry. For example under key performance indicators in its 2010 annual report, Land Securities (2010) cited that it had outperformed the IPD shopping centre performance benchmark by 6.9% and that it had outperformed by 0.75% the IPD benchmark for the performance of retail warehouses and that it had outperformed the IPD London offices benchmark by 2.3%. Of course the irony is that sometimes the index being used as a benchmark is itself in a tailspin, as was the case for the IPD index during the credit crunch. In that situation there is a quantum of solace for the fund manager who marginally outperforms the index and this represents doing less badly than the investment community generally.

The principle that portfolio diversification is a legitimate ambition has established itself among investors generally and investors in property portfolios specifically. Property company annual reports now routinely contain risk assessments which cite mitigation measures to reduce risks and these invariably mention the importance of portfolio review and diversification. Linked to the concept of diversification is the scale of the portfolio and what might the optimum number of properties need to be to have a significant risk reducing effect.

As discussed earlier in the chapter, portfolio theory suggests that the total risk posed to the financial performance of property investments can be split into two parts: systematic and unsystematic risk. The reduction of risk in a portfolio through diversification tackles the unsystematic risk, which is also sometimes referred to as the property specific risk. Diversification does not deal with systematic risk, sometimes referred to as market risk, which will remain even when a portfolio is fully diversified. Thus as a portfolio increases in size and approaches the size of the market, the variation in portfolio returns should approach the systematic level. This is because as the portfolio size increases, so the portfolio variance approaches the average covariance for all assets in the market.

Brown and Matysiak (2000: 329–37) suggest that portfolios of between 10 and 20 equally weighted properties can obtain a reduction in the unsystematic risk of between 57% and 63%. Comparable figures in the UK stock market are in the region of 50%. Research undertaken by the Investment Property Form (IPF) (2007) which examined the performance of 1,728 commercial investment properties over 10 years has also explored the relationship between the size of a property portfolio and risk reduction. The IPF confirm the general point that as portfolio size increases, its risk will converge with that of the market. This is intuitively true, in that if a portfolio grew to engulf all properties in the market it would then take on exactly the same risks borne by the market.

The IPF began by calculating the average standard deviation in individual property returns from their sample of properties and this came to 11.0%. Thus any diversification measure should be able to reduce this measure of risk. The IPD found that even by adding one property to create a portfolio of two properties reduced the risk from 11.0% to 8.8% but that risk reduction effect progressively reduced with each property added so that by 30 properties the standard deviation was down to 5.5%. The IPD calculated that a portfolio of 250 properties would be needed to reduce the risk to that of the IPD universe which has a standard deviation of 4.5%. In other words if a portfolio of 250 properties could be assembled, the risks that it faced represented by a standard deviation of 4.5% would be caused entirely by market factors as all unsystematic risk would have been eradicated by diversification. Thus the total risk to the portfolio equalled 100% of the market risk. The IPD acknowledged that there would be very few corporate investors able to assemble a portfolio of that size which based upon average lot sizes and 2005 prices they estimated to cost £3.35 billion. However a portfolio of 20 properties would still reduce unsystematic risk considerably so that the market risk represented 69% of the total risk. A portfolio of 100 properties would create a position where the market accounted for 89% of the total risk to the portfolio. The IPF found however that over a 20 year period the average size of commercial property portfolios had fallen from 93 properties to 45 simply because of the emergence of smaller funds such as property unit trusts. However even at 45 properties there would be a significant risk reduction effect.

As well as managing portfolio size, further risk reduction in property portfolios might be possible if stock could be specifically targeted which emphasized the tendency for a low correlation of returns between individual properties. Thus performance would not be unduly influenced by factors specific to individual properties or indeed particular property market sectors such as offices, retail or industrial property.

The differential risk posed by each commercial property sector as reflected by its beta value has been researched by Brown and Matysiak (2000: 324–7) over a period from 1979 to 1997. The authors note that perhaps not surprisingly macroeconomic factors and market conditions will tend to see fluctuations in the beta values for different property sectors as they adjust in different ways to economic events. However over the time period under investigation, retail property exhibited the most volatility of returns while industrial property showed the least volatility. On this basis, investors will be expecting higher levels of return from retail property and the lower returns from industrial. This goes a long way towards explaining the ranking of betas in terms of a reflection of market expectations. For example, Brown and Matysiak's estimated betas for each property sector for between 1992 and 1997 are shown in Table 11.3.

As discussed earlier, it is in practice quite difficult to achieve portfolios of property which are highly diversified and investment managers will find it very difficult to select a portfolio capable of tracking an index. In reality a portfolio containing 30 properties or more will still have some residual risk which could potentially but not practically be diversified away. In addition there is the

Table 11.3 Estimated betas for three commercial property sectors 1992–7

Commercial property sector	Beta
Retail	1.10
Office	1.01
Industrial	0.89

problem caused by smoothing which arises because the valuation of different properties and portfolios is seldom synchronized to that of a wider index of properties and so assumptions and adjustments have to be made to calibrate comparisons. Where these delicate exercises are needed, a degree of error inevitably enters the analysis.

Thus even for quite well diversified portfolios the returns will be affected by both residual components of unsystematic risk and systematic or market risk. However if the holding period is long there is a decline in systematic risk and if the portfolio is actively managed there is a further decline in unsystematic risk. Unsystematic components of risk for property include aspects such as location which will always be unique to a property and this helps to generate a low correlation coefficient between properties, thus reducing risk. The Investment Property Forum found that the average correlation in a large sample of commercial properties taken from the IPD index was only 0.18 and they thus concluded that:

> The correlations show that the returns on different property investments are only weakly related to one another. There is a high degree of heterogeneity in the market. (2007: 8)

If investors can forecast positive abnormal returns for an individual sector, then that sector will provide a better risk–reward trade-off by diversifying among properties in that sector. If the investor is unable to forecast abnormal returns then although investors should pursue a policy of diversifying, such a policy will not have the results envisaged.

For mangers of multi-asset portfolios one of the strategic questions to face is what proportion of available investment funds should be devoted to property investments. For managers of any portfolio which has a property element decisions have to be taken on the percentage of funds to be devoted to each property sector.

The answers to these questions will be different for each fund as there is an interplay of variables such as attitudes to risk, long-term and short-term strategy, the scale of funds available, the extent to which large lot sizes in property would distort the overall composition of a portfolio and crucially the historic level of real returns anticipated from the sector.

Perhaps a better way of looking at the conundrum is to consider what property might bring to a portfolio that is not delivered by other investment media. In this regard Hoesli and MacGregor (2000: 211) point out that historically property has exhibited a low correlation with competing investment opportunities such as shares and gilts and thus it is suggested that it is a good diversifier of risk in a multi-asset portfolio.

Property is also thought to be a hedge against inflation, as historically it is has shown a high correlation with the Retail Price Index. Thus property portfolios exhibit a low correlation with the FTSE 100 index, but curiously this is not true of shares in property companies because property shares are highly geared, so the equity returns are more likely to be in line with the FT all share index. The correlation coefficient between property shares and equities means that there is little diversification benefit from investing in property shares and incorporating them into a portfolio of equities.

11.6 Some practical observations on property portfolios

Thus far the discussion on portfolio theory and strategy has explored some of the key principles in a mainly abstract manner, and so the chapter is going to round up with some observations on how portfolio building has evolved in practice. In order to do this the portfolio assembled by Land Securities will be commented upon. The company is a large well established REIT listed among the FTSE 100 companies and it owns an extensive commercial property portfolio comprising offices located in London's various business districts and retail property throughout the UK. Table 11.4 summarizes the value and scale of this portfolio in 2010.

The larger part of the Land Securities' property portfolio therefore comprises retail property in different formats both in town and out of town and geographically scattered throughout the UK. That aspect of the portfolio is therefore quite diverse although there is little evidence of international exposure. The office element in the portfolio is entirely located in London, although what could be said is that there is at least exposure to the different business districts within London such as the City, West End and Mid Town. Land Securities has obviously decided not to include industrial, warehouse or leisure property in its portfolio.

Like other leading REITs Land Securities does have effective asset management with a very low void rate and a diverse tenant mix in its properties, so that the portfolio is not overexposed to any one particular business tenant. Most of the latter are reputable UK companies secured on long leases and there is modest representation from the government and public sector agencies. The company has formed joint ventures or has settled for part ownership in particularly large properties which if owned in their entirety, would distort the portfolio and present a disproportionate risk. Overall it could be said that a degree of diversity has been achieved in the portfolio. Land Securities' annual report (2010) reveals prudent stock selection and a modest degree of development activity (within the confines allowed to REITs) with a high representation of prime property. In many respects Land Securities could be thought of as a state of the art REIT and it has often outperformed the IPD index on a number of different measures.

Given that stock selection is credible and a degree of diversity has been achieved and that there is 'as good as it gets' hands-on asset management, Land Securities has probably reduced the non-market risks as far as reasonably could be expected for such a company. However a summary of the company's results as it went through the credit crunch years reveals how risk reduction through portfolio and asset management had little effect in the face of the tumultuous market swings which had particularly dramatic effects on capital asset valuation. For example there were enormous losses recorded for 2008 and 2009 shown in Table 11.5, followed by a gradual climb back into profitability in 2010.

Land Securities is no different in this respect from its peer group of leading REITs as a cursory examination of their annual reports will reveal. These companies all found the trading conditions particularly challenging with steep falls in profitability and significantly reduced returns to shareholders during the credit crunch years. Perhaps had it not been for the risk reduction measures described above, the situation would have been even worse and there would

Table 11.4 A summary of Land Securities' property portfolio in 2010

Property sector	Capital value £ billions	Floorspace millions m²	Proportions by floorspace	Top five properties
Retail	5.34	1.65	58% shopping centres throughout the UK. 22% retail warehouses throughout the UK. 12% Accor. 8% other retail throughout the UK.	White Rose Shopping Centre Leeds. Cabot Circus Bristol. Gunwharf Quays, Portsmouth. St David's Shopping Centre, Cardiff. The Centre, Livingstone.
Offices	4.20	0.77	43% London's West End. 18% City of London 18% London's Mid Town. 15% other inner London. 6 % in other locations.	Cardinal Place, West End of London. New Street Square, Mid Town, London. Queen Anne's Gate, West End of London. Bankside 2 & 3, London's South Bank. Park House, West End of London.
Totals	9.54	2.42		

Table 11.5 Key annual financial data for Land Securities 2006–10

Year	2010	2009	2008	2007	2006
Total revenue £ millions	833.4	821.2	818.0	1,641.1	1,828.7
Profit/loss £ millions	1,092.4	−5,194.6	−830.8	3,528.3	1,675.9
Net assets £ millions	5,689.0	4,820.2	9,582.9	10,791.3	7,293.9
Dividends in pence per share paid to shareholders	28p	56.5p	64p	53p	46.7p

have been a near melt down comparable to that seen in the banking sector. Companies such as Land Securities are now significantly leaner as they emerge from the recession and they are arguably now in a better position following portfolio reviews and asset disposals to grow stronger in the context of an economic recovery.

11.7 Summary

The total returns on different investment property types reflected in the annual growth in rental and capital values is driven by different economic factors. For example the growth or decline in returns to offices will be linked to the growth or decline in the financial, service and government sectors which together comprise a core user group of offices. Similarly the total returns on retail property will be related to the growth or decline in consumer expenditure and retail sales and the total returns on industrial investment property will be linked to manufacturing output.

The drivers of value underpinning the different property sectors do not move in a synchronized manner and this is of benefit to property portfolio managers seeking low correlations between investment assets in order to reduce risk though diversification. Risk can also be reduced through portfolio size, so that at a relatively modest threshold of 30 equally weighted properties, there will have been significant risk reduction relative to the risks attributed to a single property.

However despite the apparent sophistication of theory and the benefits of risk reduction and analysis around stock selection, there will always remain considerable market risks for property investors which cannot be diversified away.

References

Baum, A. (2009) *Commercial Real Estate Investment: A Strategic Approach*, 2nd edn (London: EG Books).

Baum, A. and Crosby, N. (2008) *Property Investment Appraisal*, 3rd edn (Oxford: Blackwell).

Baum, A., Nunnington, N. and Mackmin, D. (2006) *The Income Approach to Property Valuation*, 5th edn (London: EG Books).

British Land Company plc (2010) *Annual Report and Accounts 2010* (London: British Land Company plc).

Brown, G. And Matysiak, G. (2000) *Real Estate Investment: A Capital Market Approach* (Harlow: Pearson).

Hoesli, M. And MacGregor, B. (2000) *Property Investment: Principles and Practice of Portfolio Management* (Harlow: Pearson).

IPD (2009) *The IPD Index Guide*, 5th edn (London: IPD).

Investment Property Forum (2007) *Risk Reduction and Diversification in Property Portfolios* (London: Investment Property Forum).

Land Securities Group plc (2010) *Annual Report 2010* (London: Land Securities Group plc).

Markowitz, H. (1952) 'Portfolio selection', *Journal of Finance*, 7(1), March: 77–91.

Markowitz, H. (1959) *Portfolio Selection: Efficient Diversification of Investment* (New York: John Wiley).

Markowitz, H. (1991) *Portfolio Selection: Efficient Diversification of Investment* (Cambridge: Blackwell).

Sayce, S., Smith, J., Cooper, R. and Venmore-Rowland, P. (2006) *Real Estate Appraisal from Value to Worth* (Oxford: Blackwell).

Sharpe, W. F. (1964) 'Capital asset prices: a theory of market equilibrium under conditions of risk', *Journal of Finance*, 19(3), September: 425–42.

12

Conclusion

> **Aims**
> As might be expected for a conclusion, this chapter aims to bring together some key themes which have emerged in the preceding chapters. The emphasis is upon those issues which have changed significantly since the publication of the first edition of this book in 1998, when the concepts of sustainability, corporate social responsibility and BREEAM-rated buildings were not on the agenda for discussion.

12.1 Introduction

Real property fulfils a number of roles; it is a factor of production, it provides homes and shelter and the space needed by business, charities and government and as Baum (2009: 381) comments it provides the setting for work, rest and play. From an investment perspective, property can generate income and store wealth, topics which have been the focus of this book. This edition of the book has tried to create more of a balance between commercial property investment and residential property investment in recognition of the latter's resurgence in recent years. This concluding chapter will focus upon some of the key topics which have arisen in the book regarding investment appraisal, risk and how sustainability is beginning to take effect in the world of property investment.

12.2 Reflections on the credit crunch and property investment

This edition of the book has been written at a time when the UK economy was showing very fragile signs of emerging from the tumultuous events caused by the credit crunch. Those events have prompted some broader and sober reflections on what property investment is really about, how it secures value and what its prospects might be going forward.

One way to provide some perspective on the significant falls in both commercial and residential property values which took place between 2007 and 2009 is to recall some of the key fundamentals of Ricardian land rent theory. The latter suggests that the returns to land in the form of rent or its capitalized equivalent, arise where a surplus emerges between the revenue generating potential of firms and their overall costs of production. Thus the maximum returns to land are an outcome of the interplay between the ability of businesses to generate revenue set against the costs (including profit) incurred in producing that revenue. There are thus limits to what those who own land or buildings can expect to receive from this interplay.

When the economic environment makes it difficult for firms to generate revenue to meet or exceed their costs, property values are bound to be affected in a negative way. What has tended to insulate property investors to some degree against these stark realities, is the scarcity of land in an absolute sense and in the sense that there are constraints of one kind or another which limit increases in the supply of space. There has thus been competition from firms to use land (a generic term here incorporating buildings) which serves to condense and focus property values, particularly in central locations. However in economic circumstances where the gap between firms' revenue generation and costs remains static or reduces, then it is not realistic for property owners to expect that their assets will in some mysterious way buck those trends. The property market will fall and this is the reality of market risk for the property investor.

Difficult economic circumstances, or what economists prefer to call 'periods of market correction', follow periods of over-accumulation. The periodic downturns have been a feature of the business cycle for many decades and are thought to occur because over confidence creeps into the system leading to over-casual responses to risk, relaxed lending practices in the banking sector and/or over speculation in property development. Because markets are now so globally interconnected the stimulus which triggers a downturn could come from virtually anywhere in the world and is thus very unpredictable. Therefore what appeared to be a parochial residential mortgage lending problem in the sub-prime market in a part of the United States spread rapidly, because it was exposing a wider and systematic over-valuation of assets.

Investors in whatever media therefore have to philosophically accept that capitalism is not a linear process and despite the best forecasts, few seem able to predict when the next period of market correction will occur. Thus investors in any commodity in a free market situation are in reality tending to ride a wave which may have shallow or deep amplitudes depending on the asset. Investors may be able to reduce risk by careful stock selection and through building portfolios of assets which have low correlations of returns, however risks can only be mitigated, they cannot entirely be removed. Hence in a market-based system there are no rewards without risk taking.

Given the ever present risks in markets, what interest might a prudent investor have in property? At a fundamental level property investment is a process of siphoning off a proportion of the value which has been created by other entities. This creates a faint suspicion that property investment is fundamentally a parasitical activity. Thus, from a moral perspective there might be greater benefit to society if property investors were instead persuaded to put their money into and thereby take risks in genuinely wealth creating industries. The latter might for example be IT or engineering or pharmaceuticals companies where new products could be researched and developed and new markets created.

Perhaps this perspective is being a little hard on the property investor, as a constructive role is played through the provision of funds and the sharing of risks to produce valuable and sometimes very large-scale assets. It would be very difficult and risky for these assets to be created by business tenants acting alone. Thus the creation of a multi million pound regional shopping centre which provides hundreds of shop units for retailers is beyond the purview of any one of those retailers to create. Indeed it would not make financial sense for even the largest retailer among them to devote their capital to this type of venture, given their overall business ambitions. Thus in this context there is a good reason why property developers and investors play an asset creation and management role on the back of pooling funds, much of which stem from shareholders.

REITs are large property companies whose main activity is property investment, but which also take on some risky development, refurbishment and regeneration projects. These companies thus have transformational capabilities stemming from their considerable resources and expertise. REITs can therefore add value and are not therefore just large passive rent collection agencies. For example SEGRO's (2009) three-stage business model commits the company to:

1 *Buy smart* through selective acquisitions in strong locations, where the price is attractive and where there is potential to add value after thorough due diligence.
2 *Add value* through proactive asset management, increasing rents and securing long leases, developing land banks when pre-lets are achieved focusing on sustainability to protect long term value.
3 *Sell well* by disposing of non-core and stabilized assets and recycling capital assets into new opportunities.

However despite this strategy, an experienced board, highly professional staff and an extensive portfolio with a strong rental income stream SEGRO like most of its property company peers, made significant losses across the credit crunch years. This illustrates how contingent property returns are on the business cycle and how market fluctuations can seem fickle and capricious in the face of capability, resources and a credible business strategy.

Given the demonstrable fragility of property markets and their susceptibility to globally induced business cycles, it is difficult for any forecaster to be overly prescriptive about what a well managed property company should deliver for its investors. Perhaps a better way to look at the issue is to consider the underlying relationships between the macro-economy and average business performance which could be thought of as a proxy measure of the ability of businesses to pay for their premises. Thus where GDP might be increasing annually at a sustainable rate of 2% or 3% it is unrealistic for commercial property investors to expect their returns to be significantly higher than these rates of growth. If that were the case, there would ultimately have to come a point of market correction as described above. Thus the historic ability of diversified commercial property portfolios to keep ahead of inflation and to match long term pension liabilities through steady but unspectacular returns might be a realistic expectation for property investors. Performance beyond that might be viewed as a bonus but not an expectation.

Residential landlords, and in their new guise as the buy-to-let investor, have from time to time also been accused of playing a parasitical role. This is because they are thought to be capitalizing upon both the shortage of affordable housing and the inability of typically younger and less affluent households to buy their own homes. But here again the investor is arguably playing a legitimate role in keeping approximately 15% of the UK's housing stock in the private rented sector. From a national policy perspective it makes sense that a small proportion of the housing stock remains rentable on easy access terms in the private sector. This stock provides accommodation for households in transition in both a geographic and housing tenure sense. In either case, most of those households will eventually move on to become home owners.

As for the commercial property investor, private residential landlords also face financial risks. This applies particularly to buy-to-let landlords whose returns are not fundamentally about rental income, they are about the realization of capital growth from a sale after a holding period of several years. Historically the growth in house prices has proved the adage that there is no investment like bricks and mortar, and this provides a rational basis for buy-to-let landlordism.

Figure 12.1 has been produced using Department for Communities (2010) data to illustrate growth in the price of a typical London semi-detached house, which averaged 8.34% per annum between 1987 and 2009. This type of growth has outstripped growth in incomes and was fuelled by a combination of a shortage of council homes, under-building relative to demand, the availability of mortgage credit, a growing population and limitations on the supply of developable land. However this does not mean that these conditions will always exist

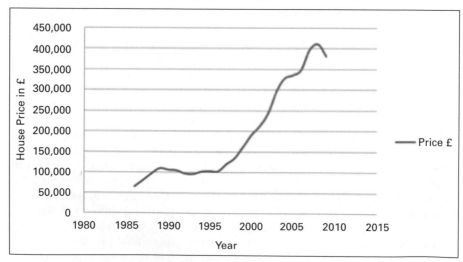

Figure 12.1 Average London semi-detached house prices 1987 to 2009

and, for example, the government is exploring the principle of a right to build as part of its new localism agenda. This could ultimately see a freeing up of land for a range of housebuilding projects and where supply increases relative to demand, prices usually fall.

Although the trend line Figure 12.1 above is obviously upwards over the longer term there is a dip in prices on the top right hand side where the data ends in 2009. The Halifax Building Society (2011) house price index recorded a 1.6% fall in the average UK house price during 2010, which stood at £162,435 by the end of that year. The Halifax was forecasting limited movement in house prices for 2011 but with some risk on the downside following widespread public spending cuts. Forecasts produced by a respected American credit rating agency: Standard & Poor's (2010) suggest that UK housing values remain overvalued at around 12% over current prices. Standard & Poor's work suggests that there is thus potential for further market correction in house prices so that they fall to a position which matches more sustainable income multiples. The messages in Standard & Poor's work will not be comforting for recent buy-to-let investors who may have to look at holding periods of 10 years or more in order to ride out the troughs in the market in order to realize the types of growth seen in the historic time-series data. Thus even where reliable historic data does exist, it is not always easy to assess future trends and it is especially difficult to predict a downturn phase of the property cycle.

12.3 Sustainability and property investment

Sustainability is a concept which had not surfaced sufficiently in the field of property investment to warrant any discussion on it in the first edition of this book in 1998. Since then however, sustainability has of course grown in prominence and is now a very fast moving agenda which is shaping attitudes and policies which bear upon every aspect of property from development to investment and asset management. There are a number of implications for property investors.

Because buildings are significant producer of CO_2 it was the environmental strand of sustainability which first surfaced for discussion in the context of measures which needed to be taken to tackle climate change. However it is now widely recognized that there are also social and economic dimensions to sustainability and there are signs that the triple bottom line concept is now being acknowledged by those who invest in and develop property.

In research on the decision-making process gone though by companies when selecting office space Dixon et al. (2009) found that in rank order of criteria, sustainability comes beneath location, availability, building quality, running costs and design. This was perhaps to some extent a predictable finding; however the sustainability of a building was beginning to move up the agenda for most companies when looking to lease office space. This is linked to change in organizational cultural and in particular to companies which have adopted an explicit policy on corporate social responsibility (CSR). It is these companies which understand and have taken ownership of the concept of sustainability as it applies to their wider procurement practices which include sourcing premises. These companies were able to articulate some sort of relationship between occupying an accredited sustainable building with better public image, improved client relations and enhanced employee satisfaction and retention.

Organizations are evolving in this respect and most now want to demonstrate in a practical way that they are trying to do something about reducing their carbon footprints.

The leading property companies are examples of organizations which are going through this cultural change and most can now point to quite developed policies on corporate social responsibility. In a manner consistent with these policies, property companies have extended their sustainability ambitions to embrace their development programmes and so for example Derwent London (2009) requires that all of its developments over 5,000 m^2 must achieve a minimum BREEAM rating of very good. Great Portland Estates (2010) requires that all of its major developments must achieve BREEAM excellent and a minimum of very good is required for refurbishment projects. Similarly British Land (2010) sets an ambition that all of its developments must achieve BREEAM excellent while Land Securities' (2010) new developments must meet a minimum BREEAM rating of very good.

Explicit property appraisal techniques which identify the NPV and IRR of a project do help commercial landlords such as those above assess options in terms of whether to retrofit a commercial building to achieve a BREEAM rating or to dispose of it or to allow the asset's returns to dwindle or to entirely redevelop a site. There are of course commercial software packages such as KEL investment valuer, which facilitate these appraisals but it is important for practitioners to understand the principles and concepts underpinning these packages.

Regarding residential property, the concept of sustainability has not been championed by private landlords or most private housebuilders but by the public sector and housing associations. The atomized nature of the private rented residential investment market, which is dominated by small investors, does not present a cohesive or vociferous lobby on most issues and this includes sustainability. Most small landlords will tend to pick up second hand stock in the market place where the average property is both dated and not particularly sustainable. Given that the private rented sector only represents something like 15% of the housing market, private landlords do not exert anything like the same degree of financial leverage over the activities of housebuilders in comparison to the influence that funding institutions exert over commercial property developers. In the latter situation, the principles of sustainability can and have been incorporated into the design and specification of new stock.

In the residential sector, private tenants are a diffuse group, many of whom see private renting as an interim measure before moving on to home ownership. Private tenants are therefore not a cohesive group who are likely to campaign around the sustainability or otherwise of what they probably see as their temporary homes. Private tenants like most other households, are very unlikely to have highly developed expectations on the sustainability of housing which they rent. These households are more likely to be concerned about the price, location and general condition of their housing rather than its sustainability characteristics. To use the jargon, there are not at present strongly developed supply chain linkages in the private rented sector which are conducive to improving the sustainability of the housing stock.

Even if the building regulations were tightened up to represent higher levels of sustainability as represented in the Code for Sustainable Homes, new housing only represents a very small proportion of the existing stock of around 26.7 million dwellings in the UK. Progress on improving the sustainability of the stock of largely unsustainable property in the UK through retro-fitting is most likely to arise where grants, financial inducements and energy trading opportunities arise, rather than through the concerted action on the part of any particular group of householders or private landlords. In the longer term the price mechanism will also begin to take effect as it is currently doing in the commercial property market, where there is a marginal uplift in value to reflect the presence of a green building accreditation of one sort or another. This is most likely to affect the private landlord at the point when a property is sold rather than in any noticeable uplift in rental value.

12.4 Research agendas

Books like this tend to conclude by recommending research agendas and this book conforms to that tradition. The specialized property investment research which has been sponsored by the Investment Property Forum (some of which has been cited in this book) stands out as being exemplary in shedding light on a number of problematic aspects of property investment practice. Research agendas which suggest themselves from a commercial property investment perspective are to do with finding more consistent link between sustainability and financial performance. This type of endeavour will probably require longitudinal studies to compare exemplary sustainable buildings (either new build or retro-fitted) against a control group of standard or 'un-badged' buildings in different property sectors. This might develop upon the valuable work already undertaken by Dixon *et al.* (2009) on the user demand for sustainable office space (discussed in Chapter 1).

In the private rented sector there is specialized reporting and data capture by organizations such as the Association of Residential Letting Agents, the Residential Landlords Association and to some extent the Council of Mortgage Lenders. This is obviously a different investment market to that for commercial property, and the concerns of the private residential landlord naturally tend to focus upon effective asset management and profitability issues. However there is perhaps scope to investigate how sustainability might begin to play a role in underpinning long term value and for example how retro-fitting housing might play a part in the buy-to-let business model. There are also issues around portfolios, optimum holding periods, optimal gearing ratios, cyclical markets, diversification and risk reduction which bear some similarities with those agendas which continue to be explored in the commercial property market.

References

Baum, A. (2009) *Commercial Real Estate Investment: A Strategic Approach*, 2nd edn (London: EG Books).
British Land Company plc (2010) *Annual Report and Accounts 2010* (London: British Land Company plc).
Department for Communities and Local Government (2010) *Table 511 Housing market: simple average house prices, by dwelling type and region, United Kingdom, from*

1986 (London: Department for Communities and Local Government). Available in e-format at: www.communites.gov.uk

Derwent London plc (2009) *Report and Accounts 2009* (London: Derwent London plc).

Dixon, T., Ennis-Reynolds, G., Roberts, C. and Simms, S. (2009) *Demand for Sustainable Offices in the UK* (London: Investment Property Forum).

Great Portland Estates (2010) *Annual Report 2010* (London: Great Portland Estates).

Halifax Building Society (2011) *House Price Index.* Available in e-format at: www.lloyds-bankinggroup.com

Land Securities Group plc (2010) *Annual Report 2010* (London: Land Securities Group plc).

SEGRO (2009) *SEGRO plc Annual Report* (London: SEGRO plc).

Standard & Poor's (2010) *Advance Signals from Europe's Housing Markets Point to Steadying Prices – For Now.* Available in e-format at: www.standardandpoors.com

Bibliography

Anderson, A. (2009) 'Defend against negligence claims', *Estates Gazette*, 28 November: 125.

Armatys, J. Askham, P. and Green, M. (2009) *Principles of Valuation* (London: EG Books).

Association of Residential Letting Agents (2010) *The ARLA Review and Index for Residential Investment, 2nd Quarter 2010* (Warwick: Association of Residential Letting Agents).

Balchin, P. and Rhoden, M. (2002) *Housing Policy: An Introduction*, 4th edn (London: Routledge).

Baiche, B. and Walliman, N. (eds) (2000) *Neufert Architects' Data*, 3rd edn (Oxford: Blackwell).

Ball, M. (2007) *Large-scale Investor Opportunities in Residential Property: An Overview* (London: Investment Property Forum).

Barker, K. (2004) *Review of Housing Supply – Delivering Stability: Securing our Future Housing Needs* (London: HM Treasury). Available in e-format at: www.barkerreview.org.uk

Barkham, R. (2002) 'Market research for office real estate', in S. Guy and J. Henneberry (eds), *Development and Developers: Perspectives on Property* (Oxford: Blackwell).

Barras, R. (1994) 'Property and the economic cycle: building cycles revisited', *Journal of Property Research*, 11(3), winter: 183–97.

Baum, A. (2009) *Commercial Real Estate Investment – A Strategic Approach*, 2nd edn (London: EG Books).

Baum, A. and Crosby, N. (2008) *Property Investment Appraisal*, 3rd edn (Oxford: Blackwell).

Baum, A., Nunnington, N. and Mackmin, D. (2006) *The Income Approach to Property Valuation*, 5th edn (London: EG Books).

Blackledge, M. (2009) *Introducing Property Valuation* (Abingdon: Routledge).

Booth, T. (2006) *The Buy to Let Handbook* (Oxford: How To Books).

Brett, M. (1990) *Property and Money* (London: Estates Gazette).

British Council for Offices (2009) *Guide to Specification* (London: British Council for Offices).

British Land Company plc (2010) *Annual Report and Accounts 2010* (London: British Land Company plc).

British Property Federation and IPD Ltd (2009) *BPF IPD Annual Lease Review 2009* (London: British Property Federation and IPD Ltd).

Brown, G. And Matysiak, G. (2000) *Real Estate Investment: A Capital Market Approach* (Harlow: Pearson).

Carsberg, B. (2002) *Property Valuation – The Carsberg Report* (London: RICS).

Cole, G. A. (2004) *Management Theory and Practice*, 6th edn (London: Thomson Publishing).

Council of Mortgage Lenders (2010) 'Buy to let lending showing modest signs of recovery' (CoML press release,11/11/10; in e-format at: www.cml.org.uk).

Council of Mortgage Lenders (2010) *Market Commentary, May 2010*. Available only in e-format at: www.cml.org.uk/cml/publications/marketcommentary

Council of Mortgage Lenders (2010) various press releases at: www.cml.org.uk

Crocker, S. (2008) 'Public houses', in R. Hayward (ed.), *Valuation Principles into Practice*, 6th edn (London: EG Books).

Darlow, C. (ed.) (1983) *Valuation and Investment Appraisal* (London: Estates Gazette).

Davidson, A. W. (ed.) (2002) *Parry's Valuation and Investment Tables*, 12th edn (London: Estates Gazette).

Department for Communities (2009) *The Code for Sustainable Homes – Case Studies* (London: Department for Communities and Local Government). Available in e-format at: www.communities.gov.uk

Department for Communities (2009) *Planning Policy Statement 4: Planning for Sustainable Economic Growth* (London: Stationery Office). Available in e-format at: www.communities.gov.uk

Department for Communities (2009) *Sustainable New Homes – The Road to Zero Carbon* (London: Stationery Office). Available in e-format at: www.communities.gov.uk

Department for Communities (2010) *Table 101 Dwelling stock: by tenure, United Kingdom (historical series)* (London: Department for Communities and Local Government). Available in e-format at: www.communities.gov.uk

Department for Communities and Local Government (2010) *Statistical Table 101: Dwelling Stock: By Tenure, United Kingdom (Historical Series)*. Available at: www.communities.gov.uk

Department for Communities and Local Government (2010) *Statistical Table 511 Housing market: Simple Average House Prices, by Dwelling Type and Region, United Kingdom, from 1986* (London: Department for Communities and Local Government). Available in e-format at: www.communites.gov.uk

Department for Communities and Local Government (2010) *Statistical Table 563: Housing market: Average valuations of residential building land with outline planning permission*. Available at: www.communities.gov.uk

Department of Trade and Industry (2004) *Queens Moat Houses plc – Investigation under Section 432(2) of the Companies Act 1985* (London: Stationery Office).

Derwent London plc (2009) *Report & Accounts 2009* (London: Derwent London plc).

Dixon, T., Ennis-Reynolds, G., Roberts, C. and Simms, S. (2009) *Demand for Sustainable Offices in the UK* (London: Investment Property Forum).

Dixon, T., Ennis-Reynolds, G., Roberts, C. and Sims, S. (2009) 'Is there demand for sustainable offices? An analysis of UK business occupier moves (2006–2008)', *Journal of Property Research*, 26(1).

Dixon, T., Thompson, B., McAllister, P., Marston, A. and Snow, J. (2005) *Real Estate and the New Economy: The Impact of Information and Communications Technology* (Oxford: Blackwell).

Drury, J. and Brebner, I. (2007) 'Industrial facilities', in D. Littlefield (ed.), *Metric Handbook: Planning and Design Data*, 3rd edn (Oxford: Architectural Press).

Dubben, N. and Sayce, S. (1991) *Property Portfolio Management: An Introduction* (London: Routledge).

Dubben, N. and Williams, B. (2009) *Partnerships in Urban Property Development* (Chichester: Wiley-Blackwell).

Edwards, C. and Krendel, P. (2007) *Institutional Leases in the 21st Century* (London: EG Books).

Eichholtz, P., Kok, N. and Quigley, J. (2009) *Doing Well by Doing Good? An Analysis of the Financial Performance of Green Buildings in the USA*. RICS Research Report (London: RICS).

Gimmy, A. E. and Johnson, B. A. (2003) *Analysis and Valuation of Golf Courses and Country Clubs* (Illinois: Appraisal Institute).

Great Portland Estates (2010) *Annual Report 2010* (London: Great Portland Estates).

Grenfell, W. (2003) 'Perfect pricing', *Estates Gazette*, 29 November: 122–3.

Grenville-Mathers, L. and Taylor, A. (2008) 'Offices', ch. 6 in R. Hayward (ed.), *Valuation: Principles into Practice*, 6th edn (London: EG Books).

Gunne-Jones, A. (2009) *Town Planning: A Practical Guide* (London: RICS).

GVA Grimley (2009) *CBI/GVA Grimley Corporate Real Estate Survey* (London: GVA Grimley). Available in e-format at: www.gvagrimley.co.uk

Hager, D. P. and Lord, D. J. (1985) The Property Market, Property Valuations and Property Performance Measurement (London: Institute of Actuaries).

Halifax Building Society (2011) *House Price Index*. Available in e-format at: www.lloyds-bankinggroup.com

Hammerson plc (2009) *Annual Report 2009* (London: Hammerson plc).

Hargitay, S. E. and Yu, S. M. (1993) *Property Investment Decisions: A Quantitative Approach* (London: Spon).

Harper, D. (2008) *Valuation of Hotels for Investors* (London: EG Books).

Havard, T. (2008) *Contemporary Property Development*, 2nd edn (London: RIBA Publishing).

Hoesli, M. And MacGregor, B. (2000) *Property Investment: Principles and Practice of Portfolio Management* (Harlow: Pearson).

Hutchinson, N. (1996) 'Variations in the capital values of UK commercial property', *Chartered Surveyor Monthly*, April: 40–1.

Investment Property Databank (2009) *IPD UK Annual Property Index* (London: Investment Property Databank). Available in e-format at: www.ipd.com

Investment Property Databank and the University of Aberdeen (1994) *Understanding the Property Cycle* (London: RICS).

Investment Property Forum (2005) *Depreciation in Commercial Property Markets: Findings and Recommendations* (London: Investment Property Forum). Available in e-format at: www.ipf.org.uk

Investment Property Forum (2005) *The Size and Structure of the UK Property Market* (London: Investment Property Forum).

Investment Property Forum (2007) *Understanding Commercial Property Investment: A Guide for Financial Advisers* (London: Investment Property Forum).

IPD (2009) *The IPD Index Guide*, 5th edn (London: IPD).

Isaac, D. and Steley, T. (2000) *Property Valuation Techniques*, 2nd edn (Basingstoke: Macmillan).

Isaac, D., O'Leary, J. and Daley, M. (2010) *Property Development, Appraisal and Finance*, 2nd edn (Basingstoke: Palgrave).

Jayne, M. R. (2008) 'Rating', in R. Hayward (ed.), *Valuation: Principles into Practice*, 6th edn (London: EG Books).

Jenkins, S. (1996) 'Valuations still highly variable', *Estates Times*, 15 March: 2.

Jones, P., Hillier, D., Comfort, D. and Clarke-Hill, C. (2009) 'Commercial property investment companies and corporate social responsibility', *Journal of Property Investment and Finance*, 27(5).

Kemp, P. (2010) 'The transformation of private renting', in P. Malpass and R. Rowlands (eds), *Housing, Markets and Policy* (Abingdon: Routledge).

Kimmet, P. (2009) 'Comparing "socially responsible" and "sustainable" commercial property investment', *Journal of Property Investment and Finance*, 27(5).

Land Securities Group plc (2010) *Annual Report 2010* (London: Land Securities Group plc).

Lawson, F. (2007) 'Retail shops and stores', in D. Littlefield (ed.), *Metric Handbook: Planning and Design Data*, 3rd edn (Oxford: Architectural Press).

London Borough of Greenwich (2006) *Unitary Development Plan* (London: Greenwich Council). Available in e-format at: www.greenwich.gov.uk

Lorenz, D. and Lutzkendorf, T. (2008) 'Sustainability in property valuation: theory and practice', *Journal of Property Investment and Finance*, 26(6).

Lumby, S. and Jones, C. (2006) *Fundamentals of Investment Appraisal* (London: Thomson Learning).

McGregor, B., Nanthakumuran, N., Key, T. and Zarkesh, F. (1994) 'Investigating property cycles', *Chartered Surveyor Monthly*, July/August: 38–9.

Markowitz, H. (1952) 'Portfolio selection', *Journal of Finance*, 7(1), March: 77–91.

Markowitz, H. (1959) *Portfolio Selection: Efficient Diversification of Investment* (New York: John Wiley).

Matysiak, G, Hoesli, M., MacGregor, B. and Nanathakumaran, N. (1995) 'Long-term inflation-hedging characteristics of UK Commercial Property', *Journal of Property Finance*, 7 (1).

Maxted, B. and Porter, T. (2007) *The UK Commercial Property Lending Market: Year End 2006 Research Findings* (Leicester: De Montfort University).

Mercer (2010) *Asset allocation survey and market profiles* (London: Mercer). Available in e-format at: www.mercer.com/assetallocation

Mullins, D. and Murie, A. (2006) *Housing Policy in the UK* (Basingstoke: Palgrave).

Mullins, L. J. (2007) *Management and Organisational Behaviour*, 8th edn (Harlow: Financial Times, Prentice Hall).

Murdoch, J. (2008) 'Negligence and valuations', ch. 23 in R. Hayward (ed.), *Valuation: Principles into Practice*, 6th edn (London: EG Books).

Office for National Statistics (2009) *Wealth in Great Britain – Executive Summary of the Main Points from the Wealth and Assets Survey 2006/2008* (ed. C. Daffin). Available in e-format at: www.statistics.gov.uk

Oprea, A. (2010) 'The importance of investment feasibility analysis', *Journal of Property Investment and Finance*, 28(1).

Pivo, G. (2005) 'Is there a future for socially responsible property investment?', *Real Estate Issues*, 30(1).

Ratcliffe, J., Stubbs, M. and Keeping, M. (2009) *Urban Planning and Real Estate Development*, 3rd edn (Abingdon: Routledge).

REITA (2009) *Understanding Commercial Property Investment*. Available in e-format at: www.reita.org

REITA (2010) *The Personal Investor's Guide to Property*. Available in e-format at: www.reita.org

RICS (2006) *Valuation Information Paper No. 8: The Analysis of Commercial Lease Transactions* (London: RICS).

RICS (2007) *Valuation Information Paper 10: The Depreciated Replacement Cost Method of Valuation for Financial Reporting* (London: RICS).

RICS (2008) *Valuation Information Paper 12: Valuation of Development Land* (London: RICS).

RICS (2009) *Valuation Information Paper 13, Sustainability and Commercial Property Valuation* (London: RICS).

RICS (2009) *Sustainability and the RICS Property Lifecycle* (London: RICS). Available in e-format at: www.rics.org

RICS (2009) *Valuation and Sale Price Report 2009* (London: RICS). Available in e-format at: www.rics.org

RICS (2010) *Property Investment Valuation in the UK: A Brief Guide for Users of Valuations* (London: RICS). Available in e-format at: www.rics.org/valuation

RICS (2010) RICS *Valuation Standards*, 6th edn (London: RICS).

RICS Economics (2010b) *RICS Commercial Market Survey, First Quarter 2010* (London: RICS). Available in e-format at: www.rics.org

Royal Institution of Chartered Surveyors (1994) *Understanding the Property Cycle: Economic Cycles and Property Cycles* (London: RICS).

Sayce, S., Smith, J., Cooper, R. and Venmore-Rowland, P. (2006) *Real Estate Appraisal: from Value to Worth* (Oxford: Blackwell).

Scarrett, D. (2008) *Property Valuation: The Five Methods*, 2nd edn (Abingdon: Routledge).

SEGRO (2009) *SEGRO plc Annual Report* (Slough: Slough Estates Group plc).

Shapiro, E., Davies, K. and Mackmin, D. (2009) *Modern Methods of Valuation*, 10th edn (London: EG Books).

Sharpe, W. F. (1964) 'Capital asset prices: a theory of market equilibrium under conditions of risk', *Journal of Finance*, 19(3), September: 425–42.

Smith, R. J. (2008) *Property Law*, 6th edn (Harlow: Longman).

Srivatsa, R., Smith, A. and Lekander, J. (2009) 'Portfolio optimisation and bootstrapping', *Journal of Property Investment and Finance*, 28(1).

Standard & Poor's (2010) *Advance Signals from Europe's Housing Markets Point to Steadying Prices – For Now*. Available in e-format at: www.standardandpoors.com

Stern, N. (2006) *Stern Review of the Economics of Climate Change* (London: HM Treasury and Cabinet Office).

Stewart, M. (2007) *The New Landlord's Guide to Letting*, 4th edn (Oxford: How To Books).

Thorne, C. (2008) 'Valuation for financial statements', in R. Hayward (ed.), *Valuation: Principles into Practice*, 6th edn (London: EG Books).

UNITE Group plc (2009) *Annual Report and Accounts 2009* (Bristol: UNITE Group plc)

United Kingdom Debt Management Office (2005) *Formulae for Calculating Gilt Prices from Yields*, 3rd edn (London: United Kingdom Debt Management Office). Available in e-format at: www.dmo.gov.uk

Universities Superannuation Scheme Limited (2010) *Statement of Investment Principles*. Available in e-format at: www.uss.co.uk

Valuation Office Agency (2010) *Property Market Report 2010*. Available in e-format at: www.voa.gov.uk

Westwick, C. A. (1980) *Property Valuation and Accounts* (London: Institute of Chartered Accountants).

Wilcox, S. (2008) *UK Housing Review 2008/2009* (Coventry: Chartered Institute of Housing; London: Building Societies Association).

Wilcox, S. (2008) 'Where next for private renting?', in S. Wilcox (ed.), *UK Housing Review 2008/2009* (Coventry: Chartered Institute of Housing; London: Building Societies Association).

World Commission on Environment and Development (Brundtland Report) (1987) *Our Common Future* (Oxford: Oxford University Press).

Index